THE GRAND OBSESSION

THE GRAND OBSESSION

An Anthology of Opera

Edited by

Rupert Christiansen

COLLINS
8 Grafton Street London W1
1988

William Collins Sons & Co. Ltd
London · Glasgow · Sydney · Auckland
Toronto · Johannesburg

BRITISH LIBRARY CATALOGUING IN PUBLICATION DATA

The grand obsession: a Collins anthology of opera
1. Opera
i. Christiansen, Rupert
728.1

ISBN 0—00—217775 7

First published 1988
Copyright in the compilation and introduction
Copyright © Rupert Christiansen 1988

Scraperboard headpieces by Val Biro

Photoset in Sabon by Ace Filmsetting Ltd, Frome
Made and printed in Great Britain by
T.J. Press (Padstow) Ltd, Padstow, Cornwall

For P, who makes
a difference

*Die Welt is lieblich, und
nicht fürchterlich dem
Mutigen – und was ist
denn Musik?*
HOFMANNSTHAL

CONTENTS

INTRODUCTION

I first came to opera at the age of twelve, an early age. It was, admittedly, nothing very demanding – schoolboy French and an acquaintance with Gilbert and Sullivan were enough to see me through Donizetti's daft but irresistible opéra-comique *La Fille du Régiment*. That introduction was fortunate: if it had been *Tannhäuser*, I dare say I would never have darkened Covent Garden's doors again. But that night it was Sutherland and Pavarotti enjoying themselves uninhibitedly, with their gorgeous extrovert voices spreading cascades of tinsel and glitter. At the end, people threw flowers and roared their approval. My friend and I crept back to the stage door and successfully solicited autographs; the next morning I bought a record of Sutherland singing the 'Mad Scene' from *Lucia*, and I was bitten, scarred, changed for life. Or rather, I had fallen in love with the sheer animal beauty of great singing, the scale and variety of the emotions communicated, the irreducible, shameless glamour of the opera house. Over the subsequent twenty years, that love has grown into a complex obsessive passion that has consumed more of my life than I care to remember. There have been months when I have felt jaded, disappointed, cynical about my mistress; but opera is an eternally fascinating courtesan who can always find some new trick to lure her admirers back, even though the relationship continues tormented and exhausting.

Good times, bad times, memories: let me start by anthologizing my supreme experiences (fellow-victims will understand the compulsion): Boulez conducting *Pelléas*, still perhaps my favourite opera; Sutherland and Pavarotti in *Lucia*, twice within a week; *Les Troyens* with Troyanos, Jessye Norman, and Domingo battling superbly with the impossible role of Enée; Tim Albery's extraordinary vision of the same piece at the Welsh National

9

Opera, an evening which left me shaking and tearful, as did Reginald Goodall's *Parsifal*; the intense humanity of Janáček's *Jenůfa* and *Katya Kabanová*; David Freeman's electrifying staging of Tippett's *The Knot Garden*; Abbado conducting Tarkovsky's production of *Boris Godunov* and Strehler's production of *Simon Boccanegra*; my first *Lulu*, my first *Elektra* (Birgit Nilsson), my second *Frau ohne Schatten*, with Böhm conducting and Rysanek as the Empress; Ligeti's *Le Grand Macabre*, witty, sensual, inventive enough to convert any scoffer at modern opera; Peter Stein's production of *Otello*, of which certain images are seared on my mind; an exquisitely sung *Idomeneo*, for me the most musically ravishing of Mozart's operas, and a quicksilver *Falstaff* (conducted by Colin Davis), the ditto of Verdi's; Cotrubas' heartbreaking Tatyana; Vickers' Otello, Tristan, and Peter Grimes; everything (except a prim Charlotte in *Werther*) that I heard Janet Baker do — my single greatest operatic regret is missing her Didon in *Les Troyens*. All these remain with me as wholly satisfying; mostly, however, the extraordinary difficulty of mounting an operatic performance means that all one can rationally hope for is a *moment* when it works. I remember, for instance, a goodish performance of Verdi's *Macbeth* suddenly transfigured by a miraculous glow cast over the grandiose finale to the first Act. Truth to tell, by the standards of Verdi's fabulous genius, the music is pretty ordinary stuff — the tempo picks up into a stately waltz, voices gather in a crescendo which depends for its effect on the use of unison. But Verdi is often most moving, most purely himself when he is being technically quite conventional; and that blossoming *tutti* seemed for a minute like a vision of the very essence of opera, falling upon me with an exhilarating immediacy which left me physically breathless, as ecstatic as a dervish.

But if I am honest there have been hours of tedium and mediocrity as well. Opera is not only damnably difficult to mount, it is also a genre which has thrown up only a small number of masterpieces. The second-rate gets disproportionate exposure. So let me pass over the times I dropped off in *Tannhäuser*, *La Favorita*, *Capriccio*; my efforts to find *Tosca* anything but deplorable; a

Forza at the Met of unremitting vulgarity; Henze's interminable *We Came to the River* and Tippett's risible *The Ice Break*; the sad anti-climax of my first exposure to Prokofiev's *War and Peace*, which I continue to find thunderously vacuous. . . .

This anthology, however, does not intend to dwell on the negative. As well as conveying some of the irrational power opera has over the emotions, I hope that it will also show some of the weird and wonderful tapestry of human existence that is woven round opera and opera houses, with all their Byzantine intensity of ritual and function; I hope, too, that it takes opera seriously, which is not to say humourlessly. Opera aims so high that it can hardly fail to fall short most of the time, but there is a regrettably suburban tendency in operatic literature to giggle about it to the point of philistinism. I have thus tried to avoid the usual run of anecdotes (although I cannot resist pointing the reader instantly to the gem on pp. 100–1) and to concentrate instead on the best writing available on the subject – from Stendhal and Chorley to Shaw, Robert Craft and Brigid Brophy, as well as some of the lesser-known biographies and memoirs. Anthologists can do little except to act on their prejudices and indulge their partialities – a mechanically comprehensive anthology would be dull indeed. Nevertheless some of the inevitable holes here have not been left empty for want of trying – I do wish, for instance, that there was something to represent Prokofiev's operatic *oeuvre* or the fabulous history of opera in South America, but I couldn't find anything that could be satisfactorily amputated from its original context. On the other hand, there are some relatively familiar pieces here, like Chorley's moving and evocative account of Pasta's last public appearance (see pp. 134–6), that I could not resist including, in the belief that at least some of my readers will not yet have encountered them.

An anthology, by its nature, contains a certain degree of randomness and meandering. It will not satisfy anyone looking for coherent and rigorously chronological history. However, anyone who wants to understand the crucial turning-points in the complex evolution of the operatic form could trace Rinuccini's letter of 1600 (pp. 46–7); Brian Trowell on *opera seria* (pp. 275–9);

Gluck's preface to *Alceste* (pp. 166–8); the 'conversation' between Verdi, Mozart and Wagner (pp. 111–14); Strauss's and Hofmannsthal's correspondence over *Ariadne auf Naxos* (pp. 225–30); and finally compare Nicholas Maw's reflections on the contemporary possibilities (pp. 116–18) with those of Pierre Boulez (pp. 186–94).

Anthologists rely heavily on research libraries which allow them the freedom to browse, and I must at this point sink to my knees in gratitude to the matchless London Library, with its gloriously deep and wide collection, its unfailingly helpful staff, and a photocopying machine that actually works. Friends are invaluable in leading you out of ruts and putting you on to their own grandly obsessive trails. Over the years, Robert Turnbull had consistently done that for me, infectious with new enthusiasms and a sweeper-away of my musical illusions; he also ploughed through mounds of books, newspapers and magazines for this book. I would also like to acknowledge the libraries, loans, casual hints, and general interest of Paul Driver (who dug up Auden's second list of desert island discs on pp. 86–7 and reminded me of Edmund Wilson's magisterial report on the first performance of *Peter Grimes*); Jane Mutch (the most assiduous reader of prima donna biographies); David Drew; Anne Olivier Bell; Ian Irvine; Jean-Jacques Gabas; Rodney Milnes and Deirdre Tilley; Patrick O'Connor; Katharine Wilkinson, Francesca Franchi, and Ken Davison of the Royal Opera House; the British Library, the Westminster City Library, and the British Sound Archive. Susie Casement valiantly sought all the permissions. Lastly and prominently, I must pay tribute to my editors, Dan Franklin and especially Ariane Goodman, who have combined practicality with vision, patience with firmness. And most heartfelt thanks of all to the operas themselves, their blessed authors and performers: thanks, for having warmed my life.

RUPERT CHRISTIANSEN
London, 1988

THE ANTHOLOGY

ABC

Reminiscent of Flaubert's Dictionary of Received Ideas, this bluffer's guide to 'what one should feel and say while listening to the Great Masters' was originally published in a French journal, La Vie Parisienne, *in 1883.*

BEETHOVEN. Mighty genius. Bow down in deepest homage. No contradiction!!! That's the way it is.

How to Act During the Performance: Deepest concentration. Everyone has to see that you are paying the closest attention. Solemn silence. Your deep emotion is betrayed only by a hardly noticeable shaking of your head.

BERLIOZ. Misunderstood during his lifetime. Since his death our ears have got used to worse things. Declare that he is extremely strong and awfully interesting. Strange. Strange. Strange.

How to Act During the Performance: Your glance should be wild and half-demented. Your hands clenched, your throat dry. And put as much cotton in your ears as you can stuff into them.

GOUNOD. Not one dissenter. The whole world is enraptured. Sway with the world in your enthusiasm. He wrote three things: *Faust, Faust,* and *Faust.* All the exclamations you can think of. Begin with 'ideal' and go on to 'divine'.

How to Act During the Performance: Crouch and clutch yourself. Tremble, shiver and give forth all signs of sensuous delight. Then murmur in an ecstatic voice inarticulate sounds like 'mmmm-oooh'.

MOZART. One either loves him to the point of insanity or one finds him insipid. It is a question of taste and temperament. Also of education. Therefore you will do well to feel your way around and get the other man's opinion before you voice your own.

How to Act During the Performance: Listen without any sign of excitement. From time to time make a noise with your closed mouth which may remind one of the bleating of a peacefully grazing sheep. This shows that these peaceful melodies are related to the pleasures of a shepherd.

MEYERBEER. Practically the whole world is agreed on admiring him. Few adversaries. Therefore you may praise safely.

How to Act During the Performance: Make a sad face as if you were making your will and repeatedly say 'terrific' in a decided, solemn tone. Nothing more, but roll the r's properly. Don't say too much. 'Terrific' covers the subject.

MASSENET. His position is not as yet clarified. A few adore him, others do not acknowledge him.

How to Act During the Performance: Cup first your right ear, then your left, not to lose anything. Your body should be in a relaxed attitude. Lean your head on your hand and give your eyes a longing expression. The safe procedure is to find everything charming. You don't have to believe it, of course.

OFFENBACH. There are some who want to burn his scores. That is exaggerated. You simply say that he has talent.

How to Act During the Performance: Do not be dignified. Rock to and fro. Put on an embarrassed air, then put your left thumb in your waistcoat and hook your right thumb in your trouser pocket. Then say, 'Crazy', and smile with a tolerant smile.

ROSSINI. Don't spare the praise. The Swan of Pesaro. The creator of *William Tell*.

How to Act During the Performance: Applaud every bar and scream, 'Bravo! Bravi! Brava!'

VERDI. You can say that you prefer to hear all the works he wrote before *Aida* performed on the barrel-organ. But that is enough criticism. Beginning with *Aida*, declaim, 'I am filled with admiration.' If you follow this suggestion you will be taken for an accomplished connoisseur.

How to Act During the Performance: Throw your arms in the air and scream at *Aida* performances. As to the rest, pfui! bah! pooh!!!

WAGNER. As a Frenchman you detest him in direct proportion to the degree of your patriotism. As a listener, it depends on how much you can stand. Say, 'I confess that it remains incomprehensible to me. Certainly that is my fault. My ears hurt me. My God! I think I am becoming deaf!'

How to Act During the Performance: Leave.

Anyone so foolish as to think of making opera their career should first contemplate this remarkable list of the alternatives.

Hendrik Appels, a Dutch tenor, was first a practising dentist.

Salvatore Baccaloni, the *basso buffo*, studied architecture.

Alfred von Bary was a qualified neurologist before his tenor voice was discovered. He returned to medicine for a time after failing eyesight terminated his musical career.

Erna Berger, coloratura soprano, was a governess.

Ingrid Bjoner, soprano, worked in an apothecary shop.

Beno Blachut, a Czechoslovakian tenor, was an ironworker.

Alessandro Bonci, tenor, was a shoemaker's apprentice.

Kim Borg, bass-baritone, began as an engineer.

Giuseppe Borgatti, a tenor and the first Andrea Chénier, started out as a mason.

John Brownlee, baritone, worked as a bookkeeper.

Aloys Burgstaller, the German tenor, studied to become a watchmaker.

Florencio Constantino, tenor, was a ship's engineer.

Régine Crespin, soprano, studied to be a pharmacist.

Charles Dalmorès, a noted French tenor, was also a horn player.

Peter Dawson, Australian bass-baritone, began as a professional boxer.

Kathleen Ferrier was a telephonist.

Mario Filippeschi, bass, started as a police official.

Miguel Fleta, tenor and first Calaf in *Turandot*, was a miner.

Alfons Fügel, German tenor, began as a tile-setter.

Beniamino Gigli worked in a pharmacy.

Apollo Granforte, the celebrated Italian baritone, began as a shoemaker.

Joseph Hislop, Edinburgh-born tenor, was a press photographer.

Dorothy Kirsten worked as a telephone operator.

Mario Lanza was a truck driver.

Emanuel List, Austrian bass, learned the tailor's trade.

Cornell MacNeil, baritone, was a machinist.

Emilio de Marchi, tenor and first Cavaradossi, began as a lieutenant.

Alfred Piccaver, the tenor idol of Vienna, worked in the laboratory of Thomas A. Edison before his voice was discovered.

Ezio Pinza was a professional bicycle rider.

Leo Slezak, the great Austrian tenor, was a gardener and a locksmith.

Thomas Stewart, baritone, worked in a government laboratory doing mathematical-physical research.

Martti Talvela, bass, was a school teacher.

Jess Thomas, tenor, started out as a child psychologist.

Jacques Urlus, the Wagnerian tenor, began as a metalworker.

Walter Widdop, English tenor, began as a wool-dyer.

ROBERT RUSHMORE, The Singing Voice

ANTIPATHY

Irrational, excessive, extravagant, ludicrous, even morally corrupting — hatred of opera has been as passionately expressed as love of it. Some even find it plain boring, like the Princess Palatine, writing from Versailles in 1709:

> In half an hour, we go to hear some music. It will be drivel, as they are only singing the old operas of Lully. I often drop off to sleep listening to them.

Or Jane Austen, writing in 1814 to her sister Cassandra in anticipation of a visit to Covent Garden for a performance of an opera by Arne, featuring the new star of the day, the soprano Catherine Stephens: 'Excepting Miss Stephens, I dare say Artaxerxes will be very tiresome...' In the event, her scepticism was unshaken:

> Fanny and Mr J. P. are delighted with Miss S, & her merit in singing is I dare say very great; that she gave *me* no pleasure is no reflection upon her, nor I hope upon myself, being what Nature made me on that article...

The philosopher and novelist Jean-Jacques Rousseau not only composed music, but also theorized about it. In his novel La Nouvelle Héloïse *(1761), he inserted the following satire on current operatic practice.*

Imagine a crate about fifteen feet long and proportionately wide: that is the stage. On each side are placed a row of screens on which the settings of the acts to be played are crudely painted. The back-drop is a big curtain, similarly daubed and almost always torn, which may represent caverns on earth or holes in the sky, depending on the perspective. Everyone who walks across the stage behind this curtain produces a sort of tremor in it which is rather attractive. The sky is represented by some bluish rags that hang from rods or ropes like laundry on a line. The sun, which is occasionally to be seen, is a torch inside a lantern. The chariot for the gods and goddesses is made of two-by-fours hung like a swing within a frame, the god sitting on a transverse board in front of which is bunched some tinted cloth – the cloud appropriate to the god's magnificence. Near the bottom of the machine stand two or three stinking candles, which, while the illuminated personage waves and shrieks in his little swing, smoke him up to his heart's content – incense worthy of the god.

Since chariots form the most important part of the Opera's equipment, you can from these infer the rest. The troubled sea consists of long structures of blue cloth or cardboard mounted on parallel rods and turned by urchins. Thunder is a heavy cart drawn across the beams – by no means the least touching instrument of this delightful band. Lightning is achieved by throwing handfuls of resinous pitch on a lighted torch; but a real bolt calls for a fuse and rocket.

The stage is provided with little square trap-doors which on being opened signify that demons are coming up from the cellar. Should they need to rise into the air, they are cleverly replaced by straw demons of brown buckram, or sometimes by actual chimney sweeps who majestically vanish into the aforementioned blue rags. But what is really tragic is when the ropes jam or break, for then the infernal spirits or immortal gods fall and break their legs and are sometimes killed. To all this you must add the monsters used to lend excitement to certain scenes (such as dragons, lizards, tortoises, crocodiles, or large toads), which, by perambulating the stage in a menacing way, permit us to witness the Temptations of Saint Anthony. Each of these characters is animated by a lout of a Savoyard who actually hasn't the sense enough to act the dumb beast.

But what you cannot imagine is the frightful cries, the prolonged bellowings, which fill the theatre during the performance. You see actresses virtually in convulsions as they rend from their lungs the most violent undulations; both fists clenched against the breast, the head thrown back, cheeks aflame, veins bursting, and diaphragm heaving. It is impossible to say which is the more unpleasantly assailed, the eye or the ear; these motions cause as much pain to those who look as the singing to those who listen, but what is still more astonishing is that the howls and cries are almost the only thing applauded by the audience. From the hand-clapping you might suppose a company of deaf-mutes in a frenzy of delight at catching here and there a few piercing sounds, and eager to encourage their repetition. For my part, I am convinced that people applaud a prima donna as they do the feats of the strong man at the fair. The sensations are painfully disagreeable, hard to endure, but one is so glad when it is all over that one cannot help rejoicing.

Opera, to a person genuinely fond of aural beauty, must inevitably appear tawdry and obnoxious, if only because it presents aural beauty in a frame of purely visual gaudiness, with overtones of the grossest sexual provocation. It is chiefly supported in all countries by the same sort of wealthy sensualists who also support musical comedy. One finds in the directors' room the traditional stock company of the stage-door alley. Such vermin, of course, pose in the newspapers as devout and almost fanatical partisans of art. But one has merely to observe the sort of opera they think is good to get the measure of their actual artistic discrimination.

The genuine music-lover may accept the carnal husk of opera to get at the kernel of actual music within, but that is no sign that he approves the carnal husk or enjoys gnawing through it. Most musicians, indeed, prefer to hear operatic music outside the opera house; that is why one so often hears such lowly things, say, as 'The Ride of the Valkyries' in the concert hall. 'The Ride of the Valkyries' has a certain intrinsic value as pure music; played by a competent orchestra it may give civilized pleasure. But as it is commonly performed in an opera house, with a posse of fat beldames throwing themselves about the stage, it can only produce the effect of a dose of ipecacuanha. The sort of person who actually delights in such spectacles is the sort of person who delights in gas-pipe furniture. Such half-wits are in a majority in every opera house west of the Rhine. They go to the opera, not to hear music, not even to hear bad music, but merely to see a more or less obscene circus. A few, perhaps, have a further purpose; they desire to assist in that circus, to show themselves in the capacity of fashionables, to enchant the yokelry with their splendor. But the majority might be content with the more modest aim. What they get for the outrageous prices they pay for seats is a chance to feast their eyes upon glittering members of the superior *demi-monde*, and to abase their groveling souls before magnificoes on their own side of the footlights. They esteem a performance, not in proportion as true music is on tap, but in proportion as the display of notorious characters on the stage is copious, and the exhibition of wealth in the boxes is lavish. A soprano who can gargle her way up to F sharp *in alt* is more to such simple souls than a whole drove of Johann Sebastian Bachs; her one real rival in the entire domain of art is the contralto who has a pension from a former grand duke and is reported to be *enceinte* by several stockbrokers.

The music that such ignobles applaud is often quite as shoddy as they are themselves. To write a successful opera a knowledge of harmony and counterpoint is not enough; one must also be a sort of Barnum. All the first-rate musicians who have triumphed in the opera house have been skilled mountebanks as well. I need cite only Wagner and Richard Strauss. The business, indeed, has almost nothing to do with music. All the actual music one finds in many a popular opera — for example, *Thaïs* — mounts up to less than one may find in a pair of Gung'l waltzes. It is not this mild flavor of tone that fetches the crowd; it is the tinpot show that goes with it. An opera may have plenty of good music in it and fail, but if it has a good enough show it will succeed.

Such a composer as Wagner, of course, could not write even an opera without getting some music into it. In all of his works, even including *Parsifal*, there are magnificent passages, and some of them are very long. Here his natural genius overcame him, and he forgot temporarily what it was about. But these magnificent passages pass unnoticed by the average opera audience. What it esteems in his music dramas is precisely what is cheapest and most mountebankish — for example, the more lascivious parts of *Tristan und Isolde*. The sound music it dismisses as tedious. The Wagner it venerates is not the musician, but the showman. That he had a king for a backer and was seduced by Liszt's daughter —

these facts, and not the fact of his stupendous talent, are the foundation stones of his fame in the opera house.

Greater men, lacking his touch of the quack, have failed where he succeeded – Beethoven, Schubert, Schumann, Brahms, Bach, Haydn. Not one of them produced a genuinely successful opera; most of them didn't even try. Imagine Brahms writing for the diamond horseshoe! Or Bach! Or Haydn! Beethoven attempted it, but made a mess of it: *Fidelio* survives today chiefly as a set of concert overtures. Schubert wrote more actual music every morning between 10 o'clock and lunch time than the average opera composer produces in 250 years, yet he always came a cropper in the opera house.   H. L. MENCKEN, 1918

APPARITIONS

Ghosts, phantasms, the slipping of the distinction between the real and the imagined are all peculiarly suited to the anti-naturalistic character of the operatic form. Here, in an extract from his autobiography, My Life, *Wagner recalls a strange encounter he had after a performance of his 'spook' opera* Der Fliegende Holländer (The Flying Dutchman).

A few days later came a second performance with the same cast, which I also conducted. What I experienced on this evening was even more singular than on the first. I had clearly gained a few allies from the first performance, who turned up again and began applauding after the overture; this aroused a lot of hissing, and throughout the entire evening nobody dared to applaud again. My old friend Heine had come from Dresden on behalf of the theater management to study the staging of *A Midsummer Night's Dream* and attended this second performance. He had persuaded me to accept an invitation from one of his Berlin

23

relatives to have supper together after the performance in a little restaurant on Unter den Linden. Very weary, I followed him to an ugly and dimly lit tavern, gulped down the proffered wine in somewhat hasty discontent in the hope of warming myself, listened to the strained conversation of my good-natured friend and his companion, and stared fixedly at the daily papers, now having ample leisure to read the reviews of the first performance of *Der Fliegende Holländer*, which had appeared that day. I felt pretty badly cut up when I saw for the first time my name and my work handled in the most contemptible tone and absolutely shameless, rampant ignorance. Our Berlin host, a thorough philistine, stated that he had known all along what would happen this evening, for he had read these reviews in the morning. The Berliners, he said, wait for the verdict of Rellstab and his cronies to determine how they should react. This singular fellow really wanted to cheer me up, and he ordered bottle after bottle of various wines; my friend Heine tried to evoke the happier memories of our *Rienzi* period in Dresden; staggering, and with my head spinning, I was finally conducted back to my hotel by the two of them. It was after midnight. When the night-clerk was lighting my way through the dark corridors to my room, a man suddenly stepped out in my path, dressed in black and of pale and distinguished countenance. He said he wanted to talk to me. He asserted he had been waiting for me since the end of the performance and in his determination to speak to me had remained here until now. I tried to excuse myself as being totally unfit for any kind of business for, as he could see, I had, without exactly giving way to unrestrained merriment, carelessly drunk a little too much wine. I got this out in a stammer; but my strange visitor was all the less willing to be rebuffed; he accompanied me to my room and declared it was now all the more imperative that he speak to me. We seated ourselves in the cold room to the feeble light of one candle, and he began telling me in fluid and impassioned speech that he too had attended that night's performance of *Der Fliegende Holländer* and could well imagine the mood in which such experiences had left me; but precisely for that reason he had decided to stop at nothing to be able to speak to me tonight in order to tell me that with *Der Fliegende Holländer* I had written an unprecedented masterpiece, and that it would be indeed terrible if I yielded to the slightest feeling of discouragement as a result of the unworthy reception accorded it by the Berlin public, as on this very evening he had made the acquaintance of a work that evoked new and undreamed-of hope for the future of German art. My hair began standing on end: one of Hoffmann's fantastic figures had entered my life in the flesh! I could think of nothing to say except to inquire his name, whereupon he seemed very surprised, as I had, he said, conversed with him the day before at Mendelssohn's house: it was there that my conduct and conversation had attracted his attention; he had suddenly regretted giving in to this general distaste for opera by not attending the first performance of *Der Fliegende Holländer* and swore to himself not to miss the second; he was, he informed me, Professor Werder. This didn't mean anything to me; he had to write it down. He hunted up pen and paper, did as requested, and we parted, after which I threw myself upon the bed, dead to the world, and enjoyed a deep and refreshing sleep.

Apparitions, dreams, and sleep figure prominently in a number of Benjamin Britten's vocal and operatic works. The following dream-notations by David Drew were originally published in a birthday anthology for Britten's lifelong collaborator Peter Pears, and refer to their Aldeburgh home, The Red House. The notations are entitled Triad — with Lydian Fourth, *and in the third dream the 'fourth' figure promises to be 'starry Vere' in* Billy Budd — *a role associated from the beginning with Pears. But when the confused sounds are finally resolved, the stellar aria that emerges is that of Peter Grimes.*

1—3—5

A dream, dreamt many years ago, in which every dimension of imaginable reality was in its proper place, although reality itself had provided no pretext or preparation for it; a dream so simple, rational, and lifelike that it would have been forgotten on waking if the conversation it consisted of had been elsewhere than in the Red House (which I had never visited) and with B. and P. (whom I had never met). Tea was served, time was most pleasantly passed, and I almost missed the train home. (Even in reality, there were still trains to be missed at Aldeburgh.)

5—1—3

Several years later the dream returned with a new start: instead of immediately finding myself in the sitting-room and being rather taken aback by the distinguished company, I was welcomed at the door with the words, 'How good of you to call again!' It was, I thought, remarkable enough that my hosts remembered my previous visit after so many years, but quite astonishing that despite their busy and celebrated lives they had apparently had the same dream as I.

#4

To this common chord that was never struck in what we call reality, a more recent dream added not only a modal colouring but also a harsh dissonance, and a resolution. Wearing a sou'wester and a yellow oilskin that dated from my West Highland schooldays, I was seemingly in a dressing-room at the Royal Opera House and about to make my wholly unrehearsed debut in a role for which I had no score, and an opera whose very name was being withheld from me. Finding that the other dressing-rooms were empty, I realized that the performance had already begun, ran breathlessly through a labyrinth of unmarked corridors, and stumbled on to the stage. The curtain was up, and I saw that I was on the deck of HMS *Indomitable*. But there was no sign of 'starry Vere' or his officers, nor was there anything recognizable as music. Since the deck was swarming with aimless figures, I abjectly tried to conceal myself among them. But at once I was picked up by a spotlight, and became aware that I was now to initiate some sort of ensemble, or be lost forever. At that immeasurably perilous moment a redemptive octave E welled up from muted double-basses, the nightmare dissolved into the clearest of dreams, and from somewhere close to me there came the familiar but disembodied voice of an incomparable artist, singing precisely as I had first and so often heard him, and with that selfsame unsurpassable phrasing –

> Now the Great Bear and Pleiades
> where earth moves
> Are drawing up the clouds
> of human grief
> Breathing solemnity in the deep night.

In these lucidly dreamt moments, as in the vividness of performance itself, the lot of those of us with lesser roles, or none at all, seemed more than merely tolerable.

APPLAUSE

It is a Folly in a Singer to grow vain at the first Applauses, without reflecting whether they are given by Chance, or out of Flattery; and if he thinks he deserves them, there is an End of him.

PIERO TOSI, *Observations on the Florid Song*, 1723

Taking a curtain call is an art in itself. I dislike seeing an artist who has just died in the most tragic circumstances bounding out to take a call with a broad grin. The illusion one has spent the previous few hours trying to create should be broken gently and I think it is most important to remain 'in character' for the first two or three calls, only gradually re-assuming one's own identity. The greatest master of the curtain call I ever saw was Boris Christoff. He would take his first curtain call after, say, *Boris* or *Don Carlos,* looking completely exhausted, and then step out of sight, listening to the applause. The moment it died a fraction he would go out again, this time, his hand on his heart. Off he would come and again gauge just the moment to reappear with a deep bow of gratitude to the audience. This would continue, ending, on one occasion, with him in a kneeling position! Audiences feed on their own applause, especially in an opera house, and Boris certainly knew how to evoke the maximum response.

MICHAEL LANGDON, *Notes from a Low Singer*

AUDEN

The poet, critic, librettist and opera buff W. H. Auden was also one of the most brilliant talkers of the century, as Robert Craft's diary reveals. I.S. is, of course, Stravinsky. See also pp. 313–15 and 420–4.

He talks about his ideas for a libretto on the *Bacchae*, confessing that 'The *Elegy [for Young Lovers*, to music by Henze] was our version of *Arabella.*' Switching to other operas, he describes the beginning of the second act of *Die Walküre* as 'a Victorian break-fast scene, Wotan meekly cracking his morning egg behind *The Times* while Fricka furiously rattles the teacups. *Pelléas,*' he says, 'is an underwater opera. Nobody can be that refined; the piece succeeds because it flatters the audience. But imagine devoting an opera to people with manias for losing things!' Apropos a line in *Vanessa*, he wonders 'where the author had seen "weeping deer",' and, in defending opera against other types of music, he remarks that 'People who attend chamber music concerts are like Englishmen who go to church when abroad.' November 1962

New York. Wystan Auden for dinner, wearing a dark brown flannel shirt, black necktie, wicker beach shoes, dark glasses (pocketed until departure, just before midnight, at which time he looks like a jazz musician), the glittering jewels of his genius. After confounding the waiters by ordering mushrooms as a 'savory' and by using 'quite' for 'yes' ('More wine sir?' – 'Quite'), he talks about 'anti-opera,' beginning with two somewhat out-of-the-way examples ('the *great* anti-operas are *Fidelio*, *Boris*, *Pelléas*), Janáček's *House of the Dead*, which 'has no characters and no tunes,' and Godard's *Dante*, pronounced 'Dant'. 'Whereas Act One of "*Dant*" merely sets the Florentine scene, the subject of Act Two is the entire *commedia*. In the third act "Dant" and Beatrice are united in, of all places, "a nunnery, near Ravenna".' But he is more at home with the Germans. 'Elektra is so definitely a non-U character,' he says, 'that a singer who does the part to perfection shouldn't attempt Isolde.' This leads to a statement that 'The first act of *Tristan* offers the greatest lessons to a librettist: nothing happens on stage, but it is drama, not oratorio, and the drama is achieved entirely by exits and entrances.' Telling I.S. of the numerous excisions in the new production of *The Rake's Progress* in Vienna, he proposes to make cutting illegal in future by pub-

29

lishers' contracts. 'And, after all, *The Rake* isn't exactly like *Götterdämmerung*, where the stage director can always claim that he has to give people a chance to pee.'

On the subject of certain more recent operas he is concerned (not unduly) 'lest the Britten pendulum swing so far the other way that people begin to say they are *all* bad.' And 'though Verdi saw that *Cleopatra* wouldn't do – but perhaps it *would* have done in Boïto's Italian – I understand that it is being tried out here nevertheless. Now, the only Shakespeare that could be turned into English-language opera is *Love's Labour's Lost*, and that would take a great deal of adapting.'

January 1966

In 1970, in collaboration with Chester Kallman, Auden did set a version of Love's Labour's Lost; *the composer was Nicolai Nabokov. Samuel Barber's adaptation of* Antony and Cleopatra *flopped disastrously when it opened the new Metropolitan Opera House in New York in 1966.*

AUDIENCES

From the astonishing snobbery of the aging connoisseur Lord Mount Edgcumbe, shaking his head as he compares 'what the opera formerly was to what it is now', to Berlioz's passionate partisanship for Gluck's classicism and George Marek's acid observations on modern auditorium philistinism, the opera audience is a fascinating and complex phenomenon, worthy of historians' and sociologists' careful attention. See also pp. 122–34.

It will scarcely be credited by those who are not old enough to

remember it, that at the period when these Reminiscences commence [c. 1770], and for many years subsequent to it, the price of a
subscription to a box for *fifty* representations was *twenty guineas*
a seat, so that there was a positive saving of five guineas on the
season to every subscriber; and that too when the theatre was
differently constructed, and the private boxes were very few in
number, not exceeding in all *thirty-six*, eighteen ranged in three
rows, on each side of the house; the front being then occupied by
open public boxes (or *amphithéâtre*, as it is called in French
theatres) communicating with the pit. Both of these were filled
exclusively with the highest classes of society, all without exception in the full dress then universally worn. The audiences thus
assembled were considered as indisputably presenting a finer
spectacle than any other theatre in Europe, and absolutely
astonished the foreign performers to whom such a sight was
entirely new. At the end of the performance, the company of the
pit and boxes repaired to the coffee-room, which was then the
best assembly in London, private ones being rarely given on opera
nights, and all the first society was regularly to be seen there. Over
the front box was the five shillings gallery, then resorted to by
respectable persons not in full dress; and above that an upper
gallery to which the admission was three shillings. Subsequently
the house was encircled by private boxes, yet still the prices
remained the same, and the pit preserved its respectability and
even grandeur till the old house was burnt down in 1789...

It was not until the second year of Catalani's engagement
[1807], when she more than doubled her demands, and obtained a
salary wholly unprecedented, that the subscription for a whole
box was at once raised from *one hundred and eighty* to *three
hundred guineas*. Thus has she permanently injured the establishment: for the price once raised, has never been lowered, or at
most in a very trifling degree; and it is become quite impossible for
persons of moderate incomes to afford so unreasonable a sum for
a mere entertainment. Hence has arisen the custom of halving and
sub-dividing the subscriptions, so that very few persons have now
the sole ownership of a box. Hence too, that of letting them for the
night, and of selling even single tickets when not used by the

proprietor. The evil of this practice is evident. Formerly every lady possessing an opera-box considered it as much her *home* as her house, and was as sure to be found there, few missing any of the performances. If prevented from going, the *loan* of her box, and the gratuitous use of the tickets was a favour always cheerfully offered and thankfully received as a matter of course, without any idea of payment. Then too it was a favour to ask gentlemen to belong to a box, when subscribing to one was actually advantageous. Now, no lady can propose to them to give her more than double the price of the admission at the door, so that having paid so exorbitantly, every one is glad to be reimbursed a part at least of the great expense which she must often support alone. Boxes and tickets therefore are no longer given, they are let for what can be got: for which traffic the circulating libraries afford an easy accommodation. Many too which are not taken for the season are disposed of in the same manner, and are almost put up to auction, their price varying from three to eight or even ten guineas, according to the performance of the evening, and other accidental circumstances. I have known an instance of a box being asked for in the morning for a particular opera, but not taken on account of the high price demanded: in the afternoon of the same day the same box was offered for half the sum, and then again rejected from the suspicious appearance of the tender. The next morning the reason was discovered; *the opera had been changed*. This artifice requires no comment....

From all these causes the whole style of the Opera House is totally changed, its audiences are of a different description, its comfort entirely lost. The pit has long ceased to be the resort of ladies of fashion, and latterly, by the innovations introduced, is no longer agreeable to the former male frequenters of it. Those who compose the best part of the audience, and who really pay the fair price, coming late to the theatre, find all the seats occupied by the holders of orders and cheap admissions, while the boxes, being frequently filled by occasional hirers of them, afford no retreat to those who would visit the friends to whom they properly belong. This is an abuse which the manager should rectify for his own sake; for that of the subscribers the rent of the boxes ought to be

lowered, if not to their original price, which may now be impossible, at least to one far beneath what is still demanded.

LORD MOUNT EDGCUMBE, *Musical Reminiscences*

Most performances at the Opéra were solemn ceremonies for
which I prepared myself diligently by reading and pondering the
work in question. I and a few of the pit regulars were fanatics for
our favourite composers. The admiration we professed for them
was equalled only by our abomination of the rest. The Jove of our
Olympus was Gluck. The most passionate music-lover of today
can have no conception how fiercely we worshipped him. But if
some of my companions were zealous adherents of the faith, I can
say in all modesty that I was its high priest. Whenever I saw any
weakening in their devotion, I would revive it with sermons
worthy of the disciples of Saint-Simon, and drag them off to the
Opéra, often paying for their tickets out of my own pocket but
pretending that I had been given them by someone in the management. Having by this means lured my men into the theatre for
the Gluck masterpiece that was being given that night, I would
station them in a particular row in the pit with strict instructions
not to change their seats, for not all places were equally good for
hearing; I had tried them all and knew the defects or advantages of
each. Thus in one you were on top of the horns, in another you
could hardly hear them. On the right the trombones were too
prominent, on the left you got an unpleasant effect from the sound
bouncing off the stall boxes. At the front you were too near the
orchestra, and the voices were drowned; on the other hand, at the
back you were too far from the stage to make out the words or the
expressions on the actors' faces. The orchestration of this work
should be heard from here, the choruses in that work from there.
In one act, where the scene was a sacred grove, the stage area was
enormous; the sound tended to disperse and lose itself about the

theatre; in that case you had to go nearer. Another act took place in the interior of a palace, and the design was what is called a box set, an apparently unimportant change which doubled the power of the voices; so it became necessary to move a little farther back to allow voices and orchestra to find a better balance.

Once these instructions had been laid down, I questioned my acolytes as to how well they knew the work which they had come to hear. If they had not read the text, I produced a libretto from my pocket, and while we waited for the curtain to go up I made them study it, to the accompaniment of copious explanations from myself on the composer's intentions in all the more important passages. We always got there early so that we could sit where we wanted to and so as not to risk missing the first notes of the overture, as well as for the pleasure that comes from savouring in anticipation a delightful experience that you know you are about to enjoy. We also loved watching the orchestra assemble. It was as empty as a piano without strings when we arrived; then it would gradually fill up with players and music. The orchestral attendant came in first and put the parts on the desks. This was always an anxious moment. Something could have happened since our arrival to make them change the opera, and instead of Gluck's monumental work they might have substituted a *Nightingale* or an *Engaged Couple*, a *Caravan from Cairo*, a *Panurge*, a *Village Magician* or *Lasthènie*, all more or less spurious creations for which we declared our sovereign contempt. The name of the work printed in large letters on the double bass parts, which were nearest to the pit, either relieved or confirmed our fears. In the latter case we would rise in a body and leave the theatre, swearing like marauding soldiers who discover water in what they had taken to be brandy casks, and including in our general execration the composer of the work substituted, the manager who had inflicted it on the public, and the government which allowed it to be performed at all.   HECTOR BERLIOZ, *Memoirs*

First and foremost, be sure not to clutter your mind with any advance idea of what the opera is about. If you know the story, if you know the dramatic reasons why the characters behave as they do, if in addition you know some of the words that are expressed in song, then there is a danger that you might enjoy the opera merely as dramatic entertainment. So 'tis folly to be wise. Be baffled! And be sure to stay baffled! If you have come to the opera-house hardly knowing what opera is being given and not caring what happens therein you must not weaken half-way through. I have seen people go staunchly into the opera without the faintest knowledge of what they were about to hear – and then during act one or two give up and hastily consult a synopsis. This is not cricket.

TIME OF ARRIVAL. Here the saddest change has taken place. Time was when every overture served as the entrance march of the guests, when people drifted in unhurriedly throughout the first act. The Met treasures a letter from a subscriber of a past day who requested that the singing of the 'Celeste Aida,' which Verdi placed at the beginning of the opera, be transferred to a later point, as she couldn't possibly arrive in time for the aria. People knew what they wanted in those days, and took seriously the admonition to be found in an old French book on etiquette: '*Ça sent la province d'arriver avant le commencement d'un concert.*' Nowadays nearly everyone is in his seat when the lights go down, and even most of the boxes, those black holes of calculation, are filled at curtain time. But make it your business to uphold tradition, never appear promptly, and when you do arrive, unwrap yourself in leisure. Just because most people are on time, a belated entrance is especially effective these days.

TIME OF DEPARTURE. For the best effect, this should be either at the beginning or in the middle of the last scene. The final portions of opera are usually great musical climaxes. They are the moments into which the composer has poured his most meaningful music. Therefore scenes like 'O terra, addio,' from *Aida*, 'Is' ein Traum kann nicht wirklich sein,' from *Der Rosenkavalier*, and, of course, the *Liebestod* are strictly to be avoided.

APPLAUSE. This should begin immediately after the tenor has run out of breath with the high C, or precisely at the moment when the love duet stops. This is particularly important in Wagnerian and the later Verdi operas because the orchestral postludes are usually beautiful.

IDENTIFYING OF CASTS. As you well know, the important thing is not what opera is being given tonight but who is singing tonight. If the tenor is not famous the opera can't be good. (This is axiomatic!) Of course, you are not likely to know beforehand who is singing. So, if in the course of the first act you are puzzled as to who is what, don't wait. Light a little pocket flashlight and look at your programme. This procedure has the additional advantage of distracting the attention of virtually everyone in your row. If you do not possess a pocket flashlight, don't hesitate to light a match. The fire-fighting equipment in most opera-houses is good.

TALKING. This is a crude though classic device; it is too elementary to need discussion and should be used only on provocation. However, talking should be kept up during orchestral interludes. This registers one's protests against the composer for providing music when the curtain is down. A young man was invited by a dowager to accompany her to a performance of *Tristan and Isolde*. 'I should love to accept your invitation to sit in your box for *Tristan*,' he replied. 'I have never heard you in *Tristan*.' This story is variously attributed to Mark Twain, George Bernard Shaw, and Bill Nye. But whoever may have originated it, there still exist members of the Old Guard who haven't heard it and who don't act accordingly.

FLUFFS. When the soprano, who has up to this moment given an intelligent and sensitive performance, makes a glaring error, be sure to show that you caught it. The best method is to jump as if stung by a bee. However, a vigorous shaking of the head will suffice. Effective, also, is an understanding veiled look at your neighbour to let him know that you know that the old grey *mère* ain't what she used to be. (See also 'Old Subscriber's Attitude'.)

CLICHES. There are two operatic clichés which should be standard equipment for all of the Old Guard. One of these is, 'All opera singers are terrible actors.' There have been and there exist to-day a number of exceptions to this rule. There are artists whose acting equipment consists of more than extending hand and arm to see whether it is raining; there are artists who sing the text and portray the character. These exceptions should not disturb your belief. You should continue firm in the faith that operatic artists should be heard but not seen, and that therefore you 'like to listen with your eyes closed.' I need not be so gauche as to point out that the closed-eye technique can be of immsense help if you have had a difficult day.

The second cliché concerns chiefly the Wagnerian music drama. It goes something like this: 'I just love Wagner's music, but the singing spoils it.' This cliché is still to-day one of the more popular ones, though it is a belief difficult to support on mere grounds of sense. Sense (musical and otherwise) would prove that Wagner knew that the voice is the most expressive and widest-ranged of musical instruments, that he wrote superbly for the voice, that if he wanted the 'Good Friday' music sung he knew what he was doing, and that if this 'Good Friday' music is played in orchestral transcription it loses something of the character the composer intended for it.

THE PROFOUND ATTITUDE. This is an entirely different approach towards the problem, but there are, of course, more ways than one to skin a category. The Profound Attitude must be handled with discretion. It is an attitude which will not work with *I Pagliacci* but does wonders for *Pelléas et Mélisande*. You imply you are here not to enjoy the music but to undergo a short-wave treatment in cultural therapy. You must wrinkle your brow, be sad and sighing, and in general display the symptoms of malaise. You must make it quite clear that this is not a piece of music written by a man for the enjoyment of everybody but a manifestation of a mystic and anomalous rite to which only presbyters hold the secret. This is perhaps most important and should be liberally studied.

IT-USED-TO-BE-BETTER or OLD SUBSCRIBER'S ATTITUDE. This is perhaps most important and should be liberally studded with references to the Golden Age of Opera. Assume this attitude and a bitter-sweet smile when you tell people who are just beginning to discover the delights of opera. Name names of the past – both the famous names and the little-known names. Aldous Huxley's advice on how to become an art connoisseur is useful here. He counsels that you should look up an unknown painter, deservedly forgotten. Then when people speak of Rembrandt or El Greco you say, 'Ah, but have you ever heard of ——?' Nobody has – so you are a connoisseur.

When talking about the old days in disparagement of present performances, select interval gatherings where your voice will carry well. GEORGE MAREK, *A Front Seat at the Opera*

I went to the *Dusk of the Gods*. Beside me in the gallery was an elderly man who smelt of garlic. He said it was a colossal opera and that it required great voices. He had heard it in Hamburg. He spoke a few words to me in English, such as, very cold, very good and beautiful. Before me was another man who said Wagner's music was splendid but intended only for Germans. It was all intellect: no heart. Every time the horn motive sounded my garlicy friend twisted to me and said confidently: Adesso viene Sigfrido. He yawned much during the third act and went away before the last scene. When Brunnhilde brought on the horse, the latter, being unable to sing, evacuated: whereat the funny Italian disyllable [*caca*, poo-poo] flew from end to end of the gallery. There were many spectators who followed the opera with scores and librettos. On the stairs coming away and in the street I heard many people hum correctly and incorrectly the nine notes of the funeral motive. Nothing in the opera moved me. I have heard the funeral march often before. Only when Siegfried died I responded from the crown of my head to his cry 'O sposa sacra.' I suppose there are a few men from time to time who really feel an impulse towards Gawd. JAMES JOYCE, 1907

AUDITION

*Rosa Ponselle records the encounter in her teacher's studio
that led to her sensational debut at the Met in 1918, when
she sang Leonora in Verdi's* La Forza del Destino *(from
which comes the aria 'Pace, pace, mio Dio'). At the time of
this audition, Ponselle had only sung in vaudeville.*

Caruso arrived punctually the afternoon of our audition. For the
first time, I saw him up close; he was slightly above average in
height, a bit overweight, blessed with a sunny disposition and a
face to match, and disarmingly charming in a boyish sort of way.
His clothes were as much a trademark as his unique voice; the
afternoon he came to audition us he was wearing a lemon-yellow
suit, with spats and a Panama hat to match.

'Hey, *scugnizz'*,' he called to me as he entered the studio. 'Do
you know you look like me?'

He spoke in Neapolitan, which of course I understood. A
scugnizza, I knew, was a ragamuffin, a sort of street urchin – an
affectionate tag that immediately put me at ease. When he said I
looked like him I knew that he meant that my features, like his,
were distinctly Neapolitan.

'I don't mind *looking* like you,' I said, joining in the banter, 'if
only I could *sing* like you!'

He laughed at my comeback, and I could sense him thinking to
himself, 'Well, now, she's certainly smart and brazen enough ...
maybe she'll make a good counterpart to me.'

Once the pleasantries were exchanged ... we got down to
business and I sang 'Pace, pace mio Dio.' Caruso gave me a hint of
what was to come when, at the end of the session, he said to me,
'You'll sing with me, you'll see.'

'I'll sing with *you*? Where? In what?' That was all I could
manage to say.

'We'll see, we'll see,' he said reassuringly. 'Maybe next year, maybe two years, maybe more. But you'll sing with me.'

At that moment he put his arm around me in a fatherly way and, letting his hand brush my throat, he said to me, 'You see, you have it there.' Next he pointed to my heart and said with a warm smile, 'And you have it there, too.' Lastly, he put his fingers to my temples and said, 'Whether you have it up there, only time will tell.' It was the finest appraisal any young singer could have been given.   ROSA PONSELLE, *A Singer's Life*

il BARBIERE DI SIVIGLIA

Seven strokes rang out across the city from the belfry of the
Signoria; fear lest I should arrive too late to find a seat at the
theatre alone had force to drag me away from this awe-inspiring
sight; for I was, so to speak, a spectator who gazed upon the very
tragedy of history. I flew like the wind to the *Hhohhomero*, for
such is the local pronunciation of the name of the Florentine
theatre, *il Cocomero*. I am resentful to the point of outragé against
the dialect of Florence, so renowned throughout the land. At first
it seemed to me that the tongue I heard was *Arabic*; and it was
impossible to pronounce it with any speed.

The overture began, and, to my delight, I found myself yet once
again in the society of that charming old friend of mine, Rossini.
By the end of the third bar, I had recognized his presence. To
confirm my supposition, I wandered down into the pit and
enquired; and indeed, as I had surmised, the *Barbiere di Siviglia*
which stood on the programme *was* his, not Paisiello's. With all
the temerity of true genius he has dared to weave new melodies
about that same *libretto* which has already won such reputation
for his rival. The part of Rosina was played tonight by signora
Giorgi, whose husband, in the days of the French occupation, was
an erstwhile judge on some tribunal. While I was in Bologna, there
was pointed out to me a young cavalry officer who is not ashamed
to play *Primo buffo* parts. In Italy no stigma attaches to any
reasonable action; in other words, the country has suffered less
corruption from that artificial principle of 'honour' inculcated by
Louis XIV.

Rossini's *Barber* has all the characteristics of a painting by
Guido Reni; its very negligence reveals the Master's hand; there is
never a hint of effort or conscientious drudgery. Rossini is a man
of infinite ideas and no education. Imagine a *Beethoven* endowed

with such a boundless inspiration: what miracles might there not result! Tonight's music struck me as being somewhat too closely borrowed from Cimarosa. The only passage of indisputably authentic Rossini was the trio of the second-act *finale*, sung by Rosina, Almaviva and Figaro, of which the only criticism I have to make is that such music is misapplied to the unravelling of a complex intrigue, and should belong rather to a situation where the text suggests energetic characterization and rank obstinacy.

When danger is imminent, when a single minute can make or mar all, it is an insult to reason to listen to the same words repeated ten times over. Yet this so-called *necessary absurdity* in music can easily be remedied. During the last three or four years, Rossini has been turning out operas which rarely contain more than one, or at the most two isolated passages worthy of the composer of *Tancredi* or of *l'Italiana in Algeri*. I was suggesting tonight a plan whereby all these scattered master-touches should be gathered together in one single score. It would give me greater satisfaction to have composed this single trio from the *Barbiere di Siviglia* than that whole monstrous rigmarole of an opera by Solliva, which delighted me so hugely in Milan.

STENDHAL, Rome, Naples, Florence

BAYREUTH

From its opening in 1876, the trip to Wagner's opera house in Bayreuth has been a great operatic pilgrimage. In its early days, however, this provincial Bavarian town did not altogether satisfy fastidious tourists' hotel and catering requirements: the ensuing comedy was often worthy of the pen of E. M. Forster. 'Food forms the chief interest of the public,' wrote Tchaikovsky; 'the artistic representations take a secondary place. Cutlets, baked potatoes, omelettes – all are discussed much more eagerly than Wagner's music.'

Bayreuth was an uncomfortable town to live in; it has changed a good deal within the last ten years, though it is still without a large hotel full of plate-glass and ferns and Liberty silks, with tennis-grounds and golf-links. In the twentieth century one gets better food in the restaurants than one did in the nineteenth, and bath-rooms have begun to appear, and the fly-haunted privy is nearly extinct. And this was the important matter that the slackening of the train's speed had reminded me of. We had written many letters, and had many interviews with the agent who apportions out the lodgings, and my last words had been to him, 'A clean privy!' He had promised that he would see to it, but from the direction in which the coachman was driving us, it would seem that the desirable accommodation was not procurable in the town. It was Edward [Moore's travelling companion] who noticed that our coachman was heading straight for the country, and standing up in the carriage, he began to expostulate – ineffec-tually, however, for Edward's German is limited and the driver only laughed, pointing with a whip towards a hillside facing the theatre, and there we saw a villa embowered and overlooking a lodging so delightful that I could not but feel interested in Edward's objection to it.

'We shall be out of the way of everything,' was all he shrieked.

'But not out of the way of the theatre!' I interjected. 'We shall walk through the cornfields to it.'

'The theatre isn't everything.'

'Everything in Bayreuth . . . surely.'

He spoke of his breakfast. He wouldn't be able to get it. He must be near a restaurant, and the cornfield did not appeal to his sense of the picturesque as Rothenburg did. Despite my entreaty, he stood up again in the carriage, and began to expostulate with the driver again, who, however, only laughed and pointed with his whip, pouring forth all the while a torrent of Bavarian German which Edward could not understand.

'How shall I stop him?' he cried, turning to me, who can speak no single word of German. After mentioning this fact, I reminded him that the people in the villa were waiting for us, and for us to go away to the town without advising them might prevent them from letting their lodgings. I said this, knowing Edward's weak spot – his moral conscience. He fell to my arrow, answering quietly that he would willingly pay for the lodging on the hillside if I would only go with him to the town in search of another. To this I consented, unwillingly, I admit, but I consented. My unwillingness, however, to live in the town, where all the decent lodgings had long ago been taken, became more marked when we were shown into a large drawing-room and two bedrooms, the cleanest we had ever seen in Bayreuth.

'We shall want a room in which to write *The Tale of the Town*.'

The mention of his play did not seem to soften Edward, and the landlord, an elderly man, who had relinquished me because I knew no German at all, attached himself to Edward – literally attached himself, taking him by the lappet of his coat; and I remember how the old man drew him along with him to the end of a passage, I following them, compelled by curiosity. We came to a door, which the old man threw open with a flourish, exhibiting to our enchanted gaze a brand-new water-closet, all varnish and cleanliness, and the pride of the old man, who entered into a long explanation, the general drift of which only pierced Edward's understanding. 'He says he has decorated the privy for us at the special request of Mr Schulz Curtis. But if we pay him for his lodging!'

'No mere payment will recompense him. Remember, he asked you if you liked the paper. He may have spent hours choosing it.'

But, blind to all the allurements of the checkered paper, Edward insisted on telling the landlord that he wished to live near a restaurant where he could get his breakfast. The German again caught him by the lappet of his coat, and there was a pretty German girl who knew a little English, the old man's daughter, smiling in the doorway, about whom I had already begun to think. But it was impossible to dissuade Edward, and we drove with our luggage here and there and everywhere, seeking a couple of rooms. It would be inopportune to describe every filthy suite of apartments that we visited; but it is not well, in a book of this kind, to omit any vivid memory, and among my memories none is more vivid than that of an iron railing dividing a sort of shallow area from the street in which some workmen were drinking beer, and of the kitchen beyond it. Uncouth women, round in the back as wash-tubs, walked about with drying-pans in their hands, great udders floating under blue blouses; and we followed a trail of inferior German cookery up a black slimy staircase to the first landing, where a bald-headed waiter, with large drops of sweat upon his brow, opened a door, exhibiting for our inspection two low-ceilinged rooms with high beds in the corners.

'Ask him if we can have clean sheets.'

'We have no others,' the waiter answered.

As I moved towards the doorway, I heard Edward saying that the rooms would do us very well, and when I explained to him their disadvantages, he answered that he would be able to get his breakfast. 'To get his breakfast!' The phrase seemed so Irish, so Catholic, that for a moment it was impossible to suppress my anger at Edward's unseemly indifference to my sense of cleanliness and comfort, and the women in the kitchen, the waiter, and the sheets horrified me, even to the extent of compelling me to tell him that I would sooner go back to England, giving up *The Ring, Parsifal*——

'I would sooner sleep anywhere, Edward; in the streets! Let us get away. Perhaps we shall find——'

'No, you'll object to all.'

'But why, Edward, should you stay here? You can have breakfast at our lodging.'

'I shan't be able to get an omelette. Can't you understand that people have habits?'

'Habits!' I said.   GEORGE MOORE, *Hail and Farewell*

Beloved,

No letter has yet come from you. I hope this heat has not turned you apoplectic: it is roasting like Hell here. We heard Parsifal yesterday – a very mysterious emotional work, unlike any of the others I thought. There is no love in it; it is more religious than anything. People dress in half mourning, and you are hissed if you try to clap. As the emotions are all abstract – I mean not between men and women – the effect is very much diffused; and peaceful on the whole. However, Saxon and Adrian say that it was not a good performance, and that I shant know anything about it until I have heard it 4 times. Between the acts, one goes and sits in a field, and watches a man hoeing turnips. The audience is very dowdy, and the look of the house is drab; one has hardly any room for ones knees, and it is very intense. I think earnest people only go – Germans for the most part, in sacks, with symbolical braid. Everything is new art – the restaurants have single lines drawn up the walls, with triangles suddenly bursting out – the kind of thing one sees in the Studio [the art magazine]. The grossness of the race is astonishing – but they seem very clean and kind.

VIRGINIA WOOLF, to her sister Vanessa, 1909

BEGINNINGS

The roots and origins of opera are matters of intense scholarly controversy, but there is no doubt that Peri's Euridice, *first performed in Florence in 1600 as part of the wedding celebrations for Henri IV of France and Maria de Medici, represents a turning-point in the early development of the form. Here its librettist Ottavio Rinuccini tries to explain to Maria the philosophy behind the spectacle she is about to witness. The alteration to 'the conclusion of the fable' mentioned by Rinuccini was the substitution of a happy ending appropriate to the mood of a wedding.*

It has been the opinion of many, most Christian Queen, that the ancient Greeks and Romans, in representing their tragedies upon the stage, sang them throughout. But until now this noble manner of recitation has been neither revived nor (to my knowledge) even attempted by anyone, and I used to believe that this was due to the imperfection of the modern music, by far inferior to the ancient.

But the opinion thus formed was wholly driven from my mind by Messer Jacopo Peri, who, hearing of the intention of Signor Jacopo Corsi and myself, set to music with so much grace the fable of *Dafne* (which I had written solely to make a simple trial of what the music of our age could do) that it gave pleasure beyond belief to the few who heard it.

Taking courage from this, Signor Jacopo gave to this same fable a better form and again represented it at his house, where it was heard and commended, not only by the entire nobility of our favoured state, but also by the most serene Grand Duchess and by the most illustrious cardinals Dal Monte and Montaldo.

But much greater favour and fortune have been bestowed upon the *Euridice*, set to music by the aforesaid Peri with wonderful art, little used by others, for the graciousness and magnificence of the most serene Grand Duchess found it worthy of representation upon a most noble stage in the presence of Your Majesty, the Cardinal Legates, and ever so many princes and lords of Italy and France.

For this reason, beginning to recognize with what favour such representations in music are received, I have wished to bring these two to light, in order that others, more skilful than myself, may employ their talents to increase the number and improve the quality of poems thus composed and cease to envy those ancients so much celebrated by noble writers.

To some I may seem to have been too bold in altering the conclusion of the fable of Orpheus, but so it seemed fitting to me at a time of such great rejoicing, having as my justification the example of the Greek poets in other fables. And our own Dante ventured to declare that Ulysses was drowned on his voyage, for all that Homer and the other poets had related the contrary. So likewise I have followed the authority of Sophocles in his *Ajax* in introducing a change of scene, being unable to represent otherwise the prayers and lamentations of Orpheus.

May Your Majesty recognize in these my labours, small though they be, the humble devotion of my mind to Your Majesty and live long in happiness to receive from God each day greater graces and greater favours.

In 1627 Monteverdi wrote to the aristocrat Alessandro Striggio (the librettist for his Orfeo *of 1607), discussing both his work on the now-lost opera* Licoris *and his views of a promising young bass, Giovanni-Battista Bisucci.*

My Most Illustrious Lord and Most Respected Master,

I beg you to forgive me for missing the previous post, not having replied to Your Lordship's most kind and courteous letter; because the many tasks I had last Saturday (the post-day) were the reason for my failure. There were two tasks: one was having to provide chamber music from 5 until 8 p.m. for the Most Serene Prince of Neuberg, who is staying incognito in the House of the English Ambassador; and this music being over, I then had to go – pressed by the entreaties of many friends – to the Carmelite Church, as it was the day of First Vespers of the Most Holy Madonna of that Order, and stay there fully occupied until almost one in the morning.

I am writing this now to let Your Lordship know what great delight I had on reading, in your very kind letter, of the pleasure you received from the first act of the brave *Licoris* of Signor Giulio Strozzi. I now have it all in my hands, given me by the same Signor Giulio, and full of many beautiful variations. At present I am having it written out at home, so that no copies, either partial or complete, can be taken.

I have already completed practically all the first act, and would be even further ahead if I had not had that little trouble with my eyes that I told Your Lordship about, and if I had not had some church music to write. From now on I shall work harder at it, and if you would like to see it, that is to read the whole of it, I shall send off to Your Lordship when I have copied it, so that you can give it a glance, and you will see that Signora Margherita [Basile, a famed soprano] will have a great deal to do on her own.

I took note of what Your Lordship proposed for the young bass [Bisucci], and it seems to me that he has firmly decided to enter His Highness's [the Duke of Mantua's] service, but I really think that the allowance is more generous than he deserves, because although it is true that he performs with assurance, he sings nevertheless in a somewhat melancholy manner; and regarding the ornaments, he does not separate them too well, because he fails most of the time to join the chest voice to the middle voice, for if the middle fails the chest voice, the ornamentation becomes harsh and hard and offensive; if the chest voice fails that of the middle, the ornamentation becomes like an almost continual deficiency in the voice, but when both function, the ornamentation comes off both sweetly and separated, and is most natural.

Although he is not in the chapel, this going around earning fees here and there (since both major and minor feasts are celebrated a great deal in this city, especially at this time) pleases him, seeing a few small coins coming into his purse, as they do come in this delightful kind of liberty. Otherwise I can give no explanation. The young man's nature is very calm, modest and humble. And here making a humble reverence to Your Lordship I pray Our Lord God for the fulfilment of every supreme joy.

BELLINI

The exquisite physical appearance of Vincenzo Bellini, 'the Swan of Catania' (his birthplace) and composer of Norma, *is described by Heinrich Heine in his* Florentine Nights, *a volume of essays and recollections published in 1836.*

He had a tall, slender figure which moved in an elegant, I might say, a coquettish manner: always *à quatre épingles*: a long, regular face, with a pale, rosy complexion; very fair, almost golden hair, twisted into small curls; high noble brows, a straight nose, pale blue eyes, a beautifully chiselled mouth, a round chin. His features had something vague and characterless; something like milk, and in this milk-face often mingled, half sweet and half bitter, an expression of sorrow. This expression compensated for the want of soul in Bellini's face, but it had a sorrow without depth: it glistened in the eyes without poetry, it played passionless about his lips. The young maestro seemed anxious to make his flat, languid sorrow conspicuous in his whole person. His hair curled in such a fanciful, melancholy style; his clothes sat so languidly about his frail body, he carried his little Spanish cane in so idyllic a way, that he always reminded me of the affected young shepherds, with their be-ribboned sticks, and bright-coloured jackets and pantaloons that we see in our pastorals. And his gait was so young-lady-like, so elegaic, so ethereal. The whole man looked like a sigh in dancing-pumps. He had received much applause among women, but I doubt if he anywhere awakened a strong passion. . . . He spoke the language (French) so badly that even in England it could scarcely be spoken worse. . . . His face, like his whole appearance, had that physical freshness, that bloom of flesh, that rosiness which makes a disagreeable impression on me – because I infinitely prefer what is death-like and marble. Later on, when I had known him a long time, I felt some liking for Bellini. This arose after I had observed that his character was thoroughly noble and good. His soul was certainly pure and unspotted by any hateful contagion. And he was not wanting in that good-natured, child-like quality which we now miss in men of genius, even if they do not wear it as an outward show.

BERG

When Alban Berg came to me in 1904, he was a very tall youngster and extremely timid. But when I saw the compositions he showed me – songs in a style between Hugo Wolf and Brahms – I recognized at once that he was a real talent. Consequently I accepted him as pupil, though at this time he was unable to pay my fee. Later his mother inherited a great fortune and told Alban, as they now had money, he could enter the conservatory. I was told that Alban was so upset by this assumption that he started to weep and could not stop weeping until his mother allowed him to continue with me.

He was always faithful to me and remained so during all of his short life. Why did I tell this story? Because I was greatly surprised when this soft-hearted, timid young man had the courage to engage in a venture which seemed to invite misfortune: to compose *Wozzeck*, a drama of such extraordinary tragedy that it seemed forbidding to music. And even more: it contained scenes of everyday life which were contrary to the concept of opera which still lived on in stylized costumes and conventionalized characters.

He succeeded. *Wozzeck* was one of the greatest successes of opera.

And why? Because Berg, this timid man, was a strong character who was faithful to his ideas, just as he was faithful to me when he was almost forced to discontinue studying with me.

He succeeded with his opera as he had succeeded in his insistence on studying with me. Making the belief in ideas one's own destiny is the quality which makes the great man.

ARNOLD SCHOENBERG, 1949

For other views of Wozzeck, *see pp. 418–19. Schoenberg, as will be evident, was a formidable egoist; the following letter, which Berg wrote to his wife in 1923, suggests the problems in their teacher–pupil relationship. (Karl Kraus, the Viennese satirist, was at the time conducting a campaign against slovenly journalism.)*

Schoenberg was again criticizing everything about me: that I'm still working on *Wozzeck* ('very Karl-Krausish, this eternal correcting'), that I smoke, that I 'shouldn't imagine *Wozzeck* will have any success, it's too difficult', and worst of all that I've still not started on the Chamber Concerto.

BISCUITS

If Proust's madeleine is the most famous cake in the history of art, then the biscuits given to Wagner by his lover Mathilde Wesendonck in 1859 also deserve commemoration as the key which unlocked a creative block. Here is his thank-you letter.

Child, child! The biscuits did help; they suddenly jerked me out of a bad patch where I had been stuck for a week, unable to go further. Yesterday my attempts to work were miserably unsuccessful. I was in a shocking humour, and gave it vent in a long letter to Liszt in which I informed him that I had come to the end of my composing days. . . . Today I was staring up at the grey sky, utterly disconsolate, simply wondering to whom I could now write something acrimonious. For a whole week had gone by since I had made any progress in the actual composition; I was stuck at the transition from 'vor Sehnsucht nicht zu sterben' to Tristan's voyage [Act 3]. So I had put that aside and turned back to work further on the beginning, the part I played to you. But today even that was making no progress, because I feel I did it much better before and cannot remember now how it was.

When the biscuits arrived, I realized what had been lacking; the biscuits I had here were much too salty, so they could not give me any sensible ideas; but when I took the sweet ones I had always been accustomed to, and dipped them in milk, everything suddenly fell into place. And so I threw aside the revision and went back to composing, on the story of the woman physician from far away. And now I am delighted; the transition is unbelievably successful, with a quite wonderful combination of two themes. Heavens, how much can be achieved by the right sort of biscuits! – Biscuits! that is the proper remedy for composers when they get stuck – but they must be the right kind. Now I have a good reserve of them; when you notice it getting low, be sure you send for more: I can see it is important. . . .

la BOHEME

The following letter from Puccini to his publisher Ricordi was written while working on his first and perhaps greatest masterpiece, in 1894. The Barrière d'Enfer eventually became the third act, and stands as one of Puccini's most sublime inspirations. Giacosa and Illica were his librettists, with whom he also collaborated on Tosca *and* Madama Butterfly.

As it is, there is no doubt about its being an original work! And such a one! The last act is most beautiful. So is that of the Quartier Latin, but very difficult. I have had the mountebank taken out. It will be necessary to eliminate other things. It would be a good thing if you would glance through it too, and rid it of certain extravagances which are really quite inessential. For example: 'The horse is the king of animals,' and 'Rivers are wines made of water,' and many other such lines which Illica loves like his own sons (if he had any). What must be shortened – and very much – is the second act, at the Barrière d'Enfer. All that stuff at the beginning is unnecessary, and we have agreed to cut it down, as also to shorten the rest, including the final quartet. This, in my opinion, is the weak act. Shall I be proved wrong? All the better! But the one which I think particularly successful is the last. The death of Mimi, with all that leads up to it, is very moving.

Kindest regards. I await the 'Quartier Latin' revised, abridged, and corrected by intervention of the Giacosian Buddha.

What is *Bohème*? Four old-time hippies in an attic. Lots of sounds (singing, drums, coughing?), sights (old attics, snow, sopranos and lights?), emotions (love, nobility and baseness?). Yeah, even sickness and yeah, love-sickness. *Bohème* is one of the few real old-time Happenings!

Advertisement of the Seattle Opera, 1967

BOOING

The headlines said 'Una *Traviata* che più traviata non si può' (A *Lost One* that couldn't have been more lost). The notoriously volatile opera aficionados of Parma outdid themselves on opening night (*La Traviata*, December 27) of the 150th anniversary season of the Teatro Regio, heckling the Violetta, Elena Mauti-Nunziata, and her tenor, Beniamino Prior, incessantly. The show ended after Flora's party, with a press attaché of the opera house announcing from the wings, 'The performance is suspended, given that Miss Nunziata, seeing the direction the evening has taken, no longer has the tranquillity or serenity to conclude it.' Conductor Fernando Previtali, even worse off than his soloists, was exhorted by the public at every appearance either to speed things up or to put down the baton and retire. With this dressy and demanding audience raging in an overcrowded auditorium, the artists backstage came to the conclusion that the riot must have been organized for political reasons, while the management upstairs summarily decided to replace conductor and all principals, apparently in deference to the audience, for a second 'prima'. . . . Miss Nunziata later commented, 'I can't imagine why this happened. I've done some ninety *Traviatas* in my life, all over the world, from the Met to Spain, England and France. I've always had success with it from critics and audiences.' The soprano would not be the first to deplore Parmesan manners if she refused to appear there again; Cornell MacNeil, for one, left the cast of *Un Ballo in Maschera* some years ago when a well-known soprano was vociferously booed. Well, at least no one threw a dead cat onstage, as someone reportedly did from the gallery of La Scala in reaction to the new production of *I Due Foscari*.

Opera News, 1980

BRITTEN

The operatic oeuvre *of some composers reveals powerful moral and philosophical consistency and depth: none more so than that of Benjamin Britten. Here the composer and critic Robin Holloway meditates on a theme which runs through not only* Owen Wingrave *(based on a story by Henry James about a victimized pacifist), but* Billy Budd *and* The Turn of the Screw *as well.*

To place all self-deception, brutality and blood-lust on one side, and all humane decency on the other is more than just simplistic and mean; it is *untrue*. And this, in a man of painfully sensitive conscience, must stand at a peculiarly vulnerable place. It is commonplace to pay pious tribute to Britten's pacifism. But Peace and its facile companion Compassion can hardly be reconciled to a preoccupation with subject-matter that sometimes seems closer to a nervous compulsion than to the spirit of 'peace on earth, good will towards men'. Owen Wingrave's fervour and the music's glittery warmth amidst so much that is angular and crashing, suggest what dare not speak its name in work after work. 'Love is the unfamiliar word' – not love as an abstract, self-possession, self-realization: 'in Peace I have found my image'. The private, almost fetishistic quality of this word in Britten's output explains itself – warrants its full warmth – only if it is understood as the pass- or code-word for his sexuality.

The wonder is that he could ever as an artist get beyond this impasse, for the extent of repression that these unresolved tensions indicate is so great as to suggest the imminence of an explosion.

CALLAS

The recording producer Walter Legge received sacks of hate mail after writing this essay on Maria Callas, published in Opera News *shortly after her mysterious death in 1976. For another view of Callas's 'superhuman inferiority complex', see pp. 342–4.*

Callas suffered from a superhuman inferiority complex. This was the driving force behind her relentless, ruthless ambition, her fierce will, her monomaniacal egocentricity and insatiable appetite for celebrity. Self-improvement, in every facet of her life and work, was her obsession. When she was first pointed out to me, a year or two before we met, she was massive, shabbily dressed in a nondescript tweed coat, and her walk had the ungainly lurch of a sailor who, after months on rough seas, was trying to adjust himself to terra firma. At our first meeting I was taken aback by her rather fearsome New York accent, which may have had a booster from GIs when she worked as interpreter for the American forces in Athens. Within months Callas was speaking what the English call the King's English until the BBC murdered it. A gifted linguist, she soon learned good Italian and French. When she had slimmed down from over 200 pounds to less than 140, she became one of the best-dressed women in Milan. Her homes in Verona, Milan and Paris paid silent tribute to her taste and love of order. Attached to every garment in her wardrobe in Milan was a list giving the date she had bought it, what it cost, where, when and in whose company she had worn it. Gloves – each pair in a transparent plastic envelope – and handbags were similarly documented, and every object had its place. These were private reflections of the meticulous care she put into her work.

A woman who worked at the Athens conservatory when Callas was a student there gave me a fascinating picture of her: bulky, shabby, serious, her pockets filled with food, which she consumed voraciously throughout the day. She neither had nor made friends. Invariably the first to arrive and the last to leave the building, when she was not having lessons she attended other classes irrespective of musical subject, listening insatiably and silently, absorbing every facet of musical information that might one day be useful to her. De Sabata later said to me, 'If the public could understand as we do how deeply and utterly musical Callas is, they would be stunned.'

CAMP

Opera's association with glamour and excess has long made it potently attractive to the camper elements of society. In his Reminiscences *of 1864, the impresario Benjamin Lumley describes a cruising-ground much frequented in the 1820s and 1830s.*

The 'Fops' Alley' is now among the traditions of the past, and younger opera-goers, among the male sex especially, may feel some interest in a description of a locality which was not unjustly reckoned among the prominent features of the opera, when the Italian Opera House stood alone.

In those days the pit was extensive; the stalls, originally introduced by M. Laporte, being comparatively few in number. From an entrance, occupying the centre of the lowest tier of boxes, a few steps descended to the back of the pit down the centre of which a broad space was left unencumbered to within a few feet of the orchestra. This formed the renowned 'Fops' Alley', the time-honoured celebrity of which I so much respected that, waving considerations of personal advantage, I objected to increase the number of the stalls. Ample room was left also between the pit seats and the boxes on the pit tier, and thus there was space allowing the *habitués* to lounge about at their leisure.

Fops' Alley, as the name implied, was an ancient institution. The very term 'Fop' had already become extinct in the earliest days of my management. The 'Dandy' was all but antiquated, while the 'Swell' had not yet risen to his recent supremacy. But no matter for the designation, the meaning of the term was fully understood and admitted as a generally recognized reality. It was the practice of the day for all the more 'exquisite' and fashionable of the male operatic patrons to quit their boxes or their scanty stalls during various portions of the performance, and to fill the vacant spaces in the centre and sides of the pit, where they could laugh, lounge, chatter, eye the boxes from convenient vantage points, and likewise criticize and applaud in common. The 'meetings and greetings' that took place in the pit of the opera were looked upon as an essential portion of the evening's entertainment. All that was aristocratic, distinguished, fashionable, or (still more) would-be fashionable, met, swarmed, greeted, babbled in an ever-seething, ever-varying crowd. Many of the young 'exquisites' of that period have since disappeared from the arena of the world as from that of the opera; many others have fallen into 'the sere and yellow leaf', and have been elbowed from their thrones by impertinently handsome young 'Dundrearys' of a later day. But the living heroes of the past may have the consolation of knowing that modern 'Fops' possess no longer this special ground whereon to display their social importance. Fops' Alley is no more.

During the first years of this century, Paris's jeunesse dorée *was seized by a mania for Debussy's opera* Pélleas et Mélisande. *In 1902,* Le Journal *wittily observed their perfumed decadence.*

Turning over with a lazy hand the score placed on the rail of the box there is a whole class of beautiful young men (nearly all the Debussyites are young, O, so young), ephebes with long hair cunningly brought in stringy locks over the forehead, with dull, smug faces, with deep sunken eyes. Their dress coats have a velvet collar and puffed sleeves; their frock coats are a little too pinched in the waist; their satin cravats are fussy over the neck or they float loosely, tied carelessly to the turn-over collar when the Debussyite is *en veston*. They all wear on their little fingers (for they all have pretty hands) precious rings of Egypt or Byzantium, rings of turquoise or of twisted greenish gold. Thus adorned, they go in couples. Orestes and Pylades commune together, or the model son accompanies his mother. They are archangels with visionary eyes, and under the spell of an impression they whisper in each other's ears, and their whispers go to the lowest depth of the soul. *The Pelléastres!*

CARMEN

Bizet died three months after Carmen's *unsuccessful first performance in 1875, tragically believing it to have failed completely. But through the 1880s it stormed the capitals of Europe, captivating audiences with its inexhaustible melodies, vibrant orchestral colouring, and frank portrayal of sexual infatuation. Tchaikovsky was one of the first to appreciate its worth: in 1880 he recorded his impressions of the score in a letter to his patron Madame von Meck.*

Yesterday evening – to take a rest from my own work – I played through Bizet's *Carmen* from cover to cover. I consider it a *chef d'oeuvre* in the fullest sense of the word: one of those rare compositions which seem to reflect most strongly the musical tendencies of a whole generation. It seems to me that our own period differs from earlier ones in this one characteristic: that contemporary composers *are engaged in the pursuit of charming and piquant effects*, unlike Mozart, Beethoven, Schubert, or

Schumann. What is the so-called New Russian School but the cult of varied and pungent harmonies, of original orchestral combinations and every kind of purely external effect? Musical ideas give place to this or that union of sounds. Formerly there was composition, creation; now (with few exceptions) there is only research and contrivance. This development of musical thought is purely intellectual, consequently contemporary music is clever, piquant and eccentric, but cold and lacking the glow of true emotion. And behold, a Frenchman comes on the scene, in whom these qualities of piquancy and pungency are not the outcome of effort and reflection, but flow from his pen as in a free stream, flattering the ear, but touching us also ... I cannot play the last scene without tears in my eyes; the gross rejoicing of the crowd who look on at the bull-fight and, side by side with this, the poignant tragedy and death of the two principal characters, pursued by an evil fate, who come to their inevitable end through a long series of sufferings.

I am convinced that ten years hence *Carmen* will be the most popular opera in the world.

CARUSO

Myths and legends accrue round every celebrated performer, and Caruso was no exception: in her biography of her husband, Dorothy Caruso tried to put the record straight on a number of small points.

Enrico was five feet nine inches tall (a half inch taller than I) and
  weighed 175 pounds.
His complexion was cream, without color in the cheeks.
His hair was black, coarse and straight.
His body was hard but not muscular.
His hands were large and strong, with square fingers.

His feet were small and broad.

He could not run well because of the formation of the Achilles tendon.

He took two baths a day.

He bathed his face with witch hazel.

He did not use face powder except on the stage.

He used Caron perfumes; he walked around the apartment with a large atomizer, spraying the rooms with scent.

He weighed three pounds less after each performance.

He did not lie down to rest during the day.

He did not ride, play golf or tennis, go for long walks, or do setting-up exercises in the morning.

He never learned to drive a car.

He did not overeat.

He never ate five plates of spaghetti for lunch! His lunch was vegetable soup with the meat of chicken left in, and a green salad.

For dinner he usually had a minute steak, two green vegetables and ice cream.

When he was to sing, he ate only the white meat of chicken or two small lamb chops.

He ate the crust of bread with every meal.

He loved ice cream and custard.

His favorite vegetable was raw fennel, which he ate like fruit.

He did not eat candies or chocolate.

Enrico was a musician who had no time for music. We never went together to hear opera. I don't believe he had heard one for twenty years, except those in which he himself sang; and even then he never stood in the wings to listen to the other singers. We never went to symphony concerts either. Once we went to a recital – the debut of Tito Schipa, who was giving a program of Neapolitan songs. We arrived late, sat in the back of the hall where no one could see us and left in fifteen minutes. 'Why did we go at all?' I asked. 'Because he is a tenor. But it's all right,' he said cryptically.

Enrico didn't play the piano, he could strike only a few chords;

but he never said he regretted not being able to play. As he concentrated on only one thing at a time, he wouldn't have accompanied himself in any case, for he refused to divide his attention.

No amateur accompanist ever played for him, nor did he ever sing 'for fun' at parties. His contract with the Metropolitan forbade his singing anywhere unless he had official permission. I know of only one time that he broke this rule. We had gone to a benefit vaudeville performance, given for soldiers and sailors, at the Manhattan Opera House. We thought no one could see us, seated in the back of a stage box, but a boy in the front row called out, 'There's Caruso!' The performance stopped, the audience shouted and stamped and the manager came to our box. 'Mr Caruso, they want you to sing "Over There."' Enrico didn't hesitate but left me immediately and went on to the stage. When he had finished, the audience wouldn't let him go. Finally, waving and called 'No more,' he hurried back to me. 'We must leave quickly,' he whispered. 'I must go and tell Gatti I broke my contract.' I waited in the car outside the stage door while he talked with Gatti. When he came out he was beaming. 'He excuse me,' he said.   DOROTHY CARUSO, *Enrico Caruso*

CASTRATI

None of the myths surrounding Caruso, however, could be as tantalizing, astonishing, or comical as those stories which survive of the eighteenth-century castrati. The operation — which involved severing the cord that runs from the testicles to the urethra — resulted in hormonal imbalances which in turn caused many bizarre physical side-effects, including a huge growth of hair on the head and a strange loping gait. From the operatic point of view, it was more significant that the vocal cords did not thicken at puberty and that the rib cage expanded, thus facilitating the breath control that constituted one of the castrati's great advantages in matters of technique.

'A very particular accident happened a few years ago to a singer of the name of Balani. This man was born without any visible signs of those parts which are taken out in castration, he was, therefore, looked upon as a true-born castrato; an opinion, which was even confirmed by his voice. He learned music, and sung for several years upon the theatre with great applause. One day, he exerted himself so uncommonly in singing an arietta, that all of a sudden those parts, which had so long been concealed by nature, dropped into their proper place. The singer from this very instant lost his voice, which became even perceptible in the same performance, and with it he lost every prospect of a future subsistence.' This strange occurrence was apparently observed in the San Carlo opera house, Naples, in about 1765; where, not long before, another unfortunate accident had taken place. The young castrato Luca Fabbris, straining after a top note of exceptionally dizzy altitude, collapsed and died on the stage, to the consternation of the composer Guglielmi, who had induced him to attempt it.   ARCHENHOLZ, quoted in ANGUS HERIOT, *The Castrati in Opera*

The sexual ambiguity of the castrati was another of their charms, as Casanova discovered while in Rome in 1762.

We went to the Aliberti theatre, where the castrato who took the prima donna's role attracted all the town. He was the complaisant favourite, the *mignon*, of Cardinal Borghese, and supped every evening *tête-à-tête* with His Eminence.

In a well-made corset, he had the waist of a nymph, and, what was almost incredible, his breast was in no way inferior, either in form or in beauty, to any woman's; and it was above all by this means that the monster made such ravages. Though one knew the negative nature of this unfortunate, curiosity made one glance at his chest, and an inexpressible charm acted upon one, so that you were madly in love before you realized it. To resist the temptation, or not to feel it, one would have had to be cold and earth-bound as a German. When he walked about the stage during the *ritornello* of the aria he was to sing, his step was majestic and at the same time voluptuous; and when he favoured the boxes with his glances, the tender and modest rolling of his black eyes brought a ravishment to the heart. It was obvious that he hoped to inspire the love of those who liked him as a man, and probably would not have done so as a woman.

Rome the holy city, which in this way forces every man to become a pederast, will not admit it, nor believe in the efforts of an illusion which it does its best to arouse.

The castrato Giusto-Fernando Tenducci ('Senesino' was his stage-name) went a good deal further than flirtation, leaving behind a story which Angus Heriot puzzles over in his excellent book The Castrati in Opera.

Tenducci had already, in 1761, made a journey to Scotland, and in 1765 he further extended his knowledge of the British Isles by a trip to Ireland, where he introduced *Artaxerxes* to the inhabitants of Dublin, causing a sensation with his singing of the aria 'Water parted from the sea'.

An even greater sensation was caused, however, the following year, when Tenducci eloped with a young girl of good family, Miss Dora Maunsell of Limerick, and married her at Cork by a Protestant ceremony. He had met her some time before while staying with some friends of her family: the horror and rage of the latter on hearing of the runaway match were almost past description.

The couple now had to endure the most grievous hardships and persecutions at the hands of the infuriated parents and various cousins, which are described in detail by the young bride herself in an account published in 1768 as *A True and Genuine Narrative of Mr. & Mrs. Tenducci*. The whole affair is reminiscent of Richardson's *Pamela*, with its traduced heroine, its poor but honest hero, its arrogant gentry and their lofty disregard of the law; for some time the pair dodged about the country and eluded their pursuers, but eventually, once more in Cork, Tenducci was thrown into jail, and his wife kidnapped and held by her inexorable relations. The singer's main preoccupation, oddly enough, seems to have been anxiety lest people believe, as his wife's family would have it, that he had seduced her while giving her lessons; and we find him writing from prison to the editor of the local newspaper:

North Goal [*sic*]
September 2nd, 1766.

Sir

I beg you will do me the justice, in your next paper, to contradict a circumstance inserted in your last, that I was married to a young lady who had been my pupil: Now, Sir, this is entirely void of foundation. I never was entertained as a singing or music master by an person, or persons, since I had the honour to perform in this kingdom; never taught the act of singing, and consequently never had a pupil; nor was I ever received by the friends of that young lady (whom I cannot mention but with the utmost respect) on any such footing, as a teacher of music, or singing, in any degree whatsoever.

I am, Sir, your humble Servant,
F. TENDUCCI.

To continue the narrative in Dora Tenducci's own words:

Some gentlemen, pitying his distressed situation ... became bail for him, and he was once more delivered from that noisome gaol. My cousin W. desired Mr T.B. not to advertise Tenducci's name in the bills for the theatre, assuring him, if he did, his house should be torn to pieces. Mr B. apprehensive of danger, advertised the Merchant of Venice, instead of an opera, for Tenducci's benefit. Mr W. not content with the scheme he had already practised, persuaded the commanding officer in Cork to withhold the usual guard from attending the play house that night, in hopes that the audience and particular friends of Tenducci might be exposed to the insults of his party; and the more effectually to answer this purpose, and to prevent company from going to his benefit play, a report was industriously spread that there would be a riot at the house that evening. However, this cruel scheme to hurt him proved abortive, for the house was filled with the best company in the city. At the end of the first act Tenducci was called on for a song; this my cousin W.'s party endeavoured to oppose but were obliged to acquiesce. When the play was over, and one given out for the next night, the audience insisted on it's being an opera: Which accordingly was performed with universal applause.

The next day after that, however, Tenducci was again warned to flee, for the cousins were again on the war-path. He did so, but after many more alarms and excursions was once more thrown into prison, where he was much maltreated and nearly died of fever. Eventually, however, the bride's father relented, and all ended happily for the time being. Tenducci and his wife remained in Ireland until 1768, when they returned to London.

Tenducci's marriage has another reason for celebrity, alluded to by Casanova: '... at Covent Garden ... the castrato Tenducci surprised me greatly by presenting me to his legitimate wife, by whom he had two children. He laughed at those who argued that, as he was a castrato, he could not produce his kind. Nature had made him a monster to keep him a man; he was a *Triorchis*, and as in the operation only two of his seminal glands had been removed, that which remained was sufficient to prove his vitality.' This story cannot be true as it stands, for Casanova was in London in 1763–4, and Tenducci was not even married till 1766: though Casanova might well have met him elsewhere at a later date, and misremembered the year and the place.

The matter is, however, altogether a strange one. The story that this castrato had become a father seems to have been widely known at the time, yet Tenducci's marriage was, in 1775, declared null and void through the influence of his wife's relatives. It is impossible to know what the real truth was.

CHALIAPIN

My parents lived in St Petersburg, or Petrograd as it was called during the First World War. The first performance of an opera that I remember at all clearly was that of *Boris Godunov* in 1916. Chaliapin, of course, sang the title role, and his enormous voice filled the Maryinsky Theatre, as much in lyrical *legato* passages as in the great dramatic monologue, and in the dialogue with Shuisky. I was seven years old at the time, and this naturally meant little to me, save that even then I noticed the enormous differences between the marvellous sensation of those huge, slow, all-sustaining, wholly delightful waves of musical sound, with their almost orchestral effect, and the voices of the other, more ordinary singers. But what absorbed my attention and fascinated me completely was the scene in which the Tsar sees the ghost of the murdered Prince in a remote corner of the stage, starts back in horror and utters panic-stricken cries. Chaliapin, on his knees, seized the table legs, burying his head in the folds of the tablecloth which hung from it and on which the map of Russia was stretched for the geography lesson of his young son in the earlier part of this act; whether deliberately or not, in an exceedingly realistic performance of the scene of panic and hysteria, he pulled the tablecloth and the map over his head: the spectacle of this gigantic figure crawling on the floor, with the rich cloth and his own robes inextricably tangled over him, crying 'Choo! Choo!', and waving his arms desperately to drive away the terrible ghostly presence, was something at once so frightening and wonderful, that I myself, apparently, began to utter cries of mixed terror and pleasure, and had to be silenced by my parents and the hissing of indignant neighbours. I do not think that I had any idea of what the hallucination really signified, but even children respond to acting of genius.

I saw Chaliapin many times after this, in *Boris* (on one occasion he sang the parts of both Boris and Varlaam in the inn scene – I wonder whether his distinguished successor, Boris Christoff, could not be induced to do this), as Khan Konchak, in *Prince Igor* as the Miller, in Dargomyzhsky's *Russalka*, as Mephistopheles in Boito's opera (I never saw him, alas, as Ivan the Terrible in Rimsky-Korsakov's *The Maid of Pskov*); but the exciting and fearful memory of that heroic frame crawling on all fours, swathed in the rich tablecloth and map, uttering wonderful cries, and singing at full-throated ease, barbarous and marvellously and consciously artistic at the same time, lingers with me to this day. For a long time after that I thought of opera as a particularly terrifying sort of entertainment. It took a good many performances of French and Italian opera to obliterate this fixed idea.

SIR ISAIAH BERLIN, *Opera*, 1975

CLAQUE

The practice of hiring members of the audience to applaud (or boo) a particular performer is a venerable operatic institution dating back to the mid eighteenth century and still not quite moribund in certain opera houses today. As this paragraph from the Musical Times *of 1888 indicates, in Paris the claque was highly organized – there was even a claque agency, run by one Monsieur Sauton, bluntly entitled 'L'Assurance des Succès Dramatiques'.*

The noble and distinguished art exercised by the 'claque' in France and elsewhere takes a less dignified form in London. In

Paris the whole force is organized in a business-like way, and the several professors find special occupations according to their talents. There are the 'bisseurs', or those whose duty it is to demand repetitions; there are the 'rieurs', the laughers, whose business it is to utter in specified places, or to break out into noisy guffaws as occasion requires; there are the 'pleureurs', who drop the briny tear, or shake the manly bosom with the bursting sob, and other sub-sections of the emotions, all evidences of an artistic division of labour. The occupation is recognized by performers, managers, and authors, and provided for accordingly. In London, where the 'profession' has no organization at present, it would appear as though a few enterprising creatures were desirous of introducing a similar custom in places of entertainment. Unfortunately, they have not laid their plans with any degree of taste and judgment like their Gallic prototypes. They have no 'bureau' where these matters can be amicably settled beforehand, and where the 'receptions' can be provided for according to a definite plan, and their own 'douceur', their 'sweetener', agreed upon. Our metropolitan reformers wait at stage doors with doubled fists and thick sticks ready to employ either or both upon the persons who decline their services. Their plan is inartistic, and although it bears the pretty and poetical name of 'chirruping', suggestive of the feathered warblers of the grove, it is apt to cause the 'chirrupers' to be deprived of their liberty for a time. In the intervals of rest between the period of practical geological studies and the disintegration of tarred rope, occupations suggested and enforced by a benign legislation, the 'chirruper' may reflect upon the disadvantages of improperly developed schemes of encouragement for the benefit of artistic designs and expositions of talents, so as to enforce their acceptance by other means than the 'argumentum ad baculinum'.

COLLABORATION

Opera has the reputation of being hysterically combative and feud-ridden (see pp. 143–51 for confirmation of this view); but it should not be forgotten that every decent performance depends on the most sensitive and sustained co-operation between singers, singers and conductor, and conductor and orchestra.

One of today's most generous singers has been the soprano Joan Sutherland who, along with her conductor husband Richard Bonynge, has promoted the careers of many younger singers, notably Marilyn Horne and Luciano Pavarotti. Their mutual collaboration has its finest memorial in the recording of their concert at the Lincoln Center in 1981; their friendship is also celebrated in Marilyn Horne's autobiography My Life.

... it was Ricky [Bonynge] who taught me how *bel canto* worked. With a dramatic composer like Verdi, you need support to carry the full weight of the sound all the way up; it's like a column of sound moving from the basement to the penthouse of the voice. In Donizetti, Rossini and Bellini roles, however, the orchestration is usually light and the middle voice is lightened. Because you don't have to sing an incredibly big middle register, you can open up on the top and let the coloratura fly. I actually 'move the center of my voice' – Ricky's term – when I do certain roles: up for Adalgisa, down for Arsace. Since that 'center' is positioned differently, however, I have to alternate my roles carefully in order to preserve my voice. I space my appearances in vehicles that call for a lightening or darkening of the voice. In 1982, over a well-spaced four-month span, I sang Handel's *Rinaldo*, returned to *Carmen* for the first time in seven years, performed *Norma* after a twelve-year layoff and then went waltzing into *Cenerentola* after twenty-five years away – and things didn't fall apart. The center of my voice held for each. It would be easier to sing roles that lie in the same range, but a lot less fun and fulfilling, and the fact that I'm still learning and adding operas to my repertoire is a tribute to careful planning as well as training. I've learned quite a bit about *bel canto* since those early days. I learned how to ornament from Ricky, but I must also mention Fritz Zweig, my coach in Los Angeles, who taught me style and ornamented for me, and, of course, my in-house coach, Henry Lewis [also Horne's first husband], who was my *real* teacher.

Joan's execution of the *bel canto* material was as phenomenal as Ricky's erudition and I wasn't the only beneficiary of her generosity. Another colleague whom Joan pulled right into the spotlight was an up-and-coming tenor of hearty proportions whom Joan dubbed 'The Big P.' You know him as Luciano Pavarotti. Luciano sang with Joan on records and in performances way before the public fell in love with him. Then he took off like a rocket.

Pavarotti is very bright, with a positive genius for salesmanship as well as music. He came to this country, saw it was good for him and learned English immediately. Foreign singers don't always master the language – they usually just get by – but somewhere in that big, wide, wonderful Pavarotti a little voice said, 'You've got to make contact, and in order to do that, you've got to speak the language.' Luciano is only *one* of a number of fine tenors of intelligence and wit performing today, but he's got a special ingredient which has made him *the* one – a quality of sound that produces goosebumps on listeners, especially women.

In October 1979, Joan and I gave a televised joint concert at the Lincoln Center. It was a smashing success, and after the performance we went to a fancy Chinese restaurant on the upper East Side. I know it was fancy because the waiter had never heard of duck sauce. I was very happy that evening, not only at being reunited with Joan and singing well, but because I'd lost a great deal of weight and really looked and felt good. Not long after we sat down to moo shoo pork without duck sauce, Joan was called to the telephone.

In a few minutes, she returned and said, 'Jackie [Horne's pet name], it's Luciano and he wants to talk to you, too.' Pavarotti was appearing with the Chicago Opera. I went to the phone and said hello.

'Jackeee,' boomed the big boy. 'Jackeee, I saw on the television, Joan an' you. Oh, Jackee, you were so wonderful, you sang so beeyootiful, you look beeyootiful, you look so ... so fuckable!'

Yes, Luciano Pavarotti has definitely mastered the language.

Our mutual history probably accounts for the special alchemy when Joan appears with him, or me, or, most magical of all, when the three of us are onstage together. Now we're *all* stars, but in the Sixties, Joan Sutherland was our fairy godmother – a wave of her wand, and we were performing. She was the sun and we reflected her glory.

COLOUR AND SOUND

The Victorian impresario Benjamin Lumley's Reminiscences of the Opera *contain this amusing exercise in vocal connoisseurship. The 'gifted friend' was doubtless Lumley himself.*

I know a person with whom music and colours are so intimately associated, that whenever this person listens to a singer, a colour corresponding to his voice becomes visible to the eyes. The greater the volume of the voice the more distinct is the colour, and when the voice is good, the high and low notes are of the same colour; whereas if different colours appear during the performance of the same singer, the voice is naturally unpleasant or has been forced out of its natural register.

To show that my gifted friend is not content with maintaining a mere theory, I give a list of celebrated singers, with the colours which, it is asserted, correspond to their voices:

GIUGLINI – Maroon. The colour softened and well blended in its gradations. Substance, a rich velvet pile.

MARIO – A beautiful violet, more like satin than velvet.

TAMBERLIK – A carmine; but unequal – on some notes the colour very strong, and on some notes scarcely any colour. The voice like a cannon when fired; a flash succeeded by haziness, but the flash very brilliant whilst it lasts.

ALBONI – A blue (cobalt). Voice like so many raised lines or divisions, mechanically and formally correct. Latterly, some of the notes with colour less bright.

GRISI – (Latter times) – Varies greatly – primrose, and sometimes changes to blue. *Mem.* – The colours change when the voice is not equal.

PICCOLOMINI – Pétillant. Many sparkling emanations as when gunpowder is thrown on fire; some portions of the voice little colour, but those that have colour very brilliant and pleasing.

PATTI – Light and dark drab, with occasional touches of coral.

BOSIO – A very beautiful moss rose colour, with a diamond-like transparency.

PAULINE VIARDOT – At least half-dozen colours – one or two like a silk shot, the shots at moments very pretty, at other times very disagreeable.

TITIENS – Red in some, and a pink in other parts of the voice. Latterly the colours faded in some of the notes.

This faculty of perceiving colours while listening to music, though it sometimes increases the pleasure of the listener, may also be a source of pain. I do not mention names, but the person bears witness to the existence of voices that have caused an appearance of the colours of snails, stale beer, sour milk, curry powder, rhubarb, mud splashes, and tea leaves from which the water has been drained.

COSTUME

This description of Ancient Egyptian couture was published in Opera News *in 1954, so that listeners to a radio broadcast of* Aida *(from the Met) could imagine what their eyes were missing – a vision of high kitsch.*

First of the sumptuous *Aida* costumes designed by Rolf Gérard and executed by Helene Pons for the 1951 revival of the opera is that of Ramfis, the High Priest, who appears throughout the action in a long white robe with a round starched yoke, heavily encrusted with black and gold embroidery.

Radames is first seen in a red cuirass, covered with fish scales outlined in sequins, a brief grey skirt and short mantle and high laced red sandals. In the Triumph Scene his tunic is of black and gold, with a gold skirt and small headdress and an orange cape. His costume in the Nile Scene is green with a brilliant green cape, but in the tomb he wears a simple earth-colored tunic.

Amneris appears first in a robe of deep rose chiffon over a long thin pleated skirt. Her veil is of a deeper color while her narrow tiara is of gold. At the beginning of the second act she dons a robe of vivid green trimmed in gold, and veiled in a sapphire cape, while her ceremonial black wig is stranded with gold. For the Triumph she adds a long cape of gold metal cloth. This is replaced by a long purple veil in the Nile Scene, while for the Finale her grief is reflected in a long black robe, trimmed with silver, with black draperies.

Aida is first seen in a simple long dress of sapphire blue, covered by a cape of blue and gold. Her dark hair is partly hidden under a blue veil. In the second act she appears in a dull purple robe cape while for both the Nile Scene and the Finale she wears a blue grey, covered in the third act by a brilliant cherry cape, and in the Finale by a thin grey blue mantle.

Amonasro discards the traditional fur cape and horned head-dress for a long black robe, trimmed with a striped over-dress of brown and gold. A long scarlet cape hangs from his shoulders.

The King of Egypt wears a rich robe of gold trimmed with simulated lapis lazuli with a broad circular starched yoke and a gold tiered hat.

Terracotta, white and variegated reds loom important in the costumes of the chorus, which is authentically arrayed for the maximum of brilliance. The ballet men are masked while Janet Collins, as soloist, is covered in a minimum of metallic harness resembling leopard skin.

Costume in the auditorium can be even more fantastic than anything on stage: George Bernard Shaw wrote the following letter to The Times *in 1905 to protest.*

Sir,—The opera management at Covent Garden regulates the dress of its male patrons. When is it going to do the same to the women?

On Saturday night I went to the Opera. I wore the costume imposed on me by the regulations of the house. I fully recognize the advantage of those regulations. Evening dress is cheap, simple, durable, prevents rivalry and extravagance on the part of male leaders of fashion, annihilates class distinctions, and gives men who are poor and doubtful of their social position (that is, the great majority of men) a sense of security and satisfaction that no clothes of their own choosing could confer, besides saving a whole sex the trouble of considering what they should wear on state occasions. The objections to it are as dust in the balance in the eyes of the ordinary Briton. These objections are that it is colorless and characterless; that it involves a whitening process which makes the shirt troublesome, slightly uncomfortable, and seriously unclean; that it acts as a passport for undesirable persons; that it fails to guarantee sobriety, cleanliness, and order on the part of the wearer; and that it reduces to a formula a very vital human habit which should be the subject of constant experiment and active private enterprise. All such objections are thoroughly un-English. They appeal only to an eccentric few, and may be left out of account with the fantastic objections of men like Ruskin, Tennyson, Carlyle, and Morris to tall hats.

But I submit that what is sauce for the gander is sauce for the goose. Every argument that applies to the regulation of the man's dress applies equally to the regulation of the woman's. Now let me describe what actually happened to me at the Opera. Not only was I in evening dress by compulsion, but I voluntarily added many graces of conduct as to which the management made no stipulation whatever. I was in my seat in time for the first chord of the overture. I did not chatter during the music nor raise my voice when the Opera was too loud for normal conversation. I did not get up and go out when the statue music began. My language was fairly moderate considering the number and nature of the improvements on Mozart volunteered by Signor Caruso, and the respectful ignorance of the dramatic points of the score exhibited by the conductor and the stage manager – if there is such a functionary at Covent Garden. In short, my behavior was exemplary.

At 9 o'clock (the Opera began at 8) a lady came in and sat down very conspicuously in my line of sight. She remained there until the beginning of the last act. I do not complain of her coming late and going early; on the contrary, I wish she had come later and gone earlier. For this lady, who had very black hair, had stuck over her right ear the pitiable corpse of a large white bird, which looked exactly as if someone had killed it by stamping on its breast, and then nailed it to the lady's temple, which was presumably of sufficient solidity to bear the operation. I am not, I hope, a morbidly squeamish person, but the spectacle sickened me. I presume that if I had presented myself at the doors with a dead snake round my neck, a collection of blackbeetles pinned to my shirtfront, and a grouse in my hair, I should have been refused admission. Why, then, is a woman to be allowed to commit such a public outrage? Had the lady been refused admission, as she should have been, she would have soundly rated the tradesman who imposed the disgusting headdress on her under the false pretence that 'the best people' wear such things, and withdrawn her custom from him; and thus the root of the evil would be struck at; for your fashionable woman generally allows herself to be dressed according to the taste of a person whom she would not let sit down in her presence. I once, in Drury Lane Theatre, sat behind a *matinée* hat decorated with the two wings of a seagull, artificially reddened at the joints so as to produce an illusion of being freshly plucked from a live bird. But even that lady stopped short of the whole seagull. Both ladies were evidently regarded by their neighbors as ridiculous and vulgar; but that is hardly enough when the offence is one which produces a sensation of physical sickness in persons of normal humane sensibility.

CRITICS

Singer David Franklin delivers a humbling riposte to those ignoramuses who dare to criticize.

Paul Jennings has turned nasty. The charm of his *Observer* column, and of the shy, boyish smile with which he is accustomed to decorate his performances in TV parlour-games, has turned into a snarl. Mr Jennings found it necessary in a recent TV programme, unaccompanied and without warning, to sing. Oddly enough, he chose for his singing debut a horn passage from a Beethoven symphony. Remembering the tense-cheeked concentration of the brass at this point, one is tempted to declare that this must have been the very first time that this horn passage has been publicly performed with a shy, boyish smile. But a TV critic ignored this remarkable technical achievement, and chose instead to accuse Mr Jennings of singing out of tune – and Mr Jennings turned nasty. 'Very well,' he wrote publicly to his critic, 'let's hear YOU sing.'

I do wish Mr Jennings hadn't done it. For the most part, artists like to pretend that they don't worry about the critics. ('No, no. Haven't seen the notices, old man. Never read 'em. Waste of time. Stands to reason – what can a bunch of ——s like that know about the business? No. Never read 'em – by the way, what did they say about me?') In fact, we do worry about them. But let sleeping dogs lie, we say – and 'dogs' will do for the moment. We don't like to do anything that may attract the attention of the critics. See what can happen to a singer who does catch the critical eye!:—

> Signor Castelmary was announced as Mefisto, but, as he would have been hopelessly out of breath after three bars or so, had he appeared, nobody was disappointed at his replacement by Signor Novero.

We artists are simple folk. We ask but little here below – only that, when we read in *Tristan and Isolde* the lovers 'undulated like startled octopuses,' or, in another opera, that 'Mr X sang by no means all the evening out of tune,' such gems of criticism should not have been written about us.

And so, we try to dodge the critics' attention. We certainly would not dream of provoking them, like the foolhardy Mr Jennings. It is true that in the past I have sometimes ventured a timid suggestion to a critic. For instance, to a lady critic, who had written of a forthcoming programme which included a harp quintet that she was 'so looking forward to hearing those five harps,' I delicately hinted that it was time she was told the facts of life, that a harp quintet wasn't necessarily to be played by five harps, nor was an oboe quartet composed of four oboes, nor – she must be brave – a piano quintet of five pianos, though I had the grace to admit that these combinations of instruments were delicious to contemplate in the imagination. Then there was a critic who had complained that my make-up in the first act was shocking, but that I had taken pains with it in the second, when it looked fine. I shyly replied that, see it wet see it dry, I hadn't touched my make-up during the interval, and its sudden-seeming improvement might be due to the fact that in the second act the stage manager had at last got his wayward and exuberant electricians under control, and had got them working for the first time to their plot.

But generally we don't dare even a whisper against the critics. We can read an account of the farewell performance of a great singer 'in Wagner's opera *Isolde*,' without so much as a twitch of a curious eyebrow. We are only too relieved when they leave us alone, overwhelmed when they throw us a scrap of praise ('Mr Smith was inoffensive in the unexacting part of A Rustic'), but mostly awed by their display of superiority. 'Tonal quality was exquisitely modulated,' we read of a rival's performance. Singers are always ready to learn from their betters, and so, after a surreptitious look at the OED, we go to the piano, and try an exquisitely modulated bash at some scales. One critic impressed us with his learning and subtlety who, examining the dreary harmony of one particular piece, was good enough to explain that it derived from the repeated frustrations of the composer's sex-life, which had led him to the extensive use of the 'inhibited second.' This penetrating analysis fascinated me, and I made a note of it. I didn't quite know where to file it, but in the end discreetly fitted in 'Second, inhibited' next to 'Fourth, diminished.'

We admire, too, the businesslike quality of the critics. We artists are gentle, dreamy, impractical creatures, and we can but admire the resolution and decision of a man who, faced with a never-ending series of familiar performances, has after experiment evolved a splendid formula to cover a wide repertory. After reading of one performance that he had seen *Rosenkavalier* without an Ochs, we were not at all surprised to read later of a *Carmen* without a Carmen, and, now that he is into his stride, we look forward to verdicts of *Macbeth* without a Macbetto, the *Masked Ball* without a mask, or indeed a ball, and a *Magic Flute* without a flute.

But, though we are over-awed by the learning and the capacity of the critics, and though we would never dream of taunting them, Mr Jennings' reckless challenge has nevertheless awakened in us longings for the might-have-been. Imagine a critic who has jeered at the slovenly playing of the wood-wind. 'Let's hear YOU do it!' says the bassoon, grimly, and we all derive the deepest pleasure from watching the critic, seated in a prominent place in the orchestra, tentatively and gingerly exploring the mysterious inter-locking of a bewildering instrument. Think of a revolt at Covent Garden — 'Let's hear YOU sing it!' says the company, defiantly. Think of the pleasures of casting amongst the critics.

The *Express* would insist on Empire parts – Raleigh in *Gloriana*, of course, but the choice of Sharpless, as an empire part, might possibly offend the American colonists. The *New Statesman?* – the Plançon roles, of course, and *how* we should look forward to hearing them. For the *Sunday Times*, there is a wide choice to be made in the caverns and amongst the mountain-tops of Wagner, but the dragon, breathing artificial fire, stands out as an attractive piece of type-casting. There surely must be a Ping, a Pang, or a Pong in the *News Chronicle*, and Miss C—— B—— may choose freely – Isolde, Pamina, Gilda, Azucena, Sophie – according to her chameleon mood of the moment. Lucky Miss B—— to be almost free of competition, though one does hear rumours of another feminine pen at work; this one behind the discreet anonymity of *The Times*. The attitude of Printing House Square towards 'moral lapses' has been so marked, that to be cast in the usual operatic soprano part would surely cause any member of their staff acute embarrassment. Violetta? Mimi? No, a thousand times, no. Gilda? – an unfortunate girl, but not the type for Printing House Square. Zerlina, Anna, Elvira were all involved, even though they were innocently involved, in unhappy incidents. Sieglinde? – the very thought of the woman's deplorable conduct shows how impossible such a piece of casting would be. No, Printing House Square must be content to ring with the impeccable male innocence in Unison of the First and Second Armed Men.

And these attractive solo performances would be supported by a Massed Choir of the critics. Imagine the billing – music-hall style – outside the opera-house:

FULL CHORUS
OF
50 LONDON CRITICS 50
with
25 voices 25

No, the mind refuses to grasp such a supreme experience. It was foolish even to attempt it. I *do* wish Mr Jennings hadn't started all this.

Opera, 1954

DEBUSSY

Exactly sixty years before this interview was given to the BBC in 1962, Mary Garden had sung Mélisande in the first performance of Debussy's Pelléas et Mélisande. *In her autobiography, published in 1951, Garden had implied that Debussy had been in love with her; at the age of eighty-five she withdraws the implication. For more of the unique Miss Garden, see pp. 249–52 and 369–70.*

Looking back on your whole career, what is the thing that stands out in your mind as the most important?

MARY GARDEN: *Pelléas* – most difficult. Debussy's the most difficult because you have to sing him as he writes – not as you want to. Everything that he wrote, every word of Mélisande or the other characters, has the right music tone. And they mustn't sing *their* way. They must sing his way. Because everything that she does, or her husband did, or Pelléas – it was perfectly human, and you had to make it that way.

How was it that you created this role of Mélisande?

Because Debussy met me and when I sang for him, at the beginning of it, he stopped, and he said, 'There's no one ever in the world sang my music like you. You don't sing it, you sing talking.'

It's true. '*Ne me touchez pas.*' It should not be sung – not hollered like some of them would. '*Ne me touchez pas.*' I don't hold the 'pas' the way they do. That'll go all over the house. Oh, I don't know. I had just my own way of doing things. I was just different from anybody else – happily. . . .

Debussy and I were great friends, but he never told me anything about Mélisande. We used to talk about Gounod and all those people. But he never said anything very much about Mélisande until I went on to the rehearsals. And then he came up and we talked about this and that and the next thing. Oh, you have to, you know – you have to know what the composer has in his brain. It's not your brain, it's his brain. Oh, fascinating! I could talk and tell you so many things, but I can't remember them very much now. . . . When you're done, you're done. . . . You can't go through life singing all these operas as a young person. And then, I used to be just as important about going and having myself weighed every first of the month, and if it was that much over what I should have, I'd just go and not eat so much. . . . Oh, you have to be so careful if you're before the public as a great success. If you're not – well, it doesn't make any difference whether you've got a stomach or not a stomach. But I tell you I was frightened to death I'd get fat.

Is it true that Debussy was in love with you?

Oh no, never. He may have been in love with my work, but I never was in love with anybody whom I created. No, no, not in the musical world. They were all crazy.

You remember that you used to dine regularly every week with Debussy and his wife, Lily.

I don't know if his wife was always there.

No? Well, regularly with Debussy. What did you talk about?

I suppose we talked about music. He may have told me about his life – I don't know.

I wondered if you discussed his music, and whether he'd asked your advice.

I don't think – well, we discussed it, but he was always right. He knew. He used to sing it when he came to my home. And he said, 'Now, Mary, that's the colour of the voice I want.' It was always the colour. You had to put your voice into the colour of the people you are singing. He loved that always, because when you sing Carmen that's entirely different from Mélisande. You have to colour your voice – but in another way, in quite another way. You have to be very impertinent, very rude – but not in Mélisande. You have to be very careful and very sad. Oh, it's a lovely opera.

You have a certain amount of correspondence of Debussy which you have kept?
No.

You haven't kept it?
No, nothing. Haven't even his photograph.

You threw all the letters away?
Everything. Why should I bother? The only thing that interested me was my work, was my engagements, was my creating operas. I created almost all I sang – the new ones, you know. Oh, it was wonderful! Nobody to touch them. . . .

But you never kept their letters? It didn't interest you?
Letters? Not a bit. No.

You threw them away?
Burnt them.

You burnt them?
Yes. Just a lot of paper in your drawers there – och, I don't care. I have it all in my mind. I think of the people I like and I forget the people I don't like, you know. So why keep them?

DEBUT

The New Zealand-born soprano Frances Alda made her debut at the Met in 1908. Gatti-Casazza, director of the Met 1908–35, later became her husband; Lillian Nordica, one of the noblest and most appealing figures in the annals of prima donnas, was an ardent feminist, cyclist, philanthropist, and an unfailingly good friend and colleague. See also pp. 314–15.

But next morning. . . .

I sat up in bed and went through one newspaper after another, caring for nothing but the reviews of *Rigoletto* at the Metropolitan. I sent Emilie downstairs for more papers, and still later editions. The bed was covered with crumpled sheets of newsprint.

The reviews were all terrible.

I had no voice . . . I showed myself too untrained for the Metropolitan. . . . If I was a sample of what Signor Gatti-Casazza meant to introduce to New York, things were just too bad. . . .

And, finally:

'The young singer who made her debut last evening comes from the land of the sheep, and she bleated like one of them. . . .'

Was I down in the blues?

My heart ached and my throat was sore. I shivered all over. I hated America.

'I'll never sing in your old opera house again,' I stormed at Gatti when he came to see me. 'I'll take the next boat back to Europe.'

He shook his beard at me gloomily.

'You can't. You are billed to sing *Le Villi* ten days from today.'

'I tell you I shall. Instantaneously. I'll break the contract. . . .'

At that moment Emilie came into the sitting-room. She carried a huge basket of roses. I reached for the card and read:

MADAME LILLIAN NORDICA

and this message:

> There was never a young singer who appeared at the Met-
> ropolitan who wasn't severely criticized on her debut.
> Melba, Sembrich, Farrar, myself . . . all of us have gone
> through what you are going through today. Have courage.
> Affectionate good wishes.

To the end of my days I shall never forget Nordica's generous
gesture towards a newcomer whom she had never met, and to
whom she had no particular reason for being kind. Years later I
was able to repay part of the debt I felt I owed her, by prompting
Gatti to arrange for her several gala performances at the Metropolitan. And always, if I have needed any urge to be cordial to
young singers, I have had the remembrance of Nordica's roses and
message, and what they meant to me on that dark morning-after.

'*Va bene*,' I said to Gatti. 'I shall not break the contract. Not
immediately. I shall sing on the seventeenth. But meanwhile I
must see a doctor. My throat is sore.'

He sent me to Doctor Clarence Rice.

That visit turned out to be the first of many visits. For more than
twenty years, until his death, Doctor Rice took care of me and
kept me in condition to sing sometimes three performances a
week.

On that first morning Doctor Rice looked at my throat, and
then he looked at me. Presumably, he had also looked at the
morning papers.

'Here is my prescription,' he said. 'Forget about your throat.
Go down to the Library in Astor Place, ask for the newspaper files,
and read the reviews of Emma Eames's, of Farrar's, of Jean de
Reszke's first performance. If your throat still bothers you tomorrow, come back and let me look at it.'

I followed his advice. In the Library I pored over the old
newspapers. The same critic who had complained of my 'bleat'
had been offended by Caruso's 'Italianate mannerisms'. They had
looked down their noses at the glorious de Reszke. Farrar, then, in
1908, at the height of her popularity, had seemed to the reviewers
of her debut '*peu de chose*'.

I gave the files back to the librarian and went out. The streets were thronged with Christmas shoppers. Salvation Army Santa Clauses tinkled bells on every corner. In front of Grace Church a street band played 'Silent Night'. I hailed a hansom, and told the driver to take me up Fifth Avenue – past Madison Square, folded in the winter's first snowfall; past the Waldorf Astoria, in whose successor I now make my home; past the banks and the clubs and the brownstone fronts of the Metropolitan's box-holders. Past the pile of masonry on the corner of Forty-Second Street where the new Public Library was in process of building.

Suddenly I felt the energy, the vitality, the thrill that *is* New York. I leaned over the hansom's apron and shook my fist at the city.

'I'm going to conquer you,' I whispered fiercely. 'See if I don't.'

FRANCES ALDA, Men, Women and Tenors

DESERT ISLAND OPERA

In November 1948, W. H. Auden listed his desert island records in the Saturday Review.

Bach: *St Matthew Passion*. The Leipzig recording, with Günther Ramin conducting, Lemnitz and Hüsch as soloists.

Bellini and others: An operatic recital by Claudia Muzio.

Donizetti: *Don Pasquale*. The La Scala recording with Tito Schipa.

Donizetti: *Lucia di Lammermoor*. The version on Parlophone, with Pagliughi and Malipiero, Tansini conducting.

Mozart: *Così Fan Tutte*. The Glyndebourne recording, Fritz Busch conducting.

Verdi: 'Ritorna vincitor' from *Aida*. Rosa Ponselle.

Verdi: *Un Ballo in Maschera*. The Rome recording with Gigli and Caniglia, Serafin conducting.

Verdi: *Requiem*. The Rome recording with Caniglia, Stignani, Gigli and Pinza, Serafin conducting.

Wagner: quintet from *Meistersinger*. Schumann, Schorr et al.

Wagner: 'Herzeleide' scene from *Parsifal*. Flagstad and Melchior.

Wagner: *Die Walküre*. Acts I and II. The composite Vienna–Berlin recording with Lehmann and Melchior.

Weber: 'Und ob die Wolke sie verhüllt' from *Freischütz*. Tiana Lemnitz (Polydor version).

Weber: 'Gebet des Hüon' from *Oberon*. Helge Roswaenge.

Shortly before his death in 1973, Auden was invited by a student music society in Oxford to discuss his desert island discs. He never gave the talk, but the secretary of the society jotted down his choice: Schumann's Fourth String Quartet (first movement), Tchaikovsky's Second Piano Concerto (second movement), the dialogue between Wotan and Fricka in Act II of Die Walküre, *the love duet from* Un Ballo in Maschera, *Chabrier's* Souvenirs de Bayreuth, *Strauss's* Four Last Songs, *Stravinsky's* Requiem Canticles, *and what he described only as three 'Biedermeier' duets by Lorenz Hart, Noël Coward and Cole Porter.*

DESTINN

The Czech soprano Emmy Destinn – 'a woman of immoderate feelings, interests and appetites', poet, novelist, gourmet, and passionate enthusiast for black magic and sex – encounters the handsome young Polish pianist Artur Rubinstein in Paris in 1907.

After the last evening at the Châtelet, Emmy Destinn invited me for supper in her suite at the Hotel Regina, where she stayed with her sister. They changed into their dressing-gowns, and the three of us sat down to a snack of cold meat and champagne. I expressed my admiration of her art to the great singer and cited some particularly impressive moments in her *Aida, Carmen,* and now *Salome*.

'The way you sing is a great lesson for me,' I said. 'you taught me how to use judiciously the rubato, that much misunderstood definition of the free expression of a melody. I try to translate your perfect breathing control into my own phrasing, and I feel certain that Chopin had exactly that on his mind when he required rubato in his works.'

Emmy Destinn listened to my long talk with frowning attention, but suddenly she picked up her glass of champagne and smashed it to bits against the fireplace.

'All right, all right,' she screamed, in a rage. 'I know I am a good singer, but I am also a woman!'

I was aghast. Her sister stood up calmly and left the room, and here I was ... expected to prove that I was a man, too! She was a strange woman, Emmy Destinn. And she really frightened me when I saw the threatening head of a serpent on her thigh. She had a bright-coloured tattoo of a boa encircling her leg from the ankle to the upper thigh; it took me some time to get over my shock. I am afraid I was not at my best that night, but she seemed not to mind; later she became quite mellow and maternal.

Well, anyway, she had to leave the next day for London to take her important part in the great season of the Covent Garden Opera. And here is another unaccountable trait of this great artist – for weeks she sent me letters in the form of poems in verse in a fine calligraphic handwriting on a special de luxe paper. Like a romantic teenager, indeed.

ARTUR RUBINSTEIN, *My Young Years*

DISASTER

There are an enormous number of things that can go wrong with opera, and an enormous number of things do – from the tragic to the ludicrous.

In April 1906, the Metropolitan Opera was on tour in San Francisco.

Historians were to write of the Mission Street Opera House that its curtain had risen on only 255 nights of grand opera in thirty years. Tonight's *Queen of Sheba* would mark its 254th. . . .

Disappointingly *The Queen of Sheba* possessed no allure for San Francisco that night. 'Opera Crowd Cold,' ran Ashton Stevens' headline.

The second night told a happier story. Caruso broke the ice; his sultry, passionate Don José swept away all the reserve of the San Francisco audience. Fremstad's Carmen seemed pale and over-shadowed. Later she claimed that she had sung with effort, fighting a strange lethargy that amounted almost to a premonition on that April 17.

Caruso felt no such foreboding. With customary expansiveness he held court in his dressing-room, then went to bed late at the Palace Hotel contented with the evening's éclat. Shaken out of a light slumber by an unusual noise, which he described as if some-one had thrown himself on the bed in the next room and then hit the wall with a 'biff, boof, br-r-am!', he dashed across the heaving floor and pulled up the window shade.

What he saw and heard made him tremble with fear – buildings toppling against the pearly dawn sky like toys knocked over by a petulant child; screams and shouts of terror. He remained spell-bound for a long, suspended moment, in which he thought of '40,000 different things' and he seemed to sing the whole of *Carmen* all over again. At last he gathered his faculties and called for his valet. Martino came immediately and solicitously helped his master into a few clothes.

In the corridor Caruso encountered Antonio Scotti. The baritone had awakened with a feeling of seasickness. He reached for the light button, but no electricity responded. When he tried to unlock the door, the key was gone; he finally found it on the floor amid scraps of fallen plaster.

On the sixth floor Bessie Abott, the new protégée of Jean de Reszke, who as Micaela had vowed in song only a few hours before not to fear anything, was nearly thrown out of bed. Everything rocked more violently than a ship at sea. She heard a noise that she could not understand – 'indescribable rumblings and grinding sounds, as if bones of earth were cracking and being crushed in the jaws of some giant monster'.

As Miss Abott tumbled out of bed great strips of plaster peeled off from the ceiling in grotesque coils, writhing through the room. The crystal chandelier hurtled past her and broke into shards on the floor. She cut her feet cruelly in gaining the door. Her maid joined her in the stumbling, panicky crowd on the staircases.

No one seemed to know what had happened. Miss Abott was ashamed to hear herself ask idiotic questions, joining the babbling chorus that echoed through the Palace. Across the street a fire had broken out; its heat penetrated scorchingly even into the lobby. Miss Abott decided to return to her room to dress.

Cursing his lame leg, Alfred Hertz pulled on a pair of trousers and a coat, ducked the falling chandelier, clutched his room key, numbered 615, and hobbled painfully down five flights.

Down the hall, Edyth Walker's trunk landed in the middle of her bed a moment after she had vacated it. Her piano danced awkwardly into the middle of the tipsy room. She hurriedly dressed and snatched up a sealskin jacket and a small sofa pillow. Several interminable moments passed before she could wrench open her door, which had bent and jammed.

Marion Weed, also from the sixth floor, reached the ground in time to see the Call Building a few doors away buckle and fall. She dashed back upstairs, packed a trunk, and lugged it down, only to abandon it because falling timber barred the exits.

Josephine Jacoby, another American singer, disregarded the hubbub in the Palace lobby and hastened back to her room to dress fully. She packed a bag with her jewels, got into a brown tailored suit, but slipped her feet into Frasquita's flimsy golden slippers.

Farther uptown in fashionable Union Square, the thirteen-story St Francis Hotel sheltered three Metropolitan singers. From a room on the top floor Andreas Dippel, the company's old reliable, looked at his heavy gold pocket watch. Its hour hand stood at 5; its minute hand moved jerkily from 12 to 13. He hurried down twelve flights, stopping at the sixth floor to see if Marcella Sembrich was safe.

The little Polish prima donna thought the world had come to an end. Shocked and crying, she ran out of her suite in her night clothes and bare feet, only coming to her senses when a gentleman gallantly placed an overcoat around her quivering shoulders. Between tremors her maid helped her into underclothes and a light blue suit.

Pol Plançon, awake in the dawn, suddenly experienced the sensation of a bird in a swinging cage. For once neglecting his usual finicky elegance, he appeared in Union Square in underwear and overcoat.

Preferring private luxury to a hotel, Emma Eames had taken up residence with friends on Taylor Street atop Nob Hill. Her coolness and sense of superiority to fate persisted through the hours that followed. Her first thought after she had extricated herself from the peril of a heavily canopied bedstead was of the matinée performance of *Le Nozze di Figaro*, in which she was billed as the Countess. She tried vainly to telephone Goerlitz and decided there would be no matinée.

Individual as always, Olive Fremstad had leased a suite at St Dunstan's Hotel in Van Ness Avenue, some distance from her colleagues. The tremor that shook the façade from her hotel loosened hardly a petal from her crimson roses of the night before. As she picked her way down stairs made rickety and railless, the flowers obsessed her. She sent a porter up to fetch them. For several hours she hugged the long-stemmed blossoms to her heart as she sat in the little park across the street and breathed the sulphurous air. Then she gave the flowers one by one to the swarming refugees.

In a less pretentious hostelry called The Oaks, orchestra players and comprimario singers fled for their lives amid showers of masonry. Taurino Parvis, a young baritone with two years' experience under Conried, managed to don his underwear and tuck a precious violin under his arm. The baritone Eugene Dufriche and his wife, a member of the orchestra, had thoughts only for the expensive Erard harp, which reposed in the Opera House. They set off toward Third and Mission Streets, but they were too late. . . .

In the first hour of the death struggle of a glamorous and bewitching city, no one spared a thought to the bundles of morning newspapers already dumped beside newsstands. Their front pages told that a great fund had been raised for sufferers from the recent eruption of Mt Vesuvius.

Caruso would not learn for many days that Blanche Partington of the *Call* wanted to rechristen the night's opera *Don José* in his honor. Fremstad would not know that Ashton Stevens of the *Examiner* had called her 'dutchy'. Bessie Abott remained happily ignorant of Stevens' appellation of 'phantom soprano'.

Caruso and Fremstad and Abott and all of their *confrères* had assumed unrehearsed roles in a more exigent drama. Few, however, thought in dramatic terms; only Hertz is credited with comparing the holocaust to *Götterdämmerung*. The 300 members of the opera company were preoccupied with reality.

Along the 270-mile trail of the San Andreas Fault, the earth cracked open from northwest to southeast that morning, shaking and grinding and tearing at everything in its path. San Franciscans knew it instantly for what it was; they had experienced the lesser stirrings of this giant before. The visitors learned fast.

In that brief and terrible April morning, water mains, gas mains, sewers, telephone connections, street car lines and telegraph cables snapped. Live wires were exposed; stoves overturned; flues cracked. As Jack London, a devoted San Franciscan, wrote for *Collier's Weekly* a few days later:

'All the cunning adjustments of a twentieth-century city had been smashed by the earthquake. . . . All the shrewd contrivances and safeguards of men had been thrown out of gear by thirty seconds' twitching of the earth-crust.'

QUAINTANCE EATON, *Opera Caravan*

In his memoir of a lifetime of concert- and opera-going, First and Last Love, Vincent Sheean movingly describes how in New York in 1933 the great Wagnerian soprano Frida Leider 'dried up' in the middle of a performance of Die Walküre. *The disaster was not fatal; Leider recovered and continued singing for another decade. Interestingly, she does not mention this traumatic incident in her autobiography.*

She was on her knees before Wotan (Friedrich Schorr) with her noble head humbly bent and her left hand at her throat. She wore a flowing white dress and a red cloak over it – traditional; but I am telling it exactly as I see and hear it even now, more than twenty years later. She had reached the point where she had to sing the phrase '*War es so schmählich?*' She sang the first two words and notes – that is, '*War es*' – after which a strange, very small sound came out of her throat and no note followed. That weird small sound is quite impossible to describe and if I had not been sitting so close I could not have heard it; I suppose most of the three thousand people there present did not. The click (if it was a click) seemed like the electrocution, the murder, of the great voice. A sound then came from the wings on the word '*schmählich*' and continued the development for five notes more.

(We all learned afterwards that Dorothee Manski from the Berlin Opera, who was one of the Walküre and had been standing in the wings anxiously watching Leider, had thus saved the day by singing her notes.)

Leider kept her head down and I saw her shake it in a kind of fury. I have never had any opportunity to ask her about this but I imagine her sensations during those few seconds must have been as acute and tumultuous as any singer has ever felt. She had been singing the whole performance over a bad cold, so bad that she could not even speak. Now the voice itself, the very sense of her existence, refused its divine grace and there she was, on her knees, with the ruin of a great career in plain view before her. Such a concentrated ordeal seldom befalls an artist.

I felt, or imagined I felt, the struggle of her will to conquer her body. Then she threw back her really grand head and looked out beyond all the three thousand of us to some utter truth beyond us, opened her mouth with confidence, it seemed to me, and by some power (I could see her throat quivering) the voice was given again.

From then on to the end of the act Leider sang with everything an artist has to give, although the sacrifice of her voice must have been tragic. My friend Janet Fairbank, who was there, spoke as we went out to Heinrich Schlusnus, the fine lyric baritone of the Berlin Opera (then singing in the Chicago Company), who had been backstage to kiss Leider's hand before the last act. Schlusnus, weeping without restraint, said that even before the act began Leider had been unable to utter a word in the spoken voice – even to an old friend and colleague like himself. My own sense of awe and terror, not from what Schlusnus told us but from what I had myself seen and felt, lasted for many hours. (I can only compare it with the terror which overwhelmed me at Toscanini's last rehearsal twenty-one years later.)

The week passed without any news of Leider's voice except that she had suffered a bronchial attack of some kind and was under treatment. The Metropolitan was extremely reluctant to make any statement for two quite obvious reasons: first, the remaining Wagner performances might have depleted audiences if it were known that Leider could not sing; second, it was not all to the credit of the Metropolitan that they had obliged this unique artist to risk an irreplaceable voice by singing when she could not even speak.

An unforgettable performance of Spontini's La Vestale *at the Wexford Festival in 1979.*

The set for Act I of the opera consisted of a platform laid over the stage, raised about a foot at the back and sloping evenly to the footlights. This was meant to represent the interior of the Temple where burned the sacred flame, and had therefore to look like marble; the designer had achieved a convincing alternative by covering the raised stage in Formica. But the Formica was slippery; to avoid the risk of a performer taking a tumble, designer and stage manager had between them discovered that an ample sprinkling of lemon juice would make the surface sufficiently sticky to provide a secure foothold. The story now forks; down one road, there lies the belief that the member of the stage staff whose duty it was to sprinkle the lifesaving liquid, and who had done so without fail at rehearsal and at the earlier performances (this was the last one of the Festival), had simply forgotten. Down the other branch in the road is a much more attractive rumour: that the theatre charlady, inspecting the premises in the afternoon, had seen to her horror and indignation that the stage was covered in the remains of some spilt liquid, and, inspired by professional pride, had thereupon set to and given it a good scrub and polish all over.

The roads now join again, for apart from the superior charm of the second version, it makes no difference what the explanation was. What matters is what happened.

What happened began to happen very early. The hero of the opera strides on to the stage immediately after the curtain has gone up. The hero strode; and instantly fell flat on his back. There was a murmur of sympathy and concern from the audience for his embarrassment and for the possibility that he might have been hurt; it was the last such sound that was to be heard that night, and it was very soon to be replaced by sounds of a very different nature.

The hero got to his feet, with considerable difficulty, and, having slid some way down the stage in falling, proceeded to stride up-stage to where he should have been in the first place; he had, of course, gone on singing throughout, for the music had not stopped. Striding up-stage, however, was plainly more difficult than he had reckoned on, for every time he took a step and tried to follow it with another, the foot with which he had taken the first proceeded to slide down-stage again, swiftly followed by its companion; he may not have known it, but he was giving a perfect demonstration of what is called *marcher sur place*, a graceful manoeuvre normally used in mime, and seen at its best in the work of Marcel Marceau.

Finding progress uphill difficult, indeed impossible, the hero wisely decided to abandon the attempt and stay where he was, singing bravely on, no doubt calculating that, since the stage was brightly lit, the next character to enter would notice him and adjust his own movements accordingly. So it proved, in a sense at least, for the next character to enter was the hero's trusted friend and confidant, who, seeing his hero further down-stage than he was supposed to be, loyally decided to join him there. Truth to tell, he had little choice, for from the moment he had stepped on to the stage he had begun to slide downhill, arms semaphoring, like Scrooge's clerk on the way home to his Christmas dinner. His downhill progress was arrested by his fetching up against his friend with a thud; this, as it happened, was not altogether inappropriate, as the opera called for them to embrace in friendly greeting at that point. It did not, however, call for them, locked in each other's arms and propelled by the impetus of the friend's descent, to career helplessly further down-stage with the evident intention of going straight into the orchestra pit with vocal accompaniment – for the hero's aria had, on the arrival of his companion, been transformed into a duet.

On the brink of ultimate disaster they managed to arrest their joint progress to destruction and, working their way along the edge of the stage like mountaineers seeking a route round an unbridgeable crevasse, most gallantly began, with infinite pain and by a form of progress most aptly described in the title of Lenin's famous pamphlet, *Four Steps Forward, Three Steps Back*, to climb up the terrible hill. It speedily became clear that this hazardous ascent was not being made simply from a desire to retain dramatic credibility; it had a much more practical object. The only structure breaking the otherwise all too smooth surface of the stage was a marble pillar, a yard or so high, on which there burned the sacred flame of the rite. This pillar was embedded firmly in the stage, and it had obviously occurred to both mountaineers at once that if they could only reach it it would provide a secure base for their subsequent operations, since if they held on to it for dear life they would at any rate be safe from any further danger of sliding downhill and/or breaking their necks.

It was soon borne in upon them that they had undertaken a labour of truly Sisyphean proportions, and would have been most heartily pardoned by the audience if they had abandoned the librettist's words at this point, and fitted to the music instead the old moral verse:

> The heights by great men reached and kept,
> Were not attained by sudden flight;
> But they, while their companions slept,
> Were toiling upwards in the night.

By this time the audience – all 440 of us – were in a state of such abandon with laughter that several of us felt that if this were to continue a moment longer we would be in danger of doing ourselves a serious internal mischief; little did we know that the fun was just beginning, for shortly after Mallory and Irvine reached their longed-for goal, the chorus entered, and instantly flung themselves *en masse* into a very freely choreographed version of *Les Patineurs*, albeit to the wrong music. The heroine herself, the priestess Giulia, with a survival instinct strong enough to suggest that she would be the one to get close to should any reader of these lines happen to be shipwrecked along with the Wexford opera company, skated into the wings and kicked her shoes off and then, finding on her return that this had hardly improved matters, skated back to the wings and removed her tights as well.

Now, however, the singing never having stopped for a moment, the chorus had come to the same conclusion as had the hero and his friend, namely that holding on to the holy pillar was the only way to remain upright and more or less immobile. The trouble with this conclusion was that there was only one such pillar on the stage, and it was a small one; as the cast crowded round it, it seemed that there would be some very unseemly brawling among those seeking a hand-hold, foot-hold, even a bare finger-hold on this tiny island of security in the terrible sea of impermanence. By an instinctive understanding of the principles of co-operation, however, they decided the matter without bloodshed; those nearest the pillar clutched it, those next nearest clutched the clutchers, those farther away still clutched those, and so on until, in a kind of daisy-chain that snaked across the stage, everybody was accommodated.

The condition of the audience was now one of fully extended hysteria, which was having the most extraordinary effect – itself intensifying the audience's condition – on the orchestra. At Wexford, the orchestra pit runs under the stage; only a single row of players – those at the edge of the pit nearest the audience, together, of course, with the conductor – could see what was happening on the stage. The rest realized that *something* out of the ordinary was going on up there, and would have been singularly dull of wit if they had not, for many members of the audience were now slumped on the floor weeping helplessly in the agony of their mirth, and although the orchestra at Wexford cannot see the stage, it can certainly see the auditorium.

BERNARD LEVIN, *Conducted Tour*

DOCTORS

What makes a doctor look like a doctor? Most actors settle for a pin-striped suit and a hint of greying over the temporoparietal muscles. They end up looking like ageing repertory playboys – which indeed many of them are. Margaret Stacey, a professor of sociology, has suggested that the pathognomonic characteristic of a doctor is clean fingernails but I suspect that we reveal our identity less in our appearance than in our behaviour.

One of the most convincing portrayals of a doctor I've seen on the stage was in, of all things, an opera – possibly because the director was a proper off-stage doctor. The occasion was the Kent Opera production of *La Traviata* and the director was Jonathan Miller. The doctor, who appears in the last act to serve the traditional operatic purpose of prognosing the imminent triumph of tubercle, looked like a doctor because of one simple piece of production.

He didn't, as the character often does, stand beside Violetta's bed and gaze down at her while he chanted a few unconvincing lies:

> 'Then we must take heart,
> Convalescence is not far away. . . .'

In the Jonathan Miller production he sat on the side of her bed and put his hand on her wrist not just to take her pulse but to establish human contact while he offered words that he and Violetta knew were only words. Her acknowledgement of their real meaning – 'Doctors are allowed a pious fib' – was a painfully accurate echo of a moment familiar to clinicians.

That actor's doctor-like qualities were so convincing that a scene that is usually played as a time filler while the audience – and Violetta – draw breath and prepare themselves for a melodic shuffling off of the coils, became one of the most poignant moments of the evening.

Doctors in opera don't often get a chance like that to steal a scene. But then they're an odd lot. I'm never happy, for instance, about the ethical behaviour of the doctor in the last act of *La Bohème* who accepts Musetta's earrings as prepayment for a visit. I don't condemn him for not making it to the garret before the final curtain – that could happen to any busy GP – but I don't think he should send 'a cordial' on ahead of him. It smacks too much of prescribing for a patient he hasn't seen. Maybe he guesses that because she's an opera singer – he may even have heard her belting

out her reprise of 'Che gelida manina' across the rooftops of Paris
– it's just another routine case of terminal phthisis.

The most irritating of operatic doctors is surely the one in
Verdi's *Macbeth*, who is addicted to the question mark. Once his
scene gets under way, his lines, apart from four 'Oh, horror!'s,
are: 'What did she speak of in her sleep?', 'She carries a light in her
hand?', 'How wide open are her eyes?', 'Why does she rub her
hands?', 'What did she say?', 'She sighs?', and 'This too?' And all
but the first of these are asked while the lady in question is singing
just a couple of yards away from him. Most of his patients must
have expired while he was still interrogating the servants.

His on-stage behaviour loses credibility when contrasted with
the off-stage behaviour of a real doctor during a performance of
the same opera at Glyndebourne. The doctor was there because
the singer playing Banquo, the late David Franklin, was suffering
from renal colic. In the story as David used to tell it, the treatment
that sustained him was morphine to dull the pain, amphetamine
to counter the depressive effect of the morphine, and champagne
because John Christie thought that it was good for everything.

David managed to keep going until the first interval but had to
be carried to his dressing-room where the doctor examined him
with some concern. Mrs Franklin, watching anxiously, was worried by the doctor's demeanour.

'Should he really go back on?' she asked.

'What's he got to do in this next act?' asked the doctor.

'A death scene.'

'He'll do that all right,' said the doctor.

Modern medicine's most dramatic contribution to opera was
surely that made in 1961 by a party of local medical students
recruited to play the walk-on firing squad in the last act of *Tosca*
at the San Francisco opera house. . . .

The students, chosen for height rather than stage experience,
knew nothing of the opera or its plot, and the producer had little
time to brief them. He wasn't worried because they didn't have to
sing. Five minutes before the start of the dress rehearsal, he told
them: 'You're a firing squad. Just follow the officer. Slow march

on in time to the music, line up, and, when the officer lowers his sword, shoot.'

'And how do we get off?'

'Just wait on stage and, at the end, exit with the principals.'

The dress rehearsal ran out of time and never reached the final scene so, on the first night, the San Francisco audience saw *Tosca* end in an unusual way.

When, at the tragic denouement, the firing squad marched slowly on, its members were momentarily confused by the fact that there were both a man and a woman on stage. However, when Cavaradossi stepped bravely in front of them they decided he was the one they had to shoot. Yet as they lined up their sights they noticed he kept nodding in a conspiratorial way towards the woman. So, as the officer dropped his sword, they swung their rifles through 180 degrees and shot Tosca.

They were clearly discomfited when she remained standing and they heard Cavaradossi, now directly behind them, hit the stage as he dropped. They gawped nervously as Tosca rushed to him, spoke to him as if he were still alive, and then screamed. And they began to grow panicky when they heard the shouts off-stage and saw Tosca mount the battlements. Then, as she flung herself off, they remembered their final instruction. As the curtain slowly descended, they rushed upstage and threw themselves after her.

MICHAEL O'DONNELL, in the *British Medical Journal*, 1984

DONIZETTI

In 1841 Donizetti wrote to the librettist Felice Romani, about a commission offered by the impresario Benjamin Lumley in London.

I hear that you have promised to write a libretto for the Italian company at London, to which I would write the music.

Is [Lumley] correct in saying you gave your word? Excuse me if I am dubious, but you have put me many times in an embarrassing situation. Truly the wrong is not completely mine if I ask you whether it is true. I spoke with Signor Lummlay [*sic*] . . . he departed for Modena and left me the charge of asking you if this libretto would be ready by the middle of January at the latest. . . . You choose the subject: but remember that, having to contend with a public that scarcely understands Italian, it would not be a bad idea to let the choice fall on some familiar subject by Sakespearre, Bayron, Valter Scott or Bulwer [*sic*]. . . . If you could write me a libretto in just two short acts that would be divine. In London after the theatre people go out in society. . . . Do not try fantastic subjects because there the stage machinery is abysmal. Speak to the heart as you know how to do. . . . I await your reply. Remember that I must give my opera [*Linda di Chamounix*] in April and that if you cannot give me the libretto by the middle of January, as Lummlay says, we are cooked [*siamo fritti*].

Donizetti writes to a friend after the fiasco of the first performance of his Caterina Cornaro *in Naples in 1844.*

A fiasco? Then let it be a fiasco! But who says that this music is not mine, or that I wrote it sleeping, or for revenge against the management? No. I assume all the responsibility, the blow and the blame for it. Why should I have others write it? Did I not perhaps have the time? Why sleeping? Don't I work perhaps with facility? Why for revenge? Could I be so ungrateful toward a public that has endured me for so many years? No! It may be that inspiration, experience and taste have deceived me, that they may be totally lacking, but that I should descend to unworthy acts, to hidden deceptions, never!

As to the echoes of other music – *eh, mon Dieu!* who does not make them? To steal (and what is worse, without wanting to), who does not steal? Note well that I do not in the least mean to justify myself. I repeat that I assume all responsibility for it. I had believed that the various pieces did not deserve all the blame that erupted, that the duets, the quartet, etc., but what use now to discuss it? I will not make the wounds shed fresh blood. If one day this score returns to my hands I will give proof to the Neapolitans that I obey their advice. It has been my error therefore to believe that this music perhaps was not unworthy of their indulgence. . . .

I want the Neapolitans to be compensated with interest by another composer more fortunate than I, and may it be soon so that my mistake is the sooner forgotten. My friends, whom I greet, will be afflicted by this, but what's the use? I am afflicted by it enough for everybody.

DRESSING-ROOM

After a disastrous performance of Don Giovanni, *the eponymous heroine of Marcia Davenport's novel* Of Lena Geyer *collapses. Her aristocratic lover seeks admittance to her dressing-room.*

My poor Lena was crouched in the far corner upon a footstool, garbed in such remnants of clothing as she had not flung all about the room. She had removed her wig, but not the ugly white bandage to which it had been pinned. This was stained with grease-paint and perspiration, and beneath it, from her streaming eyes, there flowed a torrent of tears to mingle with the greases and pigments of her make-up into an unspeakable sight. She was weeping in great racking sobs that tore my heart and filled me with terror, for this, entirely aside from its emotional danger, could only harm her voice the more. She ignored me. She was rocking to and fro upon her stool, moaning and murmuring an unintelligible garble of language which I recognized as Italian and Czech, interspersed with 'Oh, my God!' which she gasped over and over again in English. '*Ah, Maestro!*' she would say, '*carissimo mio, scusate, perdonate. Oh, my God! Oh, my God!*' – and then she would wander off into passionate phrases in her native tongue that I could not hope to reproduce here, rocking this way and that upon her stool and at last burying her face in the greasy towel upon her knees. I knew not what to do. At last I placed my hand upon her shoulder, whereupon she started violently and jumped to her feet. Her weeping and sobbing ceased instantly. She clenched her fists until I saw her knuckles whiten, and knew too well that her nails were digging into her palms.

'How did you get here?' she hissed in a low, furious tone. 'I told her to keep you out. Get out! Get out of here at once, do you understand?'

She advanced a step toward me, and even as my temper rose at the insults she was all too ready to fling at me, I could not deny a thrill of excitement at the sight of her, for she was magnificent. Ridiculous as she looked, with her face smeared in streaks of red and blue and black, with her hair wildly dishevelled above the bandage, with her underclothing falling from one shoulder and breast, with one foot bare and with the stocking she had drawn from it tangled in the towel in her hand, she was a glorious incarnation of mingled grief and anger. Her eyes seemed to have dilated to twice their usual huge size, her wide nostrils flared and trembled, her lips were pinched in her determination to suppress her sobs.

'Get out!' she said again.

'I cannot, Lena,' I replied. 'My place is here, to help you.'

'I need none of your help,' she said, struggling to keep her lips rigid. 'Help! My God, can't you see what you've done? This is your fault. You've done this to me!'

'Let us not discuss that now,' I said, making a tremendous effort not to let my temper rise, for there are times when no opera singer can fling challenges at a royal duke of France.

'We'll discuss whatever I choose!' she retorted, 'and since you have refused to leave and avoid hearing what I hoped not to say, you shall hear it. You and your love! I never want to see you again. I never want you to touch me. I ought to have known better than to make a mess of my life because of you.'

'You have made no mess,' I answered, 'and before acting upon your dismissal, I might add that you did not sing badly enough this evening to warrant this extraordinary outburst. You are merely overwrought.'

'I am?' she cried. 'And pray, who are you to tell me whether I am overwrought and how I sang? Do you think you know anything about it? You do not. You have no idea what my life is. You know nothing about me. You are a man, an animal, selfish, you only want one thing like all the rest of them. Ah, I could kill you!'

She turned to the wall and buried her face in her arms. My anger had by then risen to a point where I was making the greatest effort not to walk out of the room and out of her life, feeling that, like every vulgarian, she was only showing her mettle as I had seen many others do. Yet, as I turned actually to go, I knew that I was wrong. Whether last night's abandonment had been more my fault than hers was irrelevant. I loved this woman, and I knew that she was both a peasant and an artist. If this was the first time she had displayed the lower qualities of both, I could appreciate that she had never done so before. I removed my cloak and laid it, with my opera hat, upon the divan, seating myself quietly there in a firm determination to ride out the storm. Silence prevailed for some time; she must have thought I had taken my departure. Presently she turned toward her dressing-table and began wearily to remove her make-up. Then she saw me in the mirror. She whirled around.

'Louis!' she exclaimed, 'did I not ask you to go? Can't you understand that I must be alone? The longer you stay here the harder it is for me.'

'It is not easy for me either, Lena,' I said. 'I want only to try to make you believe that your grief is exaggerated. Nobody has an idea you sang as you think you did.'

She laid down her comb and looked at me a moment. Then she began to speak, quickly and with passion, but I could see with a tremendous effort to control her temper.

'The point is not what anybody thought,' she said. 'The point is what I know. I know I can't mix these two things, this – this love – and my work. I knew it years ago, that's why I lived the life I did before I knew you. I love you, that is the trouble. I am only human. I have learned to enjoy love and you see what I paid for it tonight.'

ELEKTRA

Both of Richard Strauss's best known one-act operas,
Salome *(1905) and* Elektra *(1909), caused enormous scandal at the time of their early performances, on account of their musical daring as much as their subject-matter.*
Elektra, *in particular, was regarded in many quarters as wantonly, cacophonously noisy.*

Elektra has known for some time that her papa was killed by mamma and her mamma's gentleman friend ... She screams and then gets down and digs up out of the dirt the axe her papa was killed with ... Her mother is afraid of her. Elektra keeps on howling ... The orchestra breaks into strange and unearthly noises ... Muted trumpets, woodwind in the lowest register and strings leaping in intervals of ninths and sevenths mingle in a medley of sounds which gives the idea of a snarling, frightened animal. In the great scene in which Elektra accuses her mother of murdering her father, the music ends with a long shrill whistle like that of a locomotive entering a tunnel. Elsewhere the music reproduces sounds of smashing glass and china, the bursting of bottles, the clashing of shovels and tongs, the groaning and creaking of rusty hinges and stubborn doors, avalanches in the mountains, the crying of babies, the squealing of rats, the grunting of pigs, the bellowing of cattle, the howling of cats and the roaring of wild beasts ... I didn't pick out a tune that I should imagine would be later on included in 'Gems from the Opera for the Parlor Organ.'

Boston Herald, 21 January 1910

Bartók admired Strauss and was considerably influenced by him; but his response to Elektra *in 1910 was guarded.*

Elektra after *Salome*: a disappointment. When a new work is begun we should more or less forget the previous ones in order to avoid subjecting ourselves to self-imitation. To repeat – I expected something from *Elektra*, but in vain. It hardly discloses an idea – hitherto unfelt, unheard, or unexpressed – that would stimulate in me the wish to hear or read it a second time. On the whole I would call it average Strauss.

It is true, however, that in Strauss – one of our outstanding composers – even the average is not devoid of interest. But we ought to expect something more, something whose composition requires higher inspiration. And *Salome* is far greater in that respect. There, already in the poetry of the first scenes, in the big scene of Herodes, in the Quintet of the Jews are many new colours, valuable pictures. In *Elektra*, on the other hand, the disintegration of the first scenes is already tiring; nor is [the] continuation very encouraging. Perhaps the most interesting scene is that of Clytemnestra.

There is an aspect of Strauss's music that I do not understand either in this opera or in his other works: how it is possible for someone, gifted enough to say so much that is musically interesting, to involve himself with such flat, 'half-hearted', '*kapellmeister*' music – that is to be found in abundance in Strauss's works – when so-called sublime feelings are expressed (for example, Elektra's boundless rejoicing at the arrival of Orestes is expressed in the most vulgar means, in never-ending A flat major).

There is a question at issue here to which perhaps only Strauss has the answer: does he actually consider this kind of music to be of a higher order or is it perhaps a sort of sugar and water to entice the plebs? The first possibility is incomprehensible, the second – ugly.

Critical opinion on the relative merits of Salome *and* Elektra *has since largely reversed, perhaps partly because of the Freudian fascination of Hofmannsthal's superb libretto for the latter.* See also pp. 370–1.

ENCORE

On Friday last, Il Barbiere was produced at Covent Garden, with Madame Patti as Rosina. Her performance in that part is too familiar to call for notice. In response to the usual *encore* in the lesson scene she sang Home, Sweet Home to the unbounded delight of her hearers. Indeed, the opera proved so intolerably wearisome that some of the audience had already displayed their appreciation of the sentiment of the ballad in the most practical way. G. B. SHAW, 1877

ESSENTIALS

In former times divers *Airs* were heard in the Theatre in this delightful Manner, preceded and accompanied with harmonious and well-modulated Instruments, that ravished the Senses of those who comprehended the Contrivance and the Melody; and if sung by one of those five or six eminent Persons abovementioned, it was then impossible for a human Soul, not to melt into Tenderness and Tears from the violent Motion of the Affections. Oh! powerful Proof to confound the idoliz'd *Mode!* Are there in these Times any, who are moved with Tenderness, or Sorrow? – No, (say all the Auditors) no; for, the continual singing of the *Moderns* in the *Allegro* Stile, though when in Perfection That deserves Admiration, yet touches very slightly one that hath a delicate Ear. The Taste of the *Ancients* was a Mixture of the *Lively* and the *Cantabile*, the Variety of which could not fail giving Delight; but the *Moderns* are so pre-possessed with Taste in *Mode*, that, rather than comply with the former, they are contented to lose the greatest Part of its Beauty. The Study of the *Pathetick* was the Darling of the former; and Application to the most difficult Divisions is the only Drift of the latter. *Those* perform'd with more Judgment; and *These* execute with greater Boldness. But since I have presum'd to compare the most celebrated Singers in both Stiles, pardon me if I conclude with saying, that the *Moderns* are arrived at the highest Degree of Perfection in singing to the *Ear;* and that the *Ancients* are inimitable in singing to the *Heart.*

PIERO TOSI, *Observations on the Florid Song*, 1723

Mozart, writing to his très cher père *in October 1787, about the composition of* Die Entführung aus dem Serail.

Now as to the libretto of the opera. You are quite right so far as Stephanie's work is concerned. Still, the poetry is perfectly in keeping with the character of stupid, surly, malicious Osmin. I am well aware that the verse is not of the best, but it fitted in and it agreed so well with the musical ideas which already were buzzing in my head, that it could not fail to please me; and I would like to wager that when it is performed, no deficiencies will be found. As for the poetry which was there originally, I really have nothing to say against it. Belmonte's aria 'O wie ängstlich' could hardly be better written for music. Except for 'Hui' and 'kummer ruht in meinem Schoss' (for sorrow – cannot rest), the aria too is not bad, particularly the first part. Besides, I should say that in an opera the poetry must be altogether the obedient daughter of the music. Why do Italian comic operas please everywhere – in spite of their miserable libretti – even in Paris, where I myself witnessed their success? Just because there the music reigns supreme and when one listens to it all else is forgotten. Why, an opera is sure of success when the plot is well worked out, the words written solely for the music and not shoved in here and there to suit some miserable rhyme (which, God knows, never enhances the value of any theatrical performance, be it what it may, but rather detracts from it) — I mean, words or even entire verses which ruin the composer's whole idea. Verses are indeed the most indispensable element for music — but rhymes — solely for the sake of rhyming — the most detrimental. Those high and mighty people who set to work in this pedantic fashion will always come to grief, both they and their music. The best thing of all is when a good composer, who understands the stage and is talented enough to make sound suggestions, meets an able poet, that true phoenix; in that case no fears need be entertained as to the applause even of the ignorant. Poets almost remind me of trumpeters with their professional tricks! If we composers were always to stick so faithfully to our rules (which were very good at a time when no one knew better), we should be concocting music as unpalatable as their libretti.

Bellini, writing to his librettist Pepoli in June 1834, about their collaboration on I Puritani.

Do not forget to bring with you the *pièce* already sketched out, so that we can settle the matter of the first act — which, if you will arm yourself with a good supply of moral patience, will emerge as an interesting, magnificent and worthy poem to music, in spite of you and all your ridiculous rules, which are good for nothing except as a subject of endless chatter that can never convince a soul who has once been introduced to the difficult art of *drawing tears by means of song.*

If my music turns out to be beautiful and the opera pleases, you can write a million letters protesting against the misuse of poetry by composers, etc., without proving anything at all. . . . Carve in your head in letters of brass: *An opera must draw tears, cause horror, bring death, by means of song* ... Poetry and music, to make their effect, must be true to nature, and that is all: anyone who forgets this is lost and will end by producing a dull, heavy work which can please only the pedants. It will never appeal to the heart, that poet which is the first to be penetrated by the passions; whereas if the heart is moved one will always be in the right, despite a flood of words that can prove nothing whatsoever. Will you or will you not grasp this in the end? I beg you to do so before beginning the libretto: and do you know why I tell you that good drama has nothing to do with good sense? It is because I know only too well what intractable animals the *literati* are, and how ridiculous, with their general rules of good sense: what I say has been proved by the facts in the world of art, for almost the majority of your famous men have gone astray in this respect....

Drawing all their statements from their own writings, Lilian Foerster Loveday assembled this ingenious 'conversation' with Mozart, Wagner and Verdi.

L.F.L.: Mr Mozart, Mr Wagner, Mr Verdi – you are the composers of some of the 'firmly embedded body of works' in the operatic repertory to which Aaron Copland referred recently in his discussion of opera in the twentieth century, and you composed three of the first four operas to be broadcast from the Metropolitan this season. I am going to ask you about the problems and conditions in your own lifetimes, in the eighteenth and nineteenth centuries. But first I should like to find out something from Mr Mozart. Aaron Copland draws a distinction between those who are 'hopelessly' opera composers, who can and will write nothing but operas (like Mr Wagner and Mr Verdi), and those who are at home in a variety of musical forms and can therefore take opera or leave it. You, Mr Mozart, are the only composer who could write – not only equally well but supremely well – in every field of music. Why did you write operas?

MOZART: It was the thing I wanted to do most of all. I had an indescribable craving to write operas!

L.F.L.: You sound as 'hopeless' as the rest of them. How did you feel while you were writing?

MOZART: When I thought things were going well with my opera, I felt as if my whole body were on fire.

WAGNER: *Tannhäuser* bewitched me; every time I touched it, I quivered and glowed with fire.... The music of *Siegfried* swarmed through my body.

L.F.L.: It is astounding that two such different people should have such similar and extraordinarily intense physical reactions to the creation of music. Now, to get on to the opera itself, what sort of story did you want for your libretto?

VERDI: I wanted plots that were great, beautiful, varied, daring – daring to an extreme – new in form and at the same time adapted to composing.

L.F.L.: Were they hard to find?

VERDI: I tried all the librettos that were sent to me, with considerable dissatisfaction.

MOZART: That was so in my day. It was very hard to find a good poem. [In 1783] I looked over at least a hundred librettos, probably more, without finding a single one that I considered satisfactory.

WAGNER: I really had no illusions about being a poet. But there were no good texts available, and I had no choice but to write my own.

L.F.L.: At least you didn't have to struggle with a librettist, or he with you! That was Mr Verdi's and Mr Mozart's problem. Mr Verdi kept a tight rein on all his librettists, and it is well known that when he came to *Aida* he practically wrote the text himself. Mr Mozart, you weren't so particular – or were you?

MOZART: I told Varesco that he would have to change and recast the [*Idomeneo*] text as much and as often as I wanted him to, and that he was not to follow his own ideas, because he had no experience or theatrical know-how.

L.F.L.: Were you as rough on Stephanie when he was writing the libretto of *Die Entführung aus dem Serail?*

MOZART: I asked him to change the whole story around. There was a charming quintet at the beginning of Act III which I wanted to use as a finale for Act II: to do this we had to add a new subplot. But he arranged the libretto for me, precisely as I wanted it – to a T – and by God, I couldn't ask any more of him!

L.F.L.: Mr Copland says that one of the most difficult things in an opera is to keep a sense of the flow of the action. How did you handle that?

MOZART: I cut the second duet in *Idomeneo* because an aria or a duet here would have made the scene cold and lifeless, and very awkward for the other actors who had to stand around.

VERDI: The single scene with Amneris alone was cold, and that type of aria at such a moment [*Aida*, Act IV, Scene 1] impossible. Ghislanzoni also wanted to make a terzet at the end of Act III, but this was not the time to stop and sing, and we had to hurry on quickly to Amneris' entrance. ... I did not criticize his poetry as poetry; I only told him what I thought its dramatic impact would be on the stage.

L.F.L.: What does the music do in an opera? How is it used? What place does it have?

VERDI: The music carves out a character, paints an emotion —

WAGNER: It has to express something in the action or the character of the actors.

VERDI: But in the theater it is sometimes necessary, when the action demands it, for the poet and the composer to have the ability to write neither poetry nor music.

MOZART: No! Music must always remain music. Even in the most horrible dramatic situations, it must delight the ear rather than offend it.

WAGNER: Either way, the drama comes first, and the music that expresses it is only secondary.

MOZART: Absolutely not! Music is the most important thing in opera. Poetry must obey it like a daughter.

L.F.L.: This is incredible! You are all diametrically opposed in theory, and yet in practice, in the operas you actually wrote, all three of you stand together at the top. But you were lucky; you lived in an operatic age. Nowadays, according to Mr Copland, it's difficult to find American operas worth performing.

VERDI: Good operas have always been rare. Eighty years ago I found them almost nonexistent.

L.F.L.: When both you and Wagner were writing? If they were nonexistent then, pity us now! Nowadays, even if someone does write an opera good enough to be performed, the situation is still risky. Mr Copland says he never knows what sort of singers he will get. What experiences did you have?

MOZART: [In *Idomeneo*] Raaff and Dal Prato were the most pathetic actors that ever encumbered a stage. Dal Prato had never been in the theater before, and Raaff was like a statue. We had to cut two scenes, because they sang the recitatives so monotonously, so utterly without spirit or fire, that everyone would have been bored.

WAGNER: What is the most important thing? Is it the voice alone? Certainly not! It is life and fire. To make the performance [of *Lohengrin*] seem shorter to the audience, I suggested that the singers deliver the recitatives as vividly and expressively as possible. Even if they were sung at the correct tempo, they would not be interesting unless they were sung with warmth and conviction.

VERDI: The voice alone is not enough [for Amneris]. I like to have a part sung as I wrote it, but I cannot provide either the voice or the spirit or that certain spark of temperament....

Opera News, 1964

Compare the following defence of opera with Pierre Boulez's attack on it, made from a not dissimilar left-wing political perspective, on pp. 186–94.

The Germans are envied the world over for their opera houses. In the USA, in England and in France people are increasingly striving to set up new opera houses or new orchestras in the provinces. In those countries it is considered culturally progressive.

For a modern city, closing down an opera house is a decisive step towards alienation. For centuries it had been a significant part of the cultural life of a city that musicians were among its citizens. It is, indeed, due to them that an appreciation of music spread and that, on the whole, there is such a natural feeling for music in our people. All that would come to an end and cannot be replaced by touring companies, especially as they are more likely to be of a token character than a permanent local institution.

The notion that opera is 'bourgeois' and an obsolete art form is itself one of the most outdated, tedious and musty notions. There are, to be sure, outmoded styles, outdated and tedious productions, and slipshod routine that make it difficult for many theatre-lovers and young comrades to grasp the content of the works being performed. (Is that the case in Dortmund? I do not know, but cannot imagine that it is.) But this art form contains riches that are among the most beautiful inventions of the human spirit. They belong to all people; they were not written for the ruling class, but in a spirit of human brotherhood. Anyone who has seen, for example, how young workers and peasants in Havana have made symphonic music and opera their own, and how they fill the opera house, *their* opera house, to listen to *their* composers, Mozart, Verdi, Caturla, Beethoven, and Brouwer, will no longer be able to retain any doubts about which direction progressive cultural work must take; certainly not that of doing away with one of the fundamental factors of our culture.

It is not opera that is reactionary. What is bourgeois is an (undialectical) belief in linear progress, titillated by fashionable notions, frustrated and elitist, which call for different forms of music and music-making as if to escape reality, to by-pass it:

forms that could not exist at all, because they would have no basis (in the political and philosophical sense). Progress in art (and in artistic life) is conceivable only in connection with social progress. One must start at the foundations.

HANS WERNER HENZE, *Music and Politics*

Nicholas Maw, composer of the delightful opera The Rising of the Moon *(1970), in interview with Paul Griffiths, in the latter's collection of conversations with younger British composers,* New Sounds, New Personalities.

Q: Is it still possible to compose opera? Is the art of libretto writing dead? Can operatic structures be supported without the narrative thread provided by the diatonic system?

I suppose the obvious answer, from the point of view of a composer in the mid eighties, is that it's not possible to compose opera in the old way. But I begin to suspect that there is no new way of composing opera, and that it's only possible to compose opera in the old way. There's one simple reason for this: that opera is by and about singing, and singing implies song, which implies phrase structure, which in turn implies cadencing, which in turn implies some kind of tonality. Basically the problem is how to make a viable song – how indeed, in this day and age, to make a melody which can be apprehended as such, lodged in the memory as an entity. I don't mean to suggest that opera has to be a long string of unbroken melodies, though some of the most successful operas have been just that. It's rather that melody is one of the essential ingredients of the art form.

Of course, it's possible to write operas of a completely different kind, but I don't think it's possible to write very many of them: there's the case of *Wozzeck*, and there's the remarkable case of *Punch and Judy*. But if one's going to create an *oeuvre* of operas, one's musical language has to be sufficiently flexible, and one way of achieving that flexibility is to make use of the speech patterns of one's language; and certainly three of this century's greatest opera composers have done that: Strauss, Janáček and Britten. But of course this question of flexibility goes far beyond that: it's a matter of dramatic tensions and relaxations, of shifts in dramatic temperature.

One of the litmus tests is whether a composer can write a comic opera. There have always been remarkably few successful comic operas, but surely never as few as in the last eighty years. Comedy demands mastery in these things in a very extreme form, and it has to be an art that conceals art: the language must not draw attention to itself but be buoyant, capable of true melody, capable of considerable kinetic energy, so that the composer can write really fast music.

There's also the question of subject matter, which is another problem in the twentieth century. In the old days characters tended to be larger than life or, in comic opera, caricatures. Auden maintained that this was necessary simply because they sang: he could never imagine somebody coming on to the stage in a business suit and singing. But I don't think that's a problem in comedy, and the problem in dramatic opera is different: operatic characters tended to be heroic, and these days it's not believable or interesting to put such characters on the stage. Two of the greatest operas of the century have been concerned rather with anti-heroes: *Wozzeck* and *Peter Grimes*, both of which feature archetypally twentieth-century figures though they're both based on early nineteenth-century texts.

Until the early twentieth century opera grew directly out of the drama of its time, but in the twentieth century this has been exceedingly difficult, partly because of the question of copyright. It's very hard for a composer to use the work of a contemporary dramatist, because he's not allowed to, or it's too expensive. I had that experience when I once approached a British playwright, who was extremely enthusiastic about the idea and even gave me a copy of the play he'd prepared for television, cutting the text by half; but the project came to naught because his agents refused to allow it.

In the past operatic characters have not been noted for

psychological depth, though of course there are exceptions: the Countess in *Figaro*, Leonore in *Fidelio*, Wotan, Hans Sachs, Othello, the Marschallin. . . . But this does seem to be an area that the twentieth-century opera composer might apply himself to.

Opera has a long tradition, begun, a touch timidly, in the eighteenth century and more than kept up in the nineteenth, of proclaiming the bliss of true love: even, or perhaps especially, impoverished true love. Admittedly, opera, like socialism, was caught in a dilemma: should it argue that the poor will never be happy until they share the wealth of the rich; or should it imply that the poor, simply by being poor, have virtues and happinesses the rich cannot share – a cogent argument for keeping the poor poor? (It was probably this argument which eighteenth-century genre painting and its patrons were implicitly putting forward when they developed a taste for sentimentalized peasants and picturesque cripples and beggars.) However, dilemma or no dilemma, contradiction or no contradiction, opera raised or at least hinted the question; and that in itself marks it as a non-monarchical entertainment. At court even so simple a competitor as true love is not permitted to challenge the theory that all the warmth and light enjoyed by the nation emanates from the Sun King. The entertainment form promoted by courts is the masque and its subsidiary the ballet, a form which is the successor to, and only in technique an improvement on, the courtly pageants of the Middle Ages. To a more than medieval extent, it was, though given to elaborate allegories and personifications, incapable of characters. All the technique, together with the spectacle and the very music, was designed to saturate the senses and drown out the sense. The difference between this and opera is precisely the difference between the absolutism of Louis XIV and the enlightened despotism of Frederick. The latter is at least based on an idea.

Opera, too, may occasionally drown out the sense, but never the emotion. It is anything but mute. At an absolute court, as

Saint-Simon shews us, only the king may have emotions freely; other people must have them in relation to his. Protocol – that is, primitive taboo – governs other people's behaviour; the king alone may twitch according to his whims, and acquires thereby a puppet's semblance of the personal and independent psychology which in reality he is not free to develop in his artificial vacuum. Puppet-psychology, together with a measure of allegory (usually through classical prototypes), which fore-ordained the characteristics of the dramatis personae as predictably as protocol fore-ordained the behaviour of courtiers, survived from the masque into the early, rhetorical days of opera. But since an emancipated public existed, opera quickly threw off the masque and fairly soon the classical masks as well, and developed into the world's most unconstrained vehicle for personal emotions.

As a form, opera is ill-adapted to depicting the massy and seemingly impersonal forces of taboo. Even its dignity, that quality most necessary to absolute monarchy, totters. (For dignity the enlightened despot substituted something opera *could* depict: panache.) Its crowd scenes are its most dangerous moments. On the stage, the chorus moves as well as sings in consort; and its drilledness, which impresses us in a church or a concert hall, easily gives us the giggles in the opera house. For re-inforcing its choruses or characters with the weight of centuries of numinous awe, opera possesses no acceptable metaphor: hence the unhistorical, fancy-dress-ball air of nineteenth-century opera's costume dramas; and hence, at another remove, the cheapness of effect when Puccini pierces his own admirably blown bubble of operatic convention by introducing touches of Christian liturgy. Opera can no more portray the mass psychology of taboo than it can tracts of landscape or lapses of historical time. (Or, at least, it could not portray those until Wagner made splendid effects of mass and time by the literal method of deploying masses of singers and instrumentalists and keeping the audience in the theatre for great lengths of time.) What opera excels in creating, by its nature (Wagner, though magnificently, was working against its nature), is, as Mozart was to shew, precisely what the enlightenment had created: not a society but a nexus of characters on whom external

social forces impose nothing more constraining than good manners and who reflect society at large only in the freedom it has
given them to form and express their personal inter-relationships.

BRIGID BROPHY, *Mozart the Dramatist*

la FANCIULLA DEL WEST

Puccini's 'wild west' opera, premièred in 1910 (see pp. 331–3), has never won the popularity of Tosca *or* Butterfly, *but has always provided good journalistic copy . . .*

An International Premiere – America Proud of *The Girl of the Golden West* – Under Two Flags, a $20,000 House Riots Over Puccini – Caruso as 'Mr Johnson' Looks and Acts his Best and All His Admirers Will Have to Hear His Lynching Aria – Sheriff Amato Shares the Big Scene – Gold Miner Gilly and Red Squaw Mattfeld Not Forgotten on the Fifty Curtain Calls.

Headlines in the New York Sun, 1910

. . . and provoked the satire of the sophisticated.

What new music have you heard recently, Mr Stravinsky?

I.S.: New to me was the *Fanciulla del West*, a remarkably up-to-date TV horse opera with a Marshall Dillon and professional Indians like the lobby Indians in the hotels at Santa Fe. These aborigines are characterized, if you could call it that, by some ineffectual reminiscences of Debussy, but most of the score is back in the land of *Butterfly*; the opera is really an Eastern western. No matter what the geography, the music – self-parodying arias, a Roxy Theater overture – is bad. Why? Is it the absence of people with whom the composer could identify (they could not identify themselves, for sure)? Or the unsuitability of the subject to that genius of sentimentality which in *La Bohème* is so perfectly matched to the dramatic substance and so superbly deployed that even I leave the theater, when I can get a ticket, humming my lost innocence? But there is one conspicuous success in *Fanciulla*, the attempt to make it American – *i.e.*, simple-minded – by having the gold miners sing in unison and by repeating a Grofé-type trot rhythm to the point of incandescence.

Interview in the *New York Review of Books*

FANS

At Princess Victoria's sixteenth birthday concert [in 1834], a present from her mother and surely one of the most dazzling collections of musical talent ever made for a private recital . . . Malibran, Grisi and all the other great interpreters – Luigi Lablache the bass, Rubini, Tamburini and Ivanoff – performed for Victoria. Malibran arrived late, 'dressed in white satin with a scarlet hat and feathers'. Victoria noted: 'Her low notes are *beautiful*, but her high notes are thick and not clear. I like *Grisi by far better* than her.' Malibran's sudden death stunned her hundreds of *aficionados*, and intense poetic tributes such as Alfred de Musset's 'Stances à la Malibran' commemorated her gift. Even Queen Victoria conceded that 'in point of cleverness and genius there is not a doubt that Malibran far surpassed Grisi . . .'

But Grisi was her favourite, not least because of her beauty. Victoria was delighted when she saw the singer out riding in the Park: 'She is pale off the stage, but has not at all a delicate appearance. On the contrary she has a very slight pinkish hue over her face. She looks very pretty and mild.' Three days later, at the première of Donizetti's *Marino Faliero* (based on Byron's play), Victoria was gripped by Grisi's intensity: 'Elena then stares wildly about her, her hand raised to her head, and giving a frantic scream falls prostrate and lifeless to the ground . . . I know no singer I like as well as Grisi. She is perfection (to my feeling). She is *very pretty* and is an *exquisite* singer and *charming* actress!' She was enraptured by Grisi's generosity in applauding warmly a rival, Albertazzi – now forgotten – in Rossini's *Cinderella*. 'She is a good-natured creature, Grisi', wrote her adorer. A special bow Grisi made to her box gave her the greatest pleasure, and the singer's appearance in person at her birthday treat, 'that delicious concert', inspired a litany of adulation. 'Such a lovely mild expression . . . such beautiful dark eyes with fine long eyelashes . . . Her beautiful dark hair . . . She is very quiet, ladylike and unaffected in her manners.' Victoria dressed herself for a ball with 'a wreath of white roses like Grisi has in the Puritani' – her favourite opera, usually referred to as '*dear* Puritani'.

The singers Grisi, Lablache, Rubini and Tamburini became known as 'the Puritani Quartet' after their unrivalled collaboration in Bellini's emotive Romeo and Juliet story set in Roundhead England. The member of the Quartet whom Victoria came to know best was Luigi Lablache, the monumental basso. Lablache had a genius for *opera buffa* roles, to which his great size but nimbleness suited him, as well as for *opera seria*, in which, as the Druid in *Norma* or the leading Roundhead in *I Puritani*, he dominated majestically. Although Lablache delighted the Princess, he did not make her heart flutter as Grisi did. Yet she drew him more often than any other figure. One particular scene from Rossini's *Otello* recurs many times: Lablache towering over the tiny figure of Grisi as Desdemona while she pleads for understanding from her father Elmiro. '*Se il padre m'abbandona, da chi sperar pietà?*' ('If ever my father abandons me, from whom else can I hope for pity?') was a line carved deep in Victoria's memory, it seems. Once again her imagination was captured by a scene of female vulnerability, intensified here by Desdemona's psychological orphanhood. Victoria, who chose to write to Uncle Leopold in Italian that he was not just '*il mio secondo padre*', but '*solo padre*', seems to have felt for the plight of the fatherless children around whom the plots of so many romantic operas are built. Amina, Grisi's role in Bellini's *Sonnambula* – one of Victoria's favourite operas – is a foster-child; Norma's lover Pollione, by whom she has two children, leaves them orphans not through his death, but his infidelity.

It would be misleading to give a neurotic edge to Victoria's love of romantic opera. She revelled in its humour too, liking particularly Lablache's Don Magnifico in *Cinderella*, and his comic improvisations in the one-act *opera buffa* by Gnecco, *La Prova di una Opera Seria*. Almost incoherent with pleasure, Victoria described the scenes: 'Signor Lablache was *beyond* every thing! He looked so funny, in his huge powdered wig and bad brown silk coat and sword. And acted – Oh! *inimitably*! He personated the distracted composer when Corilla [Grisi] sings out of tune *exquisitely* ... When he ... walks with bent legs ... and imitates her voice; she then does the same to him, and they both dance. Grisi valsed about the stage by herself in a *very funny manner*... Lablache kept us continually laughing...'

When Victoria learned that the Vernon family, whom she met on her journeys in the north of England, had been receiving lessons from Tamburini, her resolve to be taught properly herself must have stiffened. In 1836 Lablache himself came to Kensington Palace, and for twenty years continued to coach the high small voice of the Queen with his huge, deep, rolling bass. Lablache was endlessly good-natured. Victoria recorded her appreciation: 'He is so good-humoured, and though tired, or bored (as I should think he must often be, by teaching a person like me, all the lovely songs &c. which he hears Grisi, Rubini &c. sing) he is always even-tempered, merry and most obliging . . . liked my lesson extremely.' He had parts transposed to suit Victoria's voice, and patiently took her and Mama through the great arias. Victoria discussed music earnestly with him; she felt unable to agree about Mozart's supreme superiority. 'I am a terribly modern person', she wrote, 'and I must say I prefer Bellini, Rossini, Donizetti, etc., to anything else; but Lablache, who *understands* music *thoroughly*, said, "C'est le Papa de tous".' To her astonishment, Victoria discovered that her hero – with whom she spoke French – was half Irish. His father was French and he was born in Naples, where several of his enormous family were being brought up.

She also discovered, and her report has a slightly puzzled air, that Lablache did not share her own high opinion of Grisi, but criticized the singer's way of swallowing before a roulade – 'a habit she has contracted from fear of failing ... I do not think he quite *likes* her'. Indeed, when the mercurial impresario Alfred Bunn removed all the greatest singers from the King's Theatre to his new establishment at Covent Garden in 1847, Lablache refused to follow Grisi, Mario and the others. But even Lablache's reservations about Grisi could not dim her attraction for Victoria. Grisi remained the touchstone by which she judged all the great singers of the century, although slightly grudgingly she did admit later that Jenny Lind eclipsed her favourite.

MARINA WARNER, *Queen Victoria's Sketchbook*

Queen Victoria's enthusiasm for opera was affected only by her retreat from public theatres after Albert's death. In 1899, however, months before her death, she commanded a star-studded private performance of extracts from Wagner's Lohengrin *at Windsor Castle, reporting in her diary, 'I was simply enchanted': see p. 335.*

Miss Giles was a dedicated fan of the Italian tenor Mario, whose consort both onstage and off was the soprano Giulia Grisi. In 1854 she followed her idol to America and became an object of considerable public curiosity, as this newspaper article, quoted in Luigi Arditi's My Reminiscences, *shows.*

Poor thing! Everybody but Grisi must pity her in their hearts. There she sits, 'solitary and alone,' in her spacious box, dressed in the costliest of laces and brocades, perfectly indifferent to everything but Mario. The ladies of the chorus look curiously at her, lorgnettes are levelled towards the place where she sits from all parts of the house, and the bearded gentlemen of the orchestra look wonderingly up at her; but she heeds nobody, and when not looking over the fringe of her splendid fan, or through the parted petals of the white camellias of her bouquet, at the object of her burning passion, she sits like a sphynx, a tremendous riddle, which nobody has yet been able to solve. But we have lately had the pleasure of meeting a gentleman recently from London, who knew her well, and all her antecedents, from whom we learned the following particulars:

Her real name is Giles, not Gyles, as has been often said; she is a native of Gloucestershire, in England; and has lived some years in London, keeping house in a quiet way, at the West End, and going but little into society, though a constant attendant at the opera and the theatres. Her income is but £2000 a year, or $10,000, which is too small a sum to make a show with in London. At one time she conceived a passion for Charles Kean [the actor], whom she haunted in the same way she now haunts Mario, until happening to meet the latter she transferred her affections, and he has been the idol of her idolatry ever since. What will become of the poor lady when Mario retires into private life, and goes to live on his estate in Italy, unless she should in the meanwhile find some other fascination, it is not easy to conceive. Perhaps some handsome Yankee may succeed in attracting her young affections, and put an end to her unhappy passion. It is said that while Mario was indisposed at the Metropolitan Hotel, she used to call there every morning in her carriage, and when the waiter brought her word that Mario was better, she rewarded the lucky Mercury with a double eagle [dollar coin].

The *Musical World* says that a lady, who came over in the same steamer with Grisi and Mario, relates that Mario's affectionate shadow ... followed him on the embarkation, and alighted upon the deck of the steamer arrayed in a lilac-coloured silk, with flounces embellished with feather trimming, over the whole of which was work lace. Upon her head was a fragile breath of a bonnet, trimmed with orange blossoms. The lady advanced to the saloon, placed her hat in the hands of her maid, and reclined gracefully upon a lounge, whereupon the maid covered her with lace. A lady passenger entered into conversation with her, and asked if she did not think Mario was handsome. Thereupon she burst into a fit of laughter so contagious that everybody in the saloon was constrained to laugh with her.

Grisi afterwards playfully said that she wished a committee of gentlemen would incontinently drop her into the sea; adding, more earnestly, however, that she really had for her the evil eye. She had followed them wherever they went – had gone with them to St Petersburg. Twice, in such instances, had they met with comparative failure. If they failed in the United States it might be ascribed to the same evil eye.

Miss Giles met a tragic end some years later, a few days after showing Mario with rose petals during a performance of Faust *in Paris. A fallen candle set fire to her hotel room, and she burnt to death: Mario paid his respects to her charred corpse.*

Fan letters are a rich source of both the comic and the pathetic, as the American prima donna Clara Louise Kellogg discovered.

A man whose name I never learned dropped a big, fragrant bunch of violets at my feet each night for weeks. Becoming discouraged after a while because I did not seek him out in his gallery seat, he sent me a note begging for a glance and adding, for identification, this illuminating point: '*You'll know me by my boots hanging over!*'

Who could disregard such an appeal? That night my eyes searched the balconies feverishly. He had not vainly raised my hopes; his boots *were* hanging over, large boots, that looked as if they had seen considerable service. I sang my best to those boots and – dear man! – the violets fell as sweetly as before. I have conjured up a charming portrait of this individual, with a soul high enough to love music and violets and simple enough not to be ashamed of his boots. Would that all 'sincere admirers' might be of such an ingenuous and engaging a pattern.

The variety of 'admirers' that are the lot of a person on the stage is extraordinary. It is very difficult for the stage persons themselves to understand it. It has never seemed to me that actors as a class are particularly interesting. Personally I have always been too cognisant of the personalities behind the scenes to ever have any theatrical idols; but to a great many there is something absolutely fascinating about the stage and stage folk. The actor appears to the audience in a perpetual, hazy, calcium glory. We are, one and all, children with an inherent love for fairy tales and it is probably this love which is in a great measure accountable for the blind adoration received by most stage people.

I have received, I imagine, the usual number of letters from 'your sincere admirer,' some of them funny and some of them rather pathetic. Very few of them were really impertinent or offensive. In nearly all was to be found the same touching devotion to an abstract ideal for which, for the moment, I chanced to be cast. Once in a while there was some one who, like a person who signed himself 'Faust,' insisted that I had 'met his eyes' and 'encouraged him from afar.' Needless to say I had never in my life seen him; but he worked himself into quite a fever of resentment on the subject and wrote me several letters. There was also a man who wrote me several perfectly respectful, but ardent, love letters to which, naturally, I did not respond. Then, finally, he bombarded me with another type of screed of which the following is a specimen:

'Oh, for Heaven's sake, say something, – if it is only to rate me for my importunities or to tell me to go about my business! Anything but this contemptuous silence!'

But these were exceptions. Most of my 'admirers'' letters are gems of either humour or of sentiment. Among my treasures is an epistle that begins:

'Miss Clara Louise Kellogg
  Miss:
  Before to expand my feelings, before to make you known the real intent of this note, in fine before to disclose the secrets of my heart, I will pray you to pardon my indiscretion (if indiscretion that can be called) to address you unacquainted,' etc.

Isn't this a masterpiece?

There was also an absurdly conceited man who wrote me one letter a year for several years, always in the same vein. He was evidently a very pious youth and had 'gotten religion' rather badly, for in every epistle he broke into exhortation and urged me fervently to become a 'real Christian,' painting for me the joys of true religion if I once could manage to 'find it.' In one of his later letters – after assuring me that he had prayed for me night and morning for three years and would continue to do so – he ended in this impressive manner:

'... And if, in God's mercy, we are both permitted to walk "the Golden Streets," I shall there seek you out and give you more fully my reasons for writing you.'

Could anything be more entertaining than this naïve fashion of making a date in Heaven?

Not all my letters were love letters. Sometimes I would receive a few words from some woman unknown to me but full of a sweet and understanding friendliness. Mrs Elizabeth Tilton, then the centre of the stage scandal through her friendship with Henry Ward Beecher, wrote me a charming letter that ended with what struck me as a very pathetic touch:

'I am unwilling to be known by you as the defiant, discontented woman of the age – rather, as an humble helper of those less fortunate than myself——'

I never knew Mrs Tilton personally, but have often felt that I should have liked her. One of the dearest communications I ever received was from a French working girl, a corset maker, I believe. She wrote:

'I am but a poor little girl, Mademoiselle, a toiler in the sphere where you reign a queen, but ever since I was a very little child I have gone to listen to your voice whenever you have deigned to sing in New York. Those magic tone-flowers, scattering their perfumed sweetness on the waiting air, made my child heart throb with a wonderful pulsation....'

Mary Watkins Cushing, secretary and companion to the great Wagnerian soprano Olive Fremstad at the turn of the century, records a gem from her employer's correspondence. The reference to John's head relates to Strauss's Salome *in the scandalous New York première in which Fremstad sang in 1907.*

Dear Miss Fremstad:

You are unique in the world. I would bet my last dollar against a match that there is nothing in the whole universe for you but the sacred interest of art.

I too am alone in the world. I am six foot high, have a fine position, blue eyes like yours, all my hair, and much landed property.

Will you marry me? I will buy a piano.

I would rather that my head were in your hands – even if it was on a dish like John's – than that it remained on my shoulders and me to be the husband of any girl you like in the whole of Nebraska.

Here is a stamp for reply.

Yours truly,

Quoted in The Rainbow Bridge

Sir Peter Medawar was a Nobel Prize-winning scientist; Lois Kirschenbaum is a receptionist. But in their devotion to Italian opera, they are sublimely as one.

John Vincent Laborde Godefroy, known to everyone – with boyish disregard of the sensibilities of the pious – as God, was my closest friend at school. Our relationship was in no way sentimental but founded solidly upon our common love of opera. When we reached the degree of seniority that entitled us to the use of a private study we listened rapt to opera broadcasts from Rome on a small primitive radio set (a 'crystal set') that God had rigged up in his study. Our joy began when a judicious twiddling of dials brought us the beautifully modulated voice of a lady announcer: 'Radio Roma Napoli. Transmissione dell'opera Rigoletto: opera *in tre atti di Francesco Piave, musica di Giuseppe Verdi. Edizione Ricordi ... Personaggi ... Atto primo ...'*

Then we were away. Our enjoyment of opera was not merely passive; we ourselves performed. God, an extremely powerful young man with a chest like a barrel, had cultivated a powerful penetrating falsetto that had put the great *spinto* roles within his power, notably that of Aida herself. I myself, the possessor of a raucous baritone, lacking all beauty of intonation, opted for the part of Amonasro (Aida's father). God would sometimes enter my dormitory with his face blackened with burnt cork and we would embark upon the passionate duet in which Amonasro denounces his daughter at the top of his voice for declining to wheedle her lover, the commander-in-chief of the Egyptian forces, into disclosing the route of his intended attack on the forces of Ethiopia. Amonasro's thunderous denunciations alternated throughout with piteous *sforzando* (fit to bust) shrieks of mercy from Aida. (God, incidentally, later became a recognized authority on Verdi and wrote a very accomplished book entitled *The Dramatic Genius of Verdi*.)

The audience ratings could not have been more mixed. One boy who later became a Fellow of King's College Cambridge has since told me that listening to the Medawar/Godefroy duo was one of the most terrible experiences he had ever lived through. Well, you can't please everybody. On the other hand, the Reverend Canon Patey of Liverpool Cathedral – a good, genuinely pious man – once told my wife that our performances had opened his ears to the beauty of opera, of which he became a devotee.

One of God's musicological discoveries was that all operatic tunes ever written could be sung to the words 'bun' and 'apple' judiciously ordered. We would sometimes walk arm in arm singing the orchestral prelude to Act 2 of *Il Trovatore* that ushers in the Anvil chorus. It went: bun–bun, bun–bun, bun–bun, bun, apple bun–bun, apple bun, bun–bun, apple bun, bun–bun, bun–bun apple, bun ... etc. When Maclean [a schoolmaster] inadvertently killed himself by driving too fast down that icy road God was able to use this discovery to simulate the tragic course of events that led to his end. At first came the car's even progress along the road: bun–bun–bun–bun–bun–bun–bun–bun–bun–bun, with occasional warnings on the horn, apple! apple! Then an exciting roulade of buns depicted the fate of the slide down the hill followed by a huge crash – APPLE – as he crashed through the flimsy parapet of the bridge, followed by a succession of solemn legato buns rendering the plainsong *dies irae.*

PETER MEDAWAR, *Memoir of a Thinking Radish*

Every opera house of note is surrounded by a tribe of devotees of the cult. The vocal or opera buffs come in two kinds: those who prefer to live on recorded memories and those who live through live performances. The Met has its share of both kinds. The second kind, of course, is the kind most in evidence at performances, and can be typified by Lois Kirschenbaum ('Miss Cherry Tree, as Jon Vickers calls me'), the queen of the Met regulars.

Kirschenbaum, a thin, intense woman who wears heavy eye-glasses because of poor sight and on opera nights carries a big pair of binoculars, is indeed a regular. She grew up in Brooklyn, where (naturally) she was a devoted Dodgers fan; but a few years before the Bums decamped for greener, if hardly less smog-filled, pastures – perhaps Kirschenbaum subliminally sensed the future – she happened to hear a recording of *La Bohème* with Renata Tebaldi. 'I never imagined such sounds could come from the human throat.' By the time the Dodgers left town, Kirschenbaum had become an opera fanatic, and she has enlarged on her passion ever since.

'One day I was playing a record and my father came in and said, "That's Caruso – I heard him, you know." He had heard Caruso and Gigli and Chaliapin, but he had never told me – my mother never liked opera. Today he's eighty-four, and doesn't go to the Met, but now and then he sees it on television. Can you imagine – he heard Caruso live!'

By day Kirschenbaum is a telephone receptionist, and as such she acts in two capacities: that of her business and that of co-ordinator of the network of opera buffs of her acquaintance. After five, however, she heads for music. Almost every night, and twice on Saturdays and Sundays, Kirschenbaum is at a musical event. She is at the Met, during its season, three or four times a week ('depending on the schedule – sometimes it's less'); if not there, at the New York City Opera, at the ballet, or at concerts and recitals. 'Sometimes I even get to the theater or the movies.'

Since she has a limited amount of money, she often obtains free tickets or discount tickets, in ways known to all music lovers but which she is reluctant to discuss. For the Met, however, since she has little time to wait for standing room (sold at ten on the morning of the performance), Kirschenbaum arranges her season before the house opens and purchases score desk seats (the cheapest in the house) for all the performances she knows she wants.

'It's a lot of money for me to lay out, but then I don't have to worry about getting in.'

Once inside the Met, she can usually find an empty seat somewhere with a view of the stage, and sometimes a critic with an extra seat will let her have it. 'The ushers are very nice, but recently they've been cracking down, because some people – I don't know who they are – have been taking subscribers' seats and refusing to move out when the ticket holders come.'

Kirschenbaum's evening does not end with the final curtain fall. She always goes backstage ('except if I can get a ride home and they won't wait') to congratulate the artists and get them to sign her program or photographs.

'Sometimes I don't get on the subway until almost one o'clock in the morning, if it's a Wagner opera. I'm so glad Jimmy moved the *Tannhäuser* curtain to seven-thirty next year! A few nights ago I was so tired I could hardly stay awake for the last act – you don't know how wearing it is, if you have to get up every day to go to a job!'

Kirschenbaum goes to the opera primarily for the voices. Her special interest lies in following young American artists in their rising careers, often from City Opera to the Met. 'I saw Judith Raskin go up the ladder, and now I'm seeing Kathleen Battle. I grow up with them.'

Although she likes to see different artists in different roles, she is in favor of the current management's policy of broadening the operatic repertory. 'When I first heard *Mahagonny*, on the radio, I didn't like it. When I saw it in the opera house, I liked Stratas and some of the music. But it grew on me, and I can understand why they did it. It will never be my favorite opera – and *Lulu* won't be, either – but you have to give these things a chance, if they're done as well as they do them at the Met.'

Her favorite opera is *Die Frau ohne Schatten* – if it is well cast – and her second favorite is Boito's *Mefistofele*, a staple at the City Opera but unheard since the 1920s at the Met. 'After that first *Frau* I was walking on air! I never imagined opera could be like this!'

But, night after night, her favorites remain the Italian operas – Verdi, Bellini, Puccini – and she remains cool to Wagner, in part because of the lack of Wagnerian singers.

Kirschenbaum is firmly committed to the policies of the current management and is a strong supporter of the music director. 'It's much more relaxed at the Met than in the Bing days. Can you imagine Bing speaking to me? But I can talk to Jimmy about anything, when I see him after the opera, and he always gives me direct answers. There are no airs with him. The prima donna era of opera is fading: everyone is more relaxed, and there is an ensemble spirit that wasn't there before.'

She is enthusiastic about Levine's conducting. 'He's learning all the time, and he gets better and better. His Verdi is tops. I know he gets some bad press, and they say he conducts too much, but one thing: Jimmy will never put you to sleep with his conducting. He's a brilliant conductor, and an unassuming pal.'

PATRICK J. SMITH, *A Year at the Met*

FAREWELLS

Henry Chorley's account, in Thirty Years' Musical Recollections, *of Pasta's farewell concert in 1850 is often quoted, and with good reason: it is one of the most vivid and*

poignant pieces ever written about operatic performances.
See also pp. 335–9.

There remains a strange scene to be spoken of – the last appearance of this magnificent musical artist, when she allowed herself,
many years later, to be seduced into giving one performance at
Her Majesty's Theatre, and to sing in a concert for the Italian
Opera. Nothing more inadvised could have been dreamed of.
Madame Pasta had long ago thrown off the stage and all its
belongings, and any other public than those who have made their
boatmen linger on the lake of Como, hard beneath the garden
walls of her villa, with the hope of catching a glimpse of one who
in her prime had enthralled so many. Her voice, which at its best
had required ceaseless watching and practice, had been long ago
given up by her. Its state of utter ruin on the night in question
passes description. She had been neglected by those who, at least,
should have presented her person to the best advantage admitted
by time. Her queenly robes (she was to sing some scenes from
Anna Bolena [by Donizetti; a role she had created in 1830]) in
nowise suited or disguised her figure. Her hairdresser had done
some tremendous thing or other with her head – or rather, had left
everything undone. A more painful and disastrous spectacle could
hardly be looked on. There were artists present who had then, for
the first time, to derive some impression of a renowned artist –
perhaps, with the natural feeling that her reputation had been
exaggerated. Among these was Rachel [the actress], whose bitter
ridicule of the entire sad show made itself heard throughout the
whole theatre, and drew attention to the place where she sat – one
might even say, sarcastically enjoying the scene. Among the audience, however, was another gifted woman, who might far more
legitimately have been shocked at the utter wreck of every musical
means of expression in the singer, who might have been more
naturally forgiven, if some humour of self-glorification had made
her severely just – not worse – to an old prima donna; I mean
Madame Viardot. Then, and not till then, she was hearing
Madame Pasta. But truth will always answer to the appeal of
truth. Dismal as was the spectacle, broken, hoarse, and destroyed

as was the voice, the great style of the singer spoke to the great singer. The first scene was Anne Boleyn's duet with Jane Seymour. The old spirit was heard and seen in Madame Pasta's 'Sorgi!' and the gesture with which she signed to her penitent rival to rise. Later she attempted the final mad scene of the opera – that most complicated and brilliant among the mad scenes on the modern musical stage, with its two cantabile movements, its snatches of recitative, and its bravura of despair, which may be appealed to as an example of vocal display, till then unparagoned, when turned to the account of frenzy, not frivolity – perhaps as such commissioned by the superb creative artist. By that time, tired, unprepared, in ruin as she was, she had rallied a little. When, on Ann Boleyn's hearing the coronation music for her rival, the heroine searches for her own crown on her brow, Madame Pasta wildly turned in the direction of the festive sounds, the old irresistible charm broke out; nay, even in the final song, with its roulades, and its scales of shakes ascending by a semitone, the consummate vocalist and tragedian, able to combine form with meaning – the moment of the situation with such personal and musical display as form an integral part of operatic art – was indicated: at least to the apprehension of a younger artist. 'You are right!' was Madame Viardot's quick and heartfelt response (her eyes full of tears) to a friend beside her; 'You are right! It is like the *Cenacolo* of da Vinci at Milan – a wreck of a picture, but the picture is the greatest picture in the world!'

Janet Baker's farewell to opera in 1982, when she was still at the peak of her artistry, caused widespread dismay. In her diary of the period, published as Full Circle, *she explains the reasons behind her decision.*

When something comes to an end there is bound to be sadness. One feels it at the onset of autumn, when children leave home; so many sorts of little 'deaths' which we all have to face.

Quite a lot of people believe I shall change my mind. If they really knew me, they would not entertain this thought for one moment. I'm far too Yorkshire and stubborn. There will be no flirting with 'opera in concert' for me. In a letter I received today, friends of the writer had comforted her with the remark, 'Oh! she'll go back to the stage – they always do!' Well, they always *don't*. Look at Ponselle and Nan Merriman, two singers who both did what I am about to do. In my case, musical life goes on; just because opera ceases, this doesn't mean *finis*! It has been an important third of my life, but there are still two more left, the concert and Lieder worlds, both of immense importance. There has been a tradition that when a singer can no longer appear on the stage, the field of Lieder can then provide a much *less* strenuous activity, as though to sing Lieder is in some way easier! The truth of the matter is very different. One doesn't put less into singing a recital programme; in my opinion it is the most testing sphere of all, the absolute pinnacle in terms of concentration, unbroken vocal and musical responsibility. It is easy to emphasize a point by movement on a stage. It is extremely difficult to make a similar emphasis when no movement is allowed.

I put my 'all' into my theatre work; I put the same 'all' into the concert platform, and although to the outward eye the singer is only standing there, the process is just as demanding in a different way as an opera, if not more so.

Performers come and go. The music is what matters – the music is for always.

FAUST

If only the phantom would stop reappearing!
Business, if you wanted to know, was punk at the opera.
The heroine no longer appeared in *Faust*.
The crowds strolled sadly away. The phantom
Watched them from the roof, not guessing the hungers
That must be stirred before disappointment can begin.

One day as morning was about to begin
A man in brown with a white shirt reappearing
At the bottom of his yellow vest, was talking hungers
With the silver-haired director of the opera.
On the green-carpeted floor no phantom
Appeared, except yellow squares of sunlight, like those in *Faust*.

That night as the musicians for *Faust*
Were about to go on strike, lest darkness begin
In the corridors, and through them the phantom
Glide unobstructed, the vision reappearing
Of blonde Marguerite practicing a new opera
At her window awoke terrible new hungers

In the already starving tenor. But hungers
Are just another topic, like the new Faust
Drifting through the tunnels of the opera
(In search of lost old age? For they begin
To notice a twinkle in his eye. It is cold daylight reappearing
At the window behind him, itself a phantom

Window, painted by the phantom
Scene painters, sick of not getting paid, of hungers
For a scene below of tiny, reappearing
Dancers, with a sandbag falling like a note in *Faust*
Through purple air. And the spectators begin
To understand the bleeding tenor star of the opera.)

That night the opera
Was crowded to the rafters. The phantom
Took twenty-nine curtain calls. 'Begin!
Begin!' In the wings the tenor hungers
For the heroine's convulsive kiss, and Faust
Moves forward, no longer young, reappearing

And reappearing for the last time. The opera
Faust would no longer need its phantom.
On the bare, sunlit stage the hungers could begin.

JOHN ASHBERY

FEES

Nellie Melba didn't mind a fair fight: in this case losing proved to be enormously to her benefit.

One day, when I was in my flat in Paris, thinking what fun I was going to have in my coming season, Mr Hammerstein called. I had an idea of what he wanted, and I wouldn't see him.

Hammerstein went straight off to Maurice Grau [the former manager of Covent Garden and the Metropolitan Opera House] who was very ill at the time, and persuaded him to give him a letter to me. I felt obliged to give him an appointment. But I kept saying to myself: 'I'm not going to America. I'm not going to America.'

When Hammerstein arrived, my first impression was of a determined man of Jewish persuasion, shortish, thin and dark, dark, with piercing black eyes. He carried a top hat with a very wide brim in his hand, and he addressed me in a strong American accent.

HAMMERSTEIN: 'I'm out to do the big thing in opera. I am building the biggest and finest opera house in the world. And I can't do without you.'

MYSELF: 'In what way do you want me to help you?'

HAMMERSTEIN: 'I want you to come and sing.'

MYSELF: 'I'm very sorry, but I have no intention of going to New York next year.'

HAMMERSTEIN: 'I can't do without you.'

MYSELF: 'That's a great pity, because I'm not going.'

HAMMERSTEIN: 'I shall give you fifteen hundred dollars a night.'

MYSELF: 'Please don't discuss terms, Monsieur Hammerstein. I assure you it is useless.'

HAMMERSTEIN: 'Oh, you'll come all right.' (Pause.) 'What do you say to two thousand?'

MYSELF: 'If you offer me twenty thousand, I shall still say the same thing.'

HAMMERSTEIN: 'It'll be the biggest thing you have done yet. Oscar Hammerstein says so.'

MYSELF: 'And Nellie Melba says "No." I have no intention of going. Good morning, Mr Hammerstein.'

Had anybody else been so importunate, I should probably have been very angry. But there was a naïve determination about Mr Hammerstein which appealed to my own character. He knew what he wanted, and did not hesitate to say so. We therefore parted good friends, and I regarded the matter as closed.

Not so Mr Hammerstein. At intervals of six days during the next month he either called, wrote notes or telephoned, always prefacing his remarks by 'Now that you have decided to come to America ...' I merely sat tight and set my lips. On one occasion, I remember, he obtained an entry into my rooms while I was in my bath. Not in the least deterred, he came and battered at the door.

HAMMERSTEIN: 'Are you coming to America?'

MYSELF (*between splashes*): 'No!'

HAMMERSTEIN: 'I'll give you two thousand five hundred a night.'

MYSELF: 'Not for ten times the money.'

HAMMERSTEIN: 'And you can sing as many nights as you like.'

MYSELF: 'Go away.'

Shortly after that, Mr Hammerstein decided on his Napoleonic coup. I had just breakfasted and was sitting down, reading *Le Figaro*, when he burst into my rooms in a great hurry.

HAMMERSTEIN: 'It's all settled. You're to have three thousand dollars a night.'

MYSELF: 'But I've told you a hundred times –'

HAMMERSTEIN (*Interrupting*): 'Never mind about that. Three thousand dollars a night, and you open in *Traviata*.'

Here, to my astonishment, he drew from his pocket a bundle of thousand-franc notes and began scattering them over the floor like cards, until the carpet was littered with them. I was so surprised that I could say or do nothing, and before I could call him back, he had swept out of the room like a whirlwind, crying that he had to catch his train and had no time to wait.

I picked up the notes, smiling quietly, and found that in all he had strewn my carpet with one hundred thousand francs. Today it may not sound such a very vast sum, but then it meant four thousand pounds. And even nowadays one does not go strewing thousands of pounds on people's carpets.

I took the notes at the earliest possible opportunity to the Rothschild Bank, telling them they were not mine, and that they must be kept there safely until Mr Hammerstein called for them.

However, he did not call for them. Instead, he called once again for me, in the early morning.

HAMMERSTEIN: 'Well, and so you've made up your mind at last. Didn't Oscar Hammerstein say you would?'
MYSELF: 'He did, and Oscar Hammerstein was wrong. As I've told you before, I am not going to America.'
HAMMERSTEIN: 'Oh yes, you are. You've got all my money.'
MYSELF: 'The money is in the bank. It has nothing to do with me.'
HAMMERSTEIN: 'Was there ever such a woman? Still, you'll come. Mark my words.'

NELLIE MELBA, *Melodies and Memories*

Melba did go, and was received rapturously, in 1907; but Hammerstein's spectacular attempt to outbid the Metropolitan failed after four seasons.

I was once privileged enough to look through the paybooks for the Metropolitan Opera, for the years between 1898 and 1957. The following is a comparative table of singers' fees: all figures are for a single performance unless otherwise stated.

In 1898–9 Melba earned $1650; Lehmann, $1250 plus hotel expenses; Nordica, $1000; and Sembrich, $800. However, the highest earner was Jean de Reszke at 11,000 francs or $2101. His brother Edouard took $668, while the other great bass of the time, Pol Plançon, sang for $220.

1899–1900: Schumann-Heink, $9000 for 90 performances

(later renegotiated at $16,000 for 80 performances, then $24,000 for 100); Eames, $1000, payable in gold the morning after a performance; Sembrich, $1000 plus two orchestra stalls (a fee that remained the same until 1906, when it became $1200); Calvé, $1719, with a dressing-room as near the stage as possible (in 1903 this rose to $1920 for appearances outside New York).

1905–6: Melba was promised $2000 but never appeared; in 1907 Oscar Hammerstein at the rival Manhattan Opera paid her $3000; Nordica, $1250; Eames, $1500; Fremstad, $1382 for ten performances a month. An average family's annual income in New York was estimated at *c.* $850.

1907–8: Caruso, $2000; Farrar, $800; Fremstad $750; Chaliapin, $1344.

1908–9: Fremstad and Farrar level-pegged for one season at $1000; Mahler earned slightly less at $5050 a month for six performances, while Toscanini got only $4800 for twelve performances a month.

1909–10: Destinn, $900; Farrar, $1200 (making a total of forty appearances, and singing at least twice a fortnight); while Fremstad stayed at $1000 (also for forty appearances); Nordica kept to her 1905–6 fee of $1250. Hammerstein at the Manhattan paid Tetrazzini $1500 and Mary Garden $1400.

1911–12: Destinn, $1200; Farrar, $1250; Fremstad, $1000. Toscanini was still down at $7000 a month, averaging twelve performances in that period. Seats at the Met were priced, as they had been for some years, at between one and five dollars.

1914–15: Caruso, $2500; Destinn, $1300; Melanie Kurt, Fremstad's replacement, $500.

1919–20: Muzio, $625; Farrar, $1500; Ponselle's second season – she had started at $150 for up to three performances a week – $100, with guaranteed fourteen days' rehearsal: the norm was seven.

1921–2: Jeritza's first season, $1500; Farrar the same. Muzio, $800. Ponselle, $1000 per week, singing 24 times in 15 weeks; Galli-Curci, $2000; Chaliapin, $3000.

1926–7: Galli-Curci on tour commanded $3500, in New York, $2250, with Jeritza a whisker ahead at $2300; Schumann-Heink's return cost $500; Talley, $500 per week, three performances. The tenor Martinelli took $1700, the baritone Ruffo $1500; Gigli, $16,000 per month for approximately eight performances. In the mid-Twenties a motor car cost *c.* $1000, a gramophone record $1, and a round-the-world cruise *c.* $2000. A seat at the Met could cost up to $8.25 in 1929.

1930–1: the Depression had begun, but had not yet bitten into the upper end of the earnings scale. The charming and stalwart lyric soprano Lucrezia Bori, $1400; Jeritza, $2500; Ponselle (after her Covent Garden triumph), $1700; Rethberg, $1200.

1935–6: the Depression had hit. Flagstad and Lotte Lehmann, $750; Grace Moore, Ponselle, Bori, $1000; Melchior, $1000; Rethberg, $900; Martinelli, $800 – less than half what he earned in 1926–7. Average earnings in 1929, $1300; in 1935, $850.

1956–7: in the intervening twenty years, fees had not increased either in real or inflated terms. Tebaldi, Milanov, and Callas all earned the $1000 top. By comparison in 1931 it took an average wage-earner 580 hours to earn enough to buy a refrigerator; in 1956, 168 hours.

RUPERT CHRISTIANSEN, *Prima Donna*

Singers' earnings rose again dramatically in the 1960s. Today's fees are shrouded in secrecy and often involve a percentage of takings, royalties from radio or video recordings and so on. Top stars probably earn about $30,000–40,000 at the Met, but can command more elsewhere.

FEUDS

Gluck's attempts to reform and simplify the baroque conventions of opera seria caused a tremendous hoo-ha in Paris in the 1770s, another faction siding fiercely with the old-fashioned style maintained in the operas of Niccolo Pic-

cinni. Writing to the Countess von Freis in 1777, Gluck describes the first shots in what would become one of the most bitterly contested feuds in the history of music – though Gluck and Piccinni themselves remained at arms' length from it all.

Madame,

I have been so plagued about music, and am so much disgusted with it, that at present I would not write one single note for a louis; by this you may conceive, Madame, the degree of my devotion to you, since I have been able to bring myself to arrange the two songs for the harp for you, and have the honour to send them herewith. Never has a more terrible and keenly-contested *battaglia* been waged, than the one I began with my opera *Armide*. The cabals against *Iphigénie*, *Orfeo* and *Alceste* were no more than little skirmishes of light horse by comparison. The Neapolitan Ambassador, to ensure great success for Piccinni's opera, is tirelessly intriguing against me, at Court and among the nobility. He has induced Marmontel, La Harpe and several members of the Academy to write against my system of music and my manner of composing. The Abbé Arnaud, M. Suard and several others have come to my defence, and the quarrel grew so heated that from insults they would have passed to blows, but that friends of both sides brought them to order. The *Journal de Paris*, which comes out every day, is full of it. This dispute is making the Editor's fortune, for he already has more than 2500 subscribers in Paris. That's the musical revolution in France, amid the most brilliant pomp. Enthusiasts tell me: Sir, you are fortunate to be enjoying the honour of persecution; every great genius has had the same experience. – I wish them to the devil with their fine speeches. The fact is that the opera, which was said to have fallen flat, brought in 37,200 *livres* in 7 performances, without counting the boxes rented for the year, and without the subscribers. Yesterday, at the 8th performance, they took 5767 *livres*. ... The pit was so tightly packed that when a man who had his hat on his head was told by the guard to take it off, he replied: 'Come and take it off yourself, for I cannot move my arms'; which caused laughter. I have seen people coming out with their hair bedraggled and their clothes drenched as though they had fallen into a stream. Only Frenchmen would pay so dearly for a pleasure. There are passages in the opera which force the audience to lose their countenance and their composure. Come yourself, Madame, to witness the tumult, it will amuse you as much as the opera....

Rivalries between prima donnas have been one of the most fertile areas of operatic feuding, relentlessly fanned by exaggeration and misreporting from the press. One of the earliest and nastiest of such rivalries was that between the mezzo-soprano Faustina Bordoni and the soprano Francesca Cuzzoni in London during the 1720s.

Leader of the Cuzzoni faction was Mary, Countess of Pembroke, whose ardent partisanship was not of a type to cast lustre on her husband's position as a pillar of the Whig establishment. A letter to Charlotte Clayton, later Lady Sundon, favourite of the Princess of Wales, written towards the end of the 1727 season, indicates the extent to which Lady Pembroke and others were already committed. Cuzzoni had apparently received a warning that she was to be hissed off the stage at a forthcoming performance. 'She was in such concern at this,' says the Countess, 'that she had a great mind not to sing, but I ... positively ordered her not to quit the stage, but let them do what they would: though not heard, to sing on, and not to go off till it was proper.' Backed by her patroness and the applause of her supporters Cuzzoni hung on, though one of her arias was drowned by catcalling from the Faustina claque. Matters were made worse by the appearance of the king's granddaughter Princess Amelia, an ardent Handelian but an embarrassing presence at such a time.

A further lack of respect towards royalty by the heavily engaged

Haymarket audience was shown when the Directors presumed to dispute George's caution to them that if Cuzzoni were dismissed he would give up his attendance. Faustina, however, was a decided favourite, whose roster of distinguished backers included Burlington's wife Dorothy (Lord Hervey called her 'Dame Palladio'), Lady Cowper, who wrote opposite the siren's name in her *Admeto* word-book 'she is the devil of a singer' and Catherine, Lady Walpole, who engineered a social *coup* by inviting both divas to her house for a concert 'at which were all the first people of the kingdom'. As neither of the two stars would deign to sing in the other's presence, the hostess, with admirable aplomb, had each of them taken to another part of the house 'under the pretence of shewing her some curious china' while her rival obliged with an aria or two.

Matters finally came to a head in a dramatic and, so far as can be known, unique fashion on the production of a new opera which had been coaxed from Bononcini for performance as the season's last novelty. Adapted by Haym from a Salvi text originally set by the composer's brother Marc' Antonio, *Astianatte* had a respectable pedigree in Racine's *Andromaque*, and was dedicated to Bononcini's lavish patroness Henrietta Marlborough. It was his last London opera, but was to be remembered for reasons which have little to do with music.

Patrons who attended the performance on 6 June 1727 can scarcely have been surprised by what took place, but the occasion was hot news for London journalists and pamphleteers. The *British Journal* noted gleefully: 'On Tuesday-night last, a great Disturbance happened at the Opera, occasioned by the Partisans of the Two Celebrated Rival Ladies, Cuzzoni and Faustina. The Contention at first was only carried on by Hissing on one Side, and Clapping on the other; but proceeded at length to Catcalls, and other great Indecencies: And notwithstanding the Princess Caroline was present, no Regards were of Force to restrain the Rudenesses of the Opponents.' The *London Journal*, in customary style, observed that the quarrel was sustained 'by the delightful Exercise of Catcalls, and other Decencies, which demonstrated the inimitable Zeal and Politeness of that Illustrious Assembly. . . .

Neither her Royal Highness's presence, nor the laws of decorum, could restrain the glorious ardour of the combatants.' The central fact, however, was that Cuzzoni and Faustina had finally resorted to a scuffle, egged on by their partisans and perhaps even by their fellow performers.

The flavour of the event is admirably conveyed in a burlesque playlet, *The Contre Temps or Rival Queens, A Small Farce*, issued the following month. The epigraph, Virgil's '*Et cantare pares, et respondere paratae*', is slily rendered as 'Both young Italians, both alike inspir'd/To sing, or scold; just as the time requir'd. Modern Translation.' The cast, besides the three principal singers, includes Heidegger 'High-priest to the Academy of Discord', Handel himself, and the leaders of the respective claques.

Heidegger's opening speech effectively satirizes the public's preoccupation with opera in hinting at the comparative triviality of contemporary events such as the squabble over Minorca or the death of the Czarina Elizabeth. Faustina calls Cuzzoni 'that mushroom songstress of the other day', Cuzzoni tells her to 'resign the charge, you're past it now and old' and the sexual innuendo reaches a peak when the former advises:

> While you in rip'ning, like a medlar rot,
> At best a Gorgon's face, and Siren's throat,
> Help your decaying lungs, and chew *eringo*
>   [seaweed, a noted aphrodisiac]
> Thou little awkward creature! – can you *stringo*?

to which the latter ripostes:

> To do you justice tho; – I think – 'tis known
> That you to please, imploy more pipes than one.

The height of coarseness is reached in Faustina's reference to Sandoni's difficulty in making love to Cuzzoni owing to her excessively large vagina. The two women box and tear one another's headdresses, to an excited chorus of peers and tupees (beaux in smart wigs). 'The Queen and The Princess again engage; Both Factions play all their warlike Instruments; Cat-calls, Serpents and Cuckoos make a dreadful din; F-s-na lays flat C-z-ni's nose with a Sceptre; C-z-ni breaks her head with a gilt-leather crown: H-l, desirous to see an end of the battle, animates them with a kettle-drum; a glove thrown at random hits the high-priest in the temples, he staggers off the Stage....'

JONATHAN KEATES, Handel

Tenors are reputed to be as sensitive as prima donnas: matching two such delicate egos as those of Beniamino Gigli (from whose memoirs this is taken) and Maria Jeritza could only lead to trouble. The scene is the Met in 1925.

Between this lady and myself there had existed, ever since we began to sing together at the Met, what I can only presume to have been a latent conflict of temperaments. In her presence, I always felt tension. I never had any psychological difficulties with my other colleagues, but Madame Jeritza's legendary 'temperament' had a disastrous effect on me. At the least sign of it, something would boil up inside me, and I would suddenly feel capable of becoming every bit as temperamental as she was.

On the night of the *Fedora* première, she hurled herself on me with such abandon in the betrothal scene at the end of Act 2, that I was able to withstand the impact only by bracing myself firmly against a wing support. At the next performance, she wriggled so violently in my supposedly loving arms that I did actually stagger, making the audience roar with laughter at what should have been an intensely tragic moment. Yet another time, again in Act 2, when I was meant to be paying her a formal visit, my top hat dropped on the floor; with a well-placed kick, Madame Jeritza sent it spinning neatly across the stage.

Then came the evening of January 26th. The opera was drawing to an end; it was the scene of my final interview with Fedora; having discovered her to be a spy, I was supposed to spurn her. What happened then exactly I really cannot say. Did my suppressed resentment at the way in which, on all these previous occasions, she had managed to ridicule me on the stage, suddenly find an outlet? Did I miscalculate the force with which I pushed her away from me? Or did she simply slip? All I knew was that she was reeling towards the edge of the stage, and barely saved herself from tumbling over into the orchestra pit. I saw that she was hurt, and tried to help her to her feet, but she rejected my offer violently. She sang on to the end of the scene, and then rushed from the stage in a paroxysm of sobs.

She had wrenched her right wrist in falling on the glass and metal of the footlights, and had abrasions on both legs. 'He did it!' she shrieked, pointing at me. I was really sorry; I apologized profusely and assured her that it was an accident; but in vain. 'He did it! He wanted to kill me! Murderer! Murderer!'

This was too much; I protested.

'Listen to him! First he tries to murder me, then he insults me!' She turned to her husband, Baron Leopold von Popper, a tall, martial-looking Austrian, who always waited for her backstage. 'Defend my honour!' she commanded him. 'Challenge that man to a duel!'

To my relief, I received no challenge from the level-headed Baron; but next day there was an uproar of speculation, both in the newspapers and in the corridors of the Metropolitan, as to whether or not I had 'done it on purpose'. Things went so far that Gatti-Casazza, who normally refused to listen to gossip about any of the Met squabbles, much less intervene in them, felt obliged to issue a statement explaining that I had *not* done it on purpose; but for once, nobody paid any attention to him – it was more fun to let the battle rage. The cartoonists had a field-day; the European press joined in; and Madame Jeritza's wrenched wrist was lost sight of in the furious controversy that exploded between our respective followers as to which of the two of us was the leading artist of the Metropolitan.

I was horrified, but I was powerless to stop it: it was like an avalanche.

More was to come.

Madame Jeritza had declared, the day after the *Fedora* incident, that she would never sing with 'that man' again, but Gatti-Casazza calmly said 'Rubbish' – his favourite word – and reminded her that she was due to sing with me a fortnight later in

Tosca. Whatever powers of persuasion he used, he finally got her to agree.

I need hardly say that on the night of the performance, I took – or thought I took – every possible precaution to avoid offending my susceptible partner. All went well, or at least without mishap, until the very end.

The curtain had fallen; I was on the stage, waiting for it to rise again for the first call. Madame Jeritza was in the wings; I beckoned to her to join me so that we might take our bow together, but she shook her head. The curtain rose, and I took my bow alone. Then I walked off the stage to my dressing-room, leaving all subsequent curtain calls, as I thought, to her. I had attached no importance to the fact of taking the first bow alone. She had done so, as was her right, after the first and second acts; and since in the third act of *Tosca*, with 'Lucevan le stelle', the tenor rises to pre-eminence, I had thought that when she refused to join me, she was simply indicating that it was my turn.

Alas, I was mistaken. She had, I learned afterwards, refused to join me out of pique, because she thought I had no right to show myself until she had taken all her bows. When I went away, there were calls of 'Jeritza!'; but, declaring tearfully that she had been outraged, she still refused to budge from the wings. The curtain rose and fell twice on an empty stage. Most of the audience went home; but in all parts of the house a fair number of people still lingered – her *claque*, as it transpired – shouting rhythmically, insistently, 'Jeritza! We want Jeritza!'

Fifteen minutes passed, and neither she nor they showed any signs of giving in. Finally Giuseppe Bamboschek, who had conducted the orchestra that evening, took her protectively but firmly by the arm and led her out in front of the curtain. By this time her followers had hypnotized themselves into a kind of delirium. She calmed them down herself by indicating that she wished to say something. She said exactly five words: 'Gigli not nice to me!' Then she collapsed sobbing into the arms of Maestro Bamboschek.

Backstage, her sobbing developed into hysterics. Bamboschek, feeling that the situation had got beyond him, telephoned to

Gatti-Casazza, who was already at home and fast asleep. He came at once in a taxi, still muttering 'Rubbish!' and spent a couple of hours humouring and consoling the outraged heroine, with Baron Leopold von Popper a helpless onlooker.

'All right,' said Gatti-Casazza resignedly, when he saw the newspaper headlines the following morning, 'I'll never ask them to sing together again.' And I suppose it was just as well that he never did.

FIDELIO

Beethoven's Fidelio *was a problem child, which underwent extensive revisions and remains a noble torso rather than a perfectly finished work of art. Here a young tenor, Josef Röckel, remembers being summoned to sing Florestan during a playing-through of the opera, at a point when Beethoven was still being pressed to make cuts and alterations.*

We were led into a music-room with silken draperies, fitted out with chandeliers lavishly supplied with candles. On its walls rich, splendidly colourful oil paintings by the greatest masters, in broad, glittering golden frames bespoke the lofty artistic instincts as well as the wealth of the princely family owning them. We seemed to have been expected . . . tea was over, and all was in readiness for the musical performance to begin. The Princess, an elderly lady of winning amiability and indescribable gentleness, yet as a result of great physical suffering (both her breasts had been removed in former years) pale and fragile, already was sitting at the piano. Opposite her, carelessly reclining in an arm-chair, the fat Pandora-score of his unfortunate opera across his knees, sat Beethoven. At his right we recognized the author of the tragedy *Coriolan*, Court Secretary Heinrich von Collin, who was chatting with Court Counsellor Breuning of Bonn, the most intimate friend of the composer's youth. My colleagues from the opera, men and women, their parts in hand, had gathered in a half-circle not far from the piano. As before, Milder was Fidelio; Mlle. Müller sang Marzelline; Weinmüller, Rocco; Caché the doorkeeper Jacquino; and Steinkopf the Minister of State. After I had been presented to the Prince and Princess, and Beethoven had acknowledged our respectful greetings, he placed his score on the music-desk for the Princess and – the performance began.

The two initial acts, in which I played no part, were sung from the first to the last note. Eyes sought the clock, and Beethoven was importuned to drop some of the long-drawn sections of secondary importance. Yet he defended every measure, and did so with such nobility and artistic dignity that I was ready to kneel at his feet. But when he came to the chief point at issue itself, the notable cuts in the exposition which would make it possible to fuse the two acts into one, he was beside himself, shouted uninterruptedly 'Not a note!' and tried to run off with his score. But the Princess laid her hands, folded as though in prayer, on the sacred score entrusted to her, looked up with indescribable mildness at the angry genius and behold – his rage melted at her glance, and he once more resignedly resumed his place. The noble lady gave the order to continue, and played the prelude to the great aria: 'In des Lebens Frühlingstagen'. So I asked Beethoven to hand me the part of Florestan. My unfortunate predecessor, however, in spite of re-peated requests had not been induced to yield it up, and hence I was told to sing from the score, from which the Princess was accompanying at the piano. I knew that this great aria meant as much to Beethoven as the entire opera, and handled it from that point of view. Again and again he insisted on hearing it – the exertion well-nigh overtaxed my powers – but I sang it, for I was overjoyed to see that my presentation made it possible for the great Master to reconcile himself to his misunderstood work.

Midnight had passed before the performance – drawn out by reason of many repetitions – at last came to an end. 'And the revision, the curtailments?' the Princess asked the Master with a pleading look.

'Do not insist on them,' Beethoven answered sombrely, 'not a single note must be missing.'

'Beethoven,' she cried with a deep sigh, 'must your great work then continue to be misunderstood and condemned?'

'It is sufficiently rewarded with your approval, your Ladyship,' said the Master and his hand trembled slightly as it glided over her own.

Then suddenly it seemed as though a stronger, more potent spirit entered into this delicate woman. Half-kneeling and seizing his knees she cried to him as though inspired: 'Beethoven! No – your greatest work, you yourself shall not cease to exist in this way! God who has implanted those tones of purest beauty in your soul forbids it, your mother's spirit, which at this moment pleads and warns you with my voice, forbids it! Beethoven, it must be! Give in! Do so in memory of your mother! Do so for me, who am only your best friend!'

The great man, with his head suggestive of Olympian sublimity, stood for many moments before the worshipper of his Muse, then brushed his long, falling curls from his face, as though an enchanting dream were passing through his soul, and, his glance turned heavenward full of emotion, cried amid sobs: 'I will – yes, all – I will do all, for you – for my, your – for my mother's sake!' And so saying he reverently raised the Princess and offered the Prince his hand as though to confirm a vow. Deeply moved we surrounded the little group, for even then we all felt the importance of this supreme moment.

From that time onward not another word was said regarding the opera. All were exhausted, and I am free to confess that I exchanged a look of relief not hard to interpret with Mayer when servants flung open the folding-doors of the dining-room, and the company at last sat down to supper at plenteously covered tables. It was probably not altogether due to chance that I was placed opposite Beethoven who, in spirit no doubt still with his opera, ate noticeably little; while I, tormented by the most ravenous hunger, devoured the first course with a speed bordering on the ludicrous. He smiled as he pointed to my empty plate: 'You have swallowed your food like a wolf – what have you eaten?' 'I was so famished,' I replied, 'that to tell the truth, I never noticed what it was I ate.'

'That is why, before we sat down, you sang the part of Florestan, the man starving in the dungeon, in so masterly and so
natural a manner. Neither your voice nor your head deserves
credit, but your stomach alone. Well, always see to it that you
starve bravely before the performance and then we will be sure of
success.'

All those at the table laughed, and probably took more pleasure
in the thought that Beethoven had at last plucked up heart to joke
at all, rather than at his joke itself.

There are three supreme moments within the supremacy of
Fidelio as a whole. The first is that final expression of the idea (or
central truth about human existence) that man is here as fellow-
worker with God: the moment when Leonore presents her pistol
precisely as the trumpet rings out, and the trumpet rings out
precisely as Leonore presents her pistol. The second is Leonore's
spoken 'Nichts, nichts, mein Florestan' after Florestan's 'Was
hast du denn für mich getan?' (Lotte Lehmann used to move me
more by the way she spoke those four words than by all her
magnificent singing). The third of these moments is near the end:
the Minister enters, and sings, to one of the simplest as well as one
of the loveliest melodies Beethoven ever wrote, 'Es sucht der
Bruder seine Brüder, und kann er helfen hilft er gern'. A second
truth about human existence, almost as central as the first, has
been revealed: 'a brother has need of his brothers, and when a
brother can help he gladly does so'. It might be called, in the
current jargon, an existential truth: does so, not should do so.

The essence of that third moment is twofold: first, the Minister
'comes', as the trumpet-call has promised: and secondly he comes
as a brother to brothers.

Now in the Wieland Wagner production [Stuttgart, 1954; London, 1955] the Minister didn't 'come'; he was already there when
the curtain went up, sitting or standing, dominatingly remote,
above a crowd that seemed frozen, as in a cinema 'still'. And he

looked as little like a brother among brothers as could be imagined: he looked like Sarastro, with the Urim and Thummim on his breast.

But the worst has still to be told: the spoken passages were entirely or almost entirely eliminated. I complained about this to one of the officials, and he replied in effect: 'Oh, everyone knows what the work's all about, so the talk isn't necessary; and anyhow it's boring, and breaks up the music.' What was it then, a concert or a dramatic performance? That Beethoven should have made of the *Singspiel* a vehicle for his sublimities does not affect in the least its essential character as a *Singspiel*: rather, the *Singspiel* has alone been found capable of expressing those sublimities. Beethoven knew what he was about when he used spoken dialogue (just as he knew what he was about when he broke into words at the end of his last symphony), and above all in the case of 'Was hast du ...' and 'Nichts, nichts'; yet you often hear a performance of *Fidelio* in which that passage but no other of the spoken ones is cut, and the reason given is this: 'You cannot let the music down at such a moment.'

What is wanted for *Fidelio* is the simplest possible setting, with nothing outré, nothing specially emphasized, nothing the 'common man' would not immediately understand. Beethoven must be allowed to make his own unsurpassable impact. Like Shakespeare, he was a common man himself, with a common man's sensitivity, understanding and creativeness magnified a thousandfold. He was anything but a 'highbrow'; and I can imagine him shaking his fist at Wieland Wagner's doubtless reverential pretentiousness.

Peter Heyworth ... defended that prisoners' chorus as follows: 'But surely men can be oppressed to a point where they *do* lose identity? That happened in the concentration camps, and the whole point of Wieland Wagner's production was that he made us experience *Fidelio* in the light of recent history.' 'Made us experience'! Is there a living soul, capable of understanding the work at all, who does not at once, and most painfully, make the connection? That is why to hear *Fidelio,* always an overwhelming experience, is now more overwhelming than ever. The Germans understand all this as well as anyone. When I returned to Germany in 1947, after doing relief work there the previous year, I was told on my arrival that they wanted me to hear a little music. I was taken to a broken-down hall with a few scattered people in it, and as I took my seat a couple of dozen men in ordinary working clothes filed on to the platform and proceeded to sing the prisoners' chorus. I was never told anything about them except that they had 'got it up specially for me', but I suppose they and the orchestra were amateurs, though they might have been the Philharmonia chorus rehearsed by Pitz and conducted by Klemperer to judge by the effect they made on me.

VICTOR GOLLANCZ, *Journey towards Music*

FRANCE vs. ITALY

The battle between the aesthetics of French and Italian opera lasted for centuries and is based, in brief, on the question of which is paramount – clear and expressive declamation of the words (France) or melody and vocal display (Italy). The French have been more defensively articulate in the debate, as in this salvo of 1702.

There are so many things wherein the French music has the advantage over the Italian, and as many more wherein the Italian is superior to the French, that, without a particular examination into the one and the other, I think it impossible to draw a just parallel between 'em or entertain a right judgment of either. The operas are the compositions that admit of the greatest variety and extent, and they are common both to the Italians and French. 'Tis in these the masters of both nations endeavour more particularly to exert themselves and make their genius shine, and 'tis on these, therefore, I intend to build my present comparison. But in this there are many things that require a particular distinction, such as the language, the composition, the qualifications of the actors, those of the performers, the different sorts of voices, the recitative, the airs, the symphonies, the chorus, the dance, the machines, the decorations, and whatever else is essential to an opera or serves to make the entertainment complete and perfect. And these things ought to be particularly inquired into before we can pretend to determine in favour either of the Italian or French.

Our operas are writ much better than the Italian; they are regular, coherent designs; and, though repeated without the music, they are as entertaining as any of our other pieces that are purely dramatic. Nothing can be more natural and lively than their dialogues; the gods are made to speak with a dignity suitable to their character, kings with all the majesty their rank requires, and the nymphs and shepherds with a softness and innocent mirth peculiar to the plains. Love, jealousy, anger, and the rest of the passions are touched with the greatest art and nicety, and there are few of our tragedies or comedies that appear more beautiful than Quinault's operas.

On the other hand, the Italian operas are poor, incoherent rhapsodies without any connection or design; all their pieces, properly speaking, are patched up with thin, insipid scraps; their scenes consist of some trivial dialogues or soliloquy, at the end of which they foist in one of their best airs, which concludes the scene. These airs are seldom of a piece with the rest of the opera, being usually written by other poets, either occasionally or in the body of some other work. When the undertaker of an opera has fixed himself in a town and got his company together, he makes choice of the subject he likes best, such as Camilla, Themistocles, Xerxes, &c. But this piece, as I just now observed, is no better than a patchwork, larded with the best airs his performers are acquainted with, which airs are like saddles, fit for all horses alike; they are declarations of love made on one side and embraced or rejected on the other, transports of happy lovers or complaints of the unfortunate, protestations of fidelity or stings of jealousy, raptures of pleasure or pangs of sorrow, rage, and despair. And one of these airs you are sure to find at the end of every scene. Now certainly such a medley as this can never be set in competition with our operas, which are wrought up with great exactness and marvellous conduct.

Besides, our operas have a farther advantage over the Italian in respect of the voice, and that is the bass, which is so frequent among us and so rarely to be met with in Italy. For every man that has an ear will witness with me that nothing can be more charming than a good bass; the simple sound of these basses, which sometimes seems to sink into a profound abyss, has something wonderfully charming in it. The air receives a stronger concussion from these deep voices than it doth from those that are higher, and is consequently filled with a more agreeable and extensive harmony. When the persons of gods or kings, a Jupiter, Neptune, Priam, or Agamemnon, are brought on the stage, our actors, with their deep voices, give 'em an air of majesty, quite different from that of the feigned basses among the Italians, which have neither depth nor strength. Besides, the interfering of the basses with the upper parts forms an agreeable contrast and makes us perceive the beauties of the one from the opposition they meet with from the other, a pleasure to which the Italians are perfect strangers, the voices of their singers, who are for the most part castrati, being perfectly like those of their women.

Besides the advantages we claim from the beauty of our designs and the variety of voices, we receive still more from our chorus, dances, and other entertainments, in which we infinitely excel the Italians. They, instead of these decorations, which furnish our operas with an agreeable variety and give 'em a peculiar air of grandeur and magnificence, have usually nothing but some burlesque scenes of a buffoon, some old woman that's to be in love with a young footman, or a conjurer that shall turn a cat into a bird, a fiddler into an owl, and play a few other tricks of legerdemain that are only fit to divert the mob. And, for their dancers, they are the poorest creatures in the world; they are all of a lump, without arms, legs, a shape, or air.

ABBÉ FRANÇOIS RAGUENET, Parallèle des Italiens et des Français

On arriving in Milan, out of a sense of duty I made myself go to hear the latest opera. Donizetti's *L'Elisir d'Amore* was being given at the Cannobiana. I found the theatre full of people talking in normal voices, with their backs to the stage. The singers, undeterred, gesticulated and yelled their lungs out in the strictest spirit of rivalry. At least I presumed they did, from their wide-open mouths; but the noise of the audience was such that no sound penetrated except the bass drum. People were gambling, eating supper in their boxes, etc., etc. Consequently, perceiving it was useless to expect to hear anything of the score, which was then new to me, I left. It appears that the Italians do sometimes listen. I have been assured by several people that it is so. The fact remains that music to the Milanese, as to the Neapolitans, the Romans, the Florentines and the Genoese, means arias, duets, trios, well sung; anything beyond that provokes only aversion or indifference. It may be that such antipathies are mere prejudice, due above all to the feebleness of their orchestras and choruses, which prevents them from appreciating any great music outside the narrow circuit they have ploughed for so long. It may also be that they are capable to some extent of rising to the challenge of genius, provided the composer is careful not to disturb entrenched habits of mind too rudely. The striking success of *William Tell* in Florence supports this view; even the sublime *Vestale* of Spontini had a series of brilliantly successful performances in Naples twenty-five years ago. Again, if you observe people in towns under Austrian domination, you will see them flock to hear a military band and listen avidly to its rich German harmonies, so unlike the pale cavatinas they are normally fed on. Nevertheless, in general there is no denying that the Italians as a nation appreciate music solely for its physical effect and are alive only to what is on the surface.

Of all the nations of Europe, I am strongly inclined to think them the most impervious to the evocative, poetic side of music, as well as to any conception at all lofty and out of the common run. For this noble expression of the mind they have hardly more respect than for the art of cooking. They want a score that, like a plate of macaroni, can be assimilated immediately without their having to think about it or even to pay any attention to it.

We French, so paltry and mean-minded in musical matters, are as capable as any Italian of roaring our heads off at the trill or the chromatic run of a fashionable *cantatrice*, while a fine dramatic chorus or an accompanied recitative in the grandest style passes us by; but at least we listen (and if we don't understand the composer's ideas, it is *never* our fault). The behaviour of audiences beyond the Alps is so humiliating to art and to artists that I confess I would as soon sell pepper and cinnamon in a grocer's shop in the rue Saint-Denis as write for the Italians.

HECTOR BERLIOZ, *Memoirs*

As to French it is probably the most difficult to sing of any language in which there exists an important vocal literature. This language, too, pulls up the larynx to a position not suited for producing a round, full tone, and in addition requires the vocalist, if he is to sing his words with an eloquent, idiomatic pronunciation, to produce some of his notes in his nose. The concept of correct singing '*dans la masque*' is well known, but '*la masque*' has nothing to do with '*le nez*,' though the two are frequently confused. The would-be French singer, therefore, has to overcome the evolution of his resonators and pharynx over generations of his French-speaking forebears together with the negative effect of the language on the positioning of his larynx. In addition there is the absolute Gallic insistence that the tone be sacrificed to the word. Finally he has to fight a certain lack of national enthusiasm for singing – certainly not the case in England. At the Opéra and the Opéra-Comique, the French continue to go through the motions of putting on works in the standard repertory as they always have, and occasionally someone comes along and tries to stir up the thin, barely simmering broth with a new production or some guest singers. But always everything seems to fall back into the old ways with indifferent performances sung to half-filled houses by voices which, if they start out fresh, quickly degenerate into the grated, nasal sound that typifies French singing. By putting the word first, as expressed in their own cherished language, it is not surprising that among these, the most rational people in the world, a love of great singing does not seem to bind the French.

Cross the border at Ventimiglia and everything is reversed. Everyone knows that to an Italian singing comes as easily as eating or making love. It is in his blood; he adores it – though doubtless there are thousands if not millions of exceptions to the stereotype of the singing, song-loving Italian. His language, of course, is beautifully conducive to singing, with its long vowels, often connecting two words in a manner which gives added line to a musical phrase such as Violetta's 'Dite alle giovine...' and its soft words pronounced well back in the throat. No inhibitions about rude noises in this country. The Italians thrive on noise. Nor is there any particular literary mystique here. The Italians love their language, too, though to be sure over the various sections of the country they pronounce it in a multiplicity of ways, but Dante, Petrarch and possibly Manzoni hold sway over the artistic imagination of only a few, as opposed to the way Shakespeare seems to dominate that of masses of English people.

ROBERT RUSHMORE, The Singing Voice

The triumphant revival of *La Traviata* at the Opéra-Comique [1903] is more significant than the fact of the revival itself. Certain things are restored to their rightful place – in particular that peculiary Italian 'realism' which, it is held, might influence French music. Well, I suggest that it stay in Italy.

At least, these are the kinds of things said in the cafés, to liven up bigoted discussions about the so-called Latin temperament.

In *La Traviata* one meets with certain preoccupations dear to the young Italian school: the inevitable interlude, the tear-jerking romance, and so on.

Has anybody noticed their curious need to borrow French subjects of already established fame? First, there is Verdi, who used *La Dame aux Camélias*. And, closer to our time, MM. Puccini and Leoncavallo are both setting *La Vie de Bohème* to music. It is not my place to pass judgment on the literary merit of these two works, but they do represent a period that was particularly sentimental in France, and they could certainly do without being tarted up in music. Verdi is at least straightforward, going from romances to cavatinas, but there are a few pleasures to be encountered on the way, and here and there, real passion. It never pretends to be deep; it's all just a façade, and however unhappy the situation becomes, the sun always shines in the end. The aesthetics of this type of art are certainly ill-founded, for real life is not best expressed in songs. Verdi, however, speaks of a life that is perhaps more beautiful than the attempted 'realism' of the younger Italians. But Puccini and Leoncavallo pretend to character study, even to a kind of crude psychology that in reality goes no deeper than mere anecdote.

The two *Bohèmes* are striking examples. In one there is nothing more solid than triviality, with sentimentality rendered in that nasal manner peculiar to Neapolitan songs. In the other, even if M. Puccini is attempting to recapture the atmosphere of the streets and people of Paris, it is still an Italian noise he makes. Now I wouldn't hold the fact of his being Italian against him. But why the devil choose *Bohème*?

In M. Mascagni's universally celebrated *Cavalleria Rusticana* we are again faced with triviality, only it is made worse by the declamation, which attempts to be lifelike but is nothing but double Dutch! How tiresome it all is!

CLAUDE DEBUSSY, in M. *Croche the Music Hater*

But let an Englishman – D. H. Lawrence, writing from Croydon in 1911 to his girl-friend Louie Burrows – have the last word.

My dear Lou,

It is unusual for you to miss both Friday and Saturday. Are you scolding me?

I went to *Cavalleria Rusticana* and *Pagliacci* at Croydon last night – one shilling in the pit. It's an Italian company from Drury

Lane – Italians of the common class – opera in Italian. But I loved the little folk. You never saw anything in your life more natural, naïve, inartistic, and refreshing. It was just like our old charades.

I love Italian opera – it's so reckless. Damn Wagner, and his bellowings at Fate and death. Damn Debussy, and his averted face. I like the Italians who run all on impulse, and don't care about their immortal souls, and don't worry about the ultimate. My immortal soul can look after itself – what do I care about it. I don't know the creature, even. It's a relative I only know by hear say.

Comment, that, on Italian opera!

But if you were here tonight we'd go to *Carmen*, and hear those delicious little Italians love and weep. I am just as emotional and impulsive as they, by nature. It's the damned climate and upbringing and so on that make me cold-headed as mathematics.

GESAMTKUNSTWERK

*Meaning 'a unified work of art', this was an idea proposed
by Wagner to describe a form combining music, poetry and
the visual to create one overwhelming whole.*

. . . the real villain is Wagner. He has done more than any man in
the nineteenth century towards the muddling of the arts. . . .
Every now and then in history there do come these terrible
geniuses, like Wagner, who stir up all the wells of thought at once.
For a moment it's splendid. Such a splash as never was. But
afterwards – such a lot of mud; and the wells – as it were, they
communicate with each other too easily now, and not one of them
will run quite clean.
                              E. M. FORSTER, *Howards End*

Once, in the Rocky Mountains, I had a strange musical experience. In a gorge famous for its waterfalls and filled with aerial
railways, summer guests, cars, and ice-cream vendors, a well-
coordinated loud-speaker system screamed Isolde's *Liebestod* all
over the place, as part of the gorge's daily routine. I am sure the
managers of the establishment wanted to please their customers,
true to the rule which seems to be one of the leading theses of the
American way of life: enjoyment plus enjoyment gives you more
enjoyment.

We cannot blame them for the idea that the accumulation of
single enjoyments results in an accumulated sensation: that
Liebestod plus waterfalls plus ice-cream give us more pleasure
than *Liebestod* or waterfalls or ice-cream solo. After all, it was the
composer of the *Liebestod* himself who concocted the idea of the
Gesamtkunstwerk, in which singing voices, orchestra, stage, light

164

effects, horses, rivers, cardboard mountains, artificial beards, et cetera, et cetera, were part of the over-all enjoyment. The catch in this conception is that our over-all enjoyment cannot be more than one hundred per cent. Hence, three factors of enjoyment, which each by itself would provide one hundred per cent enjoyment, do not add up to three hundred per cent; they are, rather, compressed into the one hundred per cent, so that each of them, if participation is equal, has but thirty-three and a third per cent of its original effect. I personally even believe that too much of an accumulation of artistic or presumedly artistic enjoyments not only reduces the percentage of the single constituent enjoyment, but also reduces the over-all effect from its one hundred per cent to a much lower degree. Thus the effect of the aforementioned *Gesamtkunstwerk* in the mountains will most likely be that you will take your car, cursing waterfalls, *Liebestods,* and ice-cream in equal percentage and drive to a place where there is nothing but a hundred per cent view.

This time the disproportion between the composition and its performance was not, as it was in the case of the Ninth Symphony, of a musical-technical nature. Although the operatic piece was originally not written for gorges and waterfalls, the many loudspeakers provided an even distribution of sound, so that acoustically the conditions of a big opera house were reproduced not too inaptly, and thus the technical shape of the piece was not in disturbing disagreement with the space in which it was performed.

The disturbing effects in this case originated in a discrepancy between styles. The piece with all its technical, intellectual, historical, and aesthetical implications belonged to one certain sphere of style, from which the style of the pleasure-voracious crowd with their dull, indeterminate, and resistless surrender to anything sensuous is far removed – if ever such brutishness can be honored with the name style – a term that usually indicates at least a faint tendency toward a cultured life!

It is obvious that the gorge's managerial benefactors of the vacationing crowd thought: 'If *Liebestod* is good in the Metropolitan, it will be equally good in our gorge.' They forgot that the composition deals with the most refined feelings of two sub-lime lovers, expressed in exalted music for those who come espe-cially prepared for its reception, and that it should not be pro-jected into an environment which, although gigantic, has become nothing but a tremendous prop for the proverbial having-a-good-time of thousands of daily vacationists. The discrepancy between the vacationists' good time and Isolde's unfortunate experience is more than disgusting.

PAUL HINDEMITH, *A Composer's World*

GLUCK

One of the most concise and lucid summaries of Gluck's reform of opera seria (see also pp. 275–9) is contained in the Preface he wrote to his Alceste (1767), dedicated to Leopold, Duke of Tuscany.

Your Royal Highness:

When I undertook to write the music for *Alceste*, I resolved to divest it entirely of all those abuses, introduced into it either by the mistaken vanity of singers or by the too great complaisance of composers, which have so long disfigured Italian opera and made of the most splendid and most beautiful of spectacles the most ridiculous and wearisome. I have striven to restrict music to its true office of serving poetry by means of expression and by following the situations of the story, without interrupting the action or stifling it with a useless superfluity of ornaments; and I believed that it should do this in the same way as telling colours affect a correct and well-ordered drawing, by a well-assorted contrast of light and shade, which serves to animate the figures without altering their contours. Thus I did not wish to arrest an actor in the greatest heat of dialogue in order to wait for a tiresome *ritornello*, nor to hold him up in the middle of a word on a vowel favourable to his voice, nor to make display of the agility of his fine voice in some long-drawn passage, nor to wait while the orchestra gives him time to recover his breath for a cadenza. I did not think it my duty to pass quickly over the second section of an aria of which the words are perhaps the most impassioned and important, in order to repeat regularly four times over those of the first part, and to finish the aria where its sense may perhaps not end for the convenience of the singer who wishes to show that he can capriciously vary a passage in a number of guises; in short, I have sought to abolish all the abuses against which good sense and reason have long cried out in vain.

I have felt that the overture ought to apprise the spectators of the nature of the action that is to be represented and to form, so to speak, its argument; that the concerted instruments should be introduced in proportion to the interest and the intensity of the words, and not leave that sharp contrast between the aria and the recitative in the dialogue, so as not to break a period unreasonably nor wantonly disturb the force and heat of the action.

Furthermore, I believed that my greatest labour should be devoted to seeking a beautiful simplicity, and I have avoided making displays of difficulty at the expense of clearness; nor did I judge it desirable to discover novelties if it was not naturally suggested by the situation and the expression; and there is no rule which I have not thought it right to set aside willingly for the sake of an intended effect.

Such are my principles. By good fortune my designs were wonderfully furthered by the libretto, in which the celebrated author [viz. his librettist, Calzabigi], devising a new dramatic scheme, for florid descriptions, unnatural paragons, and sententious, cold morality, had substituted heartfelt language, strong passions, interesting situations and an endlessly varied spectacle. The success of the work justified my maxims, and the universal approbation of so enlightened a city has made it clearly evident that simplicity, truth and naturalness are the great principles of beauty in all artistic manifestations. For all that, in spite of repeated urgings on the part of some most eminent persons to decide upon the publication of this opera of mine in print, I was well aware of all the risk run in combating such firmly and profoundly rooted prejudices, and I thus felt the necessity of fortifying myself with the most powerful patronage of Your Royal Highness, whose August Name I beg you may have the grace to prefix to this my opera, a name which with so much justice enjoys the suffrages of an enlightened Europe. The great protector of the fine arts, who reigns over a nation that had the glory of making them arise again from universal oppression and which itself has produced the greatest models, in a city that was always the first to shake off the yoke of vulgar prejudices in order to clear a path for perfection, may alone undertake the reform of that noble spectacle in which all the fine arts take so great a share. If this should succeed, the glory of having moved the first stone will remain for me, and in this public testimonial of You Highness's furtherance of the same, I have the honour to subscribe myself, with the most humble respect,

Your Royal Highness's

Most humble, most devoted, and most obliged servant,

CHRISTOFORO GLUCK

GLYNDEBOURNE

John Christie must rank among the most visionary of English eccentrics for his achievement in establishing one of the world's finest opera houses in his (admittedly sizeable) back yard. Glyndebourne may be very expensive and exclusive, but its high standards of musical preparation and production, its adventurous repertory, and the opportunities it gives to young singers more than justify its existence.

In his autobiography 5000 Nights at the Opera, *Rudolf Bing recalls how in the 1930s he arrived to join the man-*

agement team at Glyndebourne, only to be confronted with a galère *of characters straight out of a Dickens novel or Shaw play.*

Perhaps the most remarkable was Childs, Christie's perfect butler – P. G. Wodehouse could have modelled Jeeves after him. Once in later years when I needed Christie for something and could not find him, I asked Childs where he was, and Childs told me; it was some entirely unexpected, out-of-the-way place. 'Childs,' I said, 'how do you know he is *there*? Did you ask him before he left?' Childs said, 'A good butler never asks his master where he is going, but he always knows.' On one of the first occasions that I was an overnight guest at Glyndebourne, Childs woke me with that abominable English custom, the early-morning tea, and said, 'Breakfast at eight-thirty, sir.' I said, 'Good morning, Childs. What time is it now?' 'Nine o'clock, sir,' he said. Among his other services to the household, Childs ran the local boy scout troop. For the opera company, he once acted the role of the deaf-mute in *Die Entführung*, and very successfully, too; he explained that he had once worked for a master who was deaf, and had studied all his reactions. . . . One morning, I remember, some guests and a number of county people, one of them a general, were sitting about at breakfast when Childs . . . came in and said, 'I'm sorry to disturb you, sir, but the cook is dead.' There was a moment's uncomfortable silence, broken by the general, who said, 'Under the circumstances, do you think I could have another sausage?'

RUDOLF BING, 5000 Nights at the Opera

A moving account of one of Glyndebourne's greatest triumphs – the 1986 production of Gershwin's Porgy and Bess. *Trevor Nunn is one of a new generation of directors, trained in the 'legitimate' theatre, who have brought a new vitality and imagination to the staging of opera in recent years (Patrice Chéreau, Peter Hall, Jonathan Miller, Andrei Serban, Peter Stein, and Giorgio Strehler are other significant names in this category).*

It was three years ago when I first heard about the Glyndebourne production of *Porgy and Bess*. At the time I was a member of the American Opera Center at the Juilliard School in New York. I felt unhappy and insecure. Everyone seemed to be telling me I had no future in opera, insinuating that a black television actor from Hollywood could not be taken seriously as an operatic tenor. So it was in a state of frustration and discouragement that I received news that an audition with Glyndebourne had been scheduled.

My God, I thought, Glyndebourne! *Porgy and Bess* at one of the world's most prestigious opera festivals. I felt I had to be part of this production. My history with the piece and the role of Sportin' Life had not been easy. I had always felt the majesty of the music and seen the beauty of the drama and the characters. Moreover, I believed that this was an opera – not a 'folk opera' or operetta as people said. All roles could, and should, be done in an operatic manner. Yet the productions I had seen and been involved with had never seemed to bring out the work's true greatness. I was ambivalent about being associated with the piece, and I had never found the supportive environment in which I could explore my insights and particular vision into the character of Sportin' Life.

To American musicians, Glyndebourne is seen as a kind of Disneyland. Few places in the world allow for four or more weeks of rehearsal, with the luxury of an entire cast going through the creative process together. In addition, there is an expert music staff and coaches readily available to assist the artists in discovering the nuances of the music. The Festival has a tradition of mounting fresh and revealing productions, utilizing the best talents in the theatre and music. All this is in an extraordinarily beautiful setting where everything is carefully planned to make the participants feel comfortable and relaxed. Everything about Glyndebourne and those involved in this particular production led me to believe that this *Porgy* would be a special experience, one which might reveal the piece to be the true innovative work of genius I felt it to be.

Word of Glyndebourne's interest in me arrived two days after my audition. I had had a successful career as a stage and television actor, but this marked my first major role in the top ranks of the opera world. I was excited and overjoyed. But, as the news of my upcoming debut spread, I was shocked and disappointed by the reactions. Most people seemed indifferent, acting scornfully to the novelty of Glyndebourne presenting this work and trotting out the hackneyed opinion that *Porgy* wasn't a 'real' opera. One manager said to me, 'The only thing that *Porgy and Bess* can demonstrate to me is whether or not a singer knows how to move on stage.' Many Americans still looked down on *Porgy and Bess* and it didn't matter to them that Glyndebourne and Trevor Nunn and Simon Rattle were going to be involved with this production.

So I was caught in the perennial 'Pork 'n' Beans' syndrome – that is black folks' lingo for this kind of work that provides steady employment but can be a kind of operatic ghetto for black singers. When I first expressed my interest in a career in classical music, I had been warned to stay away from *Porgy and Bess*. Experienced black singers said it wouldn't mean anything but a pay check, no one would take it seriously. As I continued to talk about Glyndebourne, the reality of this situation became clearer, but I would not allow myself to bow to these negative views. I needed to believe that my hopes and dreams would come true.

Of course, my faith was bolstered by the support of the enthusiastic few. But I wanted the world to celebrate and antici-pate this event as I did, and the growing sense of discontent persisted even as I made the journey to England. But, finally, the first day of rehearsal arrived, and there we were gathered together in the Organ Room. Tension filled the air. Trevor Nunn presided, unassuming and almost sheepish in his manner. He looked at the sea of black faces around him and quietly said, 'Glyndebourne will never be the same again, and it shouldn't.' For a moment we felt the sense of community that would eventually forge us into an ensemble, an *esprit de corps* which made us an entity independent of the Glyndebourne Festival even as we were nurtured by it.

However, a sense of community does not come easily. We had to learn to trust our guides. I vividly remember the concerns voiced at that first meeting. What image of black people would be presented to our audience? Although it was never openly expressed, the real question was, 'How do you white Englishmen dare to direct us in this piece?' (Charles Augins, our choreographer, with Alby James, the associate director, were the only blacks on the creative staff.) Trevor and Simon seemed to have considered this question but for them *Porgy and Bess* was not so much a black story as a human one. Trevor asked us to open ourselves to the discovery of the beauty and humanity of these inhabitants of Catfish Row, while Simon asked us to rediscover through his ears the special uniqueness of the music we thought we knew so well. We all had to trust. The cast had to trust that these outsiders had a true vision of the work; Trevor and Simon had to trust our knowledge of the black culture in which this piece is rooted.

The first big surprise of the rehearsal period was the meticulous and painstaking way in which Trevor and Simon approached their work. This was consistent with the tradition and legend of Glyndebourne but for those of us who had previously played our roles, often to great acclaim, I might add, the process seemed unnecessarily long. When we got frustrated and bored, Trevor would take us aside, put his arm over our shoulders and say 'Just trust me . . . and forget what you did before.' We had to relearn – sometimes painfully – our self-imposed stereotypes of our characters and our culturally-imposed stereotypes of *Porgy and Bess*. We had to open ourselves to Trevor's rethinking of every aspect of the piece.

After years of 'Pork 'n' Beans', we were defensive. We needed to prove to Glyndebourne, as well as to ourselves, that we were artists capable of doing as much as anyone else at the Festival. There was little intermingling of *Porgy* cast members with other singers during the rehearsal period. In the dining hall we sat in separate little groups. We socialized mostly with one another. We became a small segregated community not unlike Catfish Row itself. Slowly we became more and more immersed in our work. The Glyndebourne magic was indeed casting its spell. Even as an air of isolation pervaded us, we began to realize that we were becoming an ensemble of world class talent.

In fact, we were an international cast. Those of us who came from the United States had to work with black artists from not only Great Britain but Italy, South Africa and Jamaica as well. For the non-Americans in the cast there was culture shock and ignorance of what was happening in this story. The language itself often produced blank stares and questions of 'What does that mean?' Cast members had to be educated on small cultural details like the old custom of collecting burial funds in a saucer, as well as more important issues like the overwhelming injustice of overt racism as experienced in the American South in the 1930s. Friendship grew out of our working relationships. Our race was a common bond. A favorite topic of conversation was the lack of opportunity for black artists the world over. I remember my surprise at hearing a British colleague say to me, 'You mean blacks in the United States have a hard time finding work? But there are blacks in every American movie I see.'

At first, there was tension between the predominant nationalities. The English blacks seemed to feel that we had invaded their shores and robbed them of work which rightfully should be theirs. We Americans were sensitive to these attitudes. We were unused to being seen as interlopers and confused by fellow blacks who were culturally and nationally so different. The common bond of oppression which gives American blacks a sense of community was not always present with our British brothers and sisters. But the common goal of creating a community of Catfish Row brought us together. Our suspicion gave way to mutual respect and finally true fondness for one another.

As rehearsals continued, we remained unsure of what we were creating. But isolated events seemed almost miraculous. In one rehearsal of Act III Scene I in which the inhabitants of Catfish Row are mourning Clara, Jake and Crown and singing a sad and moving dirge, Cynthia Clarey, our Serena, burst into tears and had to run from the room. She was so caught up in the reality we were creating that the power and magic of the piece could not be denied. I remember being amazed at this rehearsal. But I still couldn't guess what the final verdict would be on our efforts and stature as artists.

Our first rehearsal with orchestra was another event. I have never seen so many smiling faces at the Sitzprobe. That Saturday in the large rehearsal studio, the orchestra made no attempt to hide their enormous pleasure in the music and singers. The cast in turn was stimulated and thrilled by the joy of the instrumentalists. There was electricity in the air. At the helm was Simon, thoroughly enjoying the fruits of his meticulous labour.

Finally, we came to the first public dress rehearsal, when the other singers and members of the Glyndebourne community would hear us. I think we were more nervous and excited about unveiling ourselves before our peers than before the critics. I'll never forget it. We thought the first act would never be over. There seemed to be an interminable silence from the audience. Only when Willard sang 'I got plenty o' nothin' ' was there any apparent response. Then as the story unfolded with one familiar song after another, the audience became more and more alive. We were thrilled! Our worried frowns gave way to smiles as we realized we were a HIT! But nothing could prepare us for the ovation at the final curtain. Cheers, whistles, foot stomping – general pandemonium broke loose. We were amazed and we loved it.

At last we felt welcomed into the Glyndebourne community. Backstage the tension gave way to tears and laughter, hugs and kisses. The deafening applause put us into a state of euphoric shock. Only later did I realize that we had come alive as a cast. We had become one, aware of our work, and aware of the powerful message about the glory of the human spirit which we were conveying.

Later that evening, I walked alone in the gardens of Glyndebourne, a treat which I gave myself after every performance. This night, I had an enormous sense of pride and of gratitude. I had no more ambivalence about being a part of this opera. Never before had I experienced such a sense of dignity and integrity from every member of the ensemble. On that small stage next to a manor house in the English countryside, we had become the inhabitants of Catfish Row.

On the fifth day of July, 1986, *Porgy and Bess* officially opened at the Glyndebourne Festival, the first ever British staging of the complete opera. The production was a huge critical and popular success. Over the summer, we in the cast grew used to whistles, stomping and standing ovations. Trevor's words on the first day of rehearsal came true. Glyndebourne would never be the same again. The hopes and dreams which had hatched in me when I was first approached three years before, had also come true. I wasn't sure how I had changed but I too would never be the same again.

DAMON EVANS with DAVID ELLISON

There are, however, some people who regard Glyndebourne as a little infra dig.

Not long after Glyndebourne became a place of pilgrimage for operagoers, the famous Emma Eames visited London. Though noted for her beauty she was not the easiest of people with whom to deal. She once sang Elsa in *Lohengrin* and looked so beautiful that she moved an admiring conductor to declare, 'I should love to do to you what Lohengrin did not do to Elsa.' She simply said, 'Change the conductor,' and the conductor was promptly changed. Of her cold, lady-like acting, the *New York Times* reported, 'Last night, Emma Eames sang Aida; we had skating on the Nile.'

During Madame Eames's visit to London, I was invited to meet her by Desmond Shawe-Taylor, who was later to become a distinguished music critic. 'Can I have the rare pleasure,' he asked me, 'of being able to introduce you to a *prima donna*? I now know one whom you have never met.'

Actually, I knew little of Madame Eames except that she was a famous contemporary of Melba and Calvé, and I expected to see a very old lady. There was a rustle of taffeta on the staircase, and Emma Eames swept into the room wearing a very large hat and with all the *éclat* of her first-act entry in *Tosca*. 'Madame Eames,' someone said during the party, 'you simply must see *Don Giovanni* at Glyndebourne.'

The idea appalled the great *prima donna*. 'Are you asking me,' she demanded rhetorically, 'to undergo a journey on a British railway train, and to spend a night in the discomforts of an English provincial hotel, where they stuff the mattresses with pomegranates, to hear *Don Giovanni*? I sang Donna Anna at the Metropolitan when Gustav Mahler conducted. Victor Maurel was the Don, Chaliapine the Leporello, Caruso the Don Ottavio, Lilli Lehmann the Donna Elvira and Geraldine Farrar the Zerlina. Why should I go to Glyndebourne when I have such memories of *Don Giovanni*? The remembrance of that performance will last my lifetime.'

IVOR NEWTON, *At the Piano*

GOUNOD

A base soul who poured a sort of bath-water melody down the back of every woman he met. Margaret or Madeleine, it was all the same.

GEORGE MOORE, *Memoirs of my Dead Life*

GREAT SINGING

HEYWORTH: And what do you think are the marks of really great singing?

GOLLANCZ: Heavens, what a question! I am anything but a technician, and incidentally, like my father, can't sing, hum or whistle even approximately in tune: I hear the exact notes in my head and yet can't reproduce them. But I'll have a shot at answering you so far as operatic singing is concerned. To be in the supreme class, I'd say, he (let's say he for convenience) must have a big, full voice of beautiful quality. (James Joyce once asked me, 'Don't you think

the most important thing in a tenor is that he should sing *loud*? –
referring to O'Sullivan, the Irish tenor at the Paris Opéra who
used to sing in *William Tell* and *La Juive* [see pp. 380–1]. That is
half the truth. And one of the marvels about Caruso was that,
however powerfully he might sing, you always felt he could sing
twice as powerfully if he wanted to.)

His – the great singer's – breath control must be perfect: so
must intonation and his phrasing – and he must attack with his
consonants in the middle of the note. He must be a master of
clean, steady *mezza voce* devoid of mawkishness or sentimentality. His cantilena must be beautifully smooth and even (rather like
a little Chippendale drawer going in 'with the air' as you follow it
through with your finger); and he must also be able, when occasion demands, to sing with a high sense of drama.

He must be expert in the right kind of vibrato, which enriches
the quality of a note, and be incapable of the wrong kind, which
obscures its situation and makes it unclean. There must be a
certain authority in his voice and singing. Above all, he must be
musical; and he must serve the composer in the single-minded sort
of way in which Klemperer serves Beethoven.

I have been talking of singers in the supreme class: but a singer
can be pretty great if he possesses, in a high degree, only a
considerable number of these qualities.

HEYWORTH: Well, to leave the supreme class on one side, you
presumably don't think there as many great singers nowadays as
there were when you were a boy?

GOLLANCZ: Now I must be careful. I don't possess a gramophone,
and rarely listen to one. The reason you may think rather peculiar:
though I hear a great deal of music, listening to it is always an
occasion for me, and I don't want to be able to turn the thing on
and off at my whim. Take works one can hear only once every so
often, like the Missa Solemnis or *L'Enfance du Christ* or the late
Beethoven 'cello sonatas: I like looking forward for weeks or
months to hearing them. But not having a gramophone means
that there may be many singers, unfamiliar to me except by
hearsay, who might truly be called great. Then again I should like
to leave *Lieder* singers out of account.

Finally, let me differentiate between Wagner and other forms of opera. I've never heard a really good Wagner tenor, with the possible exception of Melchior: the basses and baritones are as good, I think, as they have ever been in my time (though I've never really enjoyed a Wotan as much as van Rooy): and I am inclined to rank Birgit Nilsson with the very greatest of Wagnerian sopranos.

HEYWORTH: Well, after these reservations, what's your verdict?

GOLLANCZ: There were many great singers when I was a boy: there is only one today. Don't misunderstand me. We have a number of fine singers, a number it's a delight to listen to, a few that may even be called superb. I think at random of Lisa della Casa, of Christoff, of Ghiaurov, of Victoria de los Angeles, of Rita Gorr. But no one of these is in my opinion great.

Take the basses. Ghiaurov enraptured me the other night in *Don Carlo*; but my mind went back to Chaliapin (for all his musical naughtiness), and I couldn't help feeling that he had just the last thing that Ghiaurov misses.

HEYWORTH: And who's your exception?

GOLLANCZ: Callas. I shall never forget the first time I heard her, years and years ago, in *Norma*, and how I thought, in a sort of ecstasy, 'Here at last it is again!' Nowadays, of course, she often displeases one: and then, it may be for a minute or two, it may be for a whole aria, one says, worshipfully, 'Yes, she's in the great tradition.' Who else, nowadays, could perform that miracle of her entry into 'Dite alla giovine' in the second act of *Traviata*?

HEYWORTH: One last question. May it not be that, throughout our talk, you've been looking at the past through the rosy spectacles of remembered happiness?

GOLLANCZ: I daresay!   VICTOR GOLLANCZ, interviewed by
PETER HEYWORTH in the *Observer*, 1962

A *singer's view:*

Q: '*Of what consists artistic singing?*'

Of a clear understanding, first and foremost; of breathing, in and out; of an understanding of the form through which the breath has to flow, prepared by a proper position of the larynx, the tongue, the nose, and the palate. Of a knowledge and understanding of the functions of the muscles of the abdomen and diaphragm, which regulate the breath pressure; then, of the chest-muscle tension, against which the breath is forced, and whence, under the control of the singer, after passing through the vocal cords, it, in a roundabout way, beats against the resonating surfaces and vibrates in the cavities of the head. Of a highly cultivated skill and flexibility in adjusting all the vocal organs and in putting them into minutely graduated movements, without inducing changes through the pronunciation of words or the execution of musical figures that shall be injurious to the tonal beauty or the artistic expression of the song. Of an immense muscular power in the breathing apparatus and all the vocal organs, the strengthening of which to endure sustained exertion cannot be begun too long in advance; and the exercising of which, as long as one sings in public, must never be remitted for a single day.

As beauty and stability of tone do not depend upon excessive *pressure* of the breath, so the muscular power of the organs used in singing does not depend on convulsive rigidity, but in that snakelike power of contracting and loosening, which a singer must consciously have under perfect control.

The study needed for this occupies an entire lifetime; not only because the singer must perfect himself more and more in the rôles of his repertory – even after he has been performing them year in and year out – but because he must continually strive for progress, setting himself tasks that require greater and greater mastery and strength, and thereby demand fresh study.

LILLI LEHMANN, How to Sing

HOUSE PARTY

Two intriguingly different accounts of hospitality chez
*Adelina Patti in her Welsh castle (latterly an old people's
home) in the 1890s.*

Originally the mansion facing the 'Rock of the Night' on the road
from Brecon to Ystradgynlais had afforded somewhat limited
accommodation. Beautifully half-way down the broad northern
slope of the Swansea Valley, its ample grounds extending for
several acres along the banks of a swift trout stream, it constituted
a delightful home for a small family in search of railroad inacces-
sibility and seclusion from the world. It had been purchased on
the advice of Sir Hussey Vivian, MP (afterwards Lord Swansea),
and his brother, Mr Graham Vivian, with whom Mme Patti and
Signor Nicolini [Patti's husband] stayed when they originally
visited the neighbourhood. The fishing was not its smallest attraction in the eyes of the genial tenor: he could throw a 'fly' with
tolerable skill.

For a while the castle served its purpose well enough. But Mme
Patti liked to have her friends around her, and, finding that there
was not sufficient space to entertain a goodly number of them, she
caused some important additions to be made to the main structure. From first to last her Craig-y-Nos improvements were said to
have cost her nearly £100,000. Nicolini being an ardent devotee of
French or American billiards, a new billiard-room and a spacious
drawing-room, with several bedrooms above, were added at one
end. At the other was erected a huge conservatory, flanked in turn
by a lofty winter garden containing some splendid palms and
exotics. In this winter garden the hostess was wont in bad weather
to take her midday stroll just before *déjeuner*, stopping now and

then to converse with her favorite cockatoo, an enormous bird that was pleasanter to look upon than listen to.

Two novel features at Craig-y-Nos Castle at this period may here be mentioned. One was an installation of the electric light that was said to be among the first to be put up in a country house in the United Kingdom. The other item was a large orchestrion, made at Fribourg, in Switzerland, the musical resources of which were equally new to dwellers in an English (or Welsh) home. It stood in the billiard-room, and was worked by electricity. It had a rich pipe-organ tone, and if it could not compare, either in perfection of mechanism or variety of tonal combinations, with the more elaborate 'orchestrelle' of a later day, it was nevertheless considered a remarkable instrument of its kind, and Mme Patti was immensely proud of it. Moreover, while it was being played – generally in the evening, after dinner – the click of the billiard balls was bidden to cease, silence being requested except for the lighter pieces, such as the *España* of the gifted French composer, Chabrier (Nicolini's cousin, by the way), when the hostess would call for her castanets and accentuate the rhythm of the waltz with characteristic dash and energy. Her castanet-playing was, indeed, exceptionally good.

She did not always spare her throat on these occasions. The orchestrion had only to give out some melody that she cared for, and her gorgeous voice would instantly be ringing through the spacious room, blending deliciously with the full, deep tone of the organ pipes. Strange and lovely did the familiar golden notes of Patti sound under such conditions! But it was always something good that 'drew her out'. She was not very fond of the merely tuneful *morceaux* or the worn-out operatic selections; and as time went on she enjoyed more and more listening to Wagner and certain of the 'advanced' composers of that day.

This, then, was as a rule the nightly scene at Craig-y-Nos during the early years of the Patti-Nicolini period. Later on, after the theatre had been built, I was to have the privilege of joining the circle and witnessing it for myself, as will be seen in due course. But the picture varied little either now or in the time to come. When dinner was over there was usually an informal procession

from the conservatory or the dining-room – the former in summer, the latter in winter – headed by the 'little lady' leaning on the
arm of her principal male guest.

Always *en grande toilette* of the latest Parisian model; always
wearing some wonderful necklace, with bracelets, rings and occasionally a dazzling tiara, chosen from her priceless collection of
jewels; seated upon one of the comfortable lounges that skirted
three sides of the billiard-table, she was invariably the centre of a
bright, animated group, a veritable queen in the midst of her
courtiers. For courtiers they were, most of them, male and female,
ready with a flattering speech, ever bidding for the gracious smile
that each endeavored to win in turn. There they would drink their
coffee and smoke (Mme Patti did not object to the 'fragrant
weed', though she never indulged in it herself), while talking over
the events of the day, making plans for the morrow, discussing
various people, social and artistic, or, as has been said, listening to
the orchestrion. Gifted with an abundance of ready wit and lively
repartee, with an easy command of at least five languages, the
Queen of Song, surrounded by her court, made a striking and
alluring picture; nor could one ever forget that the personality of
the central figure was Adelina Patti.

HERMANN KLEIN, *The Reign of Patti*

The visitors to Craig-y-Nos have been able to tell many a curious
story. The life in the castle was not specially gay, as Nicolini
suffered from constant bad humour and very often threw a veil of
discontent over the whole company. He was absolutely wrapped
up in himself, as was his wife on her part, and the guests were
really invited as spectators to the most curious existence ever
witnessed. My friend, Monsieur de Saxe, told me his impressions
when he and I were guests at Etelka Gerster's castle, near Bologna.
He had just been invited by the secretary of Patti to pay a return
call at Craig-y-Nos, and I cannot help relating some of his experiences at Patti's house. This Monsieur de Saxe deserves to be
mentioned in a book about artists, as he was a sort of theatrical

Phylloxera. He is said never to have missed a first performance in any town, and to have travelled specially to places where they were given. He knew every artist on the dramatic and musical stage and was a very amusing source of information. Curiously enough, this was all he was. His temperament was a nervous one. He was exceedingly polite and had the best manners.

After he had accepted the first invitation that called him to Craig-y-Nos, his invitation was followed by a second letter from the secretary, telling him that it was the custom in coming to the house of the diva to bring a large bouquet in a cardboard box similar to a hat-box. This our friend executed painfully, as he was not very fond of expenses. All the same he arrived one fine day at Craig-y-Nos, and, when stepping out of the carriage, the footman came forward for the flowers, he was happy enough to be able to show him the jealously guarded box, which the footman took from him, disappearing into the castle.

To his great astonishment, Saxe was received by none of the family. Nicolini, who, as the host, might have come to meet him, as it is done in England, even by royalties, behaved as he pleased, and nobody received any visitor, either at the door or even in the entrance hall. A footman, in silk stockings, showed our friend the way. He took him to a greenhouse, in which he had to walk, to his terror, through two long rows of parrots and cockatoos, which were swinging wildly on their perches, shrieking at the tops of their voices and making swift dashes towards our friend, whose courage was not in proportion to his politeness. He utterly disliked this reception, and flew more than he walked through this greenhouse, which for years remained an absolute nightmare in his remembrance. When he had arrived at the end of the gallery, which, as he told me, had appeared to him twelve miles long, he was shown straight into his bedroom. The valet who accompanied him told him that the dinner started at a given hour, when he would have to appear in the drawing-room. These orders startled him, and he had not yet recovered from his astonishment and his dramatic entrance through the parrots' paradise when a knocking was heard at his door. A lady's-maid entered, carrying a big tray on her arms, covered with jewel-boxes.

'Wishing to do a special favour to her guest, her ladyship sends me to give monsieur the privilege of choosing her ladyship's jewels which she shall wear to-night at dinner,' and saying this she opened all the jewel-boxes, spreading out before him complete sets of rubies, emeralds, sapphires, diamonds and pearls, each set containing a tiara, necklaces, brooches, rings, earrings, bracelets, etc. Very embarrassed, he chose the ruby set, and with a curtsy the maid disappeared with the marvellous tray.

After having hurried through his dressing, he heard the formidable dinner-bell ringing through the house. He went to the drawing-room, and found there the other guests of the house already standing, as at Court, in two rows near a door, through which, after a few minutes, Madame Patti, in magnificent evening dress, wearing the ruby set, made a royal entrance, leaning on the arm of Monsieur Nicolini, bowing and smiling right and left, holding out her hand for a kiss here and there, and at last calling the new-comer, our friend, to greet her.

'You see, I am wearing the jewels of your choice,' said she, and with a smile took the arm of Nicolini and passed before all the guests with him into the dining-room.

What happened at table was not less curious. Several of the guests seemed to be specially trained and drilled to pay compliments over the table all the time the meal was served, and the heavier the compliments the more radiant was Patti's smile. Nothing seemed to be too much, and when at last one of the *habitués*, a young lady, called over the table to her sister, 'Is she not divine tonight?' and the sister answered, 'Be quiet, there are no words to express her beauty', she turned around to the other guests and said, 'Are they not delightful children?' It was impossible to try to start a real conversation about any subject outside the personality of Madame Patti, and after several attempts of my friend to bring some news of the world from which he came, he contented himself in contemplating the curious things that passed before his eyes. Monsieur Nicolini drank his own special wine; quite another one was served to the guests – needless to say of an inferior mark. He tasted the food put on the plate destined for Patti and, after having tasted, declared solemnly every time: 'You can eat it.' The cigars that were offered at the end of the meal were also, like the wine, different in quality for the host and for the guests. At the end of the dinner the ladies retired into the drawing-room, and Patti, leaving the room with a curtsy, answered by all the ladies in the same fashion, said: '*A tout à l'heure au théâtre.*' My friend was then told that there would be a performance at the Craig-y-Nos theatre, and that every night Madame Patti appeared to her guests and the inmates of the castle, servants and gardeners, etc., in her favourite rôles, as disposition permitted. The ringing of a bell announced the beginning of the performance, and all the guests wandered down to the little theatre. They were seated in stalls and, turning round, they saw the balcony filled with a crowd of tradesmen, farmers, villagers and servants, who were not only invited, but forced to come in turns. When the curtain rose, the diva appeared in full costume. The accompaniment was played by Mr Ganz on the piano! The stage was perfectly organized like a big one, and on that night she chose *Traviata*, to the amazement of our friend, who saw the butler of the household on the stage, playing the dummy of Alfredo, and receiving with absolute calm the smiles and tears lavished on him in the touching scene by the diva. When the scene was at its end frantic applause and torrents of bravas poured from the gallery, the noise apparently having been perfectly rehearsed and organized, and suddenly, after many curtain calls, a shower of artificial flowers and garlands were sent flying from the gallery and fell at the feet of the diva, who, smiling and sending out kisses from her finger-tips, bowed and pressed the flowers to her heart. When the curtain was rung down for the last time, footmen, provided with a huge basket, came on to the stage and picked up all the flowers that were covering the floor, putting them carefully away, to be used again the next night.

BLANCHE MARCHESI, *A Singer's Pilgrimage*

ICONOCLAST

When this interview with composer–conductor Pierre Boulez first appeared in the German newspaper Der Spiegel *in 1966, it aroused enormous controversy. Boulez has since mellowed (at least to the point of conducting at Bayreuth, Covent Garden and the Opéra), but remains solidly hostile to conventional operatic establishments.*

SPIEGEL: M. Boulez, you are the funeral orator of modern opera. Although, in Germany alone, twenty contemporary operas will have their first performance this season, you maintain that there is no such thing as modern opera.

BOULEZ: I do not allow myself to be taken in by the enormous activity of certain opera houses. I still maintain that since Alban Berg's *Wozzeck* and *Lulu* . . .

SPIEGEL: . . . in other words since 1935 . . .

BOULEZ: . . . no opera worth mentioning has been composed. And Berg probably knew that he had brought a chapter to its close.

SPIEGEL: But surely, out of the several hundred operas that have been composed since Berg's *Lulu*, there must be a few worth talking about. The world-wide success of Hans Werner Henze's operas can hardly be the result of pure chance.

BOULEZ: Henze's products are not genuinely modern operas. They always make me think of an oily hairdresser subscribing to an entirely superficial modernism. *Der Prinz von Homburg*, for example, is an unfortunate dilution of Verdi's *Don Carlos* – to say nothing of his other operas. Henze is like de Gaulle – whatever rubbish he puts out, he still believes he's the king.

SPIEGEL: If you call Henze derivate, you must surely think more of

Gunther Schuller. He is the first opera composer to have fused jazz with twelve-note music, in *The Visitation*, which had its first performance last year and was internationally applauded.

BOULEZ: That must be the fiftieth time that people have tried to blend jazz with western music. But it doesn't work. There is one kind of music which is written down and which is based on certain rules and particular intellectual configurations, and there is another kind that exists on improvization. Schuller's opera failed because the jazz forfeited its characteristic of improvization. Schoenberg was quite right when he said, 'The middle road is the only one that doesn't lead to Rome.'

SPIEGEL: John Cage, Mauricio Kagel and György Ligeti are not of course opera composers, but their works are well known as 'visible music', that is, having theatrical effects, and generally being presented as a kind of happening. Do you see in these composers any jumping-off points for a modern musical theatre?

BOULEZ: Points certainly, and these works may even be the source of a vision of the new musical theatre. But Kagel and Ligeti, in particular, lack a comprehensive understanding of the theatre. And the musical side is sometimes very thin. . . .

SPIEGEL: M. Boulez, you have now defamed composers, dethroned directors and declared a whole chapter of musical history null and void. In spite of this, you obviously believe it possible to breathe some life back into the genus Opera which, in your opinion, has been dead since Berg. For it is said that Pierre Boulez wants to write a composition for the stage.

BOULEZ: I want to – whether or not I shall is still uncertain.

SPIEGEL: How would your opera differ from, let us say, the works of Henze?

BOULEZ: In the first place, the text must really be conceived directly for the musical theatre. It must not be an adaptation of literary material, as is invariably the case today. Literature set to music is sterile.

SPIEGEL: What kind of text would it have to be that the composer Boulez could set to music?

BOULEZ: Not set to music, rather let us say make use of. It would be an experiment in which text and music would be conceived simultaneously. In other words, I would associate with a writer who feels, with every word he writes, that music belongs to it, indeed that without music the text cannot exist.

SPIEGEL: A rare gift.

BOULEZ: Yes. Brecht had it. Unfortunately he collaborated with such inconsequential musicians.

SPIEGEL: Weill and Dessau. . . .

BOULEZ: One can only dream of what might have happened in a collaboration between Stravinsky and Brecht in the 1920s. Good God, what that might have resulted in! But as it is, with both Stravinsky – particularly in *The Soldier's Tale*, for example – and Brecht, the text and the music oppose each other like two alien worlds.

SPIEGEL: If Brecht and Stravinsky had worked together. . . . Do you think that Brecht's texts would have been different, then?

BOULEZ: Of course; he would have had less of an eye on folksongs, which is what Weill brought him down to.

SPIEGEL: Do you know a playwright of our time as important as Brecht with whom you could work?

BOULEZ: I have exchanged thoughts with Jean Genet. He is one of those extraordinarily gifted writers who would be capable of a synthesis of theatre and music, who depart not only from the aesthetic and dramatic standpoint, but could fuse modern music and modern theatre together. Up to now we have only spoken about the technical aspects of modern music and the technical aspects of the theatre.

SPIEGEL: Can you give us an example of what interests you in Genet?

BOULEZ: In Genet's play *The Screens* there is a very impressive scene in which the Algerians are abusing the French, but no longer in words. They draw the insults on the walls. At the end of this scene the set is ready. You see, this is a part of the action which at the same time makes use of the technical aspects of the stage. This idea is incredibly impressive. This is why Genet was also interested in the technique of my pieces. He wanted to know how I wrote them and how they are conducted. He spoke of including the conductor's gestures in the piece, to justify the presence of the music. So there would not simply be a conductor conducting from outside the stage. For a modern opera must, I believe, be a structural mixture of technique, aesthetics and theatrical art.

SPIEGEL: Do you not think that something like this scene-painting of Genet's on an open stage has something almost accidental about it which can only now and again be artistically feasible?

BOULEZ: Of course it is a matter of luck; but everything that succeeds is, in part at least, a matter of luck. It was for this reason that I said that this is my point of departure, and that was only a comparison. On no account do I wish to repeat in music what Genet once did with painting. You will certainly not see in any piece of musical theatre that I may write an actor coming on the stage and playing an instrument. That would be a silly and ineffective copy.

SPIEGEL: M. Boulez, we would value a more precise definition of your conception of a new musical theatre.

BOULEZ: If I had written the piece then I could tell you more exactly about it. But you can't make a revolution according to a pre-digested pattern. Revolution – and this applies not only in the field of music – needs only a well-thought-out conception. Its practice then throws up continual amendments. And this practice can only be described in hindsight. So I can talk to you about my framework, as I have done.

SPIEGEL: You said that you could not yet imagine individual scenes; but surely you can say something about the things you would demand from your theme.

BOULEZ: If I collaborate with a writer, the entire conception must also be a piece of literature and not a picturesque incidental – like a treatise on social problems. People think they are making modern theatre when they're talking about Vietnam for instance.

That's not really enough.

SPIEGEL: You want a timeless theme?

BOULEZ: No, not necessarily. Genet has written about temporal themes; think of *The Blacks* or *The Screens*. But in these pieces the problems of our time were transcended. For example in *The Screens* you could substitute Cubans for Algerians without changing anything fundamental at all. I am not very keen on polemics which are tied up only with immediate politics. Such aims are short-sighted.

SPIEGEL: You want a theme that is abstracted from immediate problems – as in Genet's plays?

BOULEZ: Yes, but I do not think that one can take a play of Genet and 'set it to music'. In that case it would have to be totally changed, but that would be an adaptation. I find this solution superfluous.

SPIEGEL: How then would the music of a Boulez opera sound? Would it be essentially different from your instrumental music?

BOULEZ: No, not at all. I think the difference between stage music and pure concert music has disappeared, in any case.

SPIEGEL: Does the fact that, in your opinion, there is no such thing as modern opera result primarily from the absence of a congenial collaboration between librettist and composer? Is there anything else that represents an obstacle to contemporary opera?

BOULEZ: Yes. Opera producers, for one thing, the majority of whom are still hobbling along far behind the times.

SPIEGEL: Günther Rennert, your late friend Wieland Wagner, Franco Zeffirelli . . . ?

BOULEZ: Wieland Wagner was the only opera producer that I have known who has stimulated me into collaboration.

SPIEGEL: Can you imagine collaborating with the Italian Zeffirelli?

BOULEZ: Zeffirelli is the Henze among producers. One must of course concede that, with opera as it is at present, it is out of the question that anybody could accomplish anything adventurous in production. I have the impression that even a bourgeois producer is too adventurous for opera administrators.

SPIEGEL: Will you produce your own opera?

BOULEZ: No, it is not my profession.

SPIEGEL: Is there a producer with intentions similar to yours and Genet's with whom you could therefore collaborate, should the occasion arise?

BOULEZ: I can imagine two people: Peter Brook or Ingmar Bergman. They are real producers. I shall in any case approach a producer who is not burdened with the operatic tradition.

SPIEGEL: M. Boulez, do you think you would be able to realize your modern musical theatre in our highly conventional opera houses?

BOULEZ: Quite certainly not. That brings me to another reason why there is no modern opera today. The new German opera houses certainly look very modern – from outside; inside they have remained extremely old-fashioned. Only with the greatest difficulty can one present modern operas in a theatre in which, predominantly, repertory pieces are played. It is really unthinkable. The most expensive solution would be to blow the opera houses up. But don't you think that would also be the most elegant?

SPIEGEL: But, since no administrator is going to follow your suggestion . . .

BOULEZ: Then one can play the usual repertory in the existing opera houses, Mozart, Verdi, Wagner, up to about Berg. For new operas, experimental stages absolutely need to be incorporated. This apparently senseless demand has already been widely realized in other branches of the theatre.

SPIEGEL: This would also diminish the financial risk which every opera administrator has to run when he puts on a contemporary opera.

BOULEZ: Yes, the burden of having to present a 'successful' opera in every case – one which attracts the public – would happily be removed. And on a small stage of that kind one could risk all kinds of things, whilst the big opera houses continue to exist as museums.

SPIEGEL: You appear to find yourself quite at home in the museum, for example when you conducted *Parsifal* at the Bayreuth Festival.

BOULEZ: *Parsifal* was an exception. The conditions under which one can work at Bayreuth are unusual. Bayreuth has nothing to do with the normal business of opera. Apart from this, Wieland Wagner was a friend I admired. These two reasons were what decided me to conduct *Parsifal* in Bayreuth.

SPIEGEL: What interests you apart from *Parsifal*?

BOULEZ: Very little; a few other Wagner operas, Mozart, Mussorgsky and Debussy. That's all. If anybody asked me to conduct Verdi's *La Forza del Destino*, I'd much rather go for a walk.

SPIEGEL: That kind of opera is 'an attractive lie', as Busoni once said?

BOULEZ: Not even attractive. If you have ever seen *Rigoletto*, then you will know yourself what is wrong with it – particularly in a so-called realistic production by Zeffirelli. Idiotic! A theatre or film audience would laugh itself to death over that kind of performance. The opera audience is something else entirely. What I mean is, you can compare opera to a musty old wardrobe. But, thank God, there is only one left, and that is Vienna, where the opera house is still the centre of existence – a relic, a well-cared-for museum.

SPIEGEL: And in Paris, the capital of your own country?

BOULEZ: In the provincial town of Paris the museum is very badly looked after. The Paris Opéra is full of dust and crap, to put it plainly. The tourists still go there because you 'have to have seen' the Paris Opéra. It's on the itinerary, just like the Folies-Bergère or the Invalides, where Napoleon's tomb is.

SPIEGEL: These are obviously not the people you would like for an audience?

BOULEZ: No, these operatic tourists make me vomit. If I write a work for the stage I certainly won't write it for star-fanciers; I shall be thinking of a public which has an extensive knowledge of the theatre.

SPIEGEL: Can one split the public so easily into groups?

BOULEZ: Yes, perfectly well. At the moment I see three strata in our society. The first likes to think itself cultured and goes to the museum – and to the music-museum. When they have got bored in the museum they want to buy themselves a bit of adventure. . . . Bourgeois society needs its court jesters.

SPIEGEL: And the second stratum?

BOULEZ: This one lives in the present. It listens to the Beatles and the Rolling Stones and heaven knows what else. A Beatles record is certainly cleverer than a Henze opera, and shorter as well. But the third stratum is the one you can bet on. It is fairly independent of bourgeois society and above all of the taste of bourgeois society.

SPIEGEL: How do you explain that, in the non-bourgeois society of the Communist bloc, Henze's operas, for example, are as popular as in our bourgeois opera houses?

BOULEZ: The eastern countries are also bourgeois. Do you really believe there are still any Communist countries left?

SPIEGEL: Cuba. . . .

BOULEZ: Perhaps. I do not know the country, of course, but I do believe that if one wishes to try out some forms of the exchange between audience and artist, it is easier there. There is more unspoilt enthusiasm there – which is important. There are certainly no blasé people there who go to the opera because one must go to the opera, because that is what society likes to see, because it is a cultural duty. There is also perhaps more inspiration, more naïvety, more latent originality; but it is also possible that I would be very disappointed if I went there.

SPIEGEL: You expect nothing in this connection from the Soviet Union?

BOULEZ: No. There they prefer entirely bourgeois operas like *Eugene Onegin* and *The Queen of Spades*. Now, there would be something for the Chinese Red Guards to deal with – they could let off steam to their hearts' content!

SPIEGEL: Then you are certainly also of the opinion that our own operatic set-up would be an ideal field of activity for the Red Guards?

BOULEZ: Yes. We should import a whole lot of Red Guards! Don't forget that the French Revolution destroyed a great deal as well, and that was very healthy. If your blood-pressure is too high there is only one thing to do – get rid of the blood.

SPIEGEL: In other words, in order to be able to create a new musical theatre you have to change society?

BOULEZ: I cannot change society because I . . .

SPIEGEL: '. . . am not a revolutionary?'

BOULEZ: Not a political revolutionary, anyway. I haven't got the technique for it. So I turn to the enlightened people, people who are interested in plays by Genet, Pinter and Beckett. But opera, with its traditional audience, has felt nothing of the changes time has wrought. It lives in the ghetto. Opera can be compared to a church in which, at best, eighteenth-century cantatas are sung. I have no fond desire to liberate people who would rather suffocate in the ghetto – I've got nothing against that kind of suicide.

IMPRESARIO

The notion of making money out of mounting unsubsidized performances of opera may not seem a gilt-edged recipe for financial prosperity. Yet, occasionally and amazingly, an impresario has worked the trick, without sacrificing artistic standards. One such was Alessandro Lanari.

Lanari came from Jesi, a small town in the Marches of eastern Italy. A brother of his stayed on and seems to have had a part in running the theatre there. Alessandro is first heard of as impresario in 1819 in Lucca, by which time he was married to a successful singer, Clementina Domeniconi, a member of a well-known theatrical tribe; soon afterwards, however, they appear to have separated and from then on Lanari lived with a minor singer, Carlotta Corazza. In 1823 he took over, from an impresario who had just died, both a costume workshop in Florence and the task of running the main theatre there, La Pergola. The workshop became one of the two main influences that shaped Lanari's career; the other was the practice he developed during the 1820s of giving promising singers long-term contracts and then trying to place them at a profit.

Workshop and agency both led him to form circuits where his costumes and his singers could be exploited with the fewest possible gaps. One circuit took in Florence, Lucca, and the secondary towns of Tuscany and Umbria, particularly Pisa, Leghorn, Siena, Perugia, and Foligno. In the minor towns Lanari either put subordinates in charge of the theatre or had a regular understanding with the local impresario. In Florence he did not, like Barbaja or Jacovacci, wish to run everything himself, but he was determined to hang on to La Pergola, if not as impresario then at least as costume supplier; on two occasions when he failed in this he conducted a 'war' on La Pergola by running a season in a rival theatre.

The larger circuit on which Lanari operated took in almost the whole of operatic Italy except for Turin, Genoa, and Trieste. He had long runs of seasons at La Fenice, Venice, and at the Senigallia fair; he also worked at various times in Bologna, Parma, Verona, and Ancona, in some smaller towns of northern Italy, twice in Rome, once in Milan, and once in Naples. . . . Because he often worked in partnership with others his role has not always been clear, but he was responsible for launching two of Bellini's operas, two of Verdi's, and five of Donizetti's, including *Lucia di Lammermoor*. He also helped to launch some of the finest singers of the day, in particular the French tenor Duprez, whose discovery under Lanari's guidance in Italy of the 'chest high C' changed the development of the tenor voice.

All this was done with the impresario constantly on the move, firing off letters to partners and subordinates elsewhere while he rehearsed new works for the season he had chosen to run himself. While Lanari was away his widowed sister, a semi-literate woman, ran the costume workshop; a nephew accompanied him as secretary; other relatives and retainers, among them a couple of broken-down ex-impresari, did various jobs at his Florence headquarters.

He was running what was for Italy a fairly large and complex business. His understanding of his craft was wide. Yet he remained a harsh, narrow, driving man. The only expression of unaffected warm feeling that has come down to us dates from his youth; it was addressed to Rosa Morandi, a famous contralto, and her husband, slightly older people who both came from his native Marches and who had befriended him. He was genuinely moved at Rosa's early death. For the rest, to paraphrase Coolidge, the business of Alessandro Lanari was business.

He drove a hard bargain. When his common-law wife Carlotta exclaimed on first hearing Duprez's voice at rehearsal Lanari slapped her – by praising it she might drive up the young tenor's price. Nothing was too small for him to scrutinize. When away from Florence he insisted on trying to control the number of sequins bought for the workshop and the price paid for cloth. If the price seemed too high he complained that he was being 'assassinated'. Because he was suspicious he did not delegate authority clearly: the people he left in charge then quarrelled among themselves. He snapped at his subordinates when they failed to consult him ('I ought to be everywhere'); he snapped at them when they pestered him with detail ('I don't know how you expect me to deal with such matters from here'). An incompetent retainer, rather like an old dog, who was supposed to help in running the costume workshop once asked exceptionally for a fifth-tier box at La Pergola; Lanari let him have it but added, 'I am sure your going to the theatre won't lead you to neglect the workshop.'

A story of Duprez's rings true even though it had probably improved with time. When he saw Lanari about signing a long-term contract – he was then twenty-four – Lanari was in his bath, to which he was often confined by severe piles. Duprez tried to push up the price. ' "Alas! You want to make me die, I can see! A poor impresario who is in such pain! To torment him like that! Look! . . ." and, willy-nilly, I saw!' Hardly knowing whether to laugh or commiserate, Duprez signed.

JOHN ROSSELLI, *The Opera Industry in Italy*

ITALIAN NIGHTS

Stendhal records his first visit to the gorgeous Teatro San Carlo in Naples . . .

Among the benches which fill the pit, every seat is numbered, and *rows one to eleven* are reserved unconditionally for the military – Officers of the *Red Guards*, of the *Blue Guards*, of the *Guards of the Gateway*, etc., etc. – or else are distributed by special favour amongst the *élite* of permanent subscribers; in consequence of which, the unhappy foreigner newly arrived in the city finds himself relegated to the twelfth row. Add to this already considerable distance from the stage the vast area occupied by the orchestra, and you will realize that the unlucky tourist is mercilessly driven well back into the remoter half of the auditorium, and installed willy-nilly in a position whence he can neither see the stage nor hear the singers. No such monstrous system prevails in Milan: at *la Scala*, first come, first served is the rule for every seat. In the fair and fortunate city of Milan, every man may know himself equal of his neighbour; but in Naples, the meanest threadbare *Duke* without a thousand crowns a year to bolster up his pretensions, may invoke the prestige of the best part of a dozen *stars* and *garters* to jab his insolent elbows in my ribs. By contrast, in Milan, an honest citizen with two or three millions to his name will courteously stand aside to let me pass, should I show signs of being in a hurry, expecting me to do the same for him should need arise; and you may study in vain to recognize the bearers of many a famous name, so simple is their aspect and so modest their demeanour. Tonight, exasperated by the insolence of the *gend'armes*, I abandoned the pit and made my way towards the box; and even then, as I climbed the staircase, my temper was scarcely improved by encountering, in descending phalanx, a dozen or fifteen star-spangled Lord-High-Whatnots and Generals, ambling majestically downwards beneath the accumulated weight and grandeur of their mightiness, their braided jackets and their monumental noses. I reflected upon the inscrutable necessity of all this rag-bag of hereditary nobility, stars, privilege, garters and insolence, without which mere *courage* could never be dreamed of in an army. . . .

As I sought to leave the theatre, I found the staircase blocked by a seething mass of people. To reach the exit, there are three steep flights of stairs to be negotiated, with each man crushed hard upon his neighbour's heels. The Neapolitans refer to this as one of the 'beauties' of the place. They have built the pit of their theatre a floor above the ground; this, in terms of modern architecture, is what is described as an 'ingenious improvement'; which means that, since there is but one general staircase to accommodate some two or three thousand spectators, and since this staircase is always cluttered up in any case with a host of footmen and bootblacks, the pleasures of this forced descent may best be left to the reader's own imagination.

To sum it up, then: the *San-Carlo* is a masterpiece of operatic architecture, provided that the curtain remains *down*! I feel in no wise inclined to eat my original words: the first sight of this theatre is indeed overwhelming; but as soon as the curtain goes up, then disappointment follows disappointment, each hard upon the heels of the last. Do you wish to sit in the pit? Then our friends the *gend'armes* will see you safe installed a dozen rows from the front, whence you cannot hear a note, nor yet so much as make out with your eyes whether the actor, whose frantic gestures you dimly perceive upon the distant stage, is young or old. Do you decide to return to your box upstairs? Alas! this self-same dazzling, blinding light pursues you even here. Would you attempt to shut your ears against la Colbran's piercing ululations, by reading the paper until such time as the ballet shall begin? Impossible! Your box has no concealing curtains. Are you suffering from a cold, making it advisable to keep your hat upon your head? Inconceivable! The theatre is being *honoured* by the *presence* of Prince ***. Would you then take refuge in the coffee-house attached to the theatre? Poor comfort – it is nothing but a narrow and lugubrious corridor, of loathsome aspect. Or in the *foyer*? The staircase by which you must pass is so steep and so damnably awkward that, when you reach your goal at last, the breath is quite gone from your body.

...and to the mecca of Italian opera.

24th September [1816]. It was seven o'clock in the evening when I arrived; I was limp with exhaustion; but I dragged myself straight off to *la Scala* . . . and there, at one stroke, lay all the justification of my journey. My senses were so utterly weary that they were beyond the furthest reaches of pleasure. Yet all the fantasy that the most exotic intricacy of an oriental imagination may evolve, all that is most baroque and most bizarre, all that is most sumptuous in architectural devising, all that can be made to live and breathe through the soft brilliance of draperies, all that can be coaxed into reality through the symbolism of characters who have not merely the costume, but the very faces and gestures of their make-belief and alien lands . . . all this and more have I seen tonight. . . .

And now I am just back from *la Scala*. Dear God! My enthusiasm is still screwed to the same pitch as before! I called *la Scala* the finest opera-house in the world, because no other on earth can conjure up so much pure pleasure through the medium of music. There is not a single chandelier in the whole of the auditorium; all the illumination there is comes from the fan of light reflected from the stage. Imagination itself can conceive of nothing more grandiose, more magnificent, more impressive or more original than the *décor*, with its profoundly architectural rhythm. During this evening's performance alone there were eleven changes of scenery. Henceforward and for evermore, I am doomed to contemplate our own theatres with unalleviated disgust; this is the real price and penalty of journeying to Italy.

A box in the third tier costs me the sum of one *sequin* for each evening, on the understanding that I shall continue to reserve it for the entire duration of my stay. In spite of the almost total darkness in the auditorium, I managed perfectly well to pick out different people as they made their way into the pit. It is quite customary to give and acknowledge greetings from box to box across the theatre; I have a footing now in seven or eight different boxes, in each of which there may be five or six persons, and conversation firmly established, as in a *salon*. The tone of society is utterly *natural*, gay without being boisterous, and ruthlessly stripped of gravity.   *Rome, Naples, Florence*

Beneath the entrance arches of the opera house, and on the piazza in front of it, stand elegant policemen decked in tricorns and feathers, swords and white gloves, directing the traffic, an immense mass of Fiats and Alfa Romeos. Like the carriages in days gone by, they drive into the theatre along a proper roadway that leads right through the building. Red carpets are rolled down the steps from the foyer to this street. Liveried attendants open the door, and the ladies and gentlemen who climb out of the cars to assemble in the foyer, before occupying their private boxes, seem to possess the same affable exclusiveness as their Spanish, Bourbon and French forefathers. Hundreds of fans murmur and rustle. The stalls and the boxes pay only the most discreet attention to the opera performance – hands barely moving to offer applause; but in the gallery, and in the upper tiers as a whole, the real audience is to be found, with a fine ear, sceptical gaze, and critical comments, ready at all times for protest, praise, condemnation or encouragement, but also easily carried away by enthusiasm. Here are thin, pallid music students, impoverished lawyers with a glint of expectation beneath their half-closed eyelids, marines, *bersaglieri*, bootblacks, plump petty-bourgeois couples, and diverse representatives of indeterminate trades with elegantly knotted ties and careful suits. These are the great connoisseurs. At this level of the auditorium, where the expensive perfumes of the stalls mingle with the smell of brilliantine and cheap scent, the singers' *pianissimi* fade away, inhaled by open mouths in bewitched faces; here the human drama on the stage is mirrored in moist eyes, the truth and tragedy of life are exorcized into beautiful forms. Strange and lovable life of the San Carlo gallery! What would Verdi, Puccini, Bellini and Donizetti have been without this audience sitting and even standing up there in the dark, and how well they knew the significance of its reactions, its opinions. From here, from 'the gods', fame and love were borne, as if on wings, as if spread by birds' tongues, to the most remote corners of the city; from here the arias were made immortal; simplified, perhaps to the point of unrecognizability, only to rise again from the hot volcanic soil as a new song.

At night, when the opera is over and you are going home, in

thought perhaps still in the *belle époque* or with Taglioni or Grisi, those children are still squatting around the wood fires. It is raining slightly, the fishermen of Mergellina have put up their sad old umbrellas. The neon light in the virtually empty *pizzerie* and *trattorie* gleams pallidly out on to the damp streets. Inside, old musicians are playing dejected tunes on fiddle and mandoline. Everbody is freezing, all the guitars are out of tune. A belated whore hurries by. The fruit barrows for tomorrow morning's market are already in place on the piazza; an old man is guarding them, wedged into a niche, a picture of misery. Humidity rises, cats screech. Beneath the black clouds is a fiery reflection from the blast-furnaces of the Bagnoli industrial works, and the American warships in the harbour cast threatening shadows, or a flashing light blinks an unintelligible warning across the jetty. The sea's calm breaths beat against the walls of the Via Partenope. Everything seems good and still, subdued by the cold, muffled in the heavy mist.

Yet there is a small group of people. A young man squats on the pavement, a guitar on his lap, numb fingers plucking the jangling strings. The youth is singing. Next to him, on the road, stands a Topolino whose door is open, and from the darkness within the car emerge the arpeggios of a second guitar. If it was not for the singing and the strumming you would think they were all asleep – the singer, the invisible player in the car, and the people standing around this scene, with turned-up collars and hands buried in their pockets. Their eyes are closed, no one moves. The light from the street lamp plays on the damp fabric of their suits, amid the raindrops on blue-black hair. Old, and ageless, bitter and tart, a quivering tune floats through the Mediterranean winter's night.

HANS WERNER HENZE, *Music and Politics*

JANACEK

The work is done. And now I look back on the twelve years during which it was given to me to work with and for Janáček.

It began the moment I found myself wedged into the packed gallery standing room at the National Theatre in Prague listening to *Jenůfa*, the music of a composer wholly unknown abroad, appreciated only by a few at a time, derided as a freak by the hacks. My heart was instantly captivated by those rhythms, not only simple and natural but also laden with a new kind of power of strong sensibility. And I count it as one of my life's great blessings that I was able to find Janáček (who was already sixty-two at the time *Jenůfa* was first produced in Prague) and that I could help him gain his present unquestioned general recognition. With the translation of his *opus posthumus* I come to the end of a labor that encompasses, besides several essays, the translation of *Jenůfa, Katya Kabanová, The Cunning Little Vixen, The Makropulos Affair*, the indescribably beautiful *Diary of a Vanished Man*, several songs and choral works, as well as my monograph *Leoš Janáček*. The work is complete but it is not done – for the significance of Janáček, however highly he may be esteemed, is still not appreciated in its entirety; his choral works for example are all too little known and German opera houses have so far not seen fit to bring to life the Panic sensuality and all the innocent and joyful pagan enchantment of his tale of forests and animals, *The Cunning Little Vixen*.

The greatness and power of the *House of the Dead*, which is in some respects a dark counterpart of the joyful *Vixen*, disclose once more the full force of an elemental creative personality in whose immeasurable depths cold bloodnumbing terror slumbered alongside childlike fond play, both of them inborn and familiar to the demoniac man who here and there brought them forth to limn them as sounds. Through a careful hearing one might gather from the look and expression of the living man something of the great silence of eternity.

MAX BROD, note to the libretto of From the House of the Dead

The central point of Janáček's creative work is his opera *Jenůfa*, with libretto by Gabriela Preiss, a work into which he poured all his pain and love. His remark about it is well known: '*Jenůfa* is tied up with the black ribbon of the long illness, pains and cries of my daughter Olga, and my little boy Vladimír.' Janáček wrote on the title page of *Jenůfa*: 'In memory of my daughter Olga.'

After the completion of *Jenůfa* Janáček sent the opera to the National Theatre in Prague. The director of the opera, Karel Kovařovic, refused it and gave as his reason that there were technical faults in the score. Janáček's faith in himself as an artist was deeply shaken, but he held his own. Mrs Janáček remembers the scene: 'We were in the room where Olga was dying. My husband sat at his desk and suddenly clutched his head in his hands and tears started streaming down his face. In this sharp fit of depression, he began to blame himself for knowing nothing. This was more than I could stand. I had always believed in him as an artist, and I believed especially in the beauty and greatness of *Jenůfa*. I took his head in my arms and, crying myself, tried to comfort him. My great faith in his work enabled me to find the right words of comfort. They must have been convincing because he gradually calmed himself. After that, I kept watch over him so as to avoid the recurrence of such a shock.'

Letters and Reminiscences of Leos Janáček

JUSTICE

The New England Opera Theatre tour was interrupted in Iowa, a few weeks ago, when the driver of a bus carrying Boris Goldovsky and his troupe was arrested for speeding. Justice of the Peace Rudy Frisch, presiding over the traffic court, reduced the fine from $12 to $6 when he heard that the *Merry Masquerade* Company, which had been hurrying to open in Minnetonka, Missouri, was responsible for a *Marriage of Figaro* he had enjoyed in Boston.

Reported in *Opera News*, 1953

KNOT GARDEN

I confess to having once written that Michael Tippett's libretto for his own opera The Knot Garden *was 'an absurd sub-Eliotic farrago ... so resonant with meanings, allusions and elisions as to be completely devoid of the light of ordinary human sense'. Paul Driver argues otherwise, in his sustained scrutiny of what is certainly one of the most musically exciting and beautiful of post-war operas.*

The Knot Garden, like *The Tempest*, begins with a magic storm. Unlike *The Tempest*'s it is only half-real; it is half psychological or symbolic. Mangus, professional analyst and would-be Prospero, has conjured it as a display, for his own satisfaction and the audience's, of his magical or hypnotic power. He sits, at the centre of the whirlwind, on the couch of his profession. But then, 'at a gesture from him, the couch disappears'. The magic was not unreal.

The opera's setting is our modern urban world. The existence of the transcendent is no more excluded from this world, however, than it was from the timeless, allegoric world of *The Midsummer Marriage* or from the ancient mythological world of *King Priam*. The transcendent shadows and glints through the confused doings of the modern men and women presented, and takes them dimly by surprise. A clear perception of its significance is not permitted them; they are merely to be bewildered by it into a provisional and partial cognisance of broader scope to their lives.

What happens to them in the course of the opera may be compared to what happens to Alice in her two books of surreal adventures. Only *The Knot Garden* is a bitterer comedy; experience bites on the characters with a sharper tooth; the music that embodies them and entertains us is always 'music that's bitter-sweet'.

Mangus' storm at the outset has something of the formal function of the fall down the rabbit-hole at the beginning of *Alice in Wonderland*. Once down it, once swept by Mangus' magic, you do not find that events, however ordinary they may seem, are altogether accurate. They are liable to bump into each other, be suddenly curtailed, lack the expected definition, lose sight of the logic that brought them into being, or just 'dissolve'. The characters' environment has a corresponding instability – an urban garden can turn into a maze; a 'fabulous rose garden' materializes because of a song, and fades once the song is over. The setting is zany, yet recognisably modern; the opera is magical yet sobering.

It is true that in *The Knot Garden* the supernatural is not capable of the grand interventions it makes in the two preceding operas by Tippett. But in a more puckish way it can strike at any moment. And it is a serious mistake of production to attenuate its role: ... none of Tippett's operas, not even *The Ice Break*, can be regarded as 'secular'.

The next thing that happens in Act 1, 'Confrontation', of *The Knot Garden* is the appearance of Thea, coming slowly from 'the inner garden', which as her conversation with Mangus makes clear is her own inner world, wherein 'I touch the tap-root/ To my inward sap'. With a slightly Humpty-Dumptyish petulance she informs Mangus: 'Only I may prune this garden ... Pruning is the crown.' Or, to change the metaphor, we are in the *Looking-Glass's* Garden of Live Flowers; and promptly in runs one of them, Thea's adolescent ward Flora, with an 'Ah-ee, ah-ee'. Thea's husband Faber follows, and is given *Hamlet*-ish advice by Thea to 'cut the offensive action', his supposed flirtations with Flora. The tensions in the garden are manifest, the knots tightly drawn. Faber is almost speechlessly exasperated. He withdraws 'to the factory', and Thea sinks deeper into her garden. Mangus sees life exploding as the result, unless the 'priest-magician' intervenes.

Flora is also Alice, an Alice grown out of her childhood serenity, more susceptible, but no less alert and inquisitive. Presently she has an encounter with Tweedle-Dee and Tweedle-Dum, American and Englishman, writer and composer, Caliban and Ariel, 'black earth' and 'white roses', Mel and Dov. Like everyone in the opera, they are 'acting a scene'. Thea, bearing a tray of cocktails, disparages them as 'children at play'. But Mangus knows that 'adults too play later'.

All must act because all have lost their own selves. When Faber returns to discover Dov howling, 'like Ariel's dog' on all fours, and asks: 'Who in hell are you?' he means it literally. When Mangus comes on carrying a mass of coloured costumes for charades, he intones: 'We be but men of sin. So sounds the accusation.'

The long, intensely beautiful formal aria of Thea's freedom-fighter sister, Denise, extols a world of tortured integrity beyond the masks and game-playing of 'the beautiful and damned'. But the blues ensemble ending Act 1 immediately bombards her 'true' song with lacerated parody of negro tribulation. Whether she knows it or likes it, she too is involved in this *Alice* world; she, too, has a fuller self to discover at the end of a labyrinth.

She and her sister are the first to be whirled into that 'Labyrinth' which is the second act. And it is her collision with Mel in the middle of it that brings the most heartfelt music of the opera, a richly harmonized, cantabile melody for strings, remembering the tune of 'We shall overcome'. As Mel sings: 'A man is for real,' and Denise: 'Should I not follow such a man?' the clichés almost dissolve into the truth.

What actually stills the tumult of the act is the strange meeting of Flora and Dov. They are blown together, two delicate flowers, to rest on each other. Dov asks her whether she likes music. She replies with a verse from a Schubert song, which Dov then 'musingly' translates: '... my love's so fond of green.' He answers with a 'different song', a modern pastoral, 'I was born in a big town.' The refrain of this marvellously transformed rock-number is 'Play it cool, play it cool' – perhaps gentle advice to Flora herself. By the end of the song, the 'fabulous rose-garden' mentioned in the last line, and which has been gradually forming under the influence of

Dov's music, has completely appeared: 'the enclosing walls, the fountain, the girl, the lover, the music.'

It is the equivalent of Prospero's masque in Act 4 of *The Tempest*, and in the same way the beautiful illusion is shattered. Just as Prospero was brought news of Caliban's fresh misdeeds, so here 'a shadow enters the garden' and 'taps the lover on the shoulder'. It is Mel; 'I taught you that', he reminds Dov. And the garden fades, leaving, like Prospero's apparition, not a wrack behind.

One marvels at the skill with which this scene has been musically enacted. The Schubert melody is able to float into the texture with no disturbance of tone, and a perfectly magical evocativeness. The throbbing jazzy figurations of the electric guitar, bass clarinet and lower strings in Dov's song seem a natural, if new, item of Tippett's vocabulary; the seriousness and formality of the aria are unmistakeable, even if the operatic genre has been seachanged. The theatrical poise here is no less impressive. The scene grips the attention and complexly clinches the act. At the same time, one may let oneself be reminded of those occasions in the *Alice* books when Alice is asked to recite something, only to be interrupted by a long recitation of the questioner's own.

The 'Charade' third act moves swiftly and with brilliance. The allusiveness of the opera, which colours what Ian Kemp finds to be the work's 'expressionism' is here at its most extreme and challenging. As Mangus tells Thea, 'The play has bewildering moments.' An elaborate re-enactment of *The Tempest*, in which scenes sometimes go awry, leads the characters gradually out of their muddle and darkness into daylight sobriety (though the opera ends in a 'vast night') and a modest submission to love ('If for a timid moment...').

All sorts of peculiar confrontations occur, as when Faber-as-Ferdinand-as-a-jailor brings on Dov-Ariel in handcuffs, speech-singing with a Cockney accent: 'He's gone off his food./ His wings are drooping./ He used to sing before.'; or when Dov-Ariel unduly belabours Mel-Caliban, going beyond the script, 'As I shall always do;' or when Flora-Miranda furiously upsets the chess-board on which she has been playing with Faber-Ferdinand (and the diaphonous accompanying music also), protesting his real-life falsity, provoking him to reply, 'That scene went wrong!' and Mangus-Prospero to return, 'That scene went right!'

What we are witnessing seems part mimesis of contemporary 'family-therapy', and part reminiscence of the anarchic trial scene at the end of *Alice in Wonderland*.

A dramatic signal that the therapy is working comes with the reprise halfway through the act (just after the chess-playing scene) of the opera's opening glissandoed 12-note theme. Taking it for accompaniment, Thea sings an aria of eerie beauty, declaring: 'I am no more afraid.'

The emotional fullness of her reunion at the end with her husband Faber will be signalled in like manner by an analogous gesture, an uprushing scale-passage that nearly saturates chromatic space. Adapting words from Virginia Woolf's *Between The Acts* the couple sing 'The curtain rises'. It has risen for them, and for Mel, who has somewhat found himself in Denise, and for Flora, no longer an Alice but a private woman (she departs 'alone, radiant, dancing').

Dov remains benighted. He will live further and find himself better in the *Songs for Dov* which Tippett conceived as a pendant to the opera.

The magical metaphor is not omitted in the closing scenes of *The Knot Garden*. All characters join to sing lines adapted from a poem by Goethe which apparently were inspiration for the opera from the earliest stage of its conception: 'We sense the magic net/ That holds us veined/ Each to each to all.' Though, by this time, Mangus has already broken his staff, drowned his book and told the audience that 'Prospero's a fake'. We remember the opera's epigraph, from the mouth of the rogue Parolles in *All's Well That End's Well*: 'Simply the thing I am shall make me live.'

LADY MACBETH
OF MTSENSK

Several theatres have presented the opera *Lady Macbeth of the
Mtsensk District* by Shostakovich to this new Soviet public.
Officious music critics exalt this opera to the high heavens and
spread its fame far and wide. From the first minute the listener is
shocked by a deliberately discordant, confused stream of sounds.
Fragments of melody, embryonic phrases appear, only to disap-
pear again in the din, the grinding and the screaming. To follow
this 'music' is difficult, to remember it impossible. So it goes on
almost throughout the opera. Cries take the place of song. If by
chance the composer lapses into simple, comprehensible melody,
he is scared at such a misfortune and quickly plunges into confusion again. . . . All this is coarse, primitive and vulgar. The music
quacks, grunts and growls, and suffocates itself in order to
express the amatory scenes as naturalistically as possible. And
'love' is smeared all over the opera in this vulgar manner. The
merchant's double bed occupies the central position on the stage.
On it all problems are solved. . . . *Lady Macbeth* enjoys great
success with audiences abroad. Is it not because the opera is
absolutely unpolitical and confusing that they praise it? Is it not
explained by the fact that it tickles the perverted tastes of the
bourgeoisie with its fidgety, screaming, neurotic music?

Pravda, 1936

That article on the third page of *Pravda* changed my entire
existence. It was printed without a signature, like an editorial –
that is, it expressed the opinion of the Party. But it actually
expressed the opinion of Stalin, and that was much more important.   DMITRI SHOSTAKOVICH, *Testimony*

I heard *Lady Macbeth* by Shostakovich conducted by Rodzinski with his Cleveland Orchestra. A well-organized advertising campaign bore its fruit, exciting all the N.Y. snobs. The work is lamentably provincial, the music plays a miserable role as illustrator, in a very embarrassing realistic style. It is in recitative form with interludes between the acts – marches brutally hammering in the manner of Prokofiev, and monotonous – and each time the curtains were lowered, the conductor was acclaimed by an audience more than happy to be brutalized by the arrogance of the numerous communist brass instruments. This première (and I hope *dernière*) reminds me of the performances of Kurt Weill two years ago in Paris and all the première-goers and the snobs of my dear new country. Happily, this was the only event on this trip in the United States that did not make a very good impression on me.

STRAVINSKY, to Ernst Ansermet, 1935

LOTTE LEHMANN
AND THE LIONESS

How could anyone have suspected that luncheon with a notorious mass-murderer would be amusing and entertaining? And yet I had this sensational, even if not exactly enviable, experience.

The Scene: The Ministry of Education in Berlin. The Time: 1933 – I don't remember the date exactly. The Participants: the Minister of Education, Göring; his future wife Emmy Sonnemann; the Director of the State Opera House in Berlin – and I. The lioness came later.

I have always lived for music. Especially so during the time when the Vienna Opera was my real home, and the whole universe seemed to me merely a backdrop for the stage, to which I was devoted with every breath of my body. I had never taken any interest in politics, and, unsuspecting, had assumed that the Nazi régime would mean nothing more than an unpleasant temporary change of government in Germany. Not for one moment did I realize that it meant the beginning of a world-shattering struggle between good and evil. I knew next to nothing about Hitler, since I read only those parts of the paper that dealt with music and the arts, so whenever the conversation turned to him I would always interrupt impatiently with: 'For God's sake, why should I concern myself with politics?'

Of course, as I write this I realize that I was behaving like an idiot (and the more I think about it all, the more I recognize that indeed I was an idiot). But I must be honest, and show myself as I really was. One day, I received a telephone call from Berlin: it was the Director of the Berlin State Opera. 'Frau Kammersängerin, would you be interested in coming to Berlin for a few guest appearances? His Excellency, the Minister of Education, Herr Göring, is personally inviting you.'

'Thank you, Herr Generalintendant. But I am so happy here in Vienna that I'd leave only if it were made worth my while. Berlin doesn't pay higher salaries than Vienna, so why should I come and incur extra expenses?'

'Let's forget the question of salary, Frau Kammersängerin!'

'Oh no, that's just what I won't forget. I am an idealist when I sing, but when I draw up a contract I have both feet firmly on the ground.'

'I mean we can forget about the amount of salary. That's all taken care of. Off the record, I can tell you you will get whatever you ask.'

'Really, since when is that?'

'Since this moment, Frau Kammersängerin. . . .'

I was speechless. The Director had to repeat: 'Hello' anxiously several times before I could find words to answer him.

'Well, of course – in that case – how could I refuse? And yet, should I— What on earth has happened? Have they lost their reason in Berlin?'

'We'll discuss all that later, Frau Kammersängerin. Please! When can you come here for a conference about it? All your expenses will, of course, be refunded. No limit has been set on them. Believe me, I beg you. No limit.'

'But why is that? What's happened at the Berlin Opera? Have you all become millionaires or something?'

'Yes, yes, perhaps. . . . Please keep questions until we meet. The main thing is, that in principle you agree to come as guest artist to Berlin. That is enormously important.'

'Goodness, you're being very ceremonious! Why shouldn't I agree in principle to sing in Berlin? Especially if, as you say, there are no limits in the matter of fees. What can you be thinking? Here in Vienna we're *not* millionaires.'

'You are quite right. Why should you not agree in principle? That was a remarkably sensible answer, Frau Kammersängerin. You will be hearing from me.'

'I can't come this month, because I have a first night. But next month I shall be in Germany anyway, on a recital tour. Perhaps I can see you then. Till then, good-bye.'

'Stop, wait a moment, please. Couldn't you cancel your first night? The Berlin Opera would make themselves responsible for any losses incurred.'

'Cancel a first night?' (I nearly said: 'Have you gone mad?' But one doesn't say that to the Director of an Opera House.) 'Can't you wait for just one month?'

'It'll be difficult. But if it must be . . . Good-bye!'

A few weeks later I was giving recitals in Germany. I've forgotten in which town it was that the following took place. During my recital, in the middle of a song, I suddenly sensed a curious unrest in the audience. It irritated me immensely, and I attempted, by closing my eyes, to regain my concentration. But the unrest only grew worse. I opened my eyes, and saw, right in front of me, a man, an official of some kind, who was desperately trying to interrupt me in mid-song. Little did he know me! I again closed my eyes, and sang to the end, disregarding the mounting unrest all around me. When I had finished my song, I bent down to the interrupter and whispered: 'What's the matter? Why are you interrupting me?'

He looked at me with pleading eyes, and I noticed with astonishment that he was shaking with nerves from head to foot. 'His

Excellency, the Minister of Education, is on the telephone. He wishes to speak to you.'

I laughed in his face. It must have been a tremendous shock for him when I said: 'First I shall complete my group of songs. How dare you interrupt me like this?'

I finished the group of songs. No applause. The audience sat paralysed. Only later did I realize why. They must have thought that I had fallen into disfavour, and expected me to be arrested at any moment. I had no idea at the time, though today I can hardly comprehend how I could have been so stupid.

I did not hurry to get to the telephone. Göring's adjutant was at the other end. (Or should I say: at the other end of the *World*?)

With military curtness: 'His Excellency will be sending you his private plane! Where to, please?'

I found this very funny. 'Oh, well, if I'm allowed to choose – why not to my hotel window?'

Icy silence.

'Hallo – are you there?'

'Frau Kammersängerin, we shall be expecting you here at the aerodrome at eleven o'clock tomorrow morning. May I ask you not to be late.'

I was punctual. Soldiers stood on guard, and just as I was about to pass through their ranks towards the glittering plane, they barred my way. But my name worked wonders: I was escorted as if I had been at least a princess, and was soon sitting by the side of my accompanist Franz Rupp, who had refused to be done out of the experience of travelling in the gigantic cabin of the private aeroplane of His Excellency.

In those days flying was for me still an exciting and wonderful experience, and I relished this flight over the shimmering clouds, above which I seemed to be hurtling towards some unknown fate. But above those clouds I think Heaven must have been protecting me, not only during this romantic flight, but later, when I was saved from making a hasty decision that might have landed me unwittingly in a trap leading straight to my destruction. Of one thing I am certain: had I been foolish enough to stay in Germany I should have ended up in a concentration camp. I can never keep my mouth shut and, once I grasped the whole frightful situation, I should have said things which, during that terrible time, could have meant only my end. But I was protected and I am grateful; more grateful than I can express.

The Director of the Opera was waiting for me at the aerodrome. He was a changed man. He looked thin, and his face seemed tired and anxious. In the car on the way to Berlin he tried to explain to me that the times had changed drastically. 'Above all, do be careful, and please think before saying anything,' he whispered, nervously watching the chauffeur, who could certainly not hear a word through the dividing glass.

'Why are you whispering? He can't hear a thing.'

'Oh, one can't be certain. When we arrive let me do the talking, it would be much better if you said nothing.'

'You'd have to kill me to achieve that.'

He looked at me in horror. I didn't understand. 'Don't joke about such things,' he said, and his voice was trembling.

After a silence, interrupted only by his violent breathing, he regained control of himself. 'His Excellency is very interested in you. He wants you for the Berlin Opera, not only as a guest artist, but as a permanent member of the company.'

'Oh no! I love Vienna, and I wouldn't even think of leaving it.'

Silence.

'What would you say if I advised you in the strictest confidence to think about it most carefully. You can make whatever demands you like, and they will be granted. Understand me aright: whatever you ask, literally. Name a figure, it is yours. Make any conditions you like, mention any personal wishes, they will all be granted.' I didn't understand.

'Has everybody gone mad here?'

He heaved a sigh. Almost inaudibly he whispered: 'Yes, perhaps. Yes, perhaps that's what it is. But you can profit from this state of affairs. Only be careful, and don't blurt out everything that is in your mind. His Excellency is very sensitive, you must never make him angry. You understand? Never!'

'All this sounds as if I were going to be fed to the lions.'

For the first time he smiled slightly. 'His Excellency has a tame lioness. She is his favourite pet. It would be a good idea if you were to tell him that you liked lions.'

'That I can do with a good conscience, because I like all animals. And right now a lioness seems to me rather less terrifying than your noble master. Good God, why are you suddenly so terribly nervy? None can hear what we are saying.'

With an anxious look at the chauffeur he only answered: 'I hope not.'

We drove to the Ministry of Education. Soldiers everywhere. Swastikas everywhere. The 'Heil Hitler' greeting everywhere. It all seemed to me like rather third-rate theatre, and I said as much, which produced a very heavy fit of coughing from the Director of the Opera; no doubt in order to drown my thoughtless remark. But who could have heard me, that's what I should have liked to know.

Göring kept us waiting. It was the day of Hitler's birthday, and there was a huge parade at which, of course, Göring had to make an appearance. But he had left a message that we should make ourselves at home. Feel at home! Hardly likely, since every time I opened my mouth the Director of the Opera looked at me as if I were about to pronounce my own death sentence. (My God, how right he was!) I finally held my tongue because his caution seemed just too ridiculous. Also my stomach was showing signs of revolt: parade to the right of me, parade to the left of me, I was getting famished. I voiced my surprise that I hadn't been given an appointment at a time that involved less waiting, but the Director only smiled wanly, and murmured: 'One learns to hang about in antechambers, believe me, one learns that.'

I want to keep strictly to the truth, although it would be tempting to say that Göring's arrival was heralded with a blare of trumpets. But it seems to me that he could not simply have come in at the door like an ordinary mortal, that his entrance would have been specially staged. What a pity I love the truth so! My imagination could so easily go off into the most extravagant fantasies. As it is, I remember him very well: a fairly corpulent young man in a skyblue uniform, who greeted us in an extraordinarily friendly way, and then immediately excused himself as he had first to go and exercise his horse. Why the horse had to be exercised at this precise, and inconvenient, moment, I couldn't immediately make out. But I soon saw through the noble horseman's secret intent: childlike, he wanted to impress us, and so he rode a few times along the garden paths, magnificently mounted, glittering in his shimmering uniform, the heroic breast bedecked with a row of medals. I surveyed him, like a young girl from the age of chivalry, who looked down from her balcony and smiled proudly at her chosen suitor. It was difficult not to laugh, I must say!

My poor stomach rumbled some more when Göring announced that he would now have to take a bath.

We waited. Meanwhile Emmy Sonnemann came in, looking very lyrical and charming. I didn't know quite what to say to her, and stared in fascination at her beautiful bosom, swastika-bedecked. There was no contact between us, which is strange for two theatre people. She tried, as I did, to find a common subject of conversation, but in vain.

At last, at last: the people's darling! He was wearing a kind of tennis garb, at least that's what it looked like to me. I don't know anything about military uniforms, so I can't say whether the white jacket was part of one. He was carrying a riding crop in his hand, and had a wide knife in his belt. Curiously enough, he used this knife later at table to cut his bread.

Perhaps it will be hard to believe what I shall write about this luncheon. But that's just another proof that the truth can sound far more unlikely than some shameless lie. I want to describe, clearly and truthfully, what has remained in my memory.

Göring came straight to the point. 'I read about your success in America,' he said, between mouthfuls (at last we were having something to eat!), 'and you caused me a sleepless night. Yes. I thought of your future. You had earned a good deal of money, and you are likely to pay it into a bank in Vienna, where the Jews will deprive you of it.'

'Nonsense, my money would be perfectly safe. Anyway, I don't need other people to lose my money for me. I spend it fast enough myself. I have no talent for saving.'

'But what about your future? What will become of you – later?'

'Oh, good gracious, I've got plenty of time to think about that. In any case I shall be getting my pension from the Vienna Opera.'

He laughed about that. It was a most unpleasant laugh, and I began to feel very uncomfortable. 'The Vienna Opera! You surely don't enjoy singing for Schuschnigg?'

'But I don't sing only for Herr Schuschnigg, I sing for the whole world. In any case, I find Schuschnigg simply charming.'

The Director of the Opera seemed to be suffering from a severe cold. He coughed violently, and I saw that he had to wipe the sweat from his brow.

Curiously enough, Göring reacted not at all to my thoughtless remark. He placed the knife and the riding crop on the table, looked at me smiling, and said, in quite a friendly manner, 'Let's forget Vienna for a moment. Let's talk about your contract!'

'What contract?'

'With the Berlin Opera.'

I don't know what made me so dangerously imprudent, despite all previous warnings. I ignored the imploring looks of the Opera Director, and said very quietly to Göring:

'I am not in the habit of discussing contracts between a knife and a whip.'

Later, the Opera Director informed me that I might have had ample opportunity to bitterly regret my audacity had Göring not taken a liking to me. Not that I find that flattering. Many women found favour with Göring, and today I shudder when I think that this man should have sat next to me, and that I broke bread with him. Probably it was a completely new experience for him to be challenged in this way, and my apparent fearlessness may have pleased him. If that was the case, he greatly overrated me. I am a terrible coward, and if I had had an inkling of what this man was really like, I would have fainted from sheer terror. I hadn't the slightest idea, and the whole conversation, and his curious behaviour, amused me enormously. Looking back today, however, I feel as though I had walked where the ice lay thinnest under the glittering surface, and where terrible depths yawned beneath my feet.

Göring had only smiled. He himself proposed a fee. I have

forgotten how much it was, I only know that it was a fantastic amount. I think I could have asked double, and he would have granted it, but I was speechless at the offer.

Again and again he asked me whether I did not have any particular personal requests to make, and explained that, as well as my salary, I should be given a villa, and, naturally, a life pension of a thousand marks per month (at that time a respectable sum). A horse would always be at my disposal (so he knew about my passion for riding), and there would be opportunities of lone morning rides with him, 'the most glorious of them all'. His friend Emmy was very silent during this conversation. She watched both of us with a friendly smile – and I so wanted to know what she was thinking.

Yet again he asked me whether I did not have any special wish. I could no longer remain serious, and said, laughing: 'Oh yes! I should like a castle on the Rhine.' This ridiculous remark, which I naturally made as a joke, later went right round Germany: 'Did you hear that the Lehmann demanded a castle on the Rhine?' This strikes me as the funniest part of the whole story.

Of course Göring also had a few wishes: he expected me, as a matter of course, never to sing outside Germany again. 'You should not go out into the world,' he said dramatically. 'The world should come to us, if it wants to hear you.'

'But an artist belongs to the whole world. Why should I limit myself to one country? Music is an international language, and as one of its messengers I wish to sing everywhere, all over the world.'

Blushing furiously, Göring looked at me with icy contempt. 'First and foremost, you are a German. Or perhaps not?'

As I was about to answer hastily and thoughtlessly, I happened to glance at the Director of the Opera. His look of deathly terror stopped me.

So I half agreed to the contract with Berlin. The warning that I would be allowed to sing only in Germany I did not take very seriously. Nor did I take seriously some of the remarks that had sounded like hidden threats. I gathered only that this was a contract which it would have been sheer madness to refuse.

Göring, highly delighted, ordered the contract to be drawn up at once, adding: 'I personally stand guarantee for everything that I have promised you!' We then somehow came to speak about the critics. I don't exactly remember how we got on to the subject, and Göring said with a curious smile: 'And in Berlin you will never get bad notices!'

'Why? I may give a bad performance, and not deserve praise.'

'If I myself think you are singing well, no critic will have a different opinion. And if he dares, he will be liquidated.'

This sounded so absurd to me that I simply laughed. I didn't dream that he could be in deadly earnest. It was a joke, a childish joke, and a tactless one at that. In later years I often read descriptions of Göring, and thought that he must have changed a great deal. He was described as sinister and sickly looking. Also that he used make-up, and seemed mentally disturbed. I saw or felt nothing of all this at the time. He was already fairly corpulent, and dressed somewhat loudly. But he gave the impression of being a perfectly harmless and amiable young man. He even had charm, however strange that may sound. In any case, that's how it was at this luncheon. He laughed often and heartily, and the threatening remark about the unhappy critics seemed just a joke. How could I suspect the horrors that lived beneath the smooth brow?

Emmy spoke very little. Only once did she say, softly, and with an expression of fervent devotion: 'What good fortune it will be for you to be allowed to sing for our Führer!'

I don't remember what I murmured in reply. I remember only the beseeching and commanding looks of the Director of the Opera. But I have a feeling that Emmy understood a great deal, and that she had not taken me to her heart.

After the meal, while Emmy was talking to the Director, Göring stood a little apart with me. He was looking at me now in a way that Emmy was not meant to see. 'You will have everything that you wish for,' he said softly and secretively, 'all your wishes will come true before you even express them.'

I found him in this vein a little oppressive, and was relieved when Emmy came, and interrupted our *tête à tête*. Her graceful walk made me think of a beautiful young lioness. Lioness! I nearly forgot. 'I hear that your Excellency has a lioness. May I see her?'

'In the cage?'

'Oh no! Here, free!'

How a coward like myself could have asked for anything quite so mad is a mystery to me to the present day. But everything seemed so unreal that my feeling for the dramatic seemed to require some kind of climax. I think that's what it must have been.

The others did not share my enthusiasm. The Director of the Opera blanched. Emmy frowned, and said softly: 'Our Führer is particularly concerned over the priceless life of His Excellency. The lioness is far too big for a toy. We all tremble for His Excellency's life.'

Good God! This time I had really committed a grave folly. I felt quite sick, but not for the world must Göring suspect. So I asked him again, inwardly shaking, for the favour of seeing the lioness.

Sometimes I think that I only dreamt it all, that I only dreamt I saw a huge lioness come into the room, walk around me snarling softly, that I stroked her head because I knew Göring was only waiting for some signal of my fear, and that His Excellency, the Minister of Education, threw himself on to the sofa and romped about with her like a child. Without question, the lioness loved him. Perhaps she was the only living being that really loved him, loyally, without suspicion, and completely without respect!

Göring was delighted to tell me that the lioness had recently torn the seat of a man's trousers as he was standing on a ladder putting up a picture. 'The coward nearly died of fright,' he shouted, laughing. He thought the episode an enormous joke.

I was standing by the window. The lioness came over to me, and put her paw on the window sill. And she, Göring and I looked out of the window. That memory is, for me, an endless source of delight. Göring, the lioness and I. I wish I could paint, it's a picture that would show me in a bright heroic light: 'The fearless German woman' between two wild beasts, of which the lioness was the less dangerous.   *Opera* 66

Lotte Lehmann did not sing for the Nazis; in 1938 she emigrated to the USA.

LIBRETTOS

*A letter of Monteverdi to his librettist Alessandro Striggio,
1616.*

My Most Illustrious Lord and Most Respected Master,

I received Your Lordship's letter . . . with most hearty rejoicing,
also the little book containing the maritime fable *Le Nozze di
Tetide*. Your Lordship writes that you are sending it to me so that I
may look at it carefully and then give you my opinion, as it has to
be set to music for use at the forthcoming wedding of His Highness [Ferdinando, Sixth Duke of Mantua]. I, who long for nothing
so much as to be of some worth in His Highness's service, shall say
no more in my initial reply than this, Your Lordship – that I offer
myself readily for whatever His Highness may at any time deign to
command me, and always without question honour and revere all
that His Highness commands.

So, if His Highness approves of this fable it ought therefore to
be very beautiful and much to my taste. But if you add that I may
speak my mind, I am bound to obey Your Lordship's instructions
with all respect and promptness, realizing that whatever I may say
is a mere trifle, being a person worth little in all things, and a
person who always honours every virtuoso, in particular the
present Signor Poet (whose name I know not), and so much the
more because this profession of poetry is not mine.

I shall say, then, with all due respect – and in order to obey you
since you so command – I shall say first of all in general that music
wishes to be mistress of the air, not only of the water; I mean (in
my terminology) that the ensembles described in that fable are all
low-pitched and near to the earth, an enormous drawback to
beautiful harmony since the continuo instruments will be placed

among the bigger creatures at the back of the set – difficult for everyone to hear, and difficult to perform within the set.

And so I leave the decision about this matter to your most refined and most intelligent taste, for because of that defect you will need three theorbos instead of one, and you would want three harps instead of one, and so on and so forth: and instead of a delicate singing voice you would have a forced one. Besides this, in my opinion, the proper imitation of the words should be dependent upon wind instruments rather than upon strings and delicate instruments, for I think that the music of the Tritons and the other sea-gods should be assigned to trombones and cornetti, not to citterns or harpsichords and harps, since the action (being maritime) properly takes place outside the city; and Plato teaches us that 'the cithara should be in the city, and the tibia in the country' – so either the delicate will be unsuitable, or the suitable not delicate.

In addition, I have noticed that the interlocutors are winds, Cupids, little Zephyrs and Sirens: consequently many sopranos will be needed, and it can also be stated that the winds have to sing – that is, the Zephyrs and the Boreals. How, dear Sir, can I imitate the speech of the winds, if they do not speak? And how can I, by such means, move the passions? Ariadne moved us because she was a woman, and similarly Orpheus because he was a man, not a wind. Music can suggest, without any words, the noise of winds and the bleating of sheep, the neighing of horses and so on and so forth; but it cannot imitate the speech of winds because no such thing exists.

Next, the dances which are scattered throughout the fable do not have dance measures. And as to the story as a whole – as far as my no little ignorance is concerned – I do not feel that it carries me in a natural manner to an end that moves me. *Arianna* led me to a just lament, and *Orfeo* to a righteous prayer, but this fable leads me I don't know to what end. So what does Your Lordship want the music to be able to do? Nevertheless I shall always accept everything with due reverence and honour if by chance His Highness should so command and desire it, since he is my master without question. . . .

I also consider-it, in this respect, much too long as regards each of the speaking parts, from the Sirens onwards (and some other little discourse). Forgive me, dear Sir, if I have said too much; it was not to disparage anything, but through a desire to obey your orders, because if it has to be set to music (and were I so commanded), Your Lordship might take my thoughts into consideration. I beg you in all affection to regard me as a most devoted and most humble servant to His Highness, to whom I make a most humble reverence, and I kiss Your Lordship's hands with all affection and pray God for the fulfilment of your every happiness. From Venice, 9 December 1616.

> Your Lordship's (to whom, most affectionately, I wish
> a happy holiday)
> most humble and most devoted servant,
> CLAUDIO MONTEVERDI

Perhaps the most creative collaboration between composer and librettist was that between Richard Strauss and Hugo von Hofmannsthal. The following letters record one episode in the evolution of Ariadne auf Naxos, *in July 1911.*

Dear Herr von Hofmannsthal,

The whole of *Ariadne* is now safely in my hands and I like it well enough: I think there'll be some good use for everything. Only I should have preferred the dialogue between Ariadne and Bacchus to be rather more significant, with livelier emotional *crescendo*. This bit must soar higher, like the end of *Elektra*, sunnier, more Dionysian: harness your Pegasus for a little longer, I can give you another four weeks at least before I've caught up on you with the music.

I have just finished the entertaining dance scene: 'Die Dame gibt mit trübem Sinn.' Ariadne's expectation of the messenger of death has also come out well.

Zerbinetta's rondo is partly sketched out: you see, I'm not idle;

but for the conclusion I need something more soaring: 'Freude schöner Götterfunke.'

Shall I see you in Munich in August? Have a good rest now, stretch out under the beeches and dream a little more about Dionysus and Ariadne!

With best regards, yours,

RICHARD STRAUSS

My dear Doctor Strauss,

I must confess I was somewhat piqued by your scant and cool reception of the finished manuscript of *Ariadne*, compared with the warm welcome you gave to every single act of *Rosenkavalier* – which stands out in my memory as one of the most significant pleasures connected with that work. I believe that in *Ariadne* I have produced something at least equally good, equally original and novel, and although we certainly agree in wishing to shun anything like the false show of mutual adulation in which mediocre artists indulge, I cannot help asking myself whether any praise in the world could make up to me for the absence of yours.

You may of course have written your letter or read the manuscript when you were somewhat out of sorts, as happens so easily to creative artists; nor do I overlook the fact that a fairly subtle piece of work like this inevitably suffers seriously by being presented in manuscript rather than clear typescript (unfortunately my typist was ill). And so I am not without hope that closer acquaintance with my libretto will bring home to you its positive qualities. Set pieces like, say, the intermezzo, Zerbinetta's aria and the ensemble will not, I venture to say, be surpassed in their own line by anyone writing in Europe today. The way in which this work – though it adheres to the conventional form (which, properly understood, is full of appeal even to the librettist) – indicates and establishes its central idea quite naturally by making Ariadne and Zerbinetta represent diametrical contrasts in female character, or the manner in which I have led up to the arrival of Bacchus, first by the trio of the three women cutting each other short, next by the little Circe song, and finally by Zerbinetta's announcement which, though important in itself, gives the orchestra predominance in that hymn-like march theme – all this, I must say, seemed to me to deserve some expression of appreciation on the part of the one person for whom my work was visualized, conceived and executed. I doubt, moreover, if one could easily find in any other libretto for a one-act opera three songs of comparable delicacy, and at the same time equally characteristic in tone, as Harlekin's song, the rondo for Zerbinetta and the Circe song of Bacchus.

Not unnaturally I would rather have heard all this from you than be obliged to write it myself.

No doubt it will be possible to find a way of heightening the intensity of the end along the lines you indicate, but before we proceed to settle the degree and the manner of any such climax-building, let me try and explain in a few sentences the underlying idea or meaning of this little poetic work. What it is about is one of the straightforward and stupendous problems of life: fidelity; whether to hold fast to that which is lost, to cling to it even unto death – or to live, to live on, to get over it, to transform oneself, to sacrifice the integrity of the soul and yet in this transmutation to preserve one's essence, to remain a human being and not to sink to the level of the beast, which is without recollection. It is the fundamental theme of *Elektra*, the voice of Electra opposed to the voice of Chrysothemis, the heroic voice against the human. In the present case we have the group of heroes, demi-gods, gods – Ariadne, Bacchus, (Theseus) – facing the human, the merely human group consisting of the frivolous Zerbinetta and her companions, all of them base figures in life's masquerade. Zerbinetta is in her element drifting out of the arms of one man into the arms of another; Ariadne could be the wife or mistress of *one* man only, just as she can be only *one* man's widow, can be forsaken only by *one* man. One thing, however, is still left even for her: the miracle, the God. To him she gives herself, for she believes him to be Death: he is both Death and Life at once; he it is who reveals to her the immeasurable depths in her own nature, who makes of her an enchantress, the sorceress who herself transforms the poor little Ariadne; he it is who conjures up for her in this world another world beyond, who preserves her for us and at the same time transforms her.

But what to divine souls is a real miracle, is to the earth-bound nature of Zerbinetta just an everyday love-affair. She sees in Ariadne's experience the only thing she *can* see: the exchange of an old lover for a new one. And so these two spiritual worlds are in the end ironically brought together in the only way in which they can be brought together: in non-comprehension.

In this experience of Ariadne's, which is really the monologue of her lonely soul, Bacchus represents no mere *deus ex machina*; for him, too, the experience is vital. Innocent, young and unaware of his own divinity he travels where the wind takes him, from island to island. His first affair was typical, with a woman of easy virtue, you may say or you may call her Circe. To his youth and innocence with its infinite potentialities the shock has been tremendous: were he Harlekin, this would be merely the beginning of one long round of love affairs. But he is Bacchus; confronted · with the enormity of erotic experience all is laid bare to him in a flash – the assimilation with the animal, the transformation, his own divinity. So he escapes from Circe's embraces still unchanged, but not without a wound, a longing, not without knowledge. The impact on him now of this meeting with a being whom he can love, who is mistaken about him but is enabled by this very mistake to give herself to him wholly and to reveal herself to him in all her loveliness, who entrusts herself to him completely, exactly as one entrusts oneself to Death, this impact I need not expound further to an artist such as you.

It would be a very great joy to me if, by an early reply to this personal, friendly letter, you were to restore to me that sense of fine and intimate contact between us which I so much enjoyed during our earlier collaboration, and which has by now become indispensable to me.

Very sincerely Yours,

HOFMANNSTHAL

Dear Herr von Hofmannsthal,

I am sincerely sorry that in my dry way I failed to pay you the tribute you had hoped for and which your work certainly deserves. But I confess frankly that my first impression was one of disappointment. Perhaps because I had expected too much. I have now had your manuscript typed out and, upon a quick perusal today, got indeed a vastly better impression (except for the final conclusion, where I certainly need a bigger *crescendo*); but even so the piece did not fully convince me until after I had read your letter, which is so beautiful and explains the meaning of the action so wonderfully that a superficial musician like myself could not, of course, have tumbled to it. But isn't this a little dangerous? And isn't some of the interpretation still lacking in the action itself? If even I couldn't see it, just think of the audience and – the critics. The way you describe it it's excellent. But in the piece itself it doesn't emerge quite so clearly and plainly.

I am doubly pleased that I have again been incapable of dissembling and that my coolness has coaxed this marvellous letter out of you. I shall send you the play *and* your letter in typescript in about three days. Will you then, please, compare the letter and the play once more, and see if some of the points in the letter couldn't be put into the play so as to make the symbolism clearer. An author reads into his play things which the sober spectator doesn't see, and the fact that even I, the most willing of readers, have failed to grasp such important points must surely give you pause. Reading your piece now, after your explanation, I do indeed find in it everything, but as for the explicitness needed by any theatrical work – just think of those asses of spectators, the lot of them, starting with the composer!

Zerbinetta's scene is indeed very pretty and the scene before Bacchus's arrival, and also his song, quite excellent – as I have to admit now that you've pushed my face in it. But is this quite right? Surely, the symbolism must leap out alive from the action, instead of being dug out of it by subsequent laborious interpretation. Besides, I'm only human: I may be wrong, and am indeed out of sorts; I've been here alone without another soul for the past four weeks, I haven't touched a cigarette for four weeks – let the devil be cheerful in such circumstances! Be patient therefore: maybe my incomprehension will spur you on after all – and don't take it as anything else. After all, we want to bring out the very best in each other. As for the conclusion, we can have a chat about that in Munich. Enjoy the fine summer to the full and accept the best wishes of yours,

RICHARD STRAUSS

LIND

The American tour of the 'Swedish Nightingale' Jenny Lind in 1850–1, organized by the impresario P. T. Barnum, was one of the first instances of organized show-business 'hype'; among the stories circulated by his press agents was that her primly arranged hair disguised the fact that she had no ears. There was also a brisk trade in merchandizing 'spin-offs'.

> Oh! Manias we've had many,
> And some have raised the wind;
> But the most absurd of any
> Has been that for *Jenny Lind*.
> Causing quite a revolution
> To complement her fame; –
> From a toothpick to an Omnibus
> All are call'd by *her name*!
> > Oh! Manias we've &c.

> If you step into a grocer's
> (Upon my word it's true!)
> There is Jenny Lind's lump sugar,
> And Jenny's cocoa too.
> We shall all become great singers,
> Though Jenny Lind pipes high;
> At each snuff shop in London
> Jenny Lind's *pipes* you may buy.
> > Oh! Manias we've &c.

My wife has a Jenny Lind Bonnet,
And a Jenny Lind Visite;
With Jenny's portrait on it
My handkerchief looks neat.
My wife's a slave to fashion,
Against it never sinned;
Our baby and the kitten
Are called after Jenny Lind.
    Oh! Manias we've &c.
      W. H. C. WEST, 'The Jenny Lind Mania'

Jenny Lind died in Malvern in 1887. Nearly a century later, a poet himself in love with one of the great prima donnas of today seeks out her grave.

for Teresa Stratas

The fosses where Caractacus fought Rome
blend with grey bracken and become a blur
above the Swedish Nightingale's last home.

Somehow my need for you makes me seek her.

The Malverns darken as the dusk soaks in.
The rowan berries' dark red glaze grows dull.
The harvest moon's scraped silver and bruised tin
is only one night off from being full.

Death keeps all hours, but graveyards close at nights.
I hurry past the Malvern Hospital
where a nurse goes round small wards and puts on lights
and someone there's last night begins to fall.

'The oldest rocks this earth can boast', these hills,
packed with extinction, make me burn for you.

I ask two women leaving with dead daffodils:
Where's Jenny Lind's grave, please? They both say: *Who?*
      TONY HARRISON, 'Loving Memory'

231

LOVE

Turgenev's long, tortured and possibly unconsummated passion for the mezzo-soprano, Pauline Viardot-Garcia, Malibran's sister, makes a disturbing tale: on his deathbed in 1883 he is said to have cried out that she surpassed Lady Macbeth in her wickedness.

Turgenev's friend, Polonski, for example, said that Turgenev had admitted to him that Madame Viardot had 'some sort of special influence over him, keeping him at her feet as if by some sort of sorcery, just like witchcraft; that when he sees her, he is physically unable to do anything but submit to her, that it is beyond his strength to do otherwise, and that in her presence he feels as if in the grip of the most potent of hypnotic spells. Once he seriously assured me that Madame Viardot was a witch, and said it with such conviction that I was surprised and astonished, and started to object, laughing at Turgenev's superstition. "You shouldn't laugh, Yakov Petrovich," he replied. "There have always been witches, and always will be. They have some sort of inner power over people, no matter what one says, and there's nothing to be done about it." Turgenev also maintained that Pauline was so clever that she could see the back of a chair through the body of the person who was sitting on it.'

APRIL FITZLYON, *The Price of Genius*

When Klemperer entered the orchestral pit on Boxing Day to conduct *Lohengrin*, he appeared nervous. But he was greeted by lengthy applause and the first two acts went well. After the second interval Elisabeth Schumann, who was in a box, was alarmed to notice that her husband, supported by a few friends, had occupied some hitherto empty seats in the front row of the stalls immediately behind the conductor. Realizing that something was afoot, she tried in vain to warn Klemperer. It was, however, not until the twelve-bar coda to the final chorus of the opera that Puritz rose and shouted, 'Klemperer, turn round!' ('Klemperer, dreh um!'). As Klemperer did so, Puritz drew a riding crop out of his sleeve and with it struck him twice on the left side of his face. Neighbours immediately surrounded Puritz to prevent further violence. Meanwhile, Klemperer, who had fallen into the orchestra pit under the impact of the onslaught, clambered up 'like a huge black spider' and tried to attack Puritz, who was about to be led from the theatre by his friends. One of them, a pastor, who declared himself an intimate of the family, tried to explain the reasons for the assault, whereupon Klemperer, much to the amusement of the audience, shouted, 'Herr Puritz has attacked me, because I love his wife. Good evening.'

Shortly after midnight a hurricane howled through the streets of Hamburg. Paving stones were dragged up, window panes blown in, and in many districts a cascade of slates and tiles were hurled on to the streets. Klemperer and Schumann sought shelter in a hotel where Fritz Stiedry happened to be staying and was able to persuade the management to give the fugitives a room. The following day both parties issued statements. Puritz maintained that Klemperer's refusal to accept a duel had left him with no alternative but 'to administer a thrashing . . . in the presence of the public and in the place that had made his behaviour possible'. Klemperer's lawyer ridiculed the suggestion that Klemperer had brought any pressure on Schumann through his position in the Stadttheater and went on to declare that 'Frau Puritz and Herr Klemperer assured Herr Puritz in the most solemn manner that . . . no damage to his marital rights had occurred.'

PETER HEYWORTH, *Otto Klemperer*

The affair came to nothing, but remained for both parties an open wound throughout the rest of their lives.

Geraldine Farrar married a minor luminary of the silent movies, Lou Tellegen. It was one of the few mistakes she ever admitted to.

One midnight I was awakened by the insistent ringing of my private phone.

A call at any unusual hour always quickened an apprehension about my father, whose home was about fifteen minutes away, at the other end of our village. His health had given me concern of late; but it was happily no alarm from that source. A stranger's voice began to inquire if it were really Miss Farrar at the end of the wire? Upon such assurance and the circumlocution of an irritating preliminary, the man said, abruptly, 'Well, I'm from the Press and thought you'd probably want to know Lou Tellegen is dead – how do you feel about it, and what have you got to say?' Taken completely by surprise I replied tartly, 'I have nothing to say and am not interested,' and rang off.

The phone continued to ring repeatedly until dawn, adding nothing to soothe my humour of the moment. The following day, the curious-minded and the press hounds kept the wire humming in incessant abuse of inquiry. I left the house to escape the commotion and the attempts at interviews, to pass a few days with a friend. My father was not spared, either, in a morbid attempt to dish up some scandalous observation; of course, no news was forthcoming from him.

Mr Tellegen had been in Hollywood for some time, and the tragic finale was to be foreseen many years before it actually came to pass. I had, in the latter years, tried to think more kindly of this man who had not only misused his talents and connections, but humiliated me and my family in shameful and ungrateful fashion. It was not alone his complete indifference to the consequences and conduct of a super-ego, and condescending approach to countless women – some of whom deserved better of him than his wretched ingratitude – but his supreme contempt for those great personages who extended a helping hand up the ladder of success all during his early career. Notably Sarah Bernhardt.

Handsome and stupid, as long as physical appeal was seconded by youth, he typified romance and adventure to the casual eye. He could be charming and well-mannered when he wished, but had the perception of a moron, and no morals whatever. It was my own unwisdom to have been misled by a delightful and bland exterior, and I blame only myself for a marriage that turned out so badly for me. For him, it was only another glamorous episode, I suppose. At any rate, I was not desirous of confiding my reflections to the press for widespread relay and conjecture. In the interim since my divorce, there had been plenty of ladies in his life, and a marriage or two as well, I believe, to keep alive his interest and justify his own ego.

I learned only later of the manner of his suicide, which seems so horrible in its sordid and degrading finale, that one would not linger over it. Less than ever was I minded to discuss it, even with friends. Despite the justifiable contempt in which I held him, it was no satisfaction to view such an end to a career that could have been happy and successful. There were many qualifications that pointed that way, but other tendencies and unfortunate surroundings were too powerful for a weak character to resist, much less overcome. How dreadful an illustration on the lesson, and ending, of the fleshpots! I would not wish any human soul the task of working out such a tortured Karma.

I was harshly judged and criticized — naturally by those who never knew the proper details or sentiments of those concerned — for my apparent indifference and silence to the tawdry services that received their share of display in the tabloids. Some anonymous writers went so far as to sent me photographs of the ceremony, the casket, and the floral tributes with their pencilled criticisms. It has taken years of effort on my part to erase the many bitter memories, but I hope I have come to a fuller realization of the rewards of tolerance and understanding. May those tormented ashes rest in peace.

GERALDINE FARRAR, *Such Sweet Compulsion*

MAD SCENES

Operatic mad scenes are often regarded as curiosities of Italian
Romanticism, but their true nature is very different from what is
usually supposed. The so-called mad scene in *Lucia di Lammermoor* is the most celebrated in all Italian opera, but it is only one
of many in contemporary works. In the best-known examples it is
the heroine who is driven to distraction, as in Donizetti's own
Anna Bolena and Bellini's *I puritani*. However there are many
operas where a leading male character, nearly always a bass,
suffers a similar indignity; as in Paer's *Agnese di Fitzhenry*,
Donizetti's *Il furioso all'isola di San Domingo* and *Torquato
Tasso*, and Verdi's *Nabucco*. Why were the protagonists of
Romantic opera so prone to emotional collapse? The Italian
opera seria of the eighteenth century had been characterized by a
remarkable emotional formality and stability. One can hardly
imagine the semi-gods, kings and princes in Metastasio's librettos
losing such composure.

Some clues as to the place mad scenes had in opera can be
deduced from the guiding principles of traditional Italian opera,
that were assumed to have been derived from the ancients. Aristotle had taught that, in tragedy, the audience was exposed to the
civilizing qualities of terror (or awe) and pity. The Italians considered that this would lift the spirits of men and edify them.
Aristotle had argued against a too explicit spectacle of dreadul
scenes; and, for Italians, such *terrore* was never to descend to the
level of *orrore*. Francesco Milizia wrote in 1784 'Tragedy is supposed to arouse terror and pity, but not of course horror; spectacles of a gory nature are frightful and barbaric, and offend human
sensibilities. They transgress moral standards too, and coarsen
finer feelings, as happens to butchers and surgeons.' If violent

236

events occurred, they were supposed to happen off-stage; not like, for example, Edgardo's suicide at the end of *Lucia di Lammermoor*.

The tendency towards emotional collapse amongst soprano heroines like Lucia obviously does not derive from the very formal *opera seria* tradition. Instead, we can find scenes of madness in late-eighteenth-century *opere semiserie*. The techniques developed in comic and serious opera were fused together in the Romantic operas composed by Donizetti and Bellini, but in the eighteenth century the two genres had been kept rigidly apart. The *opera semiseria* was distinct from either; and represented a new type of sentimental pastoral, where emotional tribulations are presented and then resolved at the conclusion. One of the most celebrated was *Nina; ossia La pazza per amore (Nina; or The Girl Driven Mad Through Love)* by Giovanni Paisiello (1740–1816), which was first given at Naples in 1789. The heroine loses her reason because her father had denied her wish to be married to her Lindoro, who has therefore disappeared. Of course, the mad scenes are far removed from the frigid formality of *opera seria*; but they do not include theatrical raving or descent into horror. They portray what was termed *la dolce alienazione della mente di Nina* (Nina's gentle mental distraction); in which, significantly, she imagines her beloved has been restored to her, as happens in *Lucia*. Her father is so moved to pity by her plight that he relents, and there is a happy ending. This was a very famous opera in Naples, and was the model for similar scenes of mental distraction in Bellini's *La sonnambula* and *I puritani*.

Among the earlier operatic adaptations of Sir Walter Scott's novel of 1819 was Michele Carafa's *Le nozze di Lammermoor* (Paris, 1829), which was in fact an *opera semiseria*, though of a rather curious type. It had recitative accompanied by harpsichord, as in *opera buffa*; and some characters, particularly Lord Arturo Bucklaw, were wholly comic. However, it had either the sentimental tone of *opera semiseria* nor a mad scene. It must have given the audience a considerable jolt when, at the end, Edgardo stabbed himself on stage. This was the problem for such operas at the time: traditionally, comic and tragic elements were supposed to be kept to distinct operatic genres. The mad scene in Paer's *opera semiseria*, *Agnese di Fitzhenry*, was described as an 'insufferable medley of the lugubrious and the ludicrous', and a similar judgement might be valid for Carafa's opera. Mixing the genres risked incurring criticism for spoiling the comedy on the one hand, and for being too undignified on the other. However, by the 1830s, audiences were becoming inured to increasingly theatrical spectacles on the stage, and less satisfied by the gentle sentimentality of the *opera semiseria*. An important influence was the French Romantic stage drama. Out of the French Revolution came the melodramas of Pixérécourt and Victor Ducange (who made a successful play from Scott's novel in 1828), which were dominated by the relentless persecution of virtuous heroines by pitiless villains. The greatest playwright was Victor Hugo, who called for the fusion of the comic and tragic genres; and insisted that drama should include realistic portrayals of grotesque behaviour, reflecting man's animal nature. His *Hernani* (Paris, 1830) had scenes of violence and death onstage, and its language was considered by many to be beneath the dignity of tragedy. Bellini's librettist wanted to adapt the play later that year, but had to drop the idea as it would never have passed police censorship.

Victor Hugo had a great impact on Italian opera, providing the sources for Donizetti's *Lucrezia Borgia*, and Verdi's *Ernani* and *Rigoletto*. In particular, the new theatrical taste and fusion of old genres was responsible for establishing the mad scene from sentimental *opera semiseria* within the context of an *opera seria* such as *Lucia di Lammermoor*; and for a much more explicit presentation of violent events. Critics looked aghast at modern versions of *opere semiserie* like *Il furioso all'isola di San Domingo,* where they saw the deranged hero right from the start, and through most of the duration, of the drama. It was all too much for the conservative taste that judged it according to the criteria of terror and pity: 'It certainly is not a beautiful spectacle seeing a madman floundering about the stage with torn clothing, and ashen face, with a dazed expression, with dishevelled hair, going from one excess of fury to another ... The interest and compassion that a similar misfortune might excite, is changed to horror by the repulsiveness of the long and over realistic representation of it.' Despite his assertion that 'the audience reacted with appropriate good sense: it laughed instead of feeling terror', the opera was very successful and given all over the operatic world. In comparison, however, Lucia's mad scene would have appeared restrained.

Lucia di Lammermoor, as drafted by Salvatore Cammarano (1801–52) for Donizetti, displays some quite conservative traits as well as its advanced Romanticism; which make the characters of the protagonists unusually dissimilar. The role of Lucia in general is untheatrical for its time: she is almost completely passive throughout the opera, distanced from her only decisive action through her madness. It is a far less strong character than those displayed by Maria Stuarda, Lucrezia Borgia, or by many of Donizetti's other heroines. To find outright Romanticism we have to turn rather to the character of Edgardo; a role written for the prototype dramatic tenor, Gilbert-Louis Duprez (1806–96), who pioneered the now normal assault on top notes reinforced from the chest. It is he who transgresses the accepted norms of tragic behaviour, by issuing a curse on Lucia's marriage; and, finally, by committing suicide in front of the audience (and the chorus, who cry *Quale orror!*). In contrast, our heroine expires off stage in the approved manner.

Lucia's aria (it was not normally called a mad scene) shows many traits derived from the old *opera semiseria*, that are not found in Scott's original. The most important of these is that it is a scene of *dolce alienazione della mente*, rather than a gory, melodramatic spectacle. That is to say, in Donizetti's and Cammarano's version, there is a positive aspect to her madness, missing in the novel, where she imagines Edgardo restored to her. First she hears his voice, and later imagines herself with him by the spring. She bids him shelter with her before the altar, where a celestial wedding hymn is heard; and finally she visualizes the ceremony itself. Visions of this type appear also to Elvira in *I puritani*, and other heroines descended from Paisiello's Nina. Amina's sleepwalking scenes in *La sonnambula* are thus in the same mould; since, although not actually mad, her mind is diverted from her predicament to happier scenes in the past. What lies at the heart of such scenes is not madness; but the conjuring up of an alternative reality, through the device of mental distraction.

In Scott's novel there is no reference to any such fantasy. Instead, Lucy is described bluntly and severely; 'her head-gear dishevelled, her night-clothes torn and dabbled with blood, her eyes glazed, and her features convulsed into a wild paroxysm of insanity. When she saw herself discovered, she gibbered, made mouths, and pointed at them with her bloody fingers, with the frantic gestures of an exulting demoniac.' Donizetti's score calls for no blood-stained effects; and in some respects, his mad scene is less frightful than Scott's, although it is a great deal more extended. Lucy's 'paroxysm of insanity' is replaced by Lucia's dislocation of the mind, which makes her oblivious of the other characters and the chorus; and of course, of her crime.

Admittedly, this does not take into account the manner in which this scene might have been presented on stage, about which we know only a few details. The first reviews merely refer to Lucia's scene in the third act as one of the many greeted with much applause, and devote more interest to Donizetti's formal innovations in avoiding the repetitions of cabalettas in other scenes. Compared with some recent mad scenes in other works, it would appear that *Lucia*'s was regarded as unexceptionable. It is true that Cammarano's Lucia has actually killed Arturo Bucklaw, whereas in the novel she only wounds him; but this had already occurred in yet another adaptation, Luigi Rieschi's *La fidanzata di Lammermoor* (1831), of which only the libretto survives (described by Jerome Mitchell). The heroine evidently appeared with her blood-drenched dagger, of which there is no reference in Cammarano's version; but like Lucia, she also imagined Edgardo would now return and marry her. Donizetti's Lucia would probably not have descended to *orrore* in the eyes of contemporaries, who were becoming used to fairly theatrical representations of insanity; even if later it became conventional for her to appear blood-stained, as indeed Scott describes her.

Although Lucia's mad scene is often regarded as a prime example of Romantic extravagance, it is a relatively old-fashioned aspect of Donizetti's opera that derives from the traditions of *opera semiseria.* The distracted minds of Lucia and other similar heroines allowed the librettist to contrast their current misfortunes with scenes of happiness to be evoked musically, often using material from earlier in the opera. The technique made it at least possible for two emotional states to be portrayed at once; and this simultaneity is emphasized by the choral introductions that set the scene to these episodes in works like *Lucia* and *I puritani.* The chorus, or onlooking characters as in Paisiello's *Nina*, ensure that the conjured-up vision of happiness does not exist in isolation. Cammarano's notes for the production of *Lucia*, discovered by John Black in Naples, call for the chorus to respond to her deranged entry by expressions 'full of pity and terror' over her ordeal. A more forceful Romanticism became the norm not long afterwards; and later nineteenth-century mad scenes tend to give the protagonist a visionary quality, whereby their often wicked characters are endowed with some human insight. Examples of this can be seen in Verdi's *Nabucco* and *Macbeth*, and Mussorgsky's *Boris Godunov.* Perhaps the greatest case is Tristan's delirium in Wagner's *Tristan und Isolde.*

Finally, the musical setting of Lucia's scene is less extravagant than is generally supposed. Although much of her raving takes the form of recitative, the scene includes a regular slow aria and repeated fast finale. The notorious cadenza for flute and soprano, at the close of the slow aria, does not appear in the autograph manuscript, nor any contemporary printed score. Its precise provenance seems to be a mystery; but we can be certain that it formed no part of Donizetti's original opera. The florid flute solos in this scene were originally written for the glass harmonica (*armonica*), and played by the *maestro al cembalo.* Later Donizetti crossed most of this out and replaced it with a flute. However, the *armonica* accompaniment to the quick finale, 'Spargi d'amaro pianto', was never cancelled and remains in the autograph, complementing the wind parts. The instrument is seldom used today as, unfortunately, it fell into disuse not long afterwards; although it had been in great vogue since its invention by Benjamin Franklin in 1761. The ethereal sound of the rubbed glass would emphasize the dreamlike distractions of Lucia to perfection, in a way that the modern metallic flute cannot emulate. It was regularly associated with mental instability at the time: a contemporary Italian musical dictionary by Lichtenthal (Milan, 1826), warns that 'those of a nervous disposition should not play the *armonica*' and 'even stable people should not play it too frequently, as its extremely soft tone brings on melancholy'. To be sure, we have here a nineteenth-century Romantic *opera seria*, and not a thoroughly old-fashioned sentimental *opera semiseria* like *Nina*; but its oddities have been paraded too often, and its dramatic meanings largely ignored.

SIMON MAGUIRE

MALIBRAN

Impulsively generous, reckless, and hyperactive, the Spanish singer Maria Malibran died in 1836 at the age of twenty-eight. The impresario Augustus Bunn, for whom she sang at Drury Lane, published some of her enchanting letters. Chelard was the composer of an operetta in which Malibran was to sing.

St James's Street, Mardi

Again and again, alwais me, and eternally me, my dear Mister Bunn. I have been tormenting poor Chelard out of his wits. I want to have my part to practise it, know it, and be able to play it in 10 days the latest. I am sure if you give proper orders for the copy of the parts, *we* shall be all ready, at least I will be ready in 8 days ... but – rehearsals, parts, orders, rehearsals, no rehearsals without parts, no parts without orders, and no orders without my eternal hints, and my never ending letters, since it appears you will not do me the high honour of comming at my house for a quarter of an hour to have a little settling chit-chat. However it may be, I wait

242

your pleasure, noble cousin, and humbly beg for an answer when it may suit your Majesty. Nonsense apart, pray say YES or no...

To A Bunn !!!!!!
Esquair !!!!!!

The letter of complaint referred to below is now lost, and one can only guess at its contents.

My Dear Mr Bunn,

As I left the theatre last night I received this letter which I send to you not knowing what to do with it.

Do you know that it strikes me, if you let this letter go to the *Times*, it will only make things worse? For it seems to me that the writer takes too much notice of the King's Theatre being *well attended*, as I believe he says.

What do you think of that?

I think, if you were to answer in my name, that I would prefer that he should not take any notice of me, or if he did, not to say anything about the Italian Theatre, nor of my losing popularity in the credit of the aristocratic folks. What do you think of that?

I never take any notice of these things; but this time, as it so happens that my opinion is asked upon the question, and as I am afraid that such an article in the newspaper, *Times*, might have some bad influence upon the mind of the tender feet, *thick ankles*, and *read elbows* of the suprematy of high ranked, curled up, *tittled noses*, I think it exceedingly wise, prudent, and *circumspect* to pop into your room my letter enfolding the enclosed, upon which you must *ruminate* and deliberate, and *muse* the whole of to-morrow morning, until your ideas will be expounded on the pretious subject, and upon the many *ortographical* mistakes made, both in writing and in spelling.

By your most obedient
Scribbler and nonsense-teller
Maria, &c. &c. &c.

The performances of opera at the Teatro Fenice have come to a close. But strangely enough the day before La Malibran is due to leave Venice a Signor Gallo calls on her. He is the proprietor of the Teatro Emeronito, a dilapidated ramshackle building frequented mainly by the *petit peuple* who instinctively love music. The wretched owner of the theatre is on the brink of bankruptcy and fearful of the misery it will inflict on his many children.

If only La Malibran would consent to sing once, give only one performance at his theatre, he would be saved from disaster.

In a perfectly natural way Maria listens to his entreaty and agrees.

She allows it to be announced that on 8 April [1834] she will give Bellini's *La Sonnambula* at the Emeronito. Every seat is at once booked and the house is filled to overflowing. Elegant connoisseurs of the opera sit side by side with the populace also lovers of *bel canto*.

So many Venetians are clustered round the entrance of the theatre waiting for La Malibran that Maria, to avoid an explosion of enthusiasm, slips in through the back, avoiding the Stage Door.

The curtain rises but, alas, the tenor, a little known artist, is so overwhelmed at being chosen to sing a duet with the renowned Diva that he has a lapse of memory.

The wretched man seems totally confounded and the audience starts to murmur in protest – it is not an indulgent public, being accustomed to the best.

Then Maria, in no way disconcerted, herself sings the part of the tenor in the duet, switching fluently from one character to the other to allow her partner time to regain his composure. Incredibly she somehow succeeds in singing both parts and the audience, transported with joy at her achievement, responds with thunderous applause showing how much they appreciate the art, ability, kindness and generosity of the singer. Men wave their sticks with handkerchiefs tied to the end and ladies throw bouquets of flowers onto the stage. The Management brings a laurel wreath with a gold ribbon and doves and pigeons fly onto the stage, a living tribute, an aureole to a triumphant Diva.

The receipts for the evening amount to more than 10,000 francs and from her own purse Maria herself gives the remaining 4000 francs which were vital to save Signor Gallo and his theatre from ruin.

The following day the façade of the theatre displays the name of the Diva who saved it from disaster – TEATRO MALIBRAN. To this day the theatre still bears the same name.

SUZANNE DESTERNES and HENRIETTE CHANDET, La Malibran

MASSENET

When M. Jules Massenet descended on our shores for the first time in 1878 with an instrumental suite descriptive of scenes from Macbeth, he established his reputation as one of the loudest of modern composers. Something of that *esprit de corps* which led a celebrated artillery regiment to sing with ungrammatical enthusiasm We are the boys that fears no noise seems to have determined him not to allow even a simple chord to a recitative to pass without a pluck at the strings and a slam on the drum capable of awakening the deaf. When the curtain descends on a thrilling 'situation' he pours forth all his energy in a screeching, grinding, rasping *fortissimo* of extraordinary exuberance and vigor. He is perhaps better at a stage tumult than any living composer. Ever and anon there comes in Manon a number that stuns the hearer into drowsy good humor, and leaves him disposed to tolerate anything that gently tickles his exhausted ears and does not tax his attention too heavily. The quartet with chorus in the fourth act must be almost as audible on Waterloo Bridge as in the first row of stalls in Drury Lane Theatre.

G. B. SHAW, 1885

MAUREL

*The French baritone Victor Maurel was that rare thing in
the world of opera, a genuine intellectual, who compensated for a less than beautiful voice by the force and subtlety
of his acting. He was the first Tonio in* Pagliacci, *and at
Verdi's request created the roles of Iago (in* Otello) *and
Falstaff. Sir Thomas Beecham called him 'one of the half-
dozen supreme artistic personalities of my time'. Shaw was
another admirer, as this episode demonstrates.*

Thursday, it will be remembered, was a dark day, cold as the
seventh circle. I presently found myself prowling about a great
pile of flats, looking for a certain number at which I had to make a
call. Somebody else was prowling also; and I no sooner became
convinced that he was looking for the same number as I, and was
probably going to call on the same person, than I resolved not to
look at him; because to look at a man under such circumstances is
almost tantamount to asking what the devil he is doing there.
Consequently it was not until we got inside, and were introduced,
that I recognized in the stranger no other than Maurel.

Imagine my feelings when I found that the business upon which
he was bent was for the formulation in some fashion of his
demand as an artist for a more earnest treatment of his work and
mission. 'Of what value is your admiration of my Iago or
Rigoletto' he said, in effect 'if you do not regard the opera as a
serious entertainment? Besides, one of the conditions of a really
admirable performance is that it shall be an organic part of a
whole in which all the other parts are equally excellent in their due
degree; and how can such a whole be organized except in a place
where opera is taken seriously, both before and behind the curtain?' Maurel, having gone up and down upon the earth in search
of such places, has wisely come to the conclusion that they do not

exist readymade, and that the artists must themselves set to work to create them everywhere, by rousing the critics and educating the public to appreciate theatrical art.

As a beginning, he wishes to submit his theory of art to criticism; to give skeptical dramatic critics illustrations of the dramatic resources of stage singing; and finally to assert the claims of operatic actors to weighty social considerations, founded on a sense of the importance and dignity of their function in society, instead of the capricious fashionable vogue which they now enjoy only when they happen to be phenomenal executants. This explains the speech he made at the Hôtel Métropole the other day. He is anxious to enlarge that after-dinner sketch into a carefully considered address, giving practical examples of what he meant by saying that one should not sing the part of Rigoletto with the voice of Don Juan, and to deliver it to a select body of the critics of London, who, as profound thinkers thoroughly conversant with their subject on its philosophic, technical, and social sides, and brimful of general culture to boot, would at once seize his meaning and help him to convey it to the public.

Modesty, and loyalty to my colleagues, restrained me from warning him not to generalize too rashly from the single instance with whom he was just then conversing; so I merely hinted that though the London critics are undeniably a fine body of men, yet their *élite* are hardly sufficiently numerous to make up a crowded and enthusiastic audience. To which he replied that an audience of two would satisfy him, provided the two had his subject at heart. This was magnificent, but not war: we at once agreed that we could do better for him than that. However, prompt measures were necessary, as he has to leave London next week. So we then and there constituted ourselves an executive subcommittee, fixed the date of the lecture for the afternoon of Monday next, and chose for our platform the stage of the Lyceum Theatre, on which, as Iago, he inaugurated a new era in operatic acting. It was a cool proposal, especially as Maurel altogether declined to proceed on a commercial basis, and would only hear of putting a price upon admission on condition that the proceeds should be given to some charity. But the upshot shewed that we knew our Irving, who promptly not only placed the theatre at Maurel's disposal, but charged himself with the arrangements. To the Lyceum, therefore, I refer the critics, the students, the amateurs, the philosophers, and the experts, as well as those modest persons who only wish to hear Maurel sing again, and to be shewn how he changes the voice of William Tell into the voice of Don Juan.

G. B. SHAW, 1890

die MEISTERSINGER

... of all the bête, clumsy, blundering, boggling, baboon-blooded stuff I ever saw on a human stage that thing last night beat [all] – as far as the story and acting went; and of all the affected, sapless, soulless, beginningless, endless, topless, bottomless, topsiterviest, tuneless, scrannelpipiest, tongs-and-boniest doggerel of sounds I ever endured the deadliest of, that eternity of nothing was the deadliest, as the sound went. I was never so relieved ... in my life, by the stopping of any sound – not expecting railway whistles – as I was by the cessation of the cobbler's bellowing; even the serenader's caricatured twangle was a rest after it. As for the great 'lied' I never made out where it began or where it ended – except by the fellow's coming off the horse-block.

JOHN RUSKIN to Lady Burne-Jones, 1882

The curtain rose. The church choruses, gently lifting and subsiding, seemed to tranquilize the orchestra. Thrilling and overwhelming beauty was achieved. It was a sublime example of the power of art to triumph easily over prejudices and hatred and resentments. For Wagner was a modern German; he was a very German German; he had little use for the English. The opera is intensely German. Our troops were still occupying Germany. Only the previous week our officers had suffered outrageous insults at the hands of truculent Germans. Yet here we all were, charmed, enthralled, enthusiastic, passionately grateful! Seventy-five years since Wagner had begun the composition of this colossal and lovely work, this most singular opera whose purely philosophic theme is the conflict between the classical and the romantic! What a droll, impossible theme for an opera! But the terrific pure original force and beauty of its inspiration and execution had overcome time and us.

Arnold Bennett, Things that have Interested Me.

MELBA

If Melba was last of the old school of Victorian grande dame prima donnas, *her younger contemporary Mary Garden represented a more modern style of operatic performance. This first encounter between them occurred in the early years of this century.*

I learned that Nellie Melba was to be on the same programme with me. We didn't know each other then. Well, we arrived at Windsor Castle at the same time and were put in a large, cold room to dress. Then we were told to come upstairs where the concert was to be held. As I entered I beheld a sight of sheer grandeur that I shall never forget as long as I live. We were put into a small, round room with no door, and in front of that round room was the enormous salon, with all the chairs ready for the guests to be seated. Adjoining that room was the state dining-room, and they were all drinking the health of somebody, because they were standing with their glasses in the air, and the crowns and diamonds, the glittering uniforms of the men, the chandeliers of crystal, all was a mass of dazzling splendour such as I had never seen before and never saw again.

And little Mary Garden looked into that room and all she could say to herself was, 'My, I'm glad I came from Rome to see this!' Then they all came in and took their seats in the enormous salon, and Melba and I sang. There was also a violinist, a young boy, who was a protégé of the Queen's. I sang 'Depuis le jour' from *Louise* and 'Vissi d'arte' from *Tosca*, and Melba sang 'Mi chiamano Mimi' from *La Bohème* and 'Caro nome' from *Rigoletto*. When we were finished the kings and queens and princes and princesses all came up to congratulate us, and then they all left the room.

We were taken down to supper, and Lord Farquhar introduced everyone around, there being twenty of us at the table. While he was presenting us, Melba suddenly chirped up:

'What a dreadful concert this would have been if I hadn't come!'

Twenty pairs of eyes were fixed on me. I sat only two chairs away from Melba, and Lord Farquhar, who was very embarrassed, began to pay me a compliment to cover up Melba's remark, but I raised my hand.

'Please don't bother about me, Lord Farquhar,' I said. 'I love Melba's rudeness. It amuses me.'

Then they asked us if we wanted to go back to London in the private train or remain overnight at the castle, and Melba and I both said we preferred to go home. So we got into the carriage of the train, and before we reached London Melba and I were fast friends. During the journey she turned to me and said:

'Mary, I want you to tell me how to act Tosca. I've been studying it, and there are a lot of things about it that puzzle me. And what sort of wig should I wear?'

Well, I told Nellie Melba everything I could about Tosca, about costuming her and so forth, but I knew it was perfectly useless because she never could sing Tosca – and never did. She just wasn't made for Tosca.

I found Melba a cold person, but she could be charming when you knew her. You see, she grew to like me because I wasn't a coloratura singer. Our friendship would never have come to anything if I had been a coloratura like herself. Later she came to visit me at my villa in Monte Carlo, and we had lots of fun together, especially at the gaming tables. Both of us were incurable gamblers. Melba would win a few francs, and you'd have thought it was a million pounds.

She could be quite funny, Melba, and wherever she went she always had people laughing. In the evening she could often sit at the piano and play and sing for me – just small English songs, but she turned them all into little things of heavenly beauty. Once she asked me to go to Australia with her company, but I thought it too far away, and the repertory didn't interest me. I didn't see very much of Melba in the last part of her life. We used to write to each other at Christmas, and then she died. When you knew her, you couldn't help liking her. When you didn't know her, you thought her frightfully rude. Now I want to say something about Melba's voice.

I have no hesitation in declaring that Melba had the most phenomenal effect on me of any singer I have ever heard. I once went to Covent Garden to hear her do Mimi in *La Bohème*. Of course, Melba didn't look any more like Mimi than Schumann-Heink did. I never saw such a fat Mimi in my life. Melba didn't impersonate the rôle at all – she never did that – but, my God, how she sang it!

You know, the last note of the first act of *La Bohème* is the last note that comes out of Mimì's throat. It is a high C, and Mimì sings it when she walks out of the door with Rodolfo. She closes the door and then takes that note. The way Melba sang that high C was the strangest and weirdest thing I have ever experienced in my life. The note came floating over the auditorium of Covent Garden: it left Melba's throat, it left Melba's body, if left everything, and came over like a star and passed us in our box, and went out into the infinite. I have never heard anything like it in my life, not from any other singer, ever. It just rolled over the hall of Covent Garden. My God, how beautiful it was!

Since then I always wait for that note when I hear the first act of *Bohème*, and they reach and reach for it, and then they scream it, and it's underneath and it's false, and it rolls down the stairs, and it never comes out from behind that door, never. That note of

Melba's was just like a ball of light. It wasn't attached to anything at all – it was *out* of everything.

MARY GARDEN and LOUIS BIANCOLLI, Mary Garden's Story

In his autobiographical Great Morning, *Osbert Sitwell remembers the pre-First World War collaboration of Melba and Caruso at Covent Garden. Not the best of friends offstage – Melba's acerbic outback bluntness and bottom-less snobbery did not gel with Caruso's child-like naïveté and Italian vulgarity – onstage music united them, as one can still faintly hear from their recording of the duet from the first act of* La Bohème.

Melba and Caruso, when, fat as two elderly thrushes, they trilled at each other over the hedges of tiaras, summed up in themselves the age, no less than Sargent netted it for others. Not only was Caruso as natural a singer as the thrush he resembled, the black-bird, or the conventional nightingale to which he was compared, but contradictorily, for all its lack of art, his voice, carrying in its strains, in the sound of those notes which he was able to attain and hold as could no other singer of that or of a later day, the warm breath of southern evenings in an orange grove, and of roses, caught in the hush of dusk at the water's edge, possessed, as well as a high degree of technique, a certain kind of art. Of Melba the same cannot be said. ... Her magnificent voice was not invariably true, having about it something of the disproportion of the Australian continent from which she had emerged. But at least it can be claimed for her that, with her ample form lying on a couch, she made a surprising and unforgettable type of romantic con-sumptive.

MENOTTI

Stravinsky is interviewed in 1964 after witnessing a perfor-
mance of The Last Savage, *an opera by Gian-Carlo*
Menotti. In terms of number of performances received,
Menotti is without doubt the most successful of contem-
porary opera composers, chiefly owing to his Amahl and the
Night Visitors, *a piece cunningly designed to accommodate*
the limited resources of schools, youth groups and amateur
musicians.

SHOW MAGAZINE: What did you think of *The Last Savage*, Mr
Stravinsky?
STRAVINSKY: I did very little thinking, I assure you.
SHOW: But did you enjoy it?
I.S.: Not really. One sees everything miles away but has to wait
eons while a largely anonymous and never good-enough com-
poser slowly and without ever confounding any expectation
brings it near. And that first scene! Well, what *is* the opposite of a
flying start! A diving start?
SHOW: How would you characterize the work generally?
I.S.: As unconscious slapstick. In musical tendency it is 'farther
out' than anything in a decade, but in the wrong direction.
SHOW: Is it really so humourless? By all accounts the Metropolitan
audience...
I.S.: Exactly.
SHOW: A Met audience *is* rather special, you know.
I.S.: Yes. Many of them would have come to the late Mr Blitz-
stein's *Sacco and Vanzetti* expecting a contemporary *Romeo and
Juliet.*
SHOW: But are audiences entirely responsible for their ignorance?
I.S.: Hardly. They may 'like what they know', but before they can
'know what they like', they must be given an opportunity to

choose. If instead of *Cav* and *Pag*, *Adriana Lecouvreur*, *Manon*, *Samson*, *Andrea Chénier* and so on through the last few seasons, the Met audience had been offered good productions of a few contemporary masterpieces, could it be served with such an ear of corn as *The Last Savage*? Naturally the Met audience is palateless, and naturally it does not know how to receive anything new.

SHOW: But what *are* the masterpieces of contemporary opera?

I.S.: *Wozzeck*, *Lulu*, *Erwartung*, *Moses und Aron*, even perhaps my *Rake* and my *Rex*; even possibly something by Janáček, though the only example of which I have had any experience was the thinnest, longest, and least succulent noodle I have ever tried to swallow. Admittedly none of these is very new, but none except *Wozzeck* and the *Rake* has ever been staged by the Met. A contemporary masterpiece needs the support of a whole community of contemporary operas, however, masterpieces or not, and certainly *The Last Savage* should be one of them. But to bring it forth alone suggests the Machiavellian possibility that the Met is using it as an alibi to prove that contemporary operas are not worth doing.

SHOW: Did you find no merit in the music at all?

I.S.: I enjoyed the 'dodecaphonic' string quartet. The composer should try an entire dodecaphonic scene in his next opera. Otherwise the last nine-tenths of the music might have been composed by feeding the first tenth to a machine. Of course I appreciate that it was intended as parody, and even partly sympathize with the composer's desire that the twelve-tone system should 'drop dead'. But parody is effective only as an excursus from a home style, which is what *The Savage* lacks. Pastiche, too, requires a certain talent. Thus when the composer tries to launch an ensemble with the rhythm of '*Zitti, zitti*,' he invites and receives devastating comparison. To ridicule 'modern life' with pseudo-Mascagni is not easy, moreover – leaving aside the question of whether an assault on the kingdoms of this world is the proper business of a composer who has made it all on this side. It is somewhat later, as the saying goes, than the composer of *The Savage* thinks.

the MET

The now-demolished Metropolitan Opera in New York stood on Broadway, between 39th and 40th Streets. It opened in 1883 and closed in 1966, to be replaced with the present Metropolitan Opera House at the Lincoln Center. The old Met was a focal point for American high society – but there were certain ironies to this, noted by both Henry James and Frances Alda (see also pp. 84–6).

... the general extravagant insistence on the Opera, which plays its part as the great vessel of social salvation, the comprehensive substitute for all other conceivable vessels; the *whole* social consciousness thus clambering into it, under stress, as the whole community crams into the other public receptacles, the desperate cars of the Subway or the vast elevators of the tall buildings. The Opera, indeed, as New York enjoys it, one promptly perceives, is worthy, musically and picturesquely, of its immense function; the effect of it is splendid, but one has none the less the oddest sense of hearing it, as an institution, groan and creak, positively almost split and crack, with the extra weight thrown upon it – the weight that in worlds otherwise arranged is artfully scattered, distributed over all the ground. In default of a court-function our ladies of the tiaras and court-trains might have gone on to the opera-function, these occasions offering the only approach to the implication of the tiara known, so to speak, to the American law. Yet even here there would have been no one for them, in congruity and consistency, to curtsey to – their only possible course becoming thus, it would seem, to make obeisance, clingingly, to each other. This truth points again the effect of a picture poor in the male presence; for to what male presence of native growth is it thinkable that the wearer of an American tiara *should* curtsey? Such a vision gives the measure of the degree in which we see the social empiricism in question putting, perforce, the cart before the horse. In worlds otherwise arranged, besides there being always plenty of subjects for genuflection, the occasion itself, with its character fully turned on, produces the tiara. In New York this symbol has, by an arduous extension of its virtue, to produce the occasion.

HENRY JAMES, *The American Scene*

At first sight of the Metropolitan Opera House, I gasped. Then I laughed.

That an opera house?

It looked more like a storage warehouse. Dirty brown brick. Shabby. Old, weather-stained posters hanging in tatters in the sleety winter wind. The sordid everyday business of Broadway — the hawkers, the actors and actresses out of jobs, the hotel touts, out-of-town sightseers, sandwich men, dope peddlers, gangsters, the thousands who make a living off the weakness and ignorance of other human beings — swirling in a greasy tide around its doors.

I remembered the stately Opéra in Paris; the dignity of La Scala — a palace dedicated to music and as noble as the palazzo of any Visconti in Milan. I thought of the magnificent opera house in Buenos Aires where I had sung that summer...

And this was New York. The richest, most modern, most progressive city in the world.

It seemed to me incredible that with all the great private fortunes in America, and with the American reputation for giving education a very high place, no one person had ever come forward and built for New York an opera house worthy of the city and of the art of singing.

It still seems to me extraordinary.

I have never got used to the complaisant stagnation of America's *soi-disant* society. The sentiment among the Metropolitan's box-holders in 1908 seemed to be that what had been good enough for their fathers and for themselves back in 1883 was still good enough.

And a bit too good for the new rich who were pressing in on their sacred circle.

This childish conservatism seemed all the more incongruous considering the history of the Metropolitan. It had been built by and for the new rich of the late seventies and eighties, for whom the Academy of Music, at Fourteenth Street and Irving Place, which had succeeded the opera house in Astor Place and which was the resort of old Knickerbocker New York, was not adequate. The Astors, Vanderbilts, Goelets, Drexels, Mortons, Iselins, Warrens, and Havens who had figured prominently among the first directors and box-holders still swayed destinies and determined the policies of the company.

No Jew was permitted to own a box. Mr Otto Kahn, the President of the Board, subscribed to seats in the orchestra.

That season of my début was the first season that Mrs Astor's box, Number Seven, was not occupied by society's Queen-Dowager. She had died that year. I never witnessed what I was told was the usual procedure on Monday nights. It had been Mrs Astor's custom to arrive at the opera at exactly nine o'clock. And this no matter at what hour the curtain rose. As what she did was copied slavishly by the rest of society, it developed that the opera's first act was sung to a house more than half empty.

As nine o'clock drew near, there would be the swish and rustle of silk trains, the tramp of feet coming down the orchestra aisles, the scrape of chairs being moved to better positions in the boxes.

Interest in happenings on the stage dwindled. Opera glasses were raised and focussed on the curtains of Box Seven.

Nine o'clock.

A hand parted the curtains.

Mrs Astor came in and took her seat.

An audible sigh of satisfaction passed through the house. The prestige of Monday Night was secure. Only, then, was the attention of all but the ardent music-lovers in the audience turned to the singers and orchestra.

I laughed when all this was described to me. This, in democratic America? All this kowtowing to an old lady, the widow of a descendant of a line of pork-butchers?

I thought of the wicked, autocratic, but gallant Leopold of the Belgians; of the genuine, sincere friendliness of English royalty toward the great artists who have sung and played for them; of Duke Visconti, coming round to my dressing-room after the première of *Louise* to pay his respects to the singer, and to take me to the ducal box to meet his wife.

Well, if this was America, I must accept it.

But I couldn't take it seriously.

The interior of the Metropolitan, when it was lighted and the boxes were filled, was impressive. But backstage was a disgrace.

The dressing-rooms were ill-ventilated and unbelievably dirty. They had no toilet facilities and not even running water. There were several with no windows at all. None of the singers had her own dressing-room except Farrar, who had pre-empted a small windowless room that no one else wanted, so her possession of it remained undisputed.

I stood those conditions for years. Though not uncomplainingly.

Gatti would shake his head and motion me to be quiet whenever I protested that the whole place needed a vigorous house-cleaning. But nothing was done.

Then, one year, while Gatti was in Europe, I descended on the Metropolitan with scrubbing brush, mop, and scouring soap.

At least, figuratively speaking...

FRANCES ALDA, *Men, Women and Tenors*

Beecham told me a story of hailing a taxi in New York during the war, when he was working at the Met, and asking the driver to take him to the Metropolitan Opera. 'I'm sorry, sir,' said the driver, 'but we have gas rationing now, and the rules are that I'm not allowed to take passengers to a place of entertainment.' Sir Thomas settled into the seat and waved his hand imperiously. 'The Metropolitan Opera,' he told the driver, 'is not a place of entertainment but a place of penance.'

RUDOLF BING, *5000 Nights at the Opera*

MEYERBEER

Wagner's vendetta against the popular and powerful composer Giacomo Meyerbeer was a mixture of anti-semitism, suppressed jealousy, and genuine contempt for the musical clichés and shallow theatricality of operas like Robert le Diable.

Weber wanted a drama with which to unite his noble, spiritual melody. Meyerbeer, on the other hand, wanted an irresistibly mongrel, historico-romantic, diabolico-religious, emotionally fickle, bigoted-voluptuous, frivolously sacred, mysterioso-shameless hodge-podge to serve as subject for an extraordinarily strange music, which, owing to the leathery texture of his musical mind, never quite came off.   RICHARD WAGNER, *Opera and Drama*

Saturday, April 3 [1880] R. slept well, but he dreamed about Meyerbeer, whom he met again in a theatre and who said to him, 'Yes, I know – my long nose,' as if R. had been poking fun at his nose, whereupon R. more or less apologized, and the audience applauded their reconciliation.   COSIMA WAGNER, *Diary*

His success was incredible. No one at the time would have given a penny for anyone's chances of crashing to the top, a spot that Rossini seemed to have wrapped up exclusively for himself. There were then only two groups of composers; one was Rossini; the second, all the others trying vainly to reach the top pinnacle. And this young Jew from Germany joined the exclusive Italian group that consisted of himself and Rossini. The two were rivals, but they became and remained great friends nevertheless, though

Rossini always insisted that they could never agree on anything. 'Meyerbeer likes sauerkraut better than he does macaroni,' complained the Italian master. Rossini knew that Meyerbeer tended to be pessimistic of outlook. One day they met, and Meyerbeer asked his friend how he was. Rossini sighed. 'I've got no appetite, and what little I do eat I can't digest. I can't sleep; my rheumatism's acting up. I simply don't know what to do.' When they parted, Meyerbeer hoped that the next time they met, Rossini would feel better. A friend then asked Rossini why he had said this, being in perfect health. 'You see,' said Rossini, 'dear Meyerbeer felt so miserable, I felt it my duty to tell him something that could comfort him.'   F. G. ARNSTEIN, *The Paradox of Meyerbeer*

MORALITY

After all the fuss over Salome *and* Elektra *(see p. 106), opera's next major brush with public moral standards came in the mid 1960s, when in England 'the permissive society' was waging an ultimately successful war against the archaic censorship of theatrical performances by the Lord Chamberlain. The press showed prurient interest in some naughty goings-on inside the outwardly respectable walls of Covent Garden.*

Katerina Ismailova is the revision of Lady Macbeth of Mtsensk *which Shostakovich made in order to satisfy a rather more crushing form of censorship: see p. 211.*

OPERA SINGER AND THE BED SCENE – I HOPE IT WON'T BE BANNED – MARIE

Beautiful, dark-haired Covent Garden opera star Marie Collier stretched out cosily on a giant four-poster bed today, smiled and said: 'I hope the Lord Chamberlain will not make trouble over this.'

In fact, the problem of the Lord Chamberlain and the opera star in a shorty nightie being found in bed with a tenor, was being given some urgent consideration today.

Miss Collier was rehearsing a scene at the New London Opera Centre in the East End for the production of Shostakovich's sexy shocker of an opera, *Katerina Ismailova*, which has its Western première at Covent Garden next month.

She plays the role of Katerina, mistress of a rich Russian merchant, who is seduced by a workman named Sergei.

The score calls for Katerina to be found in bed with Sergei 'standing at the head of the bed'.

Now producer Vlado Habunek has decided Katerina and Sergei, played by tenor Charles Craig, should be found in bed together. More realistic.

Australian Miss Collier said today: 'The Lord Chamberlain has approved the score with Sergei standing by the bed. Now that we are both in the bed, I don't know what he will say.'

'I don't mind being found under the blankets with Charles Craig, but the Lord Chamberlain might.'

A special large size bed has been made for the scene. It has a foot thick foam mattress. 'I'm going to be in that bed for so long, it's got to be comfortable,' said Miss Collier.

Evening Standard, 1963

STRIPTEASE TRIAL FOR ORGY OPERA

Professional striptease girls have auditioned for the ten-minute orgy scene in the opera *Moses and Aaron*, which opens next week at the Royal Opera House in Covent Garden, London.

Yesterday an opera-house spokesman said: 'Oh dear. Not more trouble with an orgy! Really, some people will come to listen to the music. I can say nothing more at the moment, than that no stripper has actually been engaged.'

A girl in the cast of the opera said: 'A stripper who has been at rehearsals was very pretty.'

The opera's German composer, Arnold Schoenberg, who died in 1951, left a written direction calling for the sacrifice of naked virgins and 'an orgy of sexual excess'.

Producer Peter Hall was asked by the Lord Chamberlain's office yesterday to handle the orgy scene 'carefully'.

Daily Mirror, 1965

MOZART

I alone was a stickler for Mozart, and naturally enough, for he had a claim on my warmest wishes, from my adoration of his powerful genius, and the debt of gratitude I owed him, for many personal favours.

The mighty contest was put an end to by His Majesty issuing a mandate for Mozart's *Nozze di Figaro* to be instantly put into rehearsal; and none more than Michael O'Kelly, enjoyed the little great man's triumph over his rivals.

Of all the performers in this opera at that time, but one survives – myself. It was allowed that never was opera stronger cast. I have seen it performed at different periods in other countries, and well too, but no more to compare with its original performance than light is to darkness. All the original performers had the advantage of the instruction of the composer, who transfused into their minds his inspired meaning. I never shall forget his little animated countenance, when lighted up with the glowing rays of genius; – it is impossible to describe it, as it would be to paint sun-beams.

I called on him one evening, he said to me, 'I have just finished a little duet for my opera, you shall hear it.' He sat down to the piano, and we sang it. I was delighted with it, and the musical world will give me credit for being so, when I mention the duet, sung by Count Almaviva and Susan, 'Crudel perche finora farmi languire così.' A more delicious morceau never was penned by man, and it has often been a source of pleasure to me, to have been the first who heard it, and to have sung it with its greatly gifted composer. I remember at the first rehearsal of the full band, Mozart was on the stage with his crimson pelisse and gold-laced cocked hat, giving the time of the music to the orchestra. Figaro's song, 'Non piu andrai, farfallone amoroso', Bennuci gave, with the greatest animation, and power of voice.

I was standing close to Mozart, who, *sotto voce*, was repeating, Bravo! Bravo! Bennuci; and when Bennuci came to the fine passage, 'Cherubino, alla vittoria, alla gloria militar', which he gave out with Stentorian lungs, the effect was electricity itself, for the whole of the performers on the stage, and those in the orchestra, as if actuated by one feeling of delight, vociferated Bravo! Bravo! Maestro. Viva, viva, grande Mozart. Those in the orchestra I thought would never have ceased applauding, by beating the bows of their violins against the music desks. The little man acknowledged, by repeated obeisances, his thanks for the distinguished mark of enthusiastic applause bestowed upon him.

The same meed of approbation was given to the finale at the end of the first act; that piece of music alone, in my humble opinion, if he had never composed any thing else good, would have stamped him as the greatest master of his art. In the sestetto, in the second act (which was Mozart's favourite piece of the whole opera) I had a very conspicuous part, as the Stuttering Judge. All through the piece I was to stutter; but in the sestetto, Mozart requested I would not, for if I did, I should spoil his music. I told him, that although it might appear very presumptuous in a lad like me to differ with him on this point, I did, and was sure, the way in which I intended to introduce the stuttering, would not interfere with the other parts, but produce an effect; besides, it certainly was not in nature, that I should stutter all through the part, and when I came to the sestetto speak plain; and after that piece of music was over, return to stuttering; and, I added, (apologizing at the same time, for my apparent want of deference and respect in placing my opinion in opposition to that of the great Mozart), that unless I was allowed to perform the part as I wished, I would not perform it at all.

Mozart at last consented that I should have my own way, but doubted the success of the experiment. Crowded houses proved that nothing ever on the stage produced a more powerful effect; the audience were convulsed with laughter, in which Mozart himself joined. The Emperor repeatedly cried out Bravo! and the piece was loudly applauded and encored. When the opera was over, Mozart came on the stage to me, and shaking me by both hands, said 'Bravo! young man, I feel obliged to you; and acknowledge you to have been in the right, and myself in the wrong.' There was certainly a risk run, but I felt within myself I could give the effect I wished, and the event proved that I was not mistaken.

I have seen the opera in London, and elsewhere, and never saw the judge pourtrayed as a stutterer, and the scene was often totally omitted. I played it as a stupid old man, though at the time I was a beardless stripling. At the end of the opera, I thought the audience would never have done applauding and calling for Mozart, almost every piece was encored, which prolonged it nearly to the length of two operas, and induced the Emperor to issue an order on the second representation, that no piece of music should be encored. Never was any thing more complete, than the triumph of Mozart, and his 'Nozze di Figaro'...

MICHAEL KELLY, *Reminiscences*

The novelist Thomas Love Peacock, quoted below, was one of the first English admirers of Mozart; he proselytized his friend Shelley and his wife Mary to the point of taking them to see Don Giovanni *five times within a month, shortly before they left England for Italy in 1818.*

There is nothing perfect in this world except Mozart's music. Criticism has nothing to do with it, but to admire. Whatever is is right. Mozart cannot even be disparaged by comparison with himself – the detractor cannot say, 'How inferior this thing is to that!' for every composition seems to have a peculiar appropriateness to the occasion, and it is impossible to conceive any thing more suitable. There is nothing of mannerism in Mozart's music, and yet it cannot be mistaken for any other, or any other for it — it is peculiar in its excellence. The signature of the master is in an exalted sweetness of turns. In Mozart's operas there is every variety of style and expression, each having a marked style to which the varieties within it are subordinate and tributary. *Don Giovanni* and the *Zauberflöte* are both romantic operas, but of what different characters! In each the grandeur is relieved with gaiety; and here again how different the gaiety! In *Giovanni* it is touched with riot, in the *Zauberflöte* it is all fanciful and cheery. As wide a distinction is to be marked between the gaiety of *Figaro* and of *Così fan tutte*; the first is of enjoyment, the other the light laugh of the world coming more from the brain than the blood. The expression of the serious passions has as much variety in the works of Mozart as the comic. The simple sustained style of the *Clemenza* has no likeness in any of the solemn passages of his romantic operas, and the grandeur of the *Zauberflöte* is as distinguishable from the grandeur of *Giovanni*, as the devotional from the terrible. In the expression of tenderness there is most sameness in Mozart's compositions; and how could it be other than same while true to nature, which, in all states, shows herself much alike in the melting mood?

Our century, which will surely be the most execrated in history (always provided it allows history to continue so that there is someone to execrate it) has this to its credit: it is recognizing Mozart.

Mozart's orchestral music had never dropped out of the repertory. But it is his operas that lifted his genius to its highest and most sustained pitch, and operas which, as his letters make plain, he himself pre-eminently *wanted* to compose: and here, though some of the music from them was never wholly lost to the public's ears, it is the twentieth century which has resurrected the works as wholes and made it comparatively easy to hear good performances of the five major operas and not too difficult to hunt down most of the minor ones.

Even so, all that can be accurately said for the twentieth century is that it is in the process of recognizing Mozart. We have accomplished the resurrection but do not always perceive its value or even its content. Indeed, the very conjurers who have revived the operas and put them on the stage often go out of their way to prevent us from taking in their content, no doubt because they themselves do not fully believe that the operas *are* alive. Producers dare not take with Mozart today quite the liberties Victorian impresari took with Shakespeare when they mounted his plays as spectacular pantomimes: yet plenty of well sung and well played Mozart performances bury their virtues – sometimes under cheap and farcical business, but more often under picturesque and extremely expensive business. Whole 'crowds', corps de ballet or, worst of all, other singers coached ad hoc in the craft of acting are deployed to distract the eye while one singer gets on with the aria that has been reduced to a mere accompaniment. Most recent productions of Mozart have been designed on the theory that audiences would perish of boredom if the producer left them for a moment unattended with Mozart's music.

This is gross slander not only on Mozart the supreme artist and dramatist (he is more than capable of keeping audiences entertained by his own methods) but on Mozart the melodist. Mozart was probably borne back into the repertory simply on the wings of his own melodic fertility. He shares with Donizetti, Irving Berlin, Handel and Sir Arthur Sullivan the sheer gift of inventing tunes to be sung: a fertility so rare that we cannot afford to neglect for very long any composer who possesses it, but which does not in itself guarantee, though it is indispensable to, great opera. Yet if his tunes brought him back, it is fashion which makes much of him and lets producers expensively loose on him: and if we have no better reason for staging his operas, fashion may equally well carry him away again from our great-grandchildren.

BRIGID BROPHY, *Mozart the Dramatist*

MURDER

Opera, that most murderous of the fine arts, relies heavily on perforating its victims with an assortment of pointed weapons. Stabbing is not carried to the point of monotony, however; there are a respectable number of violent deaths effected by other means, some of them quite ingenious.

One would think that death by fire would be impractical on the stage, but several operas include episodes of incineration, though none could be classified as willful murder. No one would deny, for example, that Gretel is acting in self-defense when she bakes the Witch into a gingerbread cookie. The other cases, excluding self-immolations, are either executions – unjust, perhaps, but legal, like Joan of Arc or the Protestants in *Don Carlo* – or the regrettable but unavoidable inclusion of non-combatants in some general holocaust, as in *Le Prophète*. Pollione in *Norma* offers a curious instance, voluntarily facing the Druid flames with his guilty priestess.

We are spared the spectacle of opera's most gruesome death by fire, which occurred years before the beginning of *Il Trovatore*; it would be painful enough to see Azucena throw an infant into the fire, much worse to know she accidentally selected her own. (In spite of all the talk about stakes in *Il Trovatore*, no one in the opera ever does get burned at one. Manrico is supposedly beheaded – Di Luna destines him for 'the axe' – and Azucena is still alive at the end, though obviously a poor risk for fire insurance.) In *La Juive*, Halévy and Scribe were not so considerate of audience sensibility, for Rachel is boiled in oil right onstage as the Cardinal finally learns that she is his long-lost daughter.

In addition to burning and boiling, there is a scattering of other legal or quasi-legal killings: Madame Guillotine accounts for Andrea Chénier and Maddalena; the heads of Anna Bolena,

Jochanaan and *Turandot*'s Prince of Persia are removed by the executioner's sword: Aida and Radames suffer the ancient Egyptian equivalent of the gas chamber, suffocation in a vault. Magda Sorel in *The Consul* also dies from lack of air when she places her head in an oven. No one seems to be hanged, though Dick Johnson is saved only at the last minute by the Girl of the Golden West.

Shooting occurs infrequently, partly because it is too long-distance and impersonal for the passions aroused in opera. Perhaps this same element of impersonality, of killing at a remove, accounts for the comparative rarity of homicidal poisoning. Still, poison is traditionally a woman's weapon, and the opera is the world of the prima donna; also, it is probably the simplest kind of theatrical murder. Paolo Albiani is alert to its possibilities and dispatches Simon Boccanegra by putting something in his drink, but as a rule operatic poisonings are uncommon – despite some admirable opportunities.

Consider *Götterdämmerung*, for example. The Gibichungs have already ruined Siegfried's life with their hallucinating drugs; why not go back to the family medicine chest and find something really toxic? Surely it would be easier than hitting exactly the right spot in his back with a big clumsy spear. Or, if Rigoletto is at all interested in getting away with murder, poisoning the Duke's wine would be a better bet than hiring an assassin to knife him. The jester, who would not mind in the least if he did away with the whole 'vil razza dannata' of the court, is not one to shrink from poisoning a whole case of wine, if necessary. Nor is Gilda any problem; she could intercept the fatal draught sacrificially, as Hamlet's mother does by accident.

Laura Adorno, ordered by her husband to drink some fatal mixture, is saved because Gioconda substitutes a strong sleeping medicine; we cannot help wondering, however, why both ladies are so unenterprising. Laura should have shifted the glasses around somehow, letting the disagreeable Alvise drink his own poison. Even the great 'Suicidio!' aria fails to convince us that Gioconda could not have resolved her problems another way – by giving the obnoxious Barnaba a dose of her useful anaesthetic and dumping him into a canal.

Two operatic poisonings that do succeed are decidedly exotic: Adriana Lecouvreur dies rather promptly after merely smelling a bouquet sent her by the jealous Princess de Bouillon, while in *L'Amore dei Tre Re* both Avito and Manfredo succumb after kissing the poison-smeared lips of the dead Fiora. These crimes have a subtlety more worthy of Lucrezia Borgia than the mass murder of dinner guests perpetrated by that lady in Donizetti's opera of the same name.   M. EUGENIA GEIB, *Opera News*, 1964

MUSSORGSKY

In 1871 Mussorgsky and I agreed to live together and we shared rooms (or rather a room) on Pantyeleymonovskay Street. In the mornings until noon Mussorgsky used the piano while I did copying or scoring. By noon he went to his departmental duties leaving the piano to me. Moreover, twice a week I went to the conservatoire at 8.0 a.m. while Mussorgsky frequently dined out, so that the arrangement worked smoothly. That autumn and winter the two of us accomplished a good deal. Mussorgsky composed and orchestrated the Polish act of *Boris Godunoff* and the folk scene 'Near Kromy'. I finished and orchestrated my *Maid of Pskov*. The *Maid of Pskov* was performed for the first time on 1 January 1873, and favourably received. At the end of the season two scenes from *Boris Godunoff* were also given and scored a great success. Mussorgsky and all of us were delighted; after the performance Mussorgsky and other friends came to our house where we drank champagne, wishing an early performance and success to *Boris*. It was given in January 1874 and so well received that we were all jubilant. Mussorgsky was then already at work on *Khovanshtchina*. The original version of this opera had many details which have since disappeared. A whole tableau had been projected in the suburb of a German town and Mussorgsky played to us sketches of the scene composed in a quasi-Mozartian style to fit the bourgeois German scene. In Act I there was a rather long scene in which the people demolished the scrivener's booth. When, after Mussorgsky's death, I was preparing the opera for publication, I omitted this scene altogether as quite unmusical; it also delayed the action. ... There was some barbarous music of empty, perfect fourths intended for the choir of schismatics, which Mussorgsky fortunately altered later. There are now only odds and ends of the first sketch in the beautiful chorus of schismatics in the Phrygian mode.

After the production of *Boris Godunoff* Mussorgsky appeared in our midst less often; a marked change was seen in him. His conceit grew enormously and his involved manner of expression grew more marked; we could no longer understand his stories and sallies meant to be witty and amusing. At the same time he began to loiter in restaurants till the early hours drinking brandy. When he dined with us he refused wine, but after nightfall he would resort to the restaurant and drink heavily.

After his retirement from service Mussorgsky began to compose by fits and starts, going from one subject to another. ... His mental and spiritual decline was largely due to the success and failure of *Boris*. The first success made him proud and conceited, but after a time the opera began to be cut about. The splendid scene 'Near Kromy' was omitted altogether and two years later, for some inexplicable reason, the work which had been most popular disappeared from the repertory. Every barman in St Petersburg knew *Boris* and *Khovanshtchina* and honoured their composer, but the Russian Musical Society, while treating him with great affability, denied him recognition. His friends still loved him and frankly admired his brilliant flashes of creative genius, but the press was continuously scolding him. In the circumstances his craving for brandy and the desire to lounge in taverns grew stronger every day. A drinking bout which may not have affected his companions at all was poison to a man of his morbidly nervous temperament. Though still keeping up friendly relations, he began to look upon me with suspicion. My studies in harmony and counterpoint did not please him; he seemed to think

I was likely to become a pedant who would upbraid him for writing consecutive fifths. His relations with Balakireff had been strained for some time. Even in the old days Balakireff used to say that Mussorgsky had great natural talent but 'feeble brains' and a reprehensible fondness for wine.

NICHOLAS RIMSKY-KORSAKOV, *My Musical Life*

OBITUARIES

Obituaries for those operatic characters who never appeared but whose influence was crucial.

Time – Mythological

Ego Senem cecidi cum Corintho excederem, cecidi in trivio.

STRAVINSKY, Oedipus Rex

The death of Laius, King of Thebes, in mysterious and violent circumstances leaves a gap which mercifully appears likely to be filled by his staunch and loving wife, Jocasta, supported so ably by her new husband, Oedipus.

Time – Mythological

Dich ächt genannten acht' ich zu neiden; die beid' uns Brüder gebar, Frau Grimhild liess michs begreifen.

WAGNER, Götterdämmerung

After years of lingering sorrow, Frau Grimhild, mother to disappointing children by different fathers, passed on, little mourned or remembered. The hatred and envy that her son Hagen bore for his half-brother and sister, Gunther and Gutrune, was a source of great sadness during Frau Grimhild's last unhappy years, not lessened by their tragic fratricidic end.

Time — AD 30

Knie nieder am Ufer des Sees, ruf ihn an und rufe ihn beim Namen. Wenn er zu dir kommt und er kommt zu allen, die ihn rufen, dann bükke dich zu seinen Füssen, dass er dir deine Sünden vergebe.

R. STRAUSS, *Salome*

The death of Jesus of Nazareth, foretold by many 'prophets', including the one known as John the Baptist, seems likely to have more than local repercussions. Local politics in Palestine have now for a number of years provided a source of concern throughout the Roman Empire and indicate that the process of devolution — whereby local rulers control local disturbances — may not be in the best interests of the Empire.

Time — 16th century

Ella sentia quel l'Angelo, pieta delle mie pene. Solo, difforme, povero, per compassion mi amo.

VERDI, *Rigoletto*

The death of the wife of Rigoletto, court jester to the Duke of Mantua, was little noticed. She had for a number of years been something of a recluse and taken no share in her husband's public life. Among her closest confidants there was rumour of a child, Gilda, but few if any had seen her, or been aware of the close ties that bound the tiny family or of the tragic effect that her death had on her husband.

Time — 18th century

Tom Rakewell had an uncle, one long parted from his native land.

STRAVINSKY, *The Rake's Progress*

The death of Ned Rakewell in a remote part of northern New South Wales was reported recently. Rakewell's career as an

273

entrepreneur in London came to an abrupt end several years ago after an unfortunate association with a partner, Nick Shadow, whose affairs are still the subject of legal inquiries.

Time – 1800

Ma falle gli occhi neri. PUCCINI, *Tosca*

The death is announced in Rome of the Marchesa Attavanti. It is thought that she met her end in the aftermath of the troubles surrounding the assasination of the Roman Chief of Police, Scarpia, whose edict had resulted in the death of the Marchesa's brother, Cesare Angelotti – lately Consul of Rome – and the painter Mario Cavaradossi, whose execution on the ramparts of the Castle of Sant' Angelo is still the subject of legal inquiry. It is rumoured that the Marchesa, along with the singer Floria Tosca, had an amorous association with Cavaradossi.

Time – 1820

C'est votre mere qui m'envoie. BIZET, *Carmen*

News from remote villages in the Basque region of Northern Spain rarely impinges on Spanish, let alone European, society. In recent months, however, it has reached our notice that an elderly peasant woman's death has led to riots and disruption on a wide scale. It appears that the woman's son, a soldier called José, serving in Seville, had been involved in an affaire de coeur *with a southern gypsy girl, as a result of which he was charged with insubordination and subsequently met his death in a fracas at a bullfight. The woman's neighbours, convinced of discrimination against Basques, were up in arms and in the resultant demonstrations the peasant woman lost her life. We fear that the turmoil this has created will take months if not years to settle.*

Time – 1890

On the road to Campsie Ash, crushed by a cart.

BRITTEN, Albert Herring

BILLOWS, SIR BERNARD. *On April 1st, 1890, as a result of a road accident on his return from Felixstowe. Loving husband.*

HERRING, ALFRED. *On April 1st, 1890, as a result of a road accident on his return from Felixstowe. Loving husband and father. Flowers to and from the Greengrocers in Main Street.*

Time – 1905

E vostro padre? morto. E un presente del Mikado a suo padre . . . coll' invito. . . .

PUCCINI, Madama Butterfly

An example of tyrannous and medieval barbarism has reached us from Nagasaki. In recent years our fleet has made several visits to this unusual town and our brave sailors have been able to play a part in the spread of Christian civilization to heathen Japan. Our Consul in Nagasaki tells a sad story of a young Japanese girl whose father was compelled to commit suicide in a particularly bestial fashion by the 'Emperor' of Japan as a result of some minor disagreement. The story has, however, a happy end since she was fortunate enough to meet and subsequently marry one of our brave boys who was visiting her city.

PETER HEMMINGS,
Scottish Opera Yearbook 1986–7

OPERA SERIA

Opera seria – serious opera – was the most important and prestigious creation of the musical Baroque. Without its techniques, conventions and aesthetic, Handel's oratorios and Bach's mastery

275

of the aria and of melodic ornamentation could not have developed as they did. Yet it is only very recently that our opera-houses have begun to take *opera seria* seriously, on its own terms. Perhaps audiences will learn to find in its very 'artificialities' and 'unrealities' a source of strength: more than any other art-form, opera needs its conventions: an agreed framework, an expected pattern from which significant departures may be made. Yet today, when anything goes, theatre music can be poured like reinforced concrete into any shape or mould. Many a modern composer who has ventured into opera will ruefully tell you, if he is honest, that he feels hamstrung from the start by the lack of any agreed common language linking stage and audience. In such a context, the rigidities of baroque convention become a welcome strength.

It is something of a paradox that the very finest Italian *opere serie* of the Baroque should have been written by a Saxon living in London, setting libretti almost never designed specially for him, in a language which was neither his own nor that of his audience (though they probably understood Italian much better than a modern British audience, and had bi-lingual libretti to follow). But Handel's isolation gave him certain advantages. He could adapt libretti much more easily to his will, truncating the often long-winded fine sentiments of the recitatives in order to make room for more and longer arias – and, in spite of current misconceptions, it is in the succession of arias, not in the recitatives, that the essential continuity of the action lies. Handel seems to have exercised much more control over his company and his performers than might have been the case in the typical Italian opera company at an Italian or South German court: the Royal Academy of Music, though it enjoyed court patronage, was set up, in typical British fashion, as a joint-stock company. Handel must also have drawn valuable artistic support from the more discerning of his noble patrons in Augustan London, men such as the Earl of Burlington. It is easy to forget, when we read the often self-interested attacks on Italian opera by writers such as Addison and Steele, or accounts of the frivolity of the London audience, that Handel's dramatic perceptions were subtler and stronger than theirs, that he had not been nurtured on a diet of Otway and Rowe, and that much of the sensitive writing on the aesthetics of painting and architecture that he might have read in such authors as Shaftesbury was very relevant to the highly pictorial 'aria opera'. The choice of the 'significant moment', the exact narrative point or single emotional crisis with which painting or aria must deal, which gesture, tone, texture and design must combine to illuminate, is at the very heart of Handel's operatic method, which is at once highly analytical and extraordinarily concentrated and passionate.

The general themes of *opera seria* can often seem irrelevant to us today. Whether the story is classical myth, medieval history or epic fantasy, the subject-matter is essentially concerned with the behaviour of the great and powerful, of the kings, princes and dukes who had fostered the new art and used it to celebrate court occasions. Behind a typical Handel libretto we can trace the moral and social concerns of the earlier French dramatists Corneille and Racine (the former shows the individual will triumphing over its baser temptations, the latter the will failing and the individual destroyed). How should great princes behave? How use their absolute power when public duty and private love come into conflict? How choose a wife? How conduct themselves so that their 'gloire' – their good name, reputation, honour – should continue to justify the admiration and obedience of their subjects and their families? These were very important matters in an age of unfettered absolutism, when marriage and inheritance could lead to dynastic conflicts such as the War of the Spanish Succession. The French Revolution and the arrival of bourgeois constitutional monarchy naturally robbed *opera seria*, at this level, of most of its overt contemporary relevance.

All the same, Corneille and Racine reached beyond their immediate subject-matter to universal truths expressed in timeless verse and powerful dramatic portraiture, so that their dramas, greater than their local themes, still survive. The same is true of Handel's musical dramas. The individual arias, of course, were never forgotten, and many have been sung as concert pieces since the time when Walsh or Cluer first published them. That being so, and in view of the fact that the operas consist of solo arias and very little else, it is perhaps odd that we have had to wait so long to arrive at a proper understanding of the principles by which Handel used them to portray character and arranged them into significantly grouped sequences to make a scene, an act, a whole opera.

The method is like Hogarth's. His famous sets of oil-paintings, soon made into best-selling prints, such as *The Rake's Progress*, need no narration or 'recitative'. He selects for depiction various significant moments in the Rake's or the Harlot's story and arranges around his central character such a wealth of telling detail, all relevant to the main point at issue – Rakewell buying love in a brothel, Rakewell buying social admiration – that we ourselves, as we examine the detail, diffuse the imagery in our minds beyond the spatial and temporal confines of the picture; the wainscoting between the separate paintings, as we walk from one to another, becomes charged with the implications of the story. . . .

The aria opera developed perfectly naturally as the quintessence of the chief expressive and structural elements in baroque music, using an analytical method of presentation which is common in other art-forms of the time as well. Form and matter are one, and it need not disturb us that there are no concerted finales and almost no ensembles of any kind. Even the psychology of the much-scorned 'exit aria' is in fact perfectly valid: the opera is experienced as a series of wave-like crescendos of dramatic excitement, each of which ends in a crisis for one of the characters, who sings an aria; after which there is for the moment no more to be said until a new sequence of events has placed that character in a new posture requiring a new aria. (In French opera of the time, arias often begin an act, so that the ensuing action dangles after them; in practice, this usually seems less psychologically satisfying.) It has been all too easy, for the past two centuries, for historians and critics to go on repeating Gluck's censures on mid-eighteenth-century *opera seria* as if they were intended to refer to the operas of Alessandro Scarlatti and Handel, which probably Gluck, and certainly those who quote him, had never heard. It may well be that the 'caprice and vanity of singers' had increased during the lean years of the 1740s and 1750s; but the virtuosity which Handel's operas demand is never empty. He was writing for the greatest singers in the world; but their superb vocal technique would have been useless without the dramatic and musical insight, presence and sense of style, which alone make the 'impossible' conventions of *opera seria* not merely possible but vital and viable for us today.   BRIAN TROWELL

programme note for Julius Caesar

PACCHIEROTTI

Most exquisite and musicianly of the castrati, Gasparo Pacchierotti was probably the first opera singer to be recorded in conversation – by Fanny Burney in her entertaining journal.

While he was here Pacchierotti called – very grave, but very sweet. Mr G.C. asked if he spoke English.

'Oh, very well,' cried I, 'pray try him; he is very amiable, and I fancy you will like him.'

Pacchierotti began with complaining of the variable weather.

'I cannot,' he said, 'be well such an inconsistent day.'

We laughed at the word 'inconsistent', and Mr Cambridge said, 'It is curious to see what new modes all languages may take in the hands of foreigners. The natives dare not try such experiments; and, therefore, we all talk pretty much alike; but a foreigner is obliged to hazard new expressions, and very often he shows us a force and power in our words, by an unusual adaptation of them, that we were not ourselves aware they would admit.'

And then, to draw Pacchierotti out, he began a dispute, of the different merits of Italy and England; defending his own country merely to make him abuse it; while Pacchierotti most eagerly took up the gauntlet on the part of Italy.

'This is a climate,' said Pacchierotti, 'never in the same case for half an hour at a time; it shall be fair, and wet, and dry, and humid, forty times in a morning in the least. I am tired to be so played with, sir, by the climate.'

'We have one thing, however, Mr Pacchierotti,' he answered, 'which I hope you allow makes some amends, and that is our verdure; in Italy you cannot boast that.'

'But it seem to me, sir, to be of no utility so much evergreen; is rather too much for my humble opinion.'

'And then your insects, Mr Pacchierotti; those alone are a most dreadful drawback upon the comfort of your fine climate.'

'To Mr Cambridge,' cried I, meaning his father, 'I am sure they would; for his aversion to insects is quite comical.'

He wanted me to explain myself, but I dare not tell a story after Mr Cambridge, especially to his son.

'I must own,' said Pacchierotti, 'Italy is rather disagreeable for the insects; but is not better, sir, than an atmosphere so bad as they cannot live in it?'

'Why, as I can't defend our atmosphere, I must shift my ground, and talk to you of our fires, which draw together society.'

'Oh, indeed, good sir, your societies are not very invigorating! Twenty people of your gentlemen and ladies to sit about a fire, and not to pronounce one word, is very dull!'

We laughed heartily at this retort courteous, and Mr G.C. was so much pleased with is, that he kept up a sportive conversation with him the whole time he stayed, much to my satisfaction; as most of the people the poor Pac. meets with here affect a superiority to conversing with him, though he has more intelligence, ay, and cultivation too, than half of them.

Of all these dim figures of long-forgotten singers which arise, tremulous and hazy, from out of the faded pages of biographies and scores, evoked by some intense word of admiration or some pathetic snatch of melody, there is one more poetical than the rest – for all such ghosts of forgotten genius are poetical – that of Gasparo Pacchierotti, who flourished just a century ago [viz. *c.* 1780]. For in those that heard him he left so deep an impression of supreme genius, of moral and intellectual beauty, that even now we cannot read of him without falling under a sort of charm. In the pages in which the writers of the day speak of Pacchierotti there lies, as it were, a faded, crumbling flower of feeling, whose discoloured fragments still retain a perfume that goes strangely to the imagination; so that we almost fancy that we ourselves must once, vaguely and distantly, have heard that weirdly sweet voice, those subtle, pathetic intonations. Some such occult charm, acting after a century, there must be, for no story, no romance, is connected with this singer that could explain the interest he awakens. We catch a glimpse of him once or twice in Beckford and Stendhal's books, we see him oftenest in Madame d'Arblay's Diary – a gaunt youth, with plain features, but which would light up with a look of genius; proud and shy and silent, but bursting out sometimes into a strange, impassioned sort of prose-poetry, beautiful and grotesque, such as children and poets appreciate; ardent and patient, learning English and Latin and Greek with passionate eagerness, loving his own art with intense, never-satisfied enthusiasm; a curious whimsical character, always in pursuit of some indefinable excellence; equally at home in Dr Burney's parlour in Poland Street, in Mrs Thrale's garden at Streatham, and in Daddy Crispe's hermitage at Chesington, an unexpected figure by the side of Johnson, of Burke, and of Reynolds; comprehended by very few, liked by all, and especially, with a singular romantic, sisterly sort of affection, by that most sharp-witted and sharp-tongued little Fanny Burney, who, years later, when he was dead, and she an old woman, declared, that had Pacchierotti not been a singer, he must certainly have been a poet, without perceiving that the secret of his influence lay in his being both together. Strangely enough, by a curious accident, we got yet another glimpse of this singer – the glimpse, as it were, of a ghost. For rambling one day through a quiet corner of Padua – where the rows of gloomy porticoed streets have gradually thinned, and the town seems insensibly to grow into the open country, green with budding vines and corn; where you are met by bends of the sluggish, verdure-garlanded canal, which reflect faded Palladian villas, and by tracts of desolate gardens, with only mutilated statues and rows of unclipped trees, to mark their former avenues – in this remote corner of Padua we stumbled one day into a beautiful tangle of trees and grass and flowers, separated from the grand cedars and magnolias of the Orto Botanico by a bend of the

Brenta, and were informed by a gardener's boy that this garden had once belonged to a famous singer, by name Gasparo Pacchierotti (of whom your Excellency has perhaps heard? Why should we, why should any one?). The gardener led us into the house, a battered house, covered with creepers and amphorae, and sentimental inscriptions from the works of the poets and philosophers in vogue a hundred years ago – beautiful quotations, which, in their candour, grandiloquence, and sweetness, now strike us as so strangely hollow and melancholy. He showed us into a long, narrow room, in which was a large, slender harpsichord – the harpsichord, he informed us, which had belonged to Pacchierotti, the singer. It was open, and looked as if it might just have been touched, but no sound could be drawn from it. The gardener then led us into a darkened lumber-room, where hung the portrait of the singer, thickly covered with dust: a mass of dark blurs, from out of which appeared scarcely more than the pale, thin face – a face with deep dreamy eyes and tremulously tender lips, full of a vague, wistful, contemplative poetry, as if of aspirations after something higher, sweeter, fairer – aspirations never fulfilled but never disappointed, and forming in themselves a sort of perfection. This man must have been an intense instance of that highly-wrought sentimental idealism which arose, delicate and diaphanous, in opposition to the hard, materialistic rationalism of the eighteenth century; and the fascination which he exerted over the best of his contemporaries must have been due to his embodying all their vague ephemeral cravings in an art which was still young and vigorous – to his having been at once the *beautiful soul* of early romanticism and the genuine artist of yet classic music.

VERNON LEE, Studies of Eighteenth-Century Italy

PARIS

The nineteenth-century equivalent of a night out at an Andrew Lloyd Webber musical was an evening at the Paris Opéra, where Meyerbeer and his librettist Scribe produced a series of operas according to a formula cleverly calculated to satisfy the tastes and fantasies of the wealthy bourgeoisie: flash, spectacle and melodrama were paramount. See also p. 259.

The [Opéra] was both the factory in which epics were manufactured on a production line and the Crystal Palace in which they were displayed for sale. It imposed an industrial standardization on its composers, insisting for example on the insertion of ballets in the same way that a machine must flaunt a novel gadget, and punishing *Tannhäuser* for breach of commercial practice by putting the ballet in the wrong place. Meyerbeer represents the mechanization of epic; in him the creative process becomes automated. His conception of his art is actually not political . . . but industrial. His operas are assembled by a division of labor between himself, Scribe, the scene-painters and the singers. Each one is a fashionable variation on a formula which remains unchanged, like successive models of the same car. He is a musical tycoon. The 'totality of objects' which Hegel made the criterion of epic becomes, in this commercialization of the form, simply a totality of expensive and gratuitous effects, disclosing the machine at play.

Wagner jokes that Meyerbeer had commissioned Scribe to furnish a scenic equivalent of Berlioz's orchestra. Berlioz, like Wagner himself, was mocked by cartoonists for the elephantine scope and monstrous inventiveness of his orchestration; both were treated as crazed scientific projectors. Berlioz in one comic print uses a telegraph pole as a baton. Wagner was credited in a Viennese cartoon with the invention of 'Die Bayreuther Tonkunst-Dampfmaschine', a musical vapor-machine. Hanslick, describing the tinted steam and gas apparatus of Bayreuth in 1876, remarked that Wagner could not have composed the *Ring* before the invention of electric light. Wagner's imagination and that of Berlioz turn technology into art, and in the composition of their so-called epics, *Der Ring des Nibelungen* and *Les Troyens*, both approach Meyerbeer in remaking epic in the image of the mid-nineteenth century.

As Heine had attached Meyerbeer to the institutional models of democratic parliament and the army, so these works of Wagner and Berlioz resemble two other institutions characteristic of their civilization. One is the factory, in which aesthetic creation follows the logic of the industrial process by which wealth is created, and which turns works of art into assemblages of moving parts like machines. The other is the museum, a factory in which the past is organized and processed.

PETER CONRAD, *Romantic Opera and Literary Form*

PARODY

On 27 May 1847 London heard *La Fille du Régiment* for the first time, with Jenny Lind flourishing the frills and drumsticks of Marie. It was the Swedish Nightingale's greatest success in an almost hysterically successful season, which she repeated the following year. Jenny's costume was captured in a Staffordshire pottery figure, and by June 1848 there were two English 'operas' called *The Daughter of the Regiment* in performance in other theaters. Finally, twenty years later, Donizetti's opera was burlesqued by W. S. Gilbert, a London neighbor of Miss Lind.

The Victorian appetite for entertainment was omnivorous.

Like their Queen, Victorians delighted in both Van Amburgh with his performing lions and Jenny in *La Fille du Régiment* –partly, perhaps, because both performers wore uniforms. Audiences swallowed down serious operas and lapped up comic perversions of those same operas. In fact, nineteenth-century audiences liked all kinds of references to, extracts from and treatments of opera: in comic journals, as parts of other works, serious, buffa or burlesqued. J. R. Planché, for instance, in a topical revue, *Success, or, A Hit If You Like It* (1825), introduced Samiel from Weber's *Freischütz* to sing and thereby parody the popularity of the hunting chorus, 'The charming, eternal, unmerciful song'. A Cinderella pantomime by William Brough parodied the magic bullet-casting scene of the same opera, with Titania summoning a fairy chorus to enchant pumpkin, lizards and mice into coach, footmen and ponies. Many hands made light work of *Dinorah under Difficulties*; *Carmen, or, Sold for a Song*; and *L'Africaine, or, The Queen of the Cannibal Islands*.

Burlesque writers also attacked operas themselves partly or entirely comic: *The Bohemian G'yurl and the Unapproachable Pole*; *Young Fra Diavolo, The Terror of Terracini*; *Doctor Dulcamara, or, The Little Duck and the Great Quack*; *La Vivandière, or, True to the Corps!* Tightly knit comic librettos, however, were less frequently burlesqued than those with loosely constructed plots. The fewer the emotions and the higher the style in a comic opera, the less likelihood of its being parodied. *L'Elisir d'Amore* and *Don Giovanni* were each the subject of several burlesques, but none seems to have been directed against *Don Pasquale* or *Così Fan Tutte*.

Whether they dealt with comic or serious operas, the burlesque writers' techniques were essentially the same. First, the attack was almost invariably against the libretto – except when, as with Weber's hunting chorus, some opera number had become a popular street song. So little did the music matter that almost none of the original score would appear in the burlesque; airs from other operas, folk and nonce songs would take its place. Gilbert's burlesque of *La Fille du Régiment* used only two of Donizetti's numbers, while his *Pretty Druidess* retained only a chorus from

Norma. Musical parody was not the aim of such travesties.

One need not have seen the original in order to enjoy the burlesque, which often drew on a common stock of satiric subjects loosely suggested by the opera. If the original plot contained an outlaw, the travesty would likely satirize financiers or merchants who robbed within the law. The presence of a middle-aged woman like the Marquise of Berkenfield brought out jokes against the pretensions of middle age to attractiveness. Characters might be added or have their names changed, as when Donizetti's steward Hortensius becomes Gilbert's Pumpernickel. A few burlesque writers, such as Gilbert, occasionally followed the original quite closely until the denouement, which they then wrenched by introducing an inappropriately prosaic solution. *Faust and Marguerite* by F. C. Burnand stays more or less with the story until Faust, sued for breach of promise, escapes Mephistopheles by consenting to marry – Dame Martha!

This exemplifies a basic method of parody, the deflation of romanticism by introducing practical considerations. One of Brough's characters punningly points out Ernani's incapacity as an outlaw: 'This thing Ernani don't *earn-any*thing!' In *Robert the Devil, or, The Nun, the Dun, and the Son of a Gun*, Meyerbeer's magic branch turns to a policeman's club, a more efficient agent of change. Even a comic plot could be parodied by the adduction of possibilities inherent in situations or characters left unclear or undeveloped in the original. Marie's father, Captain Robert, deceased in Donizetti, is resurrected by Gilbert in *La Vivandière* as Count Roberto, 'disguised as Manfred and living on the summit of Mont Blanc'. Marie's infant presence on a battlefield is explained by Roberto's being 'the most devoted father known;/ Towards the infant he felt such attraction,/He always took it with him into action.'

The rhymed couplets of burlesque dialogue were filled with far more plays on words than the usual comic libretto. The occasional brilliance of this verbal distortion supplied something akin to the virtuosity of coloratura, and like coloratura it often became an end in itself. A strong requirement, however, was that the operas burlesqued be very popular ones. This reduced the possible target range and eliminated Wagner, even while *Punch* and other comic journals found him funny. JANE W. STEDMAN, *Opera News*

The ethereality of Maeterlinck's play Pelléas et Mélisande, *from which Debussy (much to Maeterlinck's ultimate displeasure) fashioned his libretto, lends itself readily to burlesque. Here is Marcel Proust's effort, as sketched in one of his notebooks. Compare pp. 295–7.*

MARKEL

You were wrong to leave that hat! You will never find it!	Vous avez eu tort de laisser ce chapeau! Vous ne le retrouverez jamais!

PELLEAS

Why will I never find it?	Pourquoi ne le retrouverai-je jamais?

MARKEL

One never finds anything again . . . here . . . it is lost forever.	On ne retrouve jamais rien . . . ici. . . . Il est perdu pour toujours.

PELLEAS

As we leave, we will find another which looks like it!	En nous en allant, nous en prendrons un qui lui ressemble!

MARKEL

There isn't another which looks like it!	Il n'y en a pas qui lui ressemble!

PELLEAS

What was it like then?	Comment était-il donc?

MARKEL
(very softly)

It was a poor little hat like everyone wears! Nobody could tell whose it was. . . . It looked as though it came from the end of the world!

Now we should not look for it any longer because we will not find it.

C'était un pauvre petit chapeau comme en porte tout le monde! Personne n'aurait pu dire de chez qui il venait. . . . Il avait l'air de venir du bout du monde!

Maintenant, il ne faut plus le chercher car nous ne le retrouverons pas.

PELLEAS

It seems to me that my head is going to be cold forever. It is very cold outside. It is winter! If only the sun had not yet set. Why has someone left the window open? The atmosphere in there was heavy and poisoned; several times I thought I was going to feel ill. And now all the fresh air in the world!

Il me semble que ma tête commence à avoir froid pour toujours. Il fait un grand froid dehors. C'est l'hiver! Si encore le soleil n'etait pas couché. Pourquoi avait-on laisse la fenêtre ouverte? Il faisait, là-dedans, une atmosphère lourde et empoisonnée; j'ai cru plusieurs fois que j'allais me trouver mal. Et maintenant tout l'air de toute la terre!

MARKEL

Your face, Pelléas, is serious and tearful like those who have had colds for a long time! Let us go. We will not find it. Someone who does not come from here will have

Vous avez, Pelléas, le visage grave et plein de larmes (de) ceux qui sont enrhumés pour longtemps! Allons-nous en. Nous ne le retrouverons pas. Quelqu'un qui n'est pas d'ici

taken it and God knows where it is by now. It is too late. All the other hats have gone. We could no longer take another. It is a terrible thing, Pelléas. But it is not your fault.

l'aura emporté et Dieu sait ou il est en ce moment. Il est trop tard. Tout les autres chapeaux sont partis. Nous ne pourrons plus en prendre un autre. C'est une chose terrible, Pelléas. Mais ce n'est pas votre faute.

PELLEAS

What is that noise?

Quel est ce bruit?

MARKEL

That is the carriages leaving.

Ce sont les voitures qui partent.

PELLEAS

Why are they leaving?

Pourquoi partent-elles?

MARKEL

We will have scared them. They knew that we are going a very long way from here and they have gone. They will never come back.

Nous les aurons effrayées. Elles savaient que nous en allons trés loin d'ici et elles sont parties. Elles ne reviendront jamais.

PARSIFAL

The history of *Parsifal* in New York is a special one. New York was the first city outside Bayreuth to perform *Parsifal*. Wagner intended that his 'Sacred Festival Play' be reserved for Bayreuth. It is doubtful whether he really meant this reservation to be a permanent one, because there is evidence to show that he was willing to give his favourite touring opera company, that of Angelo Neumann, permission to include *Parsifal* in the repertoire. There were no objections, either, to concert performances of the opera outside Bayreuth, and Walter Damrosch gave such a presentation in 1886, seventeen years before *Parsifal*'s New York première.

When Conried became the manager of the Metropolitan in 1903 he determined to give *Parsifal* as the second of the two sensations he set before New York during his first season. The first was the début of a tenor named Caruso. The second involved him in a legal fight which was as lucrative to the lawyers as it was productive of publicity. As soon as Conried had announced his intention of giving *Parsifal*, Cosima, Wagner's second wife, fulminating from the Wahnfried Valhalla, started the storm which was followed avidly on the front pages of the world.

Cosima first declared that any one who would have anything to do with the New York production of *Parsifal* could never again appear in Bayreuth. Felix Mottl, the conductor, therefore withdrew from participation in the New York production. Hertz took his place and conducted the New York première. Cosima then took her case to court and tried to obtain an injunction against Conried. This was denied by the United States Supreme Court on 24 November 1903, and Conried was free to proceed. But many ministers were not of the court's opinion. They preached in the pulpit against the production, and a delegation called on the Mayor of New York, Seth Low, to protest. The subject was debated in musical circles throughout the world, and it was undoubtedly the most popular subject for people who wrote letters to the editor.

It was also the favourite subject of the cartoonists. A Berlin comic paper published a picture of 'The Rape of the Grail', in which a centaur with Conried's face carried off the struggling Cosima. *Kladderadatsch*, the popular German magazine, showed a sad and resigned Cosima dancing with Uncle Sam. And the cartoonist Arpad Schmidhammer gained wide circulation for a cartoon which showed Uncle Sam, marked Conried, standing before a grail represented as a safe filled with money-bags and holding aloft a *rayonnant* dollar which all the critics worshipped, while Richard Wagner from the grave of Titurel looked on.

You can imagine how all this pro and con drove up the temperature of excitement prior to the performance. Never was a première preceded by such garish publicity. The *New York Evening Telegram* published a *'Parsifal* Extra'. Fanny Bloomfield Zeisler, pianist from Chicago, hired a special train called the *'Parsifal* Limited' to bring Chicago's curious to the occasion. From other points also special excursion trains came to New York.

The performance was scheduled for five o'clock on Christmas Eve, 1903, and people wrote letters asking whether they should or should not wear evening-dress to a performance which started at that hour. They also gladly paid the special prices which were necessary, 'owing to the unusual cost of this long-awaited production'. An orchestra seat cost ten dollars.

New York went so *Parsifal*-crazy that even the staid *New York Times* allowed itself to publish a cartoon on the subject called 'Parsifalitis'. The cartoon shows a bewildered and wobbly-kneed Father Knickerbocker reeling in the streets while newsboys around him hawk their extras, all about *Parsifal*. One extra is marked, 'How To Dress for Parsifal'. An organ-grinder stands in the middle of the street – all traffic has ceased – and he carries a sign, *'Parsifal* Selections Only.' Every building in New York is plastered with signs announcing lectures about *Parsifal*. The biggest sign says, 'Sermon Morning and Evening Denouncing *Parsifal* as Sacrilegious by Rev. Warn 'Em.' Next to him the crowd is streaming into a lecture entitled 'What *Parsifal* Means, with Maps and Diagrams.' But next-door a competitor announces, 'Only Genuine *Parsifal* Lecture Here.' He too has a competitor, a 'Grand Musical Lecture Explaining *Parsifal* to Those Who Do Not Know by One Who Saw Wagner's Picture.' All the advertising signs are completely devoted to the subject. There is a bargain sale of *Parsifal* hats; one can get *Parsifal* cough-drops, a *Parsifal* five-cent cigar; the music store displays 'Latest *Parsifal* Cakewalk'; there is a breakfast food called 'Par-see-fall'; there is a novel, '1,000,000 Edition of the New Historical Novel, Parsifal

Jr.' And upstairs in one of the buildings is housed a Signor Parsifal, 'Mind Reader and Fortune Teller'. In the background there is a beautiful new *Parsifal* skyscraper advertising *Parsifal* flats. Finally, the smoke coming out of a factory chimney writes *Parsifal* on New York's sky.

On the afternoon of the performance, a few minutes before five, several trumpeters appeared at the Broadway doors of the Metropolitan and, no doubt to the astonishment of Christmas shoppers, stenographers, and tram conductors, blew several motifs from *Parsifal*. . . .

Of the performance Richard Aldrich, writing in the *New York Times*, said:

> A vast assemblage was gathered at the Metropolitan Opera House to witness it – an assemblage most brilliant in appearance and quality, following the drama with the keenest attention, with breathless silence, and submitting early to its spell.
>
> At the very outset it may be said that yesterday's production went far to justify the bold undertaking of Mr Heinrich Conried, the new director; and that whatever else he may in future accomplish as head of the chief operatic institution in this country, he has made his incumbency long memorable by what he then achieved.
>
> The artistic value of the production was of the very highest. It was in many respects equal to anything done at Bayreuth, and in some it was superior. It was without doubt the most perfect production ever made on the American lyric stage. Those who wish to quarrel with the performance on æsthetic, moral, or religious grounds have still as much upon which to stand as before; artistically it was nothing less than triumphant.

Financially as well as artistically, *Parsifal* was a success. It was given eleven times the first season, and these performances brought in nearly 200,000 dollars in box-office receipts.

GEORGE MAREK, *A Front Seat at the Opera*

Early tea at four o'clock, and then with Katia to the Prinzregenten-Theater: *Parsifal*. Moved by the music itself. 'The harmony of sweet tones.' 'I cannot distinguish between music and tears.' The prelude has something mechanical about it, though, and at the same time a strongly authoritarian note. Beautiful colours on the stage. The tenderest and most moving part undoubtedly the foot-washing scene. Christian simplicity and, given proper distance from the stage, purity; whereas the Byzantine-domed temple scenes are overly pompous with ritual. The close is ultraromantic magic and not so powerful, in spite of its soaring highlights. The whole thing the dream of an exceedingly high-flown, tired and sensual old man. Pleasant buffet in the intermissions: vegetable soup, tomato sandwiches, red wine. Cigarettes in the theatre restaurant. Vulgar war profiteer's wife, large diamonds in her ears, picking her teeth with her stubby little finger after eating a twenty-mark portion of chicken.

THOMAS MANN, *Diary*, 1918

PASTA

Giuditta Pasta, creator of the title-roles of Norma, Anna Bolena *and* La Sonnambula: *for me, the one singer above all others I would like to have heard, and seen.*

People have frequently sounded Madame Pasta's friends as to who taught her her craft as an *actress*. The answer is—*no one*! The only instruction which she has ever received has come straight from her own heart, from her own acutely sensitive reactions to the most delicate *nuances* of human passions, and from her admiration, so boundless as to verge upon the limits of absurdity, for *ideal beauty*. Once, in Trieste, while she was walking beside the harbour with a company of friends, a little three-year-old beggar-boy came up to her and asked for alms on behalf of his blind mother; she burst into tears and gave him all she had. Her friends, who had witnessed this incident, immediately began to speak of her virtue, her charitableness and the compassion of her heart. But she merely wiped away her tears and turned on them angrily: 'I refuse to accept your commendation!' she exclaimed. 'And I am *not* virtuous! But when that child came begging to me, he begged like a great artist. In a flash, I could see in his gesture all the despair of his mother, all the poverty of their home, the clothes which they need and the biting cold which is their relentless enemy. If, when the scene called for it, *I* could discover a gesture so faithfully portraying every suggestion of indescribable misery, I should be a very great actress indeed.'   STENDHAL, *Life of Rossini*

PELLEAS ET MELISANDE

Compare Proust on pp. 288–90 for another witty demystification of Maeterlinck's problematic libretto.

The characters in *Pelléas et Mélisande* are correct, well-to-do French people. They don't talk about their business much; but they own property, wear good clothes and seem to be running some sort of kingdom. They have strong passions, kind hearts, good manners, and an intense family life. They understand about love and approve of it. What they cannot deal with is any vagueness on the subject. Mélisande's attractiveness for them seems to be due partly to the fact that she has no family ties (they can thus adopt her completely) and partly to the fact that her affections and her amorous tendencies are both powerful and imprecise. She fascinates them; they never know what to think of her. She keeps them guessing not through any plan but simply through the fact, astounding and incredible to them, that she has no plan, no conscious motives of any sort.

This lack of project, of intention on her part does not prevent her from acting with utter straightforwardness. Her one interest in life is being loved; she demands love from everybody and gets it. She pays willingly any price asked and suffers cheerfully all the consequences involved, early marriage, childbirth and death. She will do anything to avoid not being loved. She lies about a ring she has lost; she submits to a thorough beating from her husband; she refuses to hold a grudge against anyone at any time. Her famous remark at the end of the flagellation scene reveals how egocentric is all her sweetness. 'I am not happy here' is her whole comment on the incident. A lonely girl with a floating libido and no malice toward anyone can cause lots of trouble in a well-organized family.

Her husband sees trouble coming quite early, goes to bed of a minor ailment, and tries to think the situation out. 'Mélisande, be reasonable!' is his last plea. She doesn't know what he means. After that, tragedy is inevitable. Attempts on the husband's part to discipline her and to spy on her friendship with his younger brother merely bring out the relentless quality in her character, her inability to accept any discipline whatsoever. He tries to murder his brother. Then he pleads with him as man to man. But by that time the brother's sentiments are sufficiently definite so that he cannot, as an honest Frenchman, go back on them. Mélisande wouldn't have collaborated on a noble renunciation, anyway. She would never have got the idea. So the young man is ordered away on a trip. When his departure provokes a real love scene (husband having impatiently shut them both out of the house one evening), there is at last a visible justification for running the deceiver through with a sword.

Nevertheless, Mélisande has the last word. She gives birth to a child, forgives her husband his violence by saying there is nothing to forgive, and dies sweetly, like Little Eva, after refusing to answer all direct questions about her love life. The husband, reasonable and logical to the end, has wanted to know whether he has killed his brother unjustly. Also, with a legitimate curiosity, whether there is any chance he is not the father of the baby. Her reply is equivocal, 'We have done nothing to be blamed for.' The aged father, an observer from the beginning rather than an actor in the tragedy, thereupon brings out the following pearl of wisdom and of comfort for his bereaved son: 'It's terrible but it's not your fault.' The French family is thus juridical-minded to the last.

VIRGIL THOMSON

Poet Ezra Pound writes to his friend Agnes Bedford in 1921, while working on an opera of his own on the life of François Villon.

Sat through *Pelléas* the other evening and am encouraged – encouraged to tear up the whole bloomin' era of harmony and do the thing if necessary on two tins and wash-board. Anything rather than that mush of hysteria, Scandinavia strained through Belgium plus French Schwärmerei. Probably just as well I have to make this first swash without any instruments at hand. Very much encouraged by the *Pelléas*, ignorance having no further terrors if that damn thing is the result of what is called musical knowledge. . . .

PETER GRIMES

I was a little taken aback one evening for which I had vague other plans to find that I was going with G. to a new opera by Benjamin Britten which was being done at Sadler's Wells. She had bought the tickets herself and said nothing about it in advance. The only thing I had heard by Britten had been a *Requiem* that had not much impressed me, and I did not feel particularly eager to sit through an English opera called *Peter Grimes*, based on an episode from Crabbe. G. did try, with her usual lack of emphasis, to get me to read the libretto, of which she had procured a copy, but she did not explain that this work had been something of a sensation in London, where the critics, who, like me, had not at first expected anything extraordinary, had been roused from their neat routine to the point of hearing it several times and writing two or three articles about it. But she knew that I ought to hear it, and it is one of my debts to G. that she made me go to *Peter Grimes*, which I should unquestionably otherwise have missed.

For, almost from the moment when the curtain went up on the bare room in the provincial Moot Hall – which no overture had introduced – where the fisherman Peter Grimes was being examined at a coroner's inquest in connection with the death of his apprentice, I felt the power of a musical gift and a dramatic imagination that woke my interest and commanded my attention. There have been relatively few composers of the first rank who had a natural gift for the theater: Mozart, Mussorgsky, Verdi, Wagner, the Bizet of *Carmen*. To be confronted, without preparation, with an unmistakable new talent of this kind is an astonishing, even an electrifying, experience. The difficulty of describing *Peter Grimes* to someone who has not heard it is the difficulty of convincing people whose expectations are likely to be limited by having listened to too much modern music that was synthetic, arid, effortful and inadequate, that a new master has really arrived: of conveying to them the special qualities of a full-grown original artist. In my own case, I am particularly handicapped by lack of technical knowledge and training, so that I can only give an account of the opera's spell without being able to analyze it intelligently. The best I can do, then, is to report my impression – subject to expert correction – that Britten's score shows no signs of any of the dominant influences – Wagner, Debussy, Schoenberg or Prokofiev – but has been phrased in an idiom that is personal and built with a definiteness and solidity that are as English as Gilbert and Sullivan (one can find, for an English opera, no other comparison in the immediate past). And the result of this is very different from anything we have been used to. The ordinary composer of opera finds his conventions there with the stage; but, when you are watching *Peter Grimes*, you are almost completely unaware of anything that is artificial, anything 'operatic'. The composer here seems quite free from the self-consciousness of contemporary musicians. You do not feel you are watching an experiment; you are living a work of art. The opera seizes upon you, possesses you, keeps you riveted to your seat during the action and keyed up during the intermissions, and drops you, purged and exhausted, at the end.

The orchestra, in *Peter Grimes*, plays a mainly subordinate role, and the first effect on the hearer, during the opening scene in the Moot Hall, is of a drastic simplification of opera to something essential and naked, which immediately wakes one up. There is no Wagnerian web of motifs that tells you about the characters: the characters express themselves directly, either conversing or soliloquizing in a song, while the orchestra, for the most part, but comments. The music is a close continuity, though articulated rather than fluid, of vivid utterances on the part of the personages and – except in the more elaborate interludes – sharp and terse descriptive strokes, in which from time to time take shape arias, duets, trios and choruses. These – almost never regular in pattern and never losing the effect of naturalness – have their full or fragmentary developments, and give way to the next urgent pulse of the blood-stream that runs through the whole piece. In the same way, the words of the libretto, by the poet Montague Slater, which are admirably suited to the music and which the music exactly fits, shift from the colloquial and are sometimes – with no loss of dignity – left perfectly bald and flat. But we soon come to recognize in the music the extraordinary flexibility, the subtlety and the variety, which are combined with a stout British craftsmanship that has a sure hand with mortise and tenon and that knows how to plant and mass a chorus, and with a compelling theatrical sense, an instinct for tempo and point. And – what is most uncommon with opera – we find ourselves touched and stirred at listening to an eloquence of voices that does not merely charm or impress us as the performance of well-trained singers but that seems sometimes to reach us directly with the emotions of actual people. Nor do these voices find their expression exclusively through the singers' roles: one of the most effective devices of *Peter Grimes* is the use of the orchestral interludes that take place between the scenes while the curtain is down. Thus at the end of the first scene in the Moot Hall, where you have just been seeing Peter Grimes consoled by Ellen Orford, the schoolteacher, the only being in the town who cares for him, the orchestra develops a theme which seems to well up out of Ellen's heart, and then rises and falls with a plangency that, sustained through the long passage with marvellous art, conveys, as if her spirit were speaking, her sympathy and pain for Peter. And at the end of the scene that follows, when a storm has been heard coming up as Balstrode, the retired captain, has been trying to remonstrate with Peter over his plan to take another apprentice and prove to the town that he is not a monster, the winds and the waves break loose the moment the curtain falls, fiendishly yelping and slapping in a way that represents with realism – Britten was born on the Suffolk coast – the worrying raving crescendo of an equinoctial gale but that howls at the same time with the fierceness of Peter's rebellious pride and of the latent sadistic impulse of which he is half unconscious but to which the new situation will eventually give free rein. The sea's restive and pressing movement has been [present] all through the scene that preceded, and in the next, in the local tavern to which the people have resorted for warmth and cheer, the hurricane wildly intrudes whenever the door is opened and at last, with the entrance of Grimes, rushes into the room to stay. This long act, which is brought to its climax by the silence that greets Peter's appearance and that concentrates the hostility of the town, and by the arrival of the orphan whom, the carrier refusing, Ellen has herself gone to fetch and for whose welfare she hopes to make herself responsible – this act has an intensity and an impetus that carries one through, without a moment's let-down, from the opening to the end. Nor is what follows much less effective. The whole drama is a stretching of tension between the inquest and the inevitable crisis when Grimes will, if not deliberately kill, at least cause the death of, the second apprentice; and I do not remember ever to have seen, at any performance of opera, an audience so steadily intent, so petrified and held in suspense, as the audience of *Peter Grimes*. This is due partly to the dramatic skill of Britten, but it is due also to his having succeeded in harmonizing, through *Peter Grimes*, the harsh helpless emotions of wartime. This opera could have been written in no other age, and it is one of the very few works of art that have seemed to me, so far, to have spoken for the blind anguish, the hateful rancors and the will to desctruction of these horrible years. Its grip on its London audiences is clearly of the same special kind as the grip of the recent productions of *Richard III* and *The Duchess of Malfi*. Like them, it is the chronicle of an impulse to persecute and to kill which has become an obsessive compulsion, which drags the malefactor on – under a fatality which he does not understand, from which he can never get free, and which never leaves him even the lucidity for repentance or reparation – through a series of uncontrollable cruelties which will lead, in the long run, to his being annihilated himself. At first you think that Peter Grimes is Germany. He is always under the impression, poor fellow, that what he really wants for himself is to marry Ellen Orford and to live in a nice little cottage with children and fruit in the garden 'and whitened doorstep and a woman's care'. Above all, he wants to prove to his neighbors that he is not the scoundrel they think him, that he really means no harm to his apprentices and that he will make a good family man. But he cannot help flying into a fury when the boy does not respond to his will, and when he gets angry, he beats him; and his townsmen become more and more indignant. At last, shouting, 'Peter Grimes!', they go on the march against him, determined to capture him and make him pay, just at the moment when he has paused and relented, and when their approach will precipitate, in his dash to escape, his pushing the boy so that he falls over the cliff, which is finally to settle his fate. (A comparison of the text of the opera with the story as told by Crabbe in *The Borough* shows that Britten and Montague Slater – though they have used here and there a few lines from Crabbe – have put Peter in a different situation and invented for him a new significance. The outlaw fisherman in Crabbe is married, though his wife does not figure in the story, and he has no connection with Ellen Orford, who is the heroine of a separate episode. The mainspring of the original version is Peter's rebellion against his father: he is in Crabbe completely anti-social and has no hankering for middle-class decency.) But, by the time you are done with

the opera – or by the time it is done with you – you have decided
that Peter Grimes is the whole of bombing, machine-gunning,
mining, torpedoing, ambushing humanity, which talks about a
guaranteed standard of living yet does nothing but wreck its own
works, degrade or pervert its own moral life and reduce itself to
starvation. You feel, during the final scenes, that the indignant
shouting mob which comes to punish Peter Grimes is just as
sadistic as he. And when Balstrode gets to him first and sends him
out to sink himself in his boat you feel that you are in the same
boat as Grimes.   EDMUND WILSON, *Europe Without Baedeker*

PLOTS

*Throughout the nineteenth century and into the twentieth,
the plot of Mozart's and da Ponte's* Così fan Tutte *was
considered shockingly cynical on the sacred subject of sexual fidelity. This synopsis shows how the libretto was recast, in order to make it more comfortable and acceptable to
delicate moral sensibilities. In da Ponte's original, the
fidelity of Fiordiligi (who becomes Isadora here) and
Dorabella fails to withstand Don Alfonso's test, thus
confirming the truth of the opera's title.*

One day during the eighteenth century in a café in Naples, two
young cavaliers, Ferrando and Gratiano, were singing the praises
of their betrothed ladies, declaring that they had the greatest faith
in their fidelity, which would stand any test. On hearing this, their
companion, Don Alfonso, a cynical old bachelor, declared that no
woman was ever really faithful; and he laughed aloud at the
young men's indignant protestations. He then suggested that they
should allow him to put the ladies through a severe test to prove
the truth of his statement; and Ferrando and Gratiano,

thoroughly convinced that he would fail, permitted him to do so, laying a substantial wager and agreeing to obey his directions implicitly for the following few days. Don Alfonso drew up his plan of campaign and the test began forthwith.

The two young men at once repaired to the abode of their betrothed ladies, Isadora and Dorabella, two beautiful Andalusian sisters; and presently they announced that they had been ordered to depart immediately with their regiments to Havannah, where fighting was proceeding. The two girls were full of grief and anxiety on hearing this disturbing news, and they parted from their lovers with tears and many protestations of undying fidelity.

A few days later, the two young men, having, in the meantime, completely changed their appearance and disguised themselves as officers of a foreign regiment, were introduced as recently arrived strangers by Don Alfonso to Dorabella and Isadora. The latter were completely deceived by the clever disguise adopted by Ferrando and Gratiano, and failed to recognize them.

Acting upon the instructions of Don Alfonso, the newcomers proceeded to pay great attention to the young ladies, each making ardent and persuasive love to the betrothed of his friend.

Isadora and Dorabella, however, at first refused to be impressed or even interested in the 'foreigners', and expressed great indignation at the violent love made to them by their new acquaintances. Their lovers were, consequently, greatly delighted and triumphed over Don Alfonso upon this proof of their ladies' fidelity; but the wily old cynic declared that he was not yet defeated but had arranged to carry the plot deeper still.

He then persuaded the young men to keep up their present disguise a little longer, but, at their next interview, to carry their despair at the ladies' indifference to the point of attempted suicide.

The still completely confident lovers were willing enough to agree to this test also; and to carry out their plan the more successfully, they managed to bribe Despina, the ladies' waiting-maid, to assist them by admitting them after they had, as 'foreigners', been denied the house and grounds by her indignant mistress.

In this plot, Don Alfonso, to his great satisfaction, felt that he was about to succeed. Despina, entering into the joke with great spirit, being already bored by the constant supposed dolefulness of her ladies at the absence of their beloved ones, found means to introduce the 'foreigners' once more into the presence of Dorabella and Isadora.

At once, the disguised officers again made violent declarations of love, each to the betrothed of his friend, and announced that they were prepared to die rather than live without their sudden passion being returned. When the girls again indignantly refused to accept their addresses and expressed undying devotion to their 'absent' lovers, the 'strangers' then immediately produced phials of pretended poison and, swallowing the contents, fell upon the floor in a feigned dying condition.

This plan came dangerously near the point of succeeding, for Isadora and Dorabella, being kind-hearted girls, were so concerned at the seemingly terrible result of their coldness that they became full of compassion and tried to comfort the suicidal young men with the tender words and caresses so cunningly played up for.

In answer to their frantic calls for help, Despina entered, and, expressing pretended horror at the circumstance, bade her mistress hold the love-sick swains carefully in their arms until she had fetched a doctor. This the girls did, tenderly soothing the limp forms in their arms, to the triumphant satisfaction of the gloating Don Alfonso, who had managed to conceal himself near by. Presently Despina returned, having meanwhile disguised herself in the black robes and wig of a physician; and, making absurd mesmeric passes over the recumbent officers, she pretended thus to overcome the action of the poison, and to restore them to health once more.

After the revived strangers had departed, however, Despina's conscience pricked her, and she determined to remain loyal to her young mistresses after all. She sought them out, therefore, and revealed to them the whole plot, confessing how she had herself been bribed to take part in it.

At first, the two girls were very angry that such a trick should have been played upon them, and that their lovers should have dared to wager upon their fidelity with the cynical and worldly old woman-hater, Don Alfonso; and then, quickly recovering their good-humour, they determined to turn the tables upon them, and to carry the war into the enemy's camp.

Enlisting the services of Despina in their turn, they arranged a very amusing counter-plot of their own. The next time their new suitors presented themselves, again making declarations of love and offers of marriage, they pretended to have suddenly fallen in love with them since the attempted suicides and boldly accepted them as their future husbands. They even went so far as to send for a notary and to sign the necessary marriage contracts, taking care, however, that these should be faked documents, the notary being impersonated by the versatile Despina in borrowed garments; and the three girls acted so realistically that they succeeded in hood-winking completely the young men and their old arch-plotter.

Furious that the fickleness of their fiancées should thus have been proved, as they imagined, the young men hastened away to discard their disguise, returning almost immediately in their ordinary garb and natural looks, to pour forth angry reproaches upon the girls.

For some little time longer, Dorabella and Isadora kept up the deception; and then, at last, taking pity upon the sincere distress of their lovers, they laughingly revealed the fact that they had cleverly turned the tables upon them.

The young men were greatly relieved at this turn of events; and now thoroughly ashamed that they should ever have pretended to doubt the fidelity of their chosen ladies, they very contritely sued for pardon.

This being readily granted the happy couples were re-united once more; and the cynical old Don Alfonso, having lost his wager, was thus obliged to retire crestfallen, having failed to prove that fickleness and flirtation was second nature to every woman, or that, as he had declared, 'così fan tutte' – they all do it!

GLADYS DAVIDSON, *Standard Stories from the Operas*

I shall never forget one priceless American theatre programme, which illustrated the national mania for advertisement in a singularly novel fashion. A theatre programme usually contains a brief synopsis of the story of the opera, which is given immediately below the list of the characters in it and the names of the singers taking their parts. In Houston, Texas, the programme contained the following gem:

OTHELLO

Opera in 4 Acts by G. Verdi

ACT I

A Port in Cyprus

The populace are kneeling in prayer for Othello whose ship is in great danger in a violent tempest at sea. The peril is overcome, Othello enters and greets the people with the words:

> *Do all your cooking with 'Krusto' the famous cooking-fat*

'Let all rejoice! The Turk is overthrown and cast into the sea.' The people cheer Othello!

> *'Krusto' is the only cooking-fat you can use*

Iago, jealous of Cassio, who enjoys the favour of Othello, makes him intoxicated. A drinking song

> *Anybody who tries cooking without 'Krusto' is crazy*

is heard and Cassio, already under the influence of wine, attacks Montano, sword in hand. There is a great noise and Othello enters and calls out in a terrible voice:

> *'Krusto' has no rivals*

'Down with your swords!' Cassio is deposed from his captaincy, as Desdemona, the adored wife of Othello, appears in the gateway of the castle. Othello goes forward to meet her and they both sing a lovely duet,

> *Whoever has used 'Krusto' will never use any other fat*

which is generally considered to be one of the gems of operatic music. This concludes Act I.

'Krusto' cooking fat figures prominently in all four acts of the opera, at the end of which it is stated:

Having strangled Desdemona, Othello stabs himself in the breast and while dying, sings the moving words:

Always insist on 'Krusto' the only genuine cooking-fat

'Kiss me, kiss me once again,' – and expires.

LEO SLEZAK, *Songs of Motley*

The following appeared in a French opera house prog-
ramme, and was intended to elucidate Carmen *to English-*
speaking members of the audience.

On the 3rd March 1875 in the Salle Favert there was the first of Carmen. The composer is not known but none of his precedent works bought him glory. This time the history is mixed with comedy where speeches alterate with songs. Carmen's recitations have not been written by Bizet: his friend Merimée do writes them specially for the strange theatres.

For this work first welcome without interest got soon a wordy fame. The plot must captivate the tragical side and the Spanish picturesque provided his art with gifts he wonderful used and he will obtain from a beginning the effects of a seldom reached power.

Carmen is a cigar-makeress from a tabago factory who loves with Don José of the mounting guard. Carmen takes a flower from her corsets and lances it to Don José (Duet: *'Talk me of my mother'*). There is a noise inside the tabago factory and the revolting cigar-makeresses bursts into the stage. Carmen is arrested and Don José is ordered to mounting guard her but Carmen subduces him and he lets her escape.

ACT 2. The Tavern. Carmen, Frasquita, Mercedes, Zuniga, Morales. Carmen's aria (*'the sistrums are tinkling'*). Enter Escamillio, a balls-fighter. Enter two smuglers (Duet: *'We have in mind a business'*) but Carmen refuses to penetrate because Don José has liberated from prison. He just now arrives (aria: *'slop, here who comes!'*) but hear are the bugles singing his retreat. Don José will leave and draws his sword. Called by Carmen shrieks the two smuglers interfere with her but Don José is bound to dessert, he will follow into them (final chorus: *'Opening sky wandering life'*).

ACT 3. (A roky landscape, the smuglers shelter) . . . Carmen sees her death in cards and Don José makes a date with Carmen for the next balls-fight.

ACT 4, a place in Seville. Procession of balls-fighters, the roaring of the balls heard in the arena. Escamillio enters (Aria and chorus: *'Toreador, toreador. All hail the balls of a Toreador'*). Enter Don José (Aria: *'I do not threaten, I besooch you.'*) but Carmen repels himwants to join with Escamillio now chaired by the crowd. Don José stabbs her (Aria: *'Oh rupture, rupture, you may arrest me, I did kill der'*) he sings *'Oh my beautiful Carmen, my subductive Carmen'*.

With Carmen, Bizet brings a new impulsive to the lyrical theatre. Friedriche Nietsche bows to this sparkling work where he sees the triumph of the Meditteranean light. The so different elements contribute to bring Carmen to an entire fulness of he real masterpiece. Life teems to those four acts with an ever-changing scenery and a subtile music which gives the exacpt subducive atomsphere.   *About the House*, 1967

I said just now that *Die Meistersinger* was a good libretto. So it is. It has an amusing plot, it brings us a vivid picture of an interesting period, it has lots of charm, its people are believable characters and one of them is a great dramatic creation. But don't forget that the plot is supposed to revolve around a singing-contest. The competition on St John's Day is to be a public one, and anyone can enter provided he is a Meistersinger and a bachelor or, as Beckmesser says, a widower. But what kind of prize contest is this? What do we get in the last act? Where are the contestants? Did you ever hear of a contest where there are only two entrants, one of them being an illegitimate substitute? There is not the slightest suggestion that other singers are going to compete. If Hans Sachs' scheme did not work, and if Walther did not appear on cue and sing his previously rehearsed prize song or a reasonable facsimile thereof, would the prize go to Beckmesser by default, just because he was the only contestant? In the first act, when Pogner announces the contest, Kothner says enthusiastically, 'Come on, all bachelors!' Between the first and the last acts, what has happened to all the bachelors?

It is obvious that the magic music carries us over this dramatic hole so that practically no one notices the omission. I dare say that few people, even among those who know *Die Meistersinger* well, have ever thought to question the proceedings. There is a similar puzzle in another splendid libretto, *Der Rosenkavalier*. Will you tell me how it happens that the august and elegant Marschallin, Fürstin Werdenberg, comes to the shabby inn where the third act takes place? Her appearance there is even more inexplicable than the appearance of the strait-laced Germont at Flora's gambling party in *La Traviata*, at which I always ask myself, 'What is he doing here?' In *Der Rosenkavalier*, what happens between the end of the second act and the beginning of the third act? Who has talked? Who has told the Marschallin of Octavian's scheme to get rid of the Baron? Obviously not Octavian himself, because when she appears he is quite as astonished as the rest and says to her, 'We had something different in mind, Marie-Thérèse.' Neither Faninal nor Baron Ochs could possibly have informed her. But here she is, a charming and resplendent *dea ex machina*, in a *bistro*. And, of course, we are glad to see her, for she is shortly to take part in the trio, the most beautiful music of the opera. Ernest Newman in his well-known *Opera Nights* points out this dramatic inconsistency and notes that it must also have occurred to Hofmannsthal and Strauss, for the score carries at this point an added stage direction which does not appear in the original text, calling for the servant to run out when the police commissioner enters. But even this afterthought does not explain the situation. Not nearly enough time elapses for the servant to have gone to the Marschallin's palace, to have summoned her, and to have brought her to the suburban inn. Indeed, not enough time elapses for a woman like the Marschallin to have put on her hat!

What happens between acts two and three of *Tristan*? This has baffled me for years. There is no explaining the events subsequent to the fall of the curtain of the second act. Tristan draws his sword, shouts, 'On guard, Melot,' then lets his sword fall and sinks wounded into Kurvenal's arms. Isolde flings herself on him, and the curtain falls. In the next act we learn that the faithful Kurvenal has carried Tristan away on his broad shoulders and that Tristan has lain like dead since that day. Now, since the wound will not heal, Kurvenal has sent for the only physician who can heal it, for Isolde. But why did all this happen? Did Isolde turn away from the wounded Tristan and pay no further attention to him? Impossible. Then why did not Isolde flee with Tristan if Kurvenal insisted on bringing Tristan back to his native land? Did Mark hold her back? That is most unlikely. We can't believe it, knowing King Mark as we do. Did Kurvenal spirit Tristan away in secrecy? Aside from the fact that such an action would have been almost impossible without Isolde's knowing about it, why did she not follow? She intimates (in one of the most beautiful passages at the close of the second act) that she wishes to follow Tristan wherever he leads, and she knows that he leads to death. Why does she not go with him at once? Later, when the second ship arrives, Brangäne tells us that she confessed, as soon as Isolde had disappeared, the secret of the potion to the King. Learning the secret, the King himself embarked in greatest haste in order to reach Tristan and to give Isolde to him. He comes too late, and it is, of course, proper to the tragedy that he come too late. But why did Brangäne wait all this time? And what made her confess finally? None of these questions is ever resolved. It does not matter — because of the music.

GEORGE MAREK, *A Front Seat at the Opera*

PLUMBING

The essential lack in Wagner is after all a want of sanitary plumbing. No amount of sentiment or passion can wholly make up for this. One feels all the time that the connection with the main is fraudulent. JOHN JAY CHAPMAN, 1895

In 1952 *The Rape of Lucretia* was given at Covent Garden. As T. S. Eliot had published the libretto I thought he should see the piece, although I knew he cared little for opera, and as I have said, less for my collaborating with Ben. But Eliot agreed to come. I was quite surprised. . . . We sat in the Dress Circle. I had great hopes that Tom would be impressed by the work. But to my dismay, I found that the flush in the gents' lavatory behind our seats continued incessantly to interrupt and spoil Britten's music. I knew what the trouble was: a stuck ball-valve in the cistern. I'd often mended such gadgets at home. The opera reached Lucretia's Lullaby, but the urinal accompanied it.

'I'll fix that bloody thing,' I whispered to Eliot and strode to the lavatory, clambered up to the cistern and bent the copper bar up to prevent it constantly flushing. This silenced the thing. I regained my seat. Eliot listened to the rest of the opera in silence without disturbance.

As we walked out of the opera house I ventured to ask him if he'd enjoyed the work.

'Not exactly, Ronnie,' he said, 'but I was most impressed with your plumbing.' RONALD DUNCAN, *Working with Britten*

PREMIERES

Two wives comment on their composer-husbands' big nights.

Der Ring des Nibelungen

Sunday, 13 August First performance of *Rheingold* [at new Bayreuth Festspielhaus], under a completely unlucky star: Betz loses the ring, runs into the wings twice during the curse, a stagehand raises the backdrop too soon during the first scene change and one sees people standing around in shirt sleeves and the back wall of the theater, all the singers embarrassed, etc., etc. – Each of us returns home separately, R. at first very upset, but gradually regains his spirits, and the sudden visit of the Emperor of Brazil restores the mood of ebullience. We go to bed in very good spirits.

Monday, 14 August *Walküre*, this time without trouble – except for an incident which alarms R. greatly: he is summoned to the Emperor, who praises everything highly, says jokingly that, if he were an orchestra player, R. would never have got him down (into the orchestra pit), regrets not being able to remain for more than the two performances, whereupon R. replies, 'Favor is not dependent on time and place.' The Grand Duchess, however, says she is staying on. R.: 'Then you extend the favor.' The Emperor, jokingly: 'That was a dig.' He says goodbye, takes a step backward, does not notice the doorstep, stumbles so awkwardly that it takes all of R.'s strength to hold him; he is convinced that this backward fall would have meant the death of the Emperor!...

Tuesday, 15 August Herr Betz has *Siegfried* postponed! He says he is hoarse. Much ill feeling; the newspapers, already extremely malicious, will draw inferences from it. – Andrássy,

Radowitz, Keudell, all kinds of people great and small are here, everybody in fact! R. remarkably composed.

Wednesday, 16 August Siegfried goes off well, people are saying that Herr Betz was never hoarse at all! Let others attempt to explain such characters, we do not understand them.

Thursday, 17 August Götterdämmerung also goes well; in the morning the Grand Duke of Schwerin with wife and daughter (Princess Vladimir) visits us at home. The Grand Duke of Weimar also honors us with visits in the evening and morning. Among other things, he asks Prof. Helmholtz whether he is conducting here!

Friday, 18 August Calls, dinners, a tremendous amount of coming and going, in the evening a banquet; R., quite without preparation, makes a wonderful speech, paraphrasing the final chorus from *Faust* – 'All things transitory are sent but as symbols.' The idea: 'The eternally feminine leads us on.' The Reichstag deputy chooses very unfortunate words: one could not know what posterity would think of it all, but the *striving* was worthy of recognition! Following that, Count Apponyi splendidly compares R. with Siegfried; he has brought tragedy back to life, because he never learned the meaning of fear. Quite splendid.

COSIMA WAGNER, Diary, 1876

The Rake's Progress

Venice, September 11, 1951. A night of stifling heat and a sirocco that blows like a bellows. The alleys near the theater have been roped off to keep the Fourth Estate at bay during the arrival procession, though the Higher Estates come not as pedestrians but are deposited by gondolas and motor launches directly at the theater door from a strongly redolent canal. Our own (pedestrian) party includes Nadia Boulanger (who carries Igor's valises), Wystan Auden and Chester Kallman (both nervous in spite of liquid fortifications – a moat of martinis, in fact), Stephen Spender (shy, deferential), and Louis MacNeice (handsome, arrogantly silent, but perhaps pickled).

A familiar unfamiliar face veers toward me as I enter the foyer, but no sooner have I identified it as Maxim Gorky's adopted son, Zinovy Peshkov (last seen in the Caucasus during the Revolution), than others crowding around me crowd General Peshkov out. The list of old friends who have come to criticize and otherwise 'assist' at the performance is too copious to be continued.

La Fenice, the most beautiful theater in the world, has never glittered as it does tonight in honor of the debut, and as an extra garnishing, bouquets of roses, like debutantes' corsages, have been pinned to each loge. Unfortunately, the beauty of these stalls on the inside is even less than 'skin deep.' The plush seems to have had chicken – or rather, moth – pox, and it and everything else is badly in need of deodorants. Another discomfort is that the seats are like European railroad compartments. The occupants on the side nearer the stage (i.e., the men) face in the wrong direction as if their cars were encased in their legs and abdomens, like grass-hoppers.

The audience glitters, too; everyone, that is, except a New York newspaperman who has no doubt already prepared a jobbery on the event consistent with his apparel and life-long devotion to the commonplace. (*Note:* Air travel was not yet the rule at that time and therefore neither were blue denims and Beethoven sweaters.)

In Italy nothing respectable begins on time. During tonight's long delay my thoughts drift back through the weeks of preparation, to the first conferences with stage directors and music coaches, which took place in Naples. I spent the mornings in the Naples aquarium then, drawing an old *joli laide* crustacean, a 'liquid prisoner pent in walls of glass' (Shakespeare). But I also think, during the wait, about echoes in the opera of Igor's so-called private life – of how, for example, the card game stemmed from his own fondness for cards; to me, Shadow's harpsichord arpeggio is an imitation of Igor's way of shuffling cards, as the *staccato* of that instrument recalls the way he snaps playing cards on a table. Perhaps Auden had actually observed Igor playing solitaire and heard him utter Russian *gros mots* when the wrong card appeared, which may have given him the idea for 'the Dance!'

VERA STRAVINSKY, in IGOR STRAVINSKY and ROBERT CRAFT,
Themes and Episodes

PRIMA DONNAS

Katharine Tofts, whose career flourished in the early years of the eighteenth century, was the first prima donna to win herself a reputation for being jealous, cantankerous and demanding. In 1704 she was accused of arranging to have an Italian rival pelted while singing. The outraged tone of her letter to John Rich, manager of the Drury Lane Theatre, is not altogether convincing.

Sir,

I was very much surp[r]iz'd when I was inform'd that ANN BARWICK, who was lately my Servant, had committed a Rudeness last night at the Play-house, by throwing of Oranges and hissing when Mrs L'EPINE the Italian Gentlewoman Sung. I hope no one can think that it was in the least with my privity, as I assure you it was not. I abhor such Practises, and I hope you will cause her to be prosecuted, that she may be punish'd as she deserves.

I am, sir, your humble servant,

KATHARINE TOFTS

In 1707 she writes to Rich again, in an effort to secure herself a better contract with him.

She begs leave also to represent that the Principal parts being given to her, she's thereby oblig'd to be at very great Expences for several things that the house never allows for, as Locks for hair, jewells, ribbons for knots for head and body, muslin for vails, gloves, shoes, washing of vails and head-cloaths and many other things, for which she may modestly affirm that one hundred pounds is not sufficient for the season.

[She] humbly begs leave to represent the hardness of her case, concerning the cloaths that she made for the part of Camilla; For tho' she may be thought Extravagant in laying out 80 Guineys upon them, yet she hopes that nobody will think it Reasonable that she should loose the whole Sume, it being matter of fact that the cloaths that were made by Mr Rich for Camilla, and paid for by the nobility were kept for Rosamond and paid for again out of the subscription money that did arise for the said opera of Rosamond. So that Mr Rich cannot say he ever made more than 3 suits of cloaths for Mrs Tofts, tho' she has perform'd in four Operas, viz. Arsinoe, Camilla, Rosamond and Thomiris, every one of the said Operas having been Subscrib'd for, and money allowed for cloaths and Scenes, &c. The said Cloaths are newly made up and will be deliver'd to Mr Rich when agreed for.

Katharine Tofts died in Venice in 1756, where she lived in the Palazzo Balbi with her husband, a shady British consul. Among the many rumours which filtered back to London was one which claimed that she had turned Roman Catholic and sung for the Pope, who had made sexual overtures to her.

In 1789, Doctor Burney called Caterina Gabrielli 'the most intelligent and best bred virtuosa with whom I had ever conversed'. The daughter of a cardinal's cook, she had a whim of iron, an exotic love life, and a thrilling soprano and theatrical presence. On an off-night, however, nothing would budge her.

Some time ago he [the viceroy] gave a great dinner to the principal nobility of Palermo and sent an invitation to Gabrielli to be of the party. Every other person arrived at the hour of invitation. The viceroy ordered dinner to be put back, and sent to let her know that the company awaited her. The messenger found her reading in bed. She said she was sorry for having made the company wait, and begged he would make her apology, but that really she had entirely forgot her engagement. The viceroy would have forgiven this piece of insolence, but when the company came to the opera, Gabrielli repeated her part with the utmost negligence and indifference, and sang all her airs in what they call *sotto voce*, that is, so low they can scarcely be heard. The viceroy was offended; but as he is a good-tempered man, he was loth to make use of authority; but at last, by a perseverance in this insolent stubbornness, she obliged him to threaten her with punishment in case she any longer refused to sing. On this she grew more obstinate than ever, declaring that force and authority should never succeed with her; that he might make her cry, but never could make her sing. The viceroy then sent her to prison, where she remained twelve days; during which time she gave magnificent entertainments every day, paid the debts of all the poor prisoners, and distributed large sums in charity. The viceroy was obliged to give up struggling with her, and she was at last set at liberty, amidst the acclamations of the poor. GEORGE HOGARTH, *Memoirs of the Opera*

The Victorian coloratura soprano Ilma di Murska was a genuine eccentric, but also something of a nuisance.

Ilma di Murska was punctual with a punctuality which put one out quite as much as utter inability to keep an appointment would have done. She was sure to turn up on the very evening, and at the very hour when she was wanted for a representation. But she had a horror of rehearsals, and never thought it worth while, when she was travelling from some distant place on the Continent, to announce that she had started, or to give any idea as to when she might really be expected. Her geographical knowledge, too, was often at fault, and some of the routes – 'short cuts' she called them – by which she reached London from Vienna were of the most extraordinary kind. She had taken a dislike to the Railway Station at Cologne, where she declared that a German officer had once spoken to her without being introduced; and on one occasion, partly to avoid the station of which she preserved so painful a recollection, partly in order to get to London by a new and expeditious route, she travelled from Vienna to St Petersburg, and from St Petersburg took boat to Hull, where she arrived just in time to join my Opera Company at the representations that I was then giving in Edinburgh. We had not heard of her for weeks, and she came into the dressing-room to find Madame Van Zandt already attired for the part Mdlle di Murska was to have played, that of 'Lucia'. She argued, with some truth, that she was in time for the performance, and declared, moreover, that in entrusting the part of 'Lucia' to another singer she could see a desire on my part to get rid of her.

The prima donna has generally a parrot, a pet dog, or an ape, which she loves to distraction, and carries with her wherever she goes. Ilma di Murska, however, travelled with an entire menagerie. Her immense Newfoundland, Pluto, dined with her every day. A cover was laid for him as for her, and he had learned to eat a fowl from a plate without dropping any of the meat or bones on the floor or even on the table cloth.

Pluto was a good-natured dog, or he would have made short work of the monkey, the two parrots, and the Angora cat, who were his constant associates. The intelligent animal hated travelling in the dog-truck, and he would resort to any sort of device in order to join his mistress in her first-class carriage, where he would, in spite of his immense bulk, squeeze himself beneath the seat. Once I remember he sprang through the closed window, cutting himself severely about the nose in his daring leap.

The other animals were simple nuisances. But I must do the monkey the justice to say that he did his best to kill the cat, and a bare place on Minette's back showed how badly she had once been clawed by her mischievous tormentor.

The most expensive of Mdlle di Murska's pets were probably the parrots. They flew about the room, perching everywhere and pecking at everything. Once at the Queen's Hotel, Birmingham, they tore with their beaks the kid off a valuable set of chairs, for which the hotel-keeper charged £30. The hotel bill of this reckless prima donna was always of the most alarming kind. She had the most extraordinary whims, and when Signor Sinico, Mdme Sinico's first husband, in order to show the effect of parsley upon parrots, gave to one of Mdme di Murska's birds enough parsley to kill it, nothing would satisfy the disconsolate lady but to have a post-mortem examination of the bird's remains.

HENRY MAPLESON, *Memoirs*

PRODUCERS

In the Spring 1977 issue of About the House, *Elizabeth Forbes assembled accounts of the various centenary productions of Wagner's* Ring *in 1976. A tribute to the inventiveness of today's producers or an indictment of their disrespect for the composers? Here are some of the versions of* Das Rheingold.

BAYREUTH. In the industrial society the river Rhine . . . becomes an electrostatic dam, a source of generated, commercially profitable power symbolized by the gold stored underneath it. Potential thieves are warded off by the firm's enlisted call-girls, known to us as Rhinemaidens, because the only temptation stronger than financial gain is the sexual urge.

WILLIAM MANN, *The Times*

PARIS OPÉRA. The Rhinemaidens . . . are slumped in a state of sexual satiety in well worn armchairs at the bottom of the Rhine. Meanwhile their doubles swing up and down on immense gymnasium ropes past the rock with the gold. . . . Alberich fondles the ropes, gets his nose to the ladies' toes and the bottoms of their skirts, and then opts for the gold, a brilliant orange spotlight which dazzles the audience with a blaze of sun.　　JOHN HIGGINS, *The Times*

CASSEL. There were the frogwomen Rhinemaidens scooting around on fish-shaped underwater rocket ships. There was the gods' conference room with inflated green and red plastic furniture and an enormously wide, swivelling wing chair for weary boss Wotan to dream his dreams of everlasting industrial might in, with Valhalla, a 21st-century oil refinery in the background. There were the giants . . . as robots on little rolling wagons controlled by blinking computers, and Freia was a topless goddess of love in a plastic yellow hula skirt, while her brothers Froh and Donner sported radar weather helmets.   J. H. SUTCLIFFE, *Opera*

MARSEILLES. The bewildered Marseillais . . . saw three rather buxom ladies in white flowing robes precariously seated on narrow swings hanging from the flies; a Victorian oak-panelled dining-room in which a middle-aged gentleman in grey frock-coat, striped trousers and spats, his dark-haired wife in a vast black crinoline; and his blonde sister-in-law, were involved in some terrifying holdup.   TONY MAYER, *Opera*

PARIS OPÉRA. Valhalla is glimpsed as a gilded room with a chandelier, almost an opera house (Wotan and Fricka?) set in the walls. By the side an immense muddied hand guards Fasolt and Fafner; in front a white rock becomes a human head, symbol presumably of the workers who built the place. Yet the union leaders are no more trustworthy than the bosses. When Fafner leaves with the ring he puts his staff through one of the eyes of the head so that tears of blood run down to the dung around its neck.

JOHN HIGGINS, *The Times*

BAYREUTH. The motley possessions in the Nibelung's hoard include an oil painting, presumably by A. Hitler; the gold is carried up in plastic bags unceremoniously shovelled over Freia.

RONALD CRICHTON, *Financial Times*

LEIPZIG. Nibelheim, the brutal, exploiting world of Alberich, has become a gigantic factory with a mass of slaves working at fiery furnaces and highly efficient machines: a frightening picture with photos of mechanical accessories, tubes and wheels. . . . The gods'

Valhalla is a huge, ugly palace, terrible, sterile, a repulsive symbol of power. The sneering, triumphant rulers are dressed in kitschy almost cabaret-like garb.   ECKART SCHWINGER, *Opera*

PARIS OPERA. Upstage . . . a partition with tall, narrow doors and a rectangular peephole gives a glimpse of the Throne-Room ceiling in some imitation Neuschwanstein: a Valhalla for the Prince of Monaco (dinner-jacketed, without orders but carrying a spear) and Liz Taylor disguised as the young Queen Victoria (in ermine-tailed cape, armed with a golden fly whisk – it's obviously been a long, hard night), who are lying on a bed of leaves.

ANDRÉ TUBOEUF, *Lyrica*

PUCCINI

There were always two strains contending for mastery in him. There was the Puccini who dipped his thumb into the paint and drew with the thick of it, and the Puccini who was a masterly miniaturist. The two Puccinis are to be found side by side in all his works, but most of them show a decided predominance of the one or the other. *Tosca* is almost throughout gross, thick-fingered, thick-lipped, while *Madam Butterfly*, apart from the rank sentimentality of the love music, is the Puccini of the lighter touch. There are beauties and poignancies so exquisite in *Madam Butterfly* that we can hardly savour them properly in the theatre; they belong rather to chamber music. We have always to distinguish between Puccini the dramatist and Puccini the musician. His knowledge of stage effect has become a commonplace of criticism. But his musical art is generally at its grossest when he is planning these theatrical knock-down blows.

ERNEST NEWMAN, *Testament of Music*

Puccini's one-act opera, Suor Angelica, *set in a cloistered convent, embodies all the pathos that is such a potent part of Puccini's appeal.*

A curious episode in the history of *Suor Angelica* was the audition which the composer gave of it in the convent of Vicopelago near Lucca, where his eldest sister was a nun in an enclosed order.

Puccini was greatly moved when he told the story of this performance. The little nuns stood round, absorbed, breathless with attention. His sister turned the pages for him, while Giacomo played and explained the words of the songs to them. Phase by phase, the opening episodes of the novices with their mistress and the monitor, the little scene of the wishes, and then the strange secret sadness of Sister Angelica, had interested and enthralled them. It may be that each of the listeners found in that music something of her own heart. When he reached the scene of the princess aunt, Puccini stopped in embarrassment. He had to explain the heroine's story, had to tell them of her past and the sin of love which had stained her fair fame, and of that son who had been taken away from her and whose death was now brutally announced. And there was worse to come. He had to tell them of the despairing suicide and the divine pardon of the miracle.

'It was not easy,' said Puccini. 'Still, with as much tact and skill as I could summon, I explained it all. I saw many eyes that looked at me through tears. And when I came to the aria, "Madonna, Madonna, salvami per amor di mio figlio!" all the little nuns cried, with voices full of pity but firm in their decision, "Yes, yes, poor things!" '

And so with human compassion and Christian charity the real nuns absolved their phantom sister.

GIUSEPPE ADAMI, *Letters of Puccini*

RAVEL

The day came when M. Rouché asked me to write the libretto of a
fairy-tale ballet for the Opéra. I still cannot explain to myself how
I managed to produce *l'Enfant et les sortilèges* for him – I who
write so slowly and with such difficulty – in less than a week ... He
liked my little poem, and suggested the names of several composers, all of which I received with as much politeness as I could
muster.

'But,' Rouché said after a pause, 'what if I were to suggest
Ravel?'

My politeness was immediately forgotten in my excitement,
and my expressions of hope threw diplomacy to the winds.

'But we mustn't forget that it might take a long time,' Rouché
added, 'even supposing that Ravel should accept...'

He accepted. And it took a long time. He disappeared with my
libretto, and we heard nothing more about Ravel, or about
l'Enfant ... Where was Ravel working? Was he working? I was
not then aware of all that the creation of a work demanded from
him, the slow frenzy that would take hold of him and make him its
solitary prisoner, careless of the days and hours. The war claimed
Ravel, created a hermetic silence about his name, and I lost the
habit of thinking about *l'Enfant et les sortilèges*.

Five years passed. The finished work, and its creator, emerged
from the silence, escaping from the blue and nyctalopic eyes of the
Siamese cats, his confidants. But the composer did not treat me as
a privileged person; he allowed me no comments, no premature
audition of the score. His only concern seemed to be the 'miaow
duet' between the two Cats, and he asked me with great seriousness if I saw any objection to his replacing *mouao* with *mouain*, or
it may have been the other way around...

The years had stripped him by then, not only of his frilled shirt front and his side whiskers, but also of his short man's hauteur. The white hair and the black hair on his head had mingled to form a sort of plumage, and he would cross his delicate little rodent's hands as he spoke, flicking every nearby object with his squirrel's eyes...

The score of *l'Enfant et les sortilèges* – I had thoughtlessly entitled it *Divertissement pour ma fille* until the day Ravel, with icy gravity, said to me: 'But I have no daughter' – is now famous. How can I convey to you my emotion at the first throb of the tambourines accompanying the procession of the shepherd boys, the moonlit dazzle of the garden, the flight of the dragonflies and the bats ... 'It's quite amusing, don't you think?' Ravel said. But my throat was knotted tight with tears.   COLETTE, *Earthly Paradise*

RECORDING

Mary Watkins Cushing describes Olive Fremstad's sortie into the recording studio, c. 1910.

Most people have forgotten, if indeed they ever knew, what absurd places the recording studios were at that time. The Columbia headquarters were fortunately in the city, so at least we were spared the annoyance of a trip from town. Once we reached the scene of action, however, I decided that it resembled, more than anything else, a Hall of Fun at an amusement park. The whole thing was incredible. The singer, always dressed in formal attire, including hat and gloves, stood upon a small platform facing a curtain through which protruded a large tin horn. Into this she had to sing, and was required, moreover, to remember that while emitting high notes she must lean back as far as possible, but when singing low ones must sway forward almost into the horn's mouth. If, in the throes of dramatic feeling, she should happen to reverse this order, the results would resemble nothing so much as the amorous shrieks of back-fence pussies. Therefore, to facilitate these tricky gyrations, there were handles for her to grip on either side of the horn.

Behind the curtain sat the technicians, with wax disks revolving and glass cases full of instruments, cotton, and needles, like a surgery. Beyond the curtain on Madame's side was the orchestra and the conductor. The latter stood behind her where she could watch him only in a mirror; and back of him were the musicians. They supplied the comedy element in the scene, for they were not assembled in an orderly body but each was assigned his place according to the number and type of vibrations which his instrument delivered. Thus the violins – their tone augmented by tiny megaphones over the strings – were the nearest neighbors, while trombonists were banished to the outermost corners, seated on high stools near the ceiling. Percussion was barely allowed in the room at all. Madame got halfway through an aria and caught sight, in her little mirror, of a tuba player standing in a door so far away that she thought he had either been forgotten or had just arrived. She stopped at once in the middle of a phrase and turning, called to him, 'Ye gods, if I can get here on time, why can't you? This is a *Skandal*!'

The technicians swore softly, because the cutting had been perfect until then. Now it must be done all over again. The whole thing was a long and painful process, for often the trial disks, made before the singer was tired, were better than the master impression; but of course, once played, were no longer usable. It took us the better part of ten days to complete, none too satisfactorily, the repertoire which had been contracted for. At the end, in spite of a pleasing advance on royalties, elaborate expressions of regard and a large bunch of orchids from the directors, Madame swept ruthlessly from the studio never to return.

'I *du meine Güte!*' she exclaimed as she threw her orchids at Mimi and flung herself fully clothed on her bed at home. 'All that work and nothing gained! When people play those things in years to come they will say: "Oh ho, so that's the great Fremstad. Well, I guess she wasn't so much after all."'

MARY WATKINS CUSHING, *The Rainbow Bridge*

REGIME

A discreet Person will never use such affected Expressions as, *I cannot sing To-day; – I've got a deadly Cold;* and, in making his excuse, falls a Coughing. I can truly say, that I have never in my Life heard a Singer own the Truth, and say, *I'm very well to-day*: They reserve the unreasonable Confession to the next Day, when they make no difficulty to say, *In all my Days my Voice was never in better Order than it was Yesterday.*

PIERO TOSI, *Observations on the Florid Song*

'Up to forty,' she said, 'I stinted myself nothing. I ate and lived as I chose. After forty, however, I became more strict. Since then I eat no red meat and drink only white wine and soda. When I feel weak, a glass of champagne picks me up. I never touch spirits or liqueurs. My diet consists of light food and white meat and vegetables. I always sleep with the window wide open in summer and partly open in winter, so as not to get the cold air straight on my face. I never get to bed early, hardly ever before half-past twelve or one. A severe hygiene and an elaborate toilet before bed are absolutely necessary to any woman who does not want to get fat. That is my only secret of health.'

ADELINA PATTI, quoted in HERMANN KLEIN, *The Reign of Patti*

When he had finished the cigarette he went to the washstand and filled his mouth with salt water, which he inhaled – or seemed to inhale – into his lungs, then spat out before he strangled. Mario (his valet) held out a box of Swedish snuff from which he took a pinch to clear his nostrils; then he took a wineglass of whisky, next a glass of charged water and finally a quarter of an apple. Into the pockets that were placed in every costume exactly where his hands dropped, he slipped two bottles of warm salt water, in case he had to wash his throat on the stage. When all was ready Mario handed him his charms – a twisted coral horn, holy medals and old coins, all linked together on a fat little chain ... Just before he left the dressing room he called upon his dead mother for help, since the thought of her gave him courage. No one ever wished him luck because, he said, that was sure to bring disaster.

Caruso's pre-performance routine, described in ROBERT RUSHMORE,
The Singing Voice

Keeping up with Olive Fremstad's regime required considerable physical and moral stamina.

To whatever she told me to do, in those days, I gave the benefit of at least one honest trial. When she said that every good house-keeper always markets at dawn while things are fresh, I believed her and tore myself from a warm bed to go shopping in the bleak half-light of a winter morning long before seven. But Madame had overlooked the fact that this was New York, not Central Europe. I usually reached the store before the proprietor himself, and if he let me in at all, his vegetables and fruit were found to be wilted leftovers from the day before. He, as well as the cook and the maids, thought me quite crazy instead of clever.

Even more trying were the evening walks which Madame pre-scribed for herself and which consequently became my lot as well. These were taken every free night after supper on the upper paths of Riverside and often, in good weather, extended as far as Claremont and the viaduct. She had special boots made on a most un-prima-donna-like last for these excursions, and special tweeds, hats, and veils. She also inevitably wore too many or too heavy coats, so that before the promenade was half over it fell to my lot to carry them.

We went at a dizzy pace. All who remember Olive Fremstad treasure the liveliest impression of her windblown stride, both on the stage and off. It was inimitable and challenging. Although I was a husky country girl, my legs always seemed much shorter than hers, and often I had to trot in order to keep her in sight.

Then there was that maddening business of the lamp posts. These feeble luminaries were situated at regular intervals along our path, half, perhaps a third, of a block apart, and the object of a detestable game (which she had invented, I am sure, out of sheer ostentation) was to take an enormous breath and see how many lamps one could pass without releasing it. Madame filled her copious professional bellows and whizzed by five with ease, but it took me a whole season to work up to two. I was goaded to this accomplishment by the jeers of my opponent who callously met my pleas of bursting lungs and asphyxiation by the argument that it was building up my constitution. This gay diversion was supposed to be for the purpose of inducing deep, restful slumbers immediately on our return. For my part I sometimes feared such sleep might be my last as I fell into bed with parched throat and heaving sides. But Madame, whose sense of humor was unpredictable, found my severest collapses screamingly funny, and after one of our grimmer and more ruthless sprints would be sure to bid me good night in the very best of humors.

Of sleep I had little enough at best. There were always the two regular evenings a week when, after the performance, there was a ritual from which we never deviated and which ended for me, if I was lucky, about two in the morning. First, on returning from the theater, there had to be a period of 'cooling off' before we might eat; then the dinner, served by a cross and sleepy cook, which was predestined to be a failure. After that the replete and prostrate diva must be read aloud to, a rubbishy detective story usually, so that her mind could relax. When finally, after various alarms and excursions, she was safely tucked up in bed and every screen and window adjusted to the correct millimeter, I had to wrestle with the flowers. These were always dumped into her bathtub when we came in, and now had to be unwired, dethroned, and arranged, and the tub tidied up before morning.

If insomnia plagued Madame, as it often did, she would call me an hour or two later to come and talk to her. Sometimes, being so young and often so dog-weary, I would be already deep in sleep and would not hear her first summons. I always heard her second, however, and so did everyone else, for she made enough din to arouse the entire neighborhood. In order to avert what I felt to be rather just complaints from adjacent apartments, I soon devised a more silent system of communication. I tied to my toe a string which had been passed under my door and Madame's and which terminated in a ring hooked to her bedpost. This she tweaked at need, but even when, by happy chance, she slept the night through, the harness interfered considerably with my own rest. Still, at eighteen, one not only survives such things but finds them exciting.   MARY WATKINS CUSHING, *The Rainbow Bridge*

A GOOD REMEDY FOR CATARRH AND HOARSENESS

Pour boiling hot water into a saucer, and let a large sponge suck it all up. Then squeeze it firmly out again. Hold the sponge to the nose and mouth, and breathe alternately through the nose and mouth, in and out.

I sing my exercises, the great scale, passages, etc., and all the vowels into it, and so force the hot steam to act upon the lungs, bronchial tubes, and especially on the mucous membranes, while I am breathing in and out through the sponge. After this has been kept up for ten or fifteen minutes, wash the face in cold water. This can be repeated four to six times a day. The sponge should be full of water, but must be quite squeezed out. This has helped me greatly, and I can recommend it highly. It can do no injury because it is natural. But after breathing in the hot steam, do not go out immediately into the cold air.   LILLI LEHMANN, *How to Sing*

REHEARSAL

Manager of the King's Theatre in London from 1820 to 1827, John Ebers communicates the inevitable frustration and heartache of mounting a season of Italian opera.

The word rehearsal summons up, to all practically acquainted with its meaning, a scene beyond description. If the performances of a theatre are intended to represent the truth of human nature, a rehearsal is the living reality – the scene where the veil is rent in twain, and all the turmoil laid open to the view which can be produced by the undisguised operations of vanity, self-love, and jealousy. The fabled crowds who petitioned heaven to allot the parts in life otherwise than Fate had cast them, are but a type of the inmates of a theatre behind the scenes, when contending for prominent characters in an opera.

Perhaps with the very first performers there is not much of this, as their right to the principal parts cannot be disputed. But dire is the struggle among all below. A part rather better than another is an apple of contention, which, to manager, director, and conductor, proves a most bitter fruit. As every person shakes to have that character which may best serve – not the general effect of the piece, or the interests of the theatre, which are wholly immaterial – but his or her own object in making the greatest display possible; and as non-concession is the permanent rule of the place, the opera is placed in the pleasing predicament of being able to get neither one way nor the other. The prima donna, whose part is settled, attends the rehearsal, and the *seconda*, being displeased with her own station in the piece, will not go on; and the first lady, indignant at being detained to no purpose, goes away, and the business is over for the day. If the manager is positive, the lady falls ill. Biagioli, being refused a part she wanted in *Elisa e*

Claudio, took to her bed for two days, in consequence, as she said, of being so afflicted by my decision.

The refusal to proceed is the more effectual engine, because it puts all the rest of the company out of humour at their time being occupied needlessly: all complain, and a dialogue goes on in which everybody talks at once; and probably three different languages may be conceivable, but not expressible. The *signori* protest, the *signore* exclaim, the choruses are wonderfully in concert with their lamentations, the director commands, entreats, stamps, and swears, with equal success, and, in the midst of the Babel, the gentlemen of the orchestra, who wish all the singers at the devil, endeavour to get over the business of the day by playing on without the vocal music. The leader of the orchestra, finding all ineffectual, puts on his hat, and walks away, followed by violins, basses, trombones, and kettle-drums, en masse, and the scene at length concludes as it may....

JOHN EBERS, *Seven Years of the King's Theatre*

The rehearsal for the première of Puccini's La Fanciulla del West *at the Met, as reported in the New York Sun, December 1910.*

The orchestra pit, full of men and instruments, is like a cauldron of sound, boiling with preliminary tuning. At the conductor's desk Toscanini, his nose almost touching the score in the intensity of his concentration, is making rapid corrections and interlineations. Puccini himself, in derby hat, brown suit and red necktie, looks over his shoulder and does not interfere. Toscanini takes the corrected sheets to the man with the big bassoon. ... There are perhaps fifty persons waiting to see and to hear. When the curtain goes up the stage becomes the port for most of their thoughts. But there two sails in their separate offings, the hat of Puccini and the familiar head of Belasco, are the objects of many peering, curious glances. Each is the center of a little group, Puccini quiet, Belasco grumbling ominously, like Vesuvius on the point of eruption. ...

331

Through the warm shadowy gloom one recognizes faces grown familiar across the footlights. One finds one's self close to Mme Fremstad and later has a disturbing consciousness of seeing her hands clinched tightly on the top of the seat before her as she follows the music – or you would rather say by way of accuracy that it pursues her with its possibilities. When Emmy Destinn comes on and begins her lines Mme Fremstad turns and says: 'She sings beautifully. Doesn't she?' And yet they say there is no generosity of appreciation among these men and women. There is not on Manhattan Island a sound so hoarse as Toscanini's voice this week unless it is the raucous bark of an automobile horn. He has talked, he has sung, he has pom-pommed explanatory phrases till he can scarcely croak....

Caruso, who has a performance of *Aida* coming on the same evening, uses his voice cautiously. Sometimes the notes are barely audible above the climax of sounds from the orchestra. Again, when these sink to mere whispers, one hears lovely low tones, very soft, very gentle, almost like the drowsy first notes of a wonderful great bird beginning to sing at dawn. And one looks with a sort of painful incredulity at the stout gentleman in a brown business suit, who does not suggest any kind of bird – unless it is a nice plump partridge – yet who is visibly responsible for those tones. ... He makes few unnecessary motions. When he first comes in he takes off an imaginary overcoat and hat and puts them on a chair. When he goes out he possesses himself of these imperceptible articles and departs with them. That episode was repeated several times and he was always most conscientious about handling the make believe raiment. Only in the scene after he is shot does he attempt anything dramatic. This too is gone through repeatedly, and each time he is – apparently – dragged in by Destinn, his knees covered with snow and his motions animated by a sublime disregard of the possible effects on his really admirable trousers of crawling on his knees over the proverbial dust of the stage floor. Both he and Destinn work hard over his painful climb up the ladder to the half loft overhead. That eminence achieved he sits down, Turk or tailor fashion – more sublime indifference to the fate of trousers and knees – mops his forehead with his handker-

chief and gazes out into the auditorium. When he has been labori-
ously assisted to the stage again and has fallen fainting across the
table where Destinn and Amato gamble for possession of him, he
lies there inert for a while, then sits up, again mops his face and
idly watches the game, watches Toscanini, watches the cleaning
woman wiping interminable rows of chair backs in the gallery. He
seems profoundly indifferent to the whole thing. ... Destinn on
the other hand both sings and acts with more than a mere exhibition of intention. She is in a black velvet frock, almost a hobble
skirt, so that she even accentuates the difficult walk called for by
the tight slippers of the play. And she sings with dramatic intensity. Of course, she has no performance that night, and that makes
a difference. The rehearsal goes on and on. The act is finished and
there is half an hour to rest. Belasco goes on the stage, sits down at
the table and distributes embroidered advice on assorted subjects;
on how to walk like an Indian; on how to 'pull a gun' – a quite
different affair, *messieurs* and *signori*, from drawing a sword or a
stiletto; on how to shut a door in the teeth of the wind; on how to
kick one's legs against each other after fighting one's way through
a blizzard....

de RESZKE

*Jean de Reszke was not only the matinée idol of the later
Victorian opera public, but its most elegant and musicianly
tenor. In the 1890s, he moved 'up' from the French and
Italian repertory towards the vocally heavier challenges of
Tristan and Siegfried. His brother Edouard was an equally
distinguished bass-baritone.*

Without the help of the gramophone, how can we form some
notion of Jean's vocal quality and interpretative style? On two

points all who attempt to describe his singing insist. First, whatever language he sang in, he enunciated the text with exquisite art, caressing the words as tenderly as the musical phrase. As a teacher he constantly urged his pupils to cultivate 'l'amour de la parole'; and Amherst Webber, his coach, accompanist and friend for half a lifetime, declared that it was impossible to recallll any musical phrase one had heard him sing without also remembering the words and the peculiar charm he gave them. The second point concerns the relation between the volume of his voice in forte passages and the extraordinary grace and poetry of style for which he was famous: power, all are agreed, was never purchased at the expense of that sustained legato and purity of tone which are the foundation of all good singing. Yet we never read of Jean's voice having been drowned by the large Wagnerian orchestra, and it is evident that he had no need to strain or shout in order to make both notes and words fully audible throughout the largest house. Before his time, as since, the big Wagner tenor roles, despite the clear injunctions of the composer, had been almost always declaimed rather than sung. In Jean's performances, says Webber, 'incisive declamation was not wanting whenever the music called for it, but never at the sacrifice of beauty of tone, for this singing always had the quality which one of his French critics described as *"le charme dans la force"*'; his interpretations 'proved triumphantly that *bel canto* was not only possible, in the later Wagner works, but essential to a complete understanding of them'.

On such a point it is valuable to call the evidence of Cosima Wagner, who was well inured to the 'Bayreuth bark' and might have been expected to harbour a grudge against two singers who had resisted all her efforts to lure them to Bayreuth. One night, sitting by chance near Webber during a Jean de Reszke *Meistersinger* performance at Covent Garden, 'she was in ecstasies: she kept exclaiming that she caught new beauties of melody that no German singer had ever suggested.'

According to Clara Leiser, the author of the valuable standard biography of the brothers (*Jean de Reszke and the Great Days of Opera*), Jean longed to crown his career by singing Parsifal (she might have added that Edouard would have made the ideal

Gurnemanz); notwithstanding this, they refused Cosima's repeated invitations simply because the Princess of Wales (Queen
Alexandra) had extorted a promise from them 'not to go to
Germany to sing for that horrid old man' – meaning the Kaiser,
whom she detested.

Queen Victoria, by the way, who once asked Jean for his
autograph, greatly enjoyed the singing of both brothers – 'most
gentleman-like fine men, and their voices have a great likeness'.
On her eightieth birthday the two appeared at Windsor in a
command performance of *Lohengrin*, with Nordica,
Schumann-Heink and Bispham also in the fabulous cast. Though
the Queen had never heard the opera before, she found it 'the
most glorious composition' and the singing of the two brothers
'beyond praise. Jean looked so handsome in his white attire,
armour, and helmet, and the electric light was turned strong upon
him, so that he seemed surrounded by a halo.'

DESMOND SHAWE-TAYLOR, *A Gallery of Great Singers*

RETIREMENT

*Adelaide Kemble was a scion of the famous Kemble theatri-
cal family, and a famous Norma and Semiramide in the late
1830s and early 1840s. Her essay* A Recollection of Pasta *is
an evocative tribute to the first Norma, with whom Kemble
herself studied the role.*

Many years ago I had the happiness and supreme advantage of
passing some days with her at her villa on the Lake of Como. On a
lovely Sunday early in the autumn I arrived there. No servant was
at hand, but the door stood hospitably open, and in I went; a little
dog was in the doorway opposite to me, barking violently. I
passed him and went on into the inner apartment; in this second

room the only live occupant was another little dog, who came forward and greeted me with every manifestation of welcome, jumping and fawning upon me; another open door invited me still further, and here I found a huge black Newfoundland, who gazed at me with motionless mistrust as I went by. It was like a charmed palace in the 'Arabian Nights,' where, by some dire enchantment, all the human creatures have been transformed into beasts.

Across the room was a closed portal, at which I knocked for admittance. '*Chi è là? chi è là? non si può!* (Who is there? who is there? You can't come in!)' vociferated a gruff voice from within, again demanding with increased vigour, and in tones that left me quite in doubt as to the sex of the speaker, '*Chi è là?*' '*Forestieri* (Foreigners),' said I; and was then desired by the same portentous voice to go in. At a table playing at cards with several dirty-looking Italian men, sat a gigantic and most formidable old woman. She never rose from her seat, but looked at me with a good deal of solemnity, asked me who I was, and what I wanted, and then, after a pause, and without taking any further notice of me, turned to her neighbour, and simply remarking, '*Tocc'a lei* (It's your turn),' resumed her game, which my unexpected advent had for the moment suspended. This was Madama Rachele, Pasta's mother, a peasant, who had remained one in every respect, in spite of all change of life and circumstance.

Presently Pasta came in from the garden in the full slovenliness of an Italian morning costume. She was stout and under the average height, and, having one leg shorter than the other, waddled rather than walked, but for all that she looked taller than everybody else. And what a grand head it was! full of all nobleness and sweetness. She greeted me very affectionately, would not hear of my returning to Como, but insisted on keeping me, and immediately despatched her own boatmen to fetch my luggage, which had been left at the inn. She inquired eagerly into my prospects, and when she found I was studying for the artistic career, lamented that the complete retirement in which she had lived now for so long a time would make it impossible for her to be of use to me with any of the theatrical people then in power. '*Ma forse per il canto potrei essere di qualche utilità* (But perhaps for the singing I might be of some use),' she added, with a modest hesitation; and, indeed, nothing could exceed the patient kindness with which she daily gave me the most invaluable lessons while I remained with her. She made me sing to her continually, and gave me many of her own *fioriture*, always prefacing any suggestion diffidently with, '*Moi, je faisais ainsi; cela faisait de l'effet.*'

She never seemed to regret or miss the excitement of the old life, but appeared entirely absorbed in country pursuits and with the improvements she was making in the place. She had three houses on the estate – the one in which she lived and where I stayed with her, another occupied by her daughter Clelia Ferrante and her family, and another which was in process of building. She took me into her oratory, in which hung an excellent copy of Raphael's 'Saint Cecilia.' '*Quella doveva cantar bene* (She must have sung well),' she remarked, as we stood looking at the upturned rapturous face.

Over her bedroom door hung innumerable birds in cages. '*J'aime à les entendre le matin,*' she said; adding, with a comical shade of bitterness, '*Ces petits coquins, ils chantent toujours si juste!*' Even at her best, she had always sung false upon three notes in the middle of her voice – the C of the third space, with the D and E which follow, were invariably considerably too flat. One day that she was teaching me to sing 'Casta Diva,' the great air of the 'Norma,' when I came to the words '*spargi in terra,*' which fall upon these particular notes, she suddenly stopped me. '*Crescete, mia cara* (You are singing sharp, my dear),' said she. I began again, and was again stopped at the same place. Anxious to ascertain the fact, about which I had my doubts, I repeated the passage for the third time, very gently touching the piano at the concluding note, and finding myself in perfect unison with it. '*Ma non sentite che crescete sempre?* (But don't you hear that you still sing sharp?)' she exclaimed, and then herself sang the notes a full quarter of a tone too flat, after which she looked at me with an air of complacent triumph, and remarked, '*Sentite che differenza, cara mia?* (You hear the difference, my dear?)' – a very curious proof that her falseness of intonation was an imperfection of the ear, and not of the voice, for these three notes of the scale – a most remarkable peculiarity, which I have never since met with in any one. This was the only occasion upon which she opened her mouth to sing to me while I was under her roof; every service in her power, except that greatest one, she rendered me. I have often thought that my youthful and enthusiastic admiration, which almost amounted to adoration of her, was sweet to her, and that perhaps she was afraid of lessening it, or of disturbing the impression which the recollection of her singing had left upon my mind. Yet I had never heard her in her prime; nor did I see her in 'Medea', which by all accounts must have been the finest of her parts. I first heard her during the last but one of her engagements in England, when her voice had lost its freshness and often broke, and when the intonation of more than the three original false notes was becoming impaired. I saw her in 'Tancredi' when, with that gracious movement of her perfect arms, she seemed to embrace the earth, and sang, '*Oh, cara terra degli avi miei, ti bacio!* (O, dear earth of my forefathers, I kiss thee!)' How wonderful, too, was her breaking open of the coffin in 'Romeo', and the great passionate desolateness with which she lifted one lock of the dead Juliet's hair and pressed it to her lips! how glorious the upward winged look with which she said, '*Ti seguirò* (I'll follow thee),' in the recitative to the celebrated 'Ombra Adorata,' that fine song attributed to Zingarelli, but in reality composed by the soprano Crescentini. I remember, while I was sitting in my stall worshipping this great goddess and thanking Heaven for a new revelation of happiness, hearing a well-known old dandy who was just before me exclaim, while he applauded her with a sort of good-natured condescension, 'Oh, poor dear old thing! how stumpy she is! how old she has grown, to be sure! She oughtn't to have come back again!'

I saw her once again years afterwards, the last time of all that she sang in London, when love for her country induced her to consent to give 'one' representation for the benefit of the Italian refugees in England, and when, for the agony of her failure, I too could have found in my heart to cry, 'Why did she ever come again!' if afterwards I had not heard Viardot, who had seen her for the first time on this occasion, say of her, 'Yes, it is a ruin; but so is Leonardo's "Last Supper".' This tribute of one woman of genius to another reminds me of a conversation I had one day with Pasta, when at Como, about Mdme Viardot's sister, Malibran. I was speaking disapprovingly of the excess of ornament with which she was in the habit of overlaying almost everything she sang. 'Ah,' said Pasta, 'how should one not spend too much when one has such riches? If I could have done ascending scales, I should have done them too.'

And now she is gone, and Malibran; and Viardot is rarely heard, and not in public – and Grisi, who had preserved some of that tradition of beauty in power which seems to have taken such sad flight out of almost all forms of art in this the day of what is called reality, is gradually fading away also from before our eyes. To those who have seen all these glories of the olden time, the opera-house of nowadays seems an empty place.

Colette's memoir of her encounters with the famous Carmen and Santuzza, Emma Calvé, begins in Paris and ends, many years later, in Nice.

I cannot say that I knew Emma Calvé well. How could one know well a being whose starry orbit illuminated Paris?

It began by my lunching with her, in her house at the corner of the Place des Etats-Unis. Sunlight on the tablecloth made a yellow pattern from which Calvé's dark beauty had nothing to fear. As for the other guests, in her presence I had no eyes for them – and no ears either; and this was hardly surprising because she yielded, although discreetly, to the need, the sole need, of a bird: the need to sing. Constantly, as if for her own ears, she would lean her head a little to one side and throw off some marvellous high C, the beginning of some roulade, a sound of crystalline perfection. I remember that she murmured, in an astounding *pianissimo*, a snatch of the over-famous 'Air du Mysoli'...

As though listening in the dusk to a nightingale, her guests fell silent; then resumed their conversation when the luminous track of the last note had vanished. No one applauded: one does not congratulate a nightingale.

339

She always knew that I admired her, and that moreover I was attracted by her French peasant simplicity. It delighted me that she should have carried so triumphantly all over the world her fine little well-made Latin head, her delicate features, above the strong throat that concealed the treasures of her voice.

Thus, from one meeting to another, the lives of two women slipped past. Across the footlights, when I was in the theatre, Calvé would throw to me like a flower her golden notes, all the ease and accomplishment of her art. From time to time a signed photograph would cross the ocean. ... And I come to our last meeting, at Nice.

Every day, at the hour when the sun was at its height, I was faithful to a quiet restaurant in the Cours Saleya. It was reached by a path of flowers; who does not know the intoxicating flower-market divided into solid banks of carnations, roses and narcissus? Monsieur Adolphe used to send me at once a bouquet of pink radishes, baby artichokes, flageolet beans and pimentos, while I was waiting for the firm-fleshed red mullet and the carafe of Vin de Bellet.

In front of me a solidly built woman was making a very similar meal. When she turned to speak to the waitress, I could not repress a joyful exclamation, and it was not long before my table was joined to that of Emma Calvé. How old was she then? What does it matter? Ah, the beautiful old lady, the youthful old lady: with what dignity the body can grow old when it is sustained by the spirit! Impossible to tire of hearing her laugh, of savouring in her deep laughter the echo of that *pianissimo* of long ago. She told me that America wanted her to make a film of *Carmen*, but that she would not accept this sham world of the screen. She was devoted, she said, to her beloved countryside, to her mountains which kept her feet lively and her knees firm, and to the good folk who surrounded her with gratitude and affection. She was the first to rise from the table, and I proposed to call a cab for her.

'What for?' she asked in amazement. 'I have good legs. At home, every morning, I climb, I climb. When I have had enough, high up there, I sing. I sing for my mountain ... For my mountain, and also for some little shepherd boy. For a girl who beats out the washing ... For a ploughman who stops his team and listens to me...'

She bent towards me a face untouched by the arts of embellishment, and added mischievously:

'You see, they make an audience!'

Maria Callas' long and tragic retirement is the most legendary of all. The great accompanist Gerald Moore, in his Furthermoore, *describes how upset he was to witness her vocal decline during her world concert tour of 1973–4, her last public appearances. His suggestion of a panacea is deeply touching, and deeply felt.*

After the tour was over and she returned to Paris, forsaken, why did someone not speak of Schubert to her? It is unnatural that an artist with a name almost as legendary as Caruso's should have been allowed to languish in misery. Quiet study of Schubert with a sympathetic colleague would have opened up a new world for her. Naturally it was too late to cherish any hope that her marvellous *coluratura*, which had electrified the world, would be regained for she was in her fifties, but it was not too late to have preserved, or at least be capable of recapturing, much of the quality of her middle voice. Her musical instinct, though dormant at this time, was always there. The art that moved her hearers in her Violetta could have been brought to bear on 'Du bist die Ruh' ('You are Rest and Peace') with its rapturous ascending passages that need a serene melting quality of voice that she once had. She would have made that almost imperceptible *portamento* – one of her Kreisler-like virtues which nobody rivalled – on 'Hast du mein Herz' ('You warmed my heart') carrying a falling interval of a sixth in Schubert's hymn of thanksgiving 'To Music'. Her faith in herself would have been restored by 'Frühlingsglaube' ('Faith in Spring').

Schubert would have been a panacea and washed her mind of memories of the fearful Philistine who had magnetized her. Callas had forgotten that she was a musician and unless she was a musician she was nothing. Someone she trusted, someone who had her true interest in mind was needed to coax her back to her real self when she was left without aim. With her fervid musical intuition she would quickly have recognized the buoyancy and eternal spring in Schubert and would have taken his music to her heart.

Callas continued to dream of a comeback: but as Jeffrey Tate discovered when he went to coach her shortly before her death, the psychological barriers were as immense as the physical and musical ones.

'I went over to Paris in an extremely beautiful April. I rang her up from the friends' house in which I was staying – and of course everyone was agog that I was ringing Callas. I got through to her maid and then to Maria herself, and her Greek-American voice boomed down the phone and she said "Yes, John Tooley has spoken to me of you. You may come today at four o'clock." I arrived, of course, half an hour early and sat on a bench in fear and trepidation before I dared to go up. It was the same house in which Catherine Deneuve lived, it had one of those creaky old lifts. Anyway, I went up to the third floor and pressed the bell. Bruna, Callas' maid, answered the door and ushered me in and said "Madame Callas is expecting you."

'There were signed photographs of Serafin, de Sabata and all the greats and I sat there for twenty minutes, no one came near me. Then there was a sort of rustle, a noise in the other room. The door opened and two little poodles scampered through. And then the Diva herself came in, looking larger than life in a purple and gold caftan, hair scraped back. She extended me a hand graciously and we sat and talked for about three quarters of an hour – about herself, about me, about life in general. What I did not realize at that moment was that she was as nervous of me as I was of her. By that stage in her career she rarely exposed herself to working with somebody, and therefore she was insecure about what the results might be....

'We sipped tea and eventually she put a score in my hand and said, "This is Serafin's vocal score of *Don Carlos*, with the master's own markings" – which made me quiver. Then she said, "I'd like you to play for me the prelude to 'Tu che le vanità'." I thought this very curious, like an audition, but I sat down at the piano and proceeded to play, and she said "No, no. Here – this must be slower, here faster." Looking back, all she was doing was settling her nerves before she dared open her mouth and sing to me.

'She was wonderful, everything she said was absolutely right about the music. She would add, "Here are Maestro Serafin's marks, here you must do this, here I expect to hear that." Then eventually she sang – she hadn't of course got the top of the voice that she previously had, but the sound was unmistakably Callas. Work was the wrong word for it – we sang through things, one could hardly say that one worked at the beginning. The first day we sang through an hour's worth of music and then that was enough for her. I had a small drink and I went home....

'On the third day, I ventured to say "Maria, this is a little flat," or "Maria, could that be a little more legato," and she admitted to me that she had problems with the "a" vowel and that she had always had problems with it – and somehow the ice was broken the moment she admitted that she had a problem somewhere. And then from that moment on we began to work properly, but then she began to say, "I don't think I can do this," and "Is this possible? I'm frightened." In our conversation she would always refer to the past and how wonderful the past had been and how terrible the standards were now. Her view of the world was totally depressing....

'I had the terrible feeling that here was a woman who had gone beyond the edge of possibility: she lived for that concert at Covent Garden but at the same time knew that the concert wasn't possible. She wore a watch around her neck which used to ring at intervals, when she had to put drops in her eyes, because she suffered from glaucoma. It was very disconcerting to be in the middle of the aria and this little watch would ring at her breast and she would stop and say "My drops." There was a degree of hypochondria and fear. At the same time she was so beautiful that one wondered why couldn't she have gone on acting, why couldn't she have made a career out of teaching? Actually she could have done. The way she expounded that prelude to "Tu che le vanità" showed someone who could communicate a great deal. But she said, "No, I can't teach, I never had a technique. I can't teach anything, only say what is right and what is wrong." But even that would have been a great deal: she *did* know what was right. I think if she could have continued with master classes (which she taught for one season, in 1972 in New York) she would have lived longer, for I think eventually she died of neglect. She just neglected herself as a person, she abandoned her life...'

As told to Patrick O'Connor, *Harper's and Queen*, December 1983

der RING DES NIBELUNGEN

I have seen Wagner's *Valkyrie*. The performance was excellent. The orchestra surpassed itself. The best singers did all in their powers – and yet it was wearisome. What a Don Quixote Wagner is. He expends his whole force in pursuing the impossible, and all the time, if he would but follow the natural bent of his extraordinary gift, he might evoke a whole world of musical beauties. In my opinion Wagner is a symphonist by nature. He is gifted with genius, which has wrecked itself upon his tendencies; his inspiration is paralysed by theories which he has invented on his own account, and which, *nolens, volens*, he wants to bring into practice. ... But there is no doubt Wagner is a wonderful symphonist. I shall just prove to you by one example how far the symphonic prevails over the operatic style in his operas. You have probably heard the celebrated *Walkürenritt* [*The Ride of the Valkyries*]? What a great and marvellous picture! How we actually seem to see these fierce heroines flying on their magic steeds amid thunder and lightning! In the concert hall this piece makes an extraordinary impression. On the stage, in view of the cardboard rocks, the canvas clouds, and the warriors who run about awkwardly in the background – in a word, seen in this very inadequate theatrical sky, which makes a poor pretence of realizing the illimitable realm above, the music loses all its powers of expression. Here the stage does not enhance the effect but acts rather like a wet blanket. Finally I cannot understand, and never shall, why the *Nibelungen* should be considered a literary masterpiece ... Wotan, Brünnhilde, Fricka, and the rest, are so impossible, so little human, that it is very difficult to feel any sympathy with their destinies.... For three hours Wotan lectures Brünnhilde upon her disobedience.... And with it all, there are many fine and beautiful episodes of a purely symphonic description....

TCHAIKOVSKY to Madame von Meck, 1877

A clever parody of both Wagner and Gilbert and Sullivan:

THE SAVOYARD RING
OR, A TETRALOGY IN PATTER SONG

Three Little Rhinemaids
('Three Little Maids from School')

Three little Rhinemaids pert are we
Paddling around coquettishly
Guarding our gold so carefully!
Three little Rhinemaids we!

Everything is a source of fun!
Nobody's safe, for we care for none!

Three nubile naiads who take pleasure
Swimming all day in endless leisure!
No one will ever steal our treasure!
Three little Rhinemaids we!

I'm Called Little Alberich
('I'm Called Little Buttercup')

I'm called little Alberich,
Sweet little Alberich,
Everyone's favorite gnome!
And thus has come Alberich,
Dear little Alberich,
Down to the Rhinemaidens' home!

Their gold looks exciting,
And oh, so inviting!
I think that I'll snatch it away!
Though love shall evade me,
That doesn't dissuade me:
I never got much anyway!

So, gold, come to Alberich!
Let crafty Alberich
You off to Nibelheim bring!
Where talented Alberich,
Versatile Alberich,
Shall make you into a ring!

A Wandering Wälsung
('A Wandering Minstrel')

A wandering Wälsung I,
A special type of tenor,
Heroic in demeanor,
With vocal tones low and high!

I'm really quite all in,
I think I'll go to bed here,
To rest my weary head here,
And dream of my long-lost twin!
    And dream of my long-lost twin!

346

Oh, Nothung!
('Tit Willow')

In the roots of this ash tree a magic sword rests,
　　Named Nothung, called Nothung, yes, Nothung,
It was stuck there by one of my wedding-brunch guests,
　　Who said, 'Nothung, ja, Nothung, mein Nothung.
It will save you someday from your spouse, who's a pest
If you only can find someone tender and fine
Who said, 'Nothung, ja, Nothung, mein Nothung.'
　　Oh, Nothung! Ach, Nothung! It's Nothung!

Now, you look like you're rather a muscular guy,
　　Up to Nothung, strong Nothung, great Nothung!
So let's give it, for my sake, the old college try!
　　Pull Nothung! Tug Nothung! Out, Nothung!
Then off to the woods we shall gleefully flee,
And leave Hunding to rot by himself in his tree!
Then we'll both bless that guest who conveni-ent-ly
　　Left Nothung, sweet Nothung, 'our' Nothung!

A Valkyrie's Lot Is Not a Happy One
('A Policeman's Lot')

Brünnhilde:	When a daughter has been told by her dear daddy,
Valkyries:	. . . her dear daddy,
Brünnhilde:	Evil Hunding's got to do poor Siegmund in!
Valkyries:	. . . poor Siegmund in!
Brünnhilde:	And down deep inside you know how very glad he—
Valkyries:	. . . very glad he,
Brünnhilde:	Would be to see the stalwart Wälsung win!
Valkyries:	. . . the Wälsung win!
Brünnhilde:	So when you step in, trying to arrange it,
Valkyries:	. . . to arrange it,

Brünnhilde:	And Siegmund's nearly got the battle won,
Valkyries:	. . . the battle won!
Brünnhilde:	Your father barges in and goes to change it!
Valkyries:	. . . goes to change it!
Brünnhilde:	A Valkyrie's lot is not a happy one!

Brünnhilde:	So now Father's summoned me before my sisters,
Valkyries:	. . . 'fore her sisters
Brünnhilde:	And he's just about as mad as he can be!
Valkyries:	. . . as he can be!
Brünnhilde:	My ears are positively caked with blisters –
Valkyries:	. . . caked with blisters,
Brünnhilde:	For only doing what comes naturally!
Valkyries:	. . . comes naturally!
Brünnhilde:	He has clipped my wings and further aims to shame me –
Valkyries:	. . . aims to shame her,
Brünnhilde:	By putting me to sleep where anyone –
Valkyries:	. . . where anyone,
Brünnhilde:	Who wakes me up with one good smooch can claim me!
Valkyries:	. . . can claim her!
Brünnhilde:	This Valkyrie's lot is not a happy one!

All:	When a father's godly duty must be done,
	must be done,
	A Valkyrie's lot is not a happy one,
	happy one!

And Now He Is the Heldentenor of the Ring
('When I Was a Lad')

Siegfried:	When I was a lad, I was quite bored
	Till the day that I forged myself a sword
	So powerful that the stupid thing

Split my dwarf stepfather's anvil with a single
    swing!

Forest Bird: He sliced in two the anvil with one good swing,
    And now he is the Heldentenor of the *Ring*!

Siegfried: So off I went through the forest green
    Where the ugliest thing I have ever seen,
    A dragon, sat, who advised me thus:
    'Pal, this forest isn't big enough for both of us!'

Forest Bird: He polished off the dragon, that monstrous thing,
    And now he is the Heldentenor of the *Ring*!

Siegfried: Then up to this mountaintop I came,
    And I walked right through all the smoke and
      flame!
    Now I'm standing here in a state of shock,
    For 'das ist kein Mann' that's passed out here upon
      this rock!

Forest Bird: So kiss her, klutz! Or you'll have to get
    Yourself another partner for the big duet!

The Big Duet
('There Is Beauty in the Bellow of the Blast')

*Siegfried awakens Brünnhilde and inquires if she is
up to the harrowing vocal demands of the next
opera*

Siegfried: There is beauty in the bellow of the blast
    Of a music drama's orchestra and cast!

Brünnhilde: What an eloquent outpouring
When the singers all are roaring
And the pit booms forth fortissimo and fast!

Siegfried: There's a question I must pose to you.
Wagner makes demands on singers that are rough!
I'm afraid I must inquire:
Do you quickly tend to tire?
Are your lungs and larynx adequately tough?

Brünnhilde: Sir, I made it through *Walküre*,
Hence I couldn't be securer
That my vocal equipage is tough enough!

Together: If that is so,
Sing derry down dell-o
Let's heartily yell o-
ver one and all!
Away we'll go,
This girl and this fellow
Shall lustily bellow
Till curtain's fall!

The Revenge Trio
('Here's a How-de do!')

Brünnhilde: Here's a how-de do!
He's said toodle-oo!
Siegfried's gone and wed Gutrune,
Leaving me to this buffoon! Ah,
Soon this day he'll rue!
Here's a how-de-do!

Gunther: Here's a pretty mess
Words cannot express!
Though he's not so much as kissed her,
Siegfried's run off with my sister!
Witness my distress!
Here's a pretty mess!

Hagen: What a lovely thing!
Hear Brünnhilde sing!
She's so mad she's simply steaming!
Here's my chance for evil scheming!
Soon I'll wear the Ring!
What a lovely thing!

Brünnhilde's Immolation
('The Flowers that Bloom in the Spring')

The hours that take up the *Ring*, tra la,
Are finally brought to a head!
As I wearily light up the fire, tra la,
And Grane and I mount the pyre, tra la,
How I wish I'd learned Venus instead!
Alas, I'm condemned to eternally sing
My little lungs out till the end of the *Ring*!

The hours that take up the *Ring*, tra la,
Are finished, kaput and all done!
While the audience sits sound asleep, tra la,
We singers have all had to keep, tra la,
On our feet till a quarter past one!
And that's what we mean when we say, or we sing,
Our arches are glad it's the end of the *Ring*!
Tra la la la la la, etc.

ROBERT ZESCHIN, in *Opera News*, 1971

der ROSENKAVALIER

Two important hints to the actors: Just as Clytemnaestra should not be an old hag, but a beautiful proud woman of fifty, whose ruin is purely spiritual and by no means physical, the Marschallin must be a young and beautiful woman of 32 at the most who, in a bad mood, thinks herself 'an old woman' as compared with the seventeen-year-old Octavian, but who is not by any means David's Magdalena, who, by the way, is also frequently presented as too old. Octavian is neither the first nor the last lover of the beautiful Marschallin, nor must the latter play the end of the first act sentimentally as a tragic farewell to life but with Viennese grace and lightness, half-weeping, half smiling. The conductor should not slow down too much, starting with the F major 2/4. The figure which has so far been most misunderstood is that of Ochs. Most basses have presented him as a disgusting vulgar monster with a repellent mask and proletarian manners, and this has rightly shocked civilized audiences (the French and Italians). This is quite wrong: Ochs must be a rustic beau of thirty-five, who is after all a member of the gentry, if somewhat countryfied, and who is capable of behaving properly in the salon of the Marschallin without running the risk of being thrown out by her servants after five minutes. He is at heart a cad, but outwardly still so presentable that Faninal does not refuse him at first sight. Especially Ochs's first scene in the bedroom must be played with utmost delicacy and discretion if it is not to be as disgusting as the love affair of a general's elderly wife with a cadet. In other words: Viennese comedy, not – Berlin farce.

RICHARD STRAUSS, *Recollections and Reflections*

January 29th
First Production of Rosenkavalier *in England.*
Covent Garden. Began at 8.20 (20 minutes late) and finished at midnight, with many cuts. Then 30 minutes' wait nearly, for motor in procession of motors. The thing was certainly not understood by stalls and grand circle. What its reception was in the amphitheatre and gallery I was too far off to judge. First act received quite coldly. Ovation as usual at end – and an explosive sort of shout when Thomas Beecham came to bow. The beauty and symmetry of the book came out even more clearly than on reading it. An entirely false idea of this opera so far in England. Not sensual, nor perverse, nor depraved. It is simply the story of a young man providing a tragedy for an ageing woman by ceasing to love her, and an ecstatic joy for a young woman by beginning to love her. All the main theme is treated with gravity and beauty. The horse play, and the character of Ochs, and the 18th-century colour is incidental. It seemed to me to be a work of the first order.

ARNOLD BENNETT, *Journal*, 1913

In Iris Murdoch's novel The Black Prince *the sinister novelist Bradley is infatuated with the beautiful teenage girl Julian: here he relates a disastrous visit to a performance of* Rosenkavalier *at Covent Garden.*

Julian was holding my arm. I had made no attempt to take hers. She had taken mine and was squeezing it convulsively, probably unconsciously, out of excitement. We were jostling our way through a lot of noisy people in the foyer of the Royal Opera House, having just come in out of the evening sunshine into this brilliantly lit crowd scene. Julian was wearing a red silk dress, rather long, covered with an *art nouveau* design of blue tulips. Her hair, which she had been combing carefully and surreptitiously when I first caught sight of her, was unusually casque-like, glowing softly like long slightly dulled strips of flattened metal. Her face was unfocused, joyfully *distrait*, laughing with pleasure. I was feeling a sick delighted anguish of desire, as if I had been

ripped by a dagger from the groin to the throat. I also felt frightened. I fear crowds. We got into the auditorium, Julian now
pulling me, and found our seats, half-way back in the stalls.
People stood up to let us in. I hate this. I hate theatres. There was
an intense subdued din of human chatter, the self-satisfied yap of a
civilized audience awaiting its 'show': the frivolous speech of
vanity speaking to vanity. And now there began to be heard in the
background that awful and inimitably menacing sound of an
orchestra tuning up.

How I feel about music is another thing. I am not actually tone
deaf, though it might be better if I were. Music can touch me, it
can get at me, it can torment. It just, as it were, reaches me, like a
sinister gabbling in a language one can almost understand, a
gabbling which is horribly, one suspects, *about oneself*. When I
was younger I had even listened to music deliberately, stunning
myself with disorderly emotion and imagining that I was having a
great experience. True pleasure in art is a cold fire. I do not wish to
deny that there are some people – though fewer than one might
think from the talk of our self-styled experts – who derive a pure
and mathematically clarified pleasure from these medleys of
sound. All I can say is that 'music' for me was simply an occasion
for personal fantasy, the outrush of hot muddled emotions, the
muck of my mind made audible.

Julian had let go of my arm but was sitting now leaning towards
me, so that the whole length of her right arm from the shoulder to
the elbow was lightly touching my left arm. I sat stiffly in possession of this contact. At the same time I very cautiously advanced
my left shoe up against her right shoe in such a way that the shoes
were contiguous without any pressure being exerted on the foot.
As if one had secretly sent one's servant to suborn the servant of
the beloved. I was breathing very short in I hoped not audible
pants or gasps. The orchestra was continuing its jumbled keening
of crazed thirds. I felt a void the size of an opera house where my
stomach might have been and through the middle of it travelled
the great scar of desire. I felt a cringeing fear of which I could not
determine whether it was physical or mental, and a sense that
soon I might somehow lose control of myself, shout, vomit, faint.

I felt the heavenly continued steady light pressure of Julian's arm upon mine. I smelt the clean rapier smell of the silk of her dress. I felt, delicately, delicately, as if I were touching an egg shell, her shoe.

The softly cacophonous red and gold scene swung in my vision, beginning to swirl gently like something out of Blake: it was a huge coloured ball, a sort of immense Christmas decoration, a glittering shining twittering globe of dim rosy light in the midst of which Julian and I were suspended, rotating, held together by a swooning intensity of precarious feather-touch. Somewhere above us a bright blue heaven blazed with stars and round about us half-naked women lifted ruddy torches up. My arm was on fire, my foot was on fire, my knee was trembling with the effort of keeping still. I was in a golden scarlet jungle full of the chattering of apes and the whistling of birds. A scimitar of sweet sounds sliced the air and entered into the red scar and became pain. I was that sword of agony, I was that pain. I was in an arena, surrounded by thousands of grimacing nodding faces, where I had been condemned to death by pure sound. I was to be killed by the whistling of birds and buried in a pit of velvet. I was to be gilded and then flayed.

'Bradley, what's the matter?'

'Nothing.'

'You weren't listening.'

'Were you talking?'

'I was asking you if you knew the story.'

'What story?'

'Of *Rosenkavalier*.'

'Of course I don't know the story of *Rosenkavalier*.'

'Well, quick, you'd better read your programme –'

'No, you tell me.'

'Oh well, it's quite simple really, it's about this young man, Octavian, and the Marschallin loves him, and they're lovers, only she's much older than he is and she's afraid she'll lose him because he's bound to fall in love with somebody his own age –'

'How old is he and how old is she?'

'Oh I suppose he's about twenty and she's about thirty.'

'*Thirty?*'

'Yes, I think, anyway quite old, and she realizes that he just regards her as a sort of mother-figure and there can't be any real lasting relations between them, and it begins with them in bed together and of course she's very happy because she's with him but she's also very unhappy because she knows she's sure to lose him and –'

'Enough.'

'Don't you want to know what happens next?'

'No.'

At that moment there was a pattering noise of clapping, rising to a rattling crescendo, the deadly sound of a dry sea, the light banging of many bones in a tempest.

The stars faded and the red torches began to dim and a terrifying packed silence slowly fell as the conductor lifted up his rod. Silence. Darkness. Then a rush of wind and a flurry of sweet pulsating anguish has been set free to stream through the dark. I closed my eyes and bowed my head before it. Could I transform all this extraneous sweetness into a river of pure love? Or would I be somehow undone by it, choked, dismembered, disgraced? I felt now almost at once a pang of relief as, after the first few moments, tears began to flow freely out of my eyes. The gift of tears which had been given and then withdrawn again had come back to bless me. I wept with a marvellous facility, quietly relaxing my arm and my leg. Perhaps if I wept copiously throughout I could bear it after all. I was not listening to the music, I was undergoing it, and the full yearning of my heart was flowing automatically out of my eyes and soaking my waistcoat, as I hung, so easily now, together with Julian, fluttering, hovering like a double hawk, like a double angel, in the dark void pierced by sorties of fire. I only wondered if it would soon prove impossible to cry quietly, and whether I should then begin to sob.

The curtain suddenly fled away to reveal an enormous double bed surrounded by a cavern of looped-up blood-red hangings. This consoled me for a moment because it reminded me of Carpaccio's Dream of Saint Ursula. I even murmured 'Carpaccio' to myself as a protective charm. But these cooling comparisons were soon put to flight and even Carpaccio could not rescue me from what happened next. Not on the bed but upon some cushions near the front of the stage two girls were lying in a close embrace. (At least I suppose one of them was enacting a young man.) Then they began to sing.

The sound of women's voices singing is one of the bitter-sweetest noises in the world, the most humanly piercing, the most terribly significant and yet contentless of all sounds: and a duet is more than twice as bad as a single voice. (Perhaps boys' voices are worst of all: I am not sure.) The two women were conversing in pure sound, their voices circling, replying, blending, creating a trembling silver cage of an almost obscene sweetness. I did not know what language they were singing in, and the words were inaudible anyway, there was no need of words, these were not words but the highest coinage of human speech melted down, become pure song, something vilely almost murderously gorgeous. No doubt she is crying for the inevitable loss of her young lover. The lovely boy protests but his heart is free. Only it has all been changed into a sort of plump luscious heart-piercing cascade of sugary agony. Oh God, not much more of this can be endured.

I became aware that I had uttered a sort of moan, because the man on my other side, whom I noticed now for the first time, turned and stared at me. At the same moment my stomach seemed to come sliding down from somewhere else and then quickly arched itself up again and I felt a quick bitter taste in my mouth. I murmured 'Sorry!' quickly in Julian's direction and got up. There was a soft awkward scraping at the end of the row as six people rose hastily to let me out. I blundered by, slipped on some steps, the terrible relentless sweet sound still gripping my shoulders with its talons. Then I was pushing my way underneath the illuminated sign marked *Exit* and out into the brightly lit and completely empty and suddenly silent foyer. I walked fast. I was definitely going to be sick.

ROSSINI

Rossini's sparkling vulgarity, his devil-may-care technique mixing brilliant invention with cliché and repetition, his marvellous fecundity of melody, his essential irresponsibility were all excitedly debated by his contemporaries. Members of the vieil école *like Lord Mount Edgcumbe put their hands over their ears; young radicals like Pushkin, Byron, and Stendhal adored the charm and energy.*

That he is possessed of genius and invention cannot be denied, but they are not guided by good taste, and may be deemed too fanciful; neither are they inexhaustible, for he is so rapid and so copious a writer that his imagination seems already to be nearly drained, as no one is so great a plagiarist of himself. His compositions are so similar and bear so strong a stamp of peculiarity and *mannerism*, that while it is impossible not to recognize instantly a piece of music as his, it is frequently difficult to distinguish one from another...

Of the operas of Rossini that have been performed here in London, that of *La Gazza Ladra* is most peculiarly liable to all the objections I have made ... its finales, and many of its numerous *pezzi concertati* are uncommonly loud, and the lavish use made of the *noisy* instruments appears to my judgment singularly inappropriate to the subject, which though it might have been rendered touching, is far from calling for such warlike accompaniments.   Lord Mount Edgcumbe, *Musical Reminiscences*

After reading through the score of Il Barbiere di Siviglia, *a greater contemporary musical genius, Beethoven, remarked, 'Rossini would have become a great composer if*

358

his teacher had frequently smacked his bottom.' The two composers met, quite amicably, during Rossini's visit to Vienna in 1822. 'Ah Rossini,' Beethoven said,

'you are the composer of *Il Barbiere di Siviglia*? I congratulate you; it is an excellent *opera buffa*; I read it with pleasure, and it delights me. It will be played as long as Italian opera exists. Never try to do anything but *opera buffa*; wanting to succeed in another genre would be trying to force your destiny.'

Two contrasting versions of how the beautiful prayer in the third act of Mosé in Egitto *came to be written – an addition to the score which transformed performances of the opera from failure into triumph.*

On the eve of the first performance, Rossini, who was as usual lounging in bed and holding court to a score or so of acquaintances, was interrupted (to the immense delight of everyone present) by the appearance of the librettist Totola, who came rushing into the room, utterly unmindful of the assembled company, and shrieked at the top of his voice: *Maestro! maestro! ho salvato l'atto terzo! – E che hai fatto..?* [Saved the third act? And how have you done that?] demanded Rossini, mimicking the curious mixture of burlesque and pedantry which made up the wretched poet's manner: 'My poor friend, what on earth *could* you do? They'll laugh this time, just as they always do!' '*Maestro*, I've written a prayer for the Jews just before the passage of the Red Sea,' cried the wretched, snivelling hack, hauling from his pocket an immense wad of papers, all docketed like a lawyer's brief, and handing them to Rossini, who promptly lay down again in bed to decipher the tangle of hieroglyphic jottings scribbled in the margin of the principal document. While he was reading, the silly little poetaster was circling the room with a nervous smile, shaking hands and whispering over and over again: *Maestro, è lavoro d'un' ora* [it is the work of an hour]. Rossini glared at him: *E lavoro d'un' ora, he!* The scribbler, half terrified out of his wits, and more than ever apprehensive of some catastrophic practical joke, tried to make himself inconspicuous, tittered awkwardly, and glanced at Rossini: *Sì, signor, sì, signor maestro!* 'Very well, then,' exclaimed the composer, 'if it only took *you* an hour to write the words, *I* shall manage to write the music in fifteen minutes!' Whereupon he leapt out of bed and, sitting down to a table (still in his night-shirt), dashed off the music for the *Prayer* in eight or ten minutes at the most, without a piano, and undeterred by the conversation of his friends, which continued as loud as ever regardless of his preoccupations, everyone talking away at the top of his voice, as is normal in Italy. 'Here's your music – take it!' he barked finally at the librettist, who promptly vanished, leaving Rossini to jump back into bed, convulsed with laughter at Totola's fright. STENDHAL, *Life of Rossini*

'My immortality?' said Rossini; 'do you know what will survive me? (*sais-tu ce qui restera après moi?*) The third act of *Tell*, the second act of *Otello*, and *The Barber of Seville* from one end to the other.'

Strange to say, of the Prayer of Moses, that piece magnificent in its simplicity, he only once spoke to me, but what he then said is well worth repeating. I asked him was he in love, or very hungry and miserable, when he wrote that inspired page; for hunger as well as love has the power of making people write with lofty inspiration.

'I will tell you,' he said, and from his ironical smile I saw some fun was coming; 'I had a little misfortune; I had known a Princess B—g—e, and she, one of the most passionate women living, and with a magnificent voice, kept me up all night with duos and talking, etc. A short time after this exhausting performance, I had to take a tisane which stood before me, while I wrote that prayer. When I was writing the chorus in G minor I suddenly dipped my pen into the medicine bottle instead of the ink; I made a blot, and when I dried it with sand (blotting paper was not invented then) it took the form of a natural, which instantly gave me the idea of the effect which the change from G minor to G major would make, and to this blot all the effect – if any – is due.'

LOUIS ENGEL, *From Mozart to Mario*

SALOME AT HOME

Acté Talks About her Dance of the Seven Veils

Mme Aino Acté, the beautiful prima-donna, who is going to
introduce Salome to a gasping world at Covent Garden tomorrow
night, was in hiding yesterday in her cosy suite of rooms at the St
Ermin's Hotel, with thick carpets and double windows to keep
out the roar and the draughts of London, and Mademoiselle, her
Swedish companion, to do all the talking. As an old acquaintance,
however, Mme Acté was gracious enough to steal out of her
zareba and to talk to 'H.A.' about *Salome, Strauss, Oscar Wilde,
London* ('grande, triste – magnifique – impossible!'), Paris, Berlin, and – *Salome.*

Whispers

'I can give you five-minutes only,' said madame, in a tragic
whisper. 'Five minutes pre-cisely; and even then I must whisper in
your ear, for to-day my voice is to me more precious than rubies!'
Mme Acté's bright eyes flashed in whimsical misery.

'I want to sing, I want to laugh, I want to shout!' she whispered,
'but I daren't. For days and nights I have been living Salome –
awake and asleep. I cannot shake her off, and I don't want to! For
a person with imagination – a woman with imagination – no such
part has ever been conceived. It is splendid, gorgeous, real,
throbbing——'

Her voice rose, squandering several rubies.

'Madame!' cried Mademoiselle, rapping sharp warnings upon
the table with her fingers.

'Oh, pardon!' whispered Salome. 'Pray, you do the talking, my
dear!'

When Strauss Rubbed His Eyes

Mademoiselle rushed in blithely – for just twenty words. 'You must know,' she said, 'Mme Acté was the special and particular choice of Strauss, who himself schooled her in the part——'

'No, no!' cried Acté, rising from her chair, forgetting her shredded voice, and striking an attitude as though Herod himself were in the room. 'Not the part! Only the singing! Strauss said, "I will show you how to sing Salome"; and he whistled me through the music – tore my throat to tatters, and broke my heart! And when all that was done, it was I who said, "Now I will show you how to act Salome". Though singing is my profession, acting is the fibre of my soul. So before Richard Strauss I acted Salome, and I danced Salome, and the great master of music rubbed his eyes and said it was good. Before this, another woman had sung the part, and wonderfully she sang it. But her acting was too – well – mild; and when she was expostulated with and asked (mildly, as they ask great artists) to do this and to do that, she said, "I cannot do these things."

Salome No School Miss

'Pouf!' cried Acté, snapping her jewelled fingers. 'Cannot! Is not that ridiculous? Imagine Salome standing with her hands behind her back, twiddling her thumbs, and singing her feelings like a school miss! You must have a woman with a soul, a woman with a heart to feel and passions to let loose like floods if she is to be the Salome Herod shuddered at. I say it with a whisper – a real whisper this time – that Salome is essentially a modern part, and that there is more than a spice of Salome in every modern woman. But for heaven's sake do not print that: it is a heresy; it is treason!'

Salome's own view of the temperament of Salome is too good to lose.

The five minutes had long since fled, but Acté, spurred on by her emotional enthusiasm, rattled on and let the soup grow cold, forgot her tragedy-whisper and continued to squander her rubies of melodic phrases, whilst mademoiselle held up her little white fingers in horror.

Wait and See

'You think that the modern woman——?' said I, and paused aghast as Salome, disguised in a morning gown, bared her pretty white teeth and flashed unfathomable things with her unfathomable eyes.

'Enough!' she cried, attacking the cold soup. 'You shall drag me no further into the meshes. Come and see my dance – and you may learn something of the modern woman! The dance is all my own: every movement of it and every gesture. The music is Strauss, the words are Oscar Wilde; but the dance is Acté! It is the Dance of the Seven Veils. It begins slowly, and as I cast off each veil one by one, so the fiercer it grows – the wilder, and the more alluring, until King Herod is squirming, and the whole Court is aghast. My soul is in that dance.'

The Dance of the Veils

'Of course, the whole performance is terribly trying. The music alone is enough to wrench the heart out of one. The opera lasts an hour and a half, and out of that my Dance of the Veils takes quite fifteen minutes. And that is why I am supposed to be whispering to you today! There is a full rehearsal this afternoon, and a dress rehearsal to-morrow afternoon. Even then must I whisper and move through the opera like a ghost with never a "boo!" in his throat! I shall not sing until Thursday. I dare not! Another —*nous verrons!*'

'Madame,' cried Mademoiselle. 'The feesh is cold!'

'Terrible!' said Acté. 'It is really too bad! You have ruined my voice and spoilt my luncheon!' she whispered, with a bright smile. 'But I will have my revenge on Thursday night. I will sing you and I will dance you into subjugation! *Au revoir!*'   *The Star*, 1910

SCHOENBERG

Die Glückliche Hand, with its great black cat crouching like an incubus or succubus on the hero, and its green-faced chorus peering through dark violet hangings is in the purest Edgar Allan

Poe tradition, while *Erwartung*, with its vague hints of nec-rophily, brings in the Kraft Ebbing touch (Jung at the prow and Freud at the helm) which is the twentieth century's only gift to the 'nineties. I am not suggesting for a moment that Schönberg rises no higher than the weak decadence of Giraud. There is in his music a fierce despair, an almost flamelike disgust which recalls the mood of Baudelaire's *La Charogne* and places it far above the watercolour morbidities of his chosen text. But at the moment I am not trying to determine the purely musical value of Schön-berg's various works — I merely wish to indicate the undoubted neurasthenic strain that is symptomatic of his period, and which can be found in works like Strauss's *Salomé* and *Elektra* which, musically speaking, are widely differentiated from Schönberg's in technique. CONSTANT LAMBERT, *Music Ho!*

SCHWARZKOPF

Soprano Elisabeth Schwarzkopf married recording pro-ducer Walter Legge in 1953. They worked together until Legge's death in 1979.

Since Schwarzkopf has so often spoken of herself as 'Her Master's Voice', casting me as Svengali, let me give some indication of how we worked together. My predecessor in the recording world was Fred Gaisberg. He believed that his job was to get the best artists into the studio and get onto wax the best sound pictures of what those artists habitually did in public, intermittently using his persuasive diplomatic skill as nurse-maid and tranquillizer to temperaments. Having watched him at work, I decided that recording must be a collaboration between artists and what are now called 'producers'. I wanted better results than are normally possible in public performance: I was determined to put onto disc the best that artists could do under the best possible conditions. From the start of the Hugo Wolf Society, when I began to exercise my craft (with Elena Gerhardt, Alexander Kipnis, Herbert Janssen, and others), the new approach was a success. After the war I found in Schwarzkopf, Karajan, and Lipatti (to mention but three) ideal and incurable perfectionists – self-critical, hungry for informed criticism, untiring, and acutely aware that their recorded performances were the true proof of their qualities and the cornerstones and keystone of their careers.

When Schwarzkopf came to London in 1947, she had never owned a gramophone. My first and favourite toy had been an ancient cylinder model: I had learned to read from record labels and catalogues, saved my pocket money to buy records, and over the years built up a mammoth collection. Her father's profession, teaching the classics, meant that he and she changed schools every two or three years through the German provinces. She was nineteen before she heard decent singing. She had started with piano at seven, viola and organ at ten, and taken part in school opera performances, including Kurt Weill's *Der Jasager*.

First I set out to widen by recorded examples her imaginative concept of the possibilities of vocal sound. Rosa Ponselle's vintage port and thick cream timbre and noble line; the Slavic brilliance of Nina Koshetz; a few phrases from Farrar's Carmen, whose insinuations were later reflected in Schwarzkopf's 'Im Chambre séparée'; one word only from Melba, 'Bada' in 'Donde lieta'; some Rethberg; and large doses of Meta Seinemeyer to show how essentially Teutonic voices can produce brilliant Italianate sound. Then Lehmann's all-embracing generosity, Schumann's charm and lightness, McCormack's incredible octave leap in 'Care selve', Frida Leider's dramatic tension – all these were nectar and ambrosia for Schwarzkopf's musical appetite. Instrumentalists, too: Fritz Kreisler for the dark beauty of his tone, his nobility and elegance, his vitality in upbeats, his rubato and cavalier nonchalance; Schnabel for concentrated thinking over long musical periods, firmly rhythmical, seemingly oblivious to bar lines. From the analysis of what we found most admirable in these diverse models we made our own synthesis, most adaptable to what we believed would best develop her voice for the repertory we were to concentrate on.

We made it our aim to recreate to the best of our abilities the intensity and emotions that music and words had in their authors' minds in the moment of creation. Therefore utmost obedience to every composer's markings – he knew best. This has involved and still does involve hours of merciless rehearsal, domestically known as 'Walter crucifying the pianist'. She has had rare luxury in pianists as partners – Furtwängler and Karajan, Sawallisch, Ackermann and Rosbaud, Edwin Fischer, Gieseking and Ciccolini, and, for over twenty years as a steady diet, the incomparable London-based pair, Gerald Moore and now Geoffrey Parsons. And in the summer of 1975, Sviatoslav Richter, for three recitals after twenty days' rehearsal.

From the outset I sat in with a secretary in opera rehearsals and performances, quickly dictating detailed notes on musical and acting nuances, sometimes having these passed to her in the wings. At performances I sat whenever possible in a stage box to watch both what she was doing and how the audience reacted – the exact moment when women fumbled in their handbags for handkerchiefs and men tugged them from their breast pockets. This is *not* calculation; it is in my view obedience to composers' intentions, to involve the audience in the action. We tried for years and once or twice succeeded in achieving Pamina's 'Ach, ich fühl's' so heart-breakingly that there was no applause. The length of the silence after Strauss's 'Morgen' is more eloquent than clapping.

We have tried to communicate and stir emotions like painters, by beauty and truth of line and colours in the voice. From what we have heard, most of her best younger colleagues have different aims. In two consecutive evenings at the Paris Opéra we listened to galaxies of stars singing beautifully, obeying every dynamic marking and conveying nothing but the glory of their voices and their technical skill – no trace of emotion or the meaning and overtones of the words for which composers had so tenaciously wrestled with their librettists. For this the producers and conductors are most to blame.   WALTER LEGGE, *On and Off the Record*

In Furthermoore, *however, Gerald Moore took a rather different view of the relationship.*

Unquestionably Walter indulged in delusions of grandeur, the most unacceptable being the Svengali pose towards Elisabeth. His conviction was that he was the source from which the virtuoso technique, the consummate musicianship and artistry, even the quality of tone, flowed. The great singer did nothing to undeceive him and angelically yielded pride of place and all the glory to him. After a strenuous recital, to which Walter had been listening in comfort, it was *he* who was exhausted, *he* who had given out so much, though he might concede that Elisabeth could, perhaps, be physically fatigued. He remained, during his entire life, unaware of the strain of public performance. His wife accepted this without demur, but to those of us who were associated with and admired her, this attitude was insupportable.

SELLING OUT

Madame Calvé, who endowed opera roles with an abundance of Latin temperament, did not abate her vivacity when it came time to make recordings. Taken to the door of the Maiden Lane building in a luxurious four-wheeler by Landon Ronald, she at first refused to budge from the carriage. Dismayed at the shabby appearance of the building and the sinister atmosphere of the narrow street, she cried out: 'Never in my life will I enter such a place. It is a tavern – not a manufactory. I shall be robbed there. You have brought me to a thieves' den.' Ronald was inured to the outbursts of prima donnas and knew well how to cope with this one: he excused himself for a moment, ran into the accountant's office, and returned bearing the company's payment for Calvé's services (100 guineas for six records). This acted as a strong restorative, and soon she was upstairs – ready to perform for the gramophone. But the troubles had only begun. She had the disconcerting habit of commenting on her performance in the midst of a recording – even uttering shrieks of joy or groans of disgust, depending on whether she had turned a particular phrase to her liking – and in the 'Séguedille' from *Carmen* she insisted on dancing in front of the recording horn just as she was wont to do on stage. Despite her antics, Calvé's 1902 recordings came off fairly creditably, though their improvisatory quality seems rather grotesque beside the studio-perfect renditions that we are accustomed to hearing on records today.

ROLAND GELLATT, *The Fabulous Phonograph*

Many opera singers have tried to make it in the movies, seldom with any sustained success: one of the more persevering was Mary Garden.

Miss Garden was making a silent film version of the opera *Thaïs*, a rather hazardous innovation for opera singers at that time. Just how hazardous it actually was would have been difficult to imagine had we not accepted an invitation to witness a portion of it in the making. Olive Fremstad had then already received certain intimations that her membership in the Metropolitan might not be eternal and was tentatively casting about for other fields of profitable activity. She was enormously impressed by Miss Garden's enterprise and hardihood in essaying this new medium and readily agreed to visit the studio and observe with her own eyes the mysteries in operation.

So, on the coldest possible morning of a very snowy February, we crossed the Hudson to Fort Lee on this novel errand. There, in a vast and echoing steel, concrete and glass structure, which provided as much illusion of North African glamour and warmth as might an empty carbarn wide open to the arctic blasts, we were escorted to a relatively sheltered corner where a rather pallid evocation of Alexandrian revels was in progress. Miss Garden, simply clad in two or three odd wisps of rose-colored chiffon (a wide departure from that ultra-respectable and opaque garment which, on the operatic stage, was supposed so wildly to inflame all beholders), was standing a little apart from the cavortings of a meager *corps de ballet*, her chattering teeth greatly impeding the welcoming smile with which she attempted to greet us. She was listening with pardonably frigid politeness to the words of a stage director.

'Look, dear,' the man was saying, 'you'll be lying on this couch, see, and you've got this mirror in your hand. You hold it up high, like this – get me? And then you . . .' He rambled on and on while Miss Garden fixed a glazed eye upon him and stoically heard him through to the end. When at last he ran out of words, she tossed her head, strode firmly over to the couch and said, 'Thank you: now I will show you how *I'm going* to do it!'

A little later, during a brief intermission between endless repetitions of the couch episode, while poor Thaïs, her flesh blue and quivering beneath her garish ocher make-up, was sipping some lukewarm tea, Fremstad exclaimed, 'My God, Mary, you must be quite mad! Why do you let yourself in for anything like this?'

Miss Garden answered by tracing with one stiff finger in the icy air the cabalistic sign of the dollar. 'Only that and nothing else!' she declared, adding, 'But even so, it's not worth it . . . SO DON'T!'

MARY WATKINS CUSHING, The Rainbow Bridge

STRAUSS

For several years Strauss has had a belittling press in this country in certain quarters, where romanticism has been attacked with a petulant wistfulness, for reasons doubtless as much phyiological as aesthetic. *Arabella* was dismissed at its first performance in London nearly twenty years ago as a pale imitation of *Rosenkavalier*. I cannot resist saving my face in this connection by quoting from my notice of this first performance at Covent Garden, printed publicly on 18th May, 1934: 'Up to a point *Arabella* is charming enough with instrumentation as stylish and more light-fingered than anything Strauss has ever done before. The tissue is often beautifully woven; there are taste and poise in the orchestra, and plenty of lovely sounds. *Arabella* is proof that Strauss is still the best composer of a Strauss opera. . . .'

Action and reaction being equal and opposite, the chances are that criticism will soon go to the length of praising Strauss for virtue not in character. It need not be argued, for it is not necessary so to argue to clinch the fact of his genius, that old age brought to him any new vision or conception of his art. He had no more need than Sir Toby Belch to refine himself finer than he was; he remained the man of the world and a master of all the elements of his craft, a consummate artificer, always responsive to the comedy of manners played in the mirrored drawing-rooms of civilized men and women — women especially. Of much of the weightier or bulkier Strauss we might say that here is perishable stuff; even with *Salome* and *Elektra* the future is uncertain. In the long run criticism conceivably might discover that Strauss, not less than his antipodean Mahler, was a miniaturist too heavily burdened by the elephantine Teuton Zeitgeist. He was at bottom a middle-class sensualist (I use the term without its English Victorian implications); a comedian, not even a tragic comedian, but one whose intent was all for our delight. *Der Rosenkavalier* is the perfect opera for all who know what it is to have a savour for leisured living. The work is poised in a period, in spite of mixture of style; with every woman's destiny, which is the passing of time as the sands run out and the wrinkles come in, the ironic informing spirit and *deux ex machina*. Sentiment and costume and mask, power and pastiche and the belch of Ochs, who is Pan blown-out in disguise, ogling through the horse-collar, and knowing the 'secret of the bull and lamb'. It is doubtful if any composer has enjoyed himself more than Strauss as he made his music.

NEVILLE CARDUS, *Talking of Music*

SUPERSTITION

Neither Jean nor Edouard de Reszke would walk under a ladder, and both of them disliked being photographed, for they believed it brought them bad luck. Edouard would never ride a white horse. Lilli Lehmann used to come to the opera-house two or three hours before the beginning of the performance, put on her costume and make-up, and then sit for an hour in stony and regal silence on a chair – all for luck. Scotti could not sing unless a certain rag doll was on his dressing-table – a doll his mother had given him when he was a boy. Pinza now has the same foible; his doll has a grey knitted dress and a very broken face. Tetrazzini had a special superstition concerning a dagger. It was one which she first used in *Lucia di Lammermoor* and which one night, when she happened to be singing unusually well, fell from her hand and stuck upright in the floor. Thereafter she used the dagger as a barometer: she would drop it each time before going on-stage; if it again stood upright that meant she would have a success – or, if it fell flat, a failure!

Selma Kurz, the Viennese coloratura, believed that she would sing well if she saw a chimney-sweep before the performance. Her manager used to hire one to saunter accidentally past the stage-door. On one occasion, seeing the sooted man, she called him over, reached into her purse, and gave him a tip; whereupon the honest fellow said, 'Not necessary, Madame. I have already been paid.'

The *credo in superstitionem* has by no means diminished in our own times. It is of course elementary that no one must ever wish a singer good luck before a performance. If you visit Lauritz Melchior back-stage you must wish him, '*Hals und Beinbruch.*' This, though German, is now an international wish, all rights reserved for all singers, including the Scandinavian. It means, 'Here's wishing you a broken neck or leg.' Another traditional wish is,

'*Imbocca lupo*'; it means, 'Your head in the wolf's mouth', and it is used with gusto by Metropolitan Manager Edward Johnson. Spitting three times – or saying 'toi, toi, toi', the more refined form of the same thing – is another potent charm. Gertrude Wettergren always asked to be kicked three times before she went on-stage. In the French opera the good-luck word is one which cannot be printed in a family book like this. It means what you think it means.

Rosa Ponselle used to walk to the opera-house from her hotel. Risë Stevens believes that it is bad luck to put a pair of shoes on the table. Kerstin Thorborg's good-luck charm is a little elephant, and she is convinced that snow also augurs well for her singing. Zinka Milanov hates the number seven. Gerhard Pechner believes that stepping on the stub of a burning cigarette will bring him good luck – a belief shared by the New York Fire Department. Licia Albanese is a serious student of dreams, and Wilfred Pelletier a collector of good-luck penguins. . . .

Lotte Lehmann (like Martinelli) had pictures of all her family in her dressing-room and meticulously kissed each picture before going on the stage. Helen Traubel, inspired possibly by the Lone Ranger, cuts a notch in her spear every time she sings Brünnhilde. Every time she sings Isolde she cuts a notch in the handle of the torch.   GEORGE MAREK, *A Front Seat at the Opera*

TCHAIKOVSKY

Very probably you are quite right in saying that my opera is not effective for the stage. I must tell you, however, I do not care a rap for such effectiveness. It has long been an established fact that I have no dramatic vein, and now I do not trouble about it. If it is really not fit for the stage, then it had better not be performed! I composed this opera because I was moved to express in music all that seems to cry out for such expression in *Eugene Onegin*. I did my best, working with indescribable pleasure and enthusiasm and thought very little of the treatment, the effectiveness and all the rest. I spit upon 'effects'! Besides, what are effects? For instance, if *Aida* is effective, I can assure you I would not compose an opera on a similar subject for all the wealth of the world; for I want to handle human beings, not puppets. I would gladly compose an opera which was completely lacking in startling effects, but which offered characters resembling my own, whose feelings and experiences I shared and understood. The feelings of an Egyptian Princess, a Pharaoh, or some mad Nubian, I cannot enter into, or comprehend. .... Had I a wider acquaintance with the literatures of other countries, I should no doubt have discovered a subject which was both suitable for the stage and in harmony with my taste. Unfortunately I am not able to find such things for myself, nor do I know anyone who could call my attention to such a subject as Bizet's *Carmen*, for example, one of the most perfect operas of our day. You will ask what I actually require? I will tell you. Above all I want no kings, no tumultuous populace, no gods, no pompous marches – in short, none of those things which are the attributes of 'grand opera'. I am looking for an intimate yet thrilling drama, based upon such a conflict of circumstance as I myself have experienced or witnessed, which is capable of touching me to the quick. I have nothing to say against the fantastic element, because it does not restrict me, but rather offers unlimited freedom. I feel I am not expressing myself very clearly. In a word, Aida is so remote, her love for Radames touches me so little – since I cannot picture it in my mind's eye – that my music would lack the vital warmth which is essential to good work....

The opera *Onegin* will never have a success; I feel already assured of that. I shall never find singers capable, even partially, of fulfilling my requirements. The routine which prevails in our theatres, the senseless performances, the system of retaining invalided artists and giving no chance to younger ones: all this stands in the way of my opera being put on the stage. ... It is the outcome of an invincible inward impulse. I assure you one should only compose opera under such conditions. It is only necessary to think of stage effects to a certain extent. If my enthusiasm for *Eugene Onegin* is evidence of my limitations, my stupidity and ignorance of the requirements of the stage, I am very sorry; but I can at least affirm that the music proceeds in the most literal sense from my inmost being.... TCHAIKOVSKY to Serge Taneiev, 1878

TEACHERS

Dear Piroli,

In view of the musical conditions and tendencies of our day, this is what, in my opinion, a Commission called to reorganize training should suggest. These are general ideas which I have often put to you, both orally and in writing, and which I also mentioned in my letter to Florimo.

I shall speak only of composition and of singing, because I believe that on the instrumental side (which has always produced good results) there is little need for reform. So, then, I should like to see young composers doing very long and thorough studies in all branches of counterpoint. Study of old compositions, both sacred and profane. It must be noted, however, that not everything among these works of the past is beautiful, and so it will be necessary to choose.

No study of the moderns! That will seem strange to many. But when I hear and see so many works today, constructed the way bad tailors make clothes based on a model, I cannot change my opinion. I know well that one can find many modern works which are as worthwhile as those of the past, but what does that prove? When a young man has undergone strict training, when he has found his own style and has confidence in his own powers, he can then, if he thinks it useful, study these works somewhat, and there will be no danger of his turning into an imitator. You may object: 'Who will teach this young man instrumentation? Who will teach him the theory of composition?' His own head and his own heart, if he has any.

For singing, I should like the students to have a wide knowledge of music; exercises in voice production; very long courses in solfeggi, as in the past: exercises for singing and speaking with clear and perfect enunciation. Then, without having any teacher perfect him in vocal style, I should like the young students, who by now should have a strong knowledge of music and a well-trained voice, to sing, guided only by his own feelings. This will be singing, not of such-and-such a school, but of inspiration. The artist will be an individual. He will be himself, or, better still, he will be the character he has to represent in the opera. I don't need to say that these musical studies must be combined with a broad literary education.

Those are my ideas. Would they be approved by a Commission? If so, then the Minister has only to command me. If not, then it's better for me to return to Sant'Agata.

VERDI to Giuseppe Piroli, 1871

I was once shown a large piece of lead, round and uninteresting-looking, which the pupil of a Dresden teacher had to put on the point of her tongue to keep it down when singing. This teacher, like some others, drew excessive and exclusive attention to the position of the tongue, making it the principal point in teaching, thus avoiding answering other questions that would arise and referring to the tongue as the principal promoter and factor in the production of the sound. These lessons were a great torture, as the weight of the lead tired the tongue and the fear of swallowing it made the pupil stiffen the root of the tongue so much that after a few minutes the action of the larynx seemed paralysed. The drying up of the mouth added to the worry of the cramped tongue and it became a real agony to sing, so it happened that one day the lady *did* swallow the lead.

It is easy to picture what followed. The case was serious, as the piece of lead was very large. All the doctors of the town, both great and small, were called and the patient was submitted to every torture conceivable, as her life was despaired of for several days, lead poisoning being one of the great dangers to be overcome. At last, by means of X-rays, the doctors triumphed, but the lady spent a fortune on doctors and nurses (she happily belonged to a wealthy Lancashire family) before she could be brought back to England, accompanied by most of her nearest relatives, who had been summoned to Dresden when danger was at its height. Had she died – a thing that was quite possible – what would the trial before judge and jury have been like? After all, one could not have condemned the teacher, any more than a doctor or surgeon can be condemned for making a mistake which ends with fatal results for the patient. Pupils who will *not* open their mouths at all, and whose voices one cannot train in consequence, have been given by my mother a small piece of wood to hold between their front teeth to accustom them to keep their mouths open, but a piece of thread was always attached to this little piece of wood, the other end of it being held by the pupil in order to avoid any danger of swallowing it. Placing the pupil in front of a looking-glass helps in many cases, as the eye controls exterior defects, whilst the intelligence can be occupied by more difficult problems at the same time.

Mrs M. B., an American lady, handed me a list of her former teachers at her first interview and, smiling, said: 'Madame, this is the list of my fourteen teachers, the last of whom was Madame votre mère.' 'Madame,' I replied, returning the folded paper to her, 'please keep your list. I am not desirous at all to know the names of your former teachers. That you come to me proves that you have not been content. But how is it that you left my mother?' 'This, madame,' she answered, 'I can promise, that there has been nothing disagreeable between your mother and me, but she has been so ill lately that for several weeks she had to give up her lessons, and her great age does not permit uninterrupted studies. The few times I have had the honour to receive her advice it has been invaluable to me.' When I examined her voice I understood at once that her case was a most difficult and complicated one, which, indeed, my beloved aged mother, who was nearing her ninetieth year, could not have undertaken. This lady had been taught to sing with the so-called fixed larynx, the pernicious result of which was obvious, and everything had to be undone and done over again. However, we both had patience, and at the end of long and painful studies she reaped a beautiful contralto voice, but was forced to retire into private life through domestic circumstances.

At the end of our first meeting she said: 'Here is a little present for you,' handing me a sort of small wire cage. 'This, madame,' she added, 'is an instrument of torture that my teacher, No. 4, sold to every new-comer for one guinea. He called it a phonatone.' The instrument was larger and higher in front, touching the teeth, and was bent and made smaller at the back, pushing the root of the tongue down, at the same time keeping the mouth wide open. Human faces and mouths are all shapes and sizes, but this man sold only one size, and the suffering that the pupils had to endure in fixing this instrument into their mouths, and the scenes that used to take place at this studio, as some people can open their mouths twice as much as others, and some people cannot bear anything on the back of their tongues without feeling deadly sick, can be imagined. A maid would appear with a glass of water to refresh, and some smelling-salts to revive, the student. I forgot to ask her if it was the same man who tortured her to sing with the larynx in fixed position. Needless to say that she soon fled from the inventor of the 'mouth cage.'

One man explained to his pupils that the cheeks touching the teeth hampered sonority, that filling each side of the mouth with dried prunes or chestnuts would double the sound. The discomfort of singing with a larder in one's mouth can be imagined. This case was more funny than dangerous, just as funny as the teacher who insisted that the only way to sing was *without* the larynx. This is indeed a method nothing short of a miracle.

The latest insane and most painful method has been reported to me by a pupil whilst writing this present chapter. The young man suffered from severe headache, and especially eyeache, having been forced to make the wildest contortions with *his eyes*, the teacher actually teaching that the *sound* has to be produced through the eyes! And such a thing can be said and taught in the year 1920! BLANCHE MARCHESI, *A Singer's Pilgrimage*

TENORS

In operatic lore, the tenor's top C (as at the end of 'Di quella pira' in Il Trovatore*) is a sound with an unfathomable mystique. Hitting it fair and square is hard enough, even for the best of the breed; holding it steadily, without bleating, is every tenor's prayer; bringing the house down with it some sort of ultimate achievement. Pavarotti has a fabulously powerful top C; Domingo's is more beautiful in tone, but more tentative. Most of the rest of today's tenors either sing it flat, push on it as though constipated, or wobble horribly when they get there.*

The first celebrated purveyor of the 'chesty' full-blooded top C was the Frenchman Gilbert-Louis Duprez. In 1849, his rival Gustave Roger recorded his impact in a performance of Rossini's Otello.

Duprez, today, electrified us all. What daring! A terrifying old lion! How he hurled his guts in the audience's face! For those are no longer notes that one hears. They are the explosion of a breast crushed by an elephant's foot! That's his own blood, his own life, that he is squandering to entice from the public those cries of 'Bravo!' with which the Romans honoured the dying gladiator. There is a certain nobility about it. For despite the inequalities of a voice more blemished by passion than time, his good schooling prevails, and he finds even in his deficiencies the means of sustaining style. When this man is gone the world will not hear his like again. I was amused by the critics and lesser musicians talking about him in the foyer. Some find that he drags, that he opens his mouth too wide, and God knows what else. And what does it all add up to? It's molten ore that he pours into those broadened rhythms, and when he opens his mouth so wide it is to show us his heart!

James Joyce's infatuation with the Irish tenor John O'Sullivan led him to compose this letter, on O'Sullivan's behalf, to the editor of the New York Herald *in 1930.*

De La Musique avant toute chose...

Your musical critic Mr Louis Schneider, in his notice of the recent performance at the Paris Opéra of *Guillaume Tell*, with Mr Lauri-Volpi in the tenor role, informs the numerous readers of your journal that this was an exceptional performance, such as only a really great artist could have given. As I have, for many years, sustained this part, notably the most difficult ever written for the tenor voice, at the National Academy of Music here, where I am to-day *titulaire du rôle*, I claim the right, under your favor, to state publicly in these columns that Mr Lauri-Volpi, quite departing from the tradition upheld at this theatre for the last hundred years by all who have preceded him, cut out more than half of the singing part assigned to him by the composer. To be precise, all the arduous recitatives, without one exception, were suppressed. The duet with Tell in the first set was reduced to one third of its length and vocal difficulty, as was the duet with the soprano in the second act and the celebrated and trying trio which immediately follows. As if this were not enough, Mr Lauri-Volpi most prudently avoided the perilous duel with the chorus which was written to form the climax of the whole Opera.

These being the facts, I courteously invite Mr Lauri-Volpi to sing this part in its entirety and as it was composed by his fellow countryman Rossini and as I myself have sung it over two hundred times throughout France, Belgium, Spain and North and South America, but especially in all the principal cities of Italy. I had, indeed, the honor of being chosen by Mr Tullio Serafin when this Opera was revived by him at the San Carlo Theatre of Naples in 1923, after a lapse of thirty four years, during which time no tenor had been found in all Italy to sustain the part after the death of the celebrated Tamagno. If Mr Lauri-Volpi will sing this role, without transpositions or omissions at any Paris theatre or concert hall, where I may be allowed to sing it also, I am willing to accept Mr Louis Schneider as judge. Nay more, to facilitate him in coming to his verdict, I shall be most happy to present to him an elegantly bound edition of the operatic score, feeling sure that such an eminent musician will welcome this opportunity of becoming re-acquainted with a masterpiece which he would appear to have very successfully forgotten.

Et tout le reste est ... publicité. Sincerely yours

JOHN SULLIVAN

The stunt went further. In June 1930 Joyce created a furore at a performance of Tell *at the Opéra. After O'Sullivan had sung an aria, Joyce leaned forward in his box, took off the heavy dark glasses he habitually wore to protect his poor eyesight, and shouted out,* 'Merci, mon dieu, pour ce miracle. Après vingt ans, je revois la lumière.'

O hark! 'tis the voice of the Schmaltztenor!
It swells in his bosom and hangs in the air.
Like lavender-scent in a spinster's drawer
It oozes and percolates everywhere.
So tenderly glutinous,
Soothing the brute in us,
Wholly unmutinous
Schmalztenor.

Enchanting, his smile for the third encore
(Cherubic complexion and glossy curls),
His nasal nostalgia, so sweetly sore,
Vibrates on the sternums of swooning girls.
Emerging and merging,
Suggestively urging,
Receding and surging —
The Schmalztenor.

The Absolute Last of the Schmalztenor
Is heard in Vienna in lilac-time.
He's steaming and quivering more and more
And dowagers whisper, 'He's past his prime!'
Young maidens have drowned for him:
Pass the hat round for him:
Open the ground for him —
Schmalztenor.   M. W. BRANCH, *Punch*

TRANSLATION

This Maxim [that nothing is capable of being well set to music
that is not nonsense] was no sooner received, but we immediately
fell to translating the *Italian* Operas; and as there was no great

Danger of hurting the Sense of those extraordinary Pieces, our Authors would often make Words of their own which were entirely foreign to the Meaning of the Passages they pretended to translate; their chief Care being to make the numbers of the *English* verse answer to those of the *Italian*, that both of them might go to the same Tune. Thus the famous song in *Camilla* [by Bononcini],

Barbara si t'intendo &c.

Barbarous woman, yes, I know your Meaning,

which expresses the Resentments of an angry Lover, was translated into that *English* Lamentation,

Frail are a Lover's Hopes &c

And it was pleasant enough to see the most refined Persons of the *British* Nation dying away and languishing to Notes that were filled with a Spirit of Rage and Indignation. It happened also very frequently, where the Sense was rightly translated, the necessary Transposition of words, which were drawn out of the Phrase of one Tongue into that of another, made the Musick appear very absurd in one Tongue that was very natural in the other. I remember an *Italian* Verse that ran thus Word for Word,

And turn'd my Rage into Pity

which the *English* for Rhime sake translated

And into Pity turn'd my Rage

By this means the soft Notes that were adapted to *Pity* in the *Italian*, fell upon the Word *Rage* in the *English*; and the angry Sounds that were turned to *Rage* in the Original, were made to express *Pity* in the Translation. It oftentimes happened likewise, that the finest Notes in the Air fell upon the most insignificant Words in the Sentence. I have known the Word *And* pursued through the whole Gamut, have been entertained with many a melodious *The*, and have heard the most beautiful Graces, Quavers, and Divisions bestowed upon *Then*, *For*, and *From*; to the eternal Honour of our *English* Particles.

JOSEPH ADDISON, *Spectator*, 1711

les TROYENS

Berlioz never heard anything approaching a complete per-
formance of his sublime masterpiece during his lifetime. In
1863, a heavily cut version of the second part was staged in
Paris; but its failure with public and critics was more than
Berlioz could bear. 'I am sure I have written a great work,
greater and nobler than anything done hitherto,' he had
written to his son in 1861.

The following pieces in *The Trojans at Carthage* were cut at the
Théâtre-Lyrique, as many during rehearsals as after the first performance:
1. The entry of the builders
2. The entry of the sailors
3. The entry of the farm-workers
4. The orchestral interlude (Royal Hunt and Storm)
5. The scene between Anna and Narbal
6. The second ballet
7. Iopas' air
8. The sentries' duet
9. Hylas' song
10. The big duet for Aeneas and Dido, 'Errante sur tes pas'.

Carvalho [director of Théâtre-Lyrique] found the first three
numbers dull; in any case the stage was not big enough for a
procession of this size. The hunting interlude was lamentably
staged. Instead of several real waterfalls, I was given a painted
representation of a stream. The leaping satyrs were represented by
a troupe of twelve-year-old girls, who brandished no flaming
branches in their hands, the firemen having forbidden it for fear of
a conflagration. There were no nymphs flying dishevelled through
the forest with cries of 'Italy!' The female choristers were
stationed in the wings; their cries were not strong enough to
penetrate to the auditorium. Even the stage thunder could

scarecely be heard, despite the fact that the orchestra was thin and lacking in vigour. And when this miserable travesty came to an end, the scene-shifter always needed at least forty minutes to change his scenery. So I myself asked for the interlude to be removed. Carvalho, against my furious resistance, remorselessly insisted on cutting out the scene between Narbal and Anna, the second ballet, and the sentries' duet (whose homely style he found out of place in an epic work). Iopas' stanzas disappeared with my approval, the singer charged with the part being incapable of singing them well. It was the same with the duet between Aeneas and Dido; I had realized that Madame Charton's voice was unequal to the vehemence of this scene, which took so much out of her that she would not have had the strength left to deliver the tremendous recitative 'Dieux immortels! il part', the final aria and the scene on the pyre. As for Hylas' song, which had been greatly liked at the early performances and was well sung by young Cabel, it vanished while I was in bed with bronchitis. Cabel was needed for the opera which was due to follow *The Trojans*, and since his contract required him to sing only fifteen times a month, he had to be paid two hundred francs for each additional performance; so Carvalho, without telling me, removed the song on grounds of economy. I was so numbed and stupefied by this long torture that when the publisher of the vocal score, who shared Carvalho's view that it should conform as closely as possible to the performance, proposed to omit several of these pieces, I consented to it instead of opposing it with all my remaining strength. Happily the full score has not yet been published. I spent a month putting it back into shape and carefully tending all its wounds. It will appear in its pristine integrity, exactly as I wrote it.

But oh, the agony of seeing a work of this kind laid out for sale with the scars of the publisher's surgery upon it! A score lying dismembered in the window of a music shop like the carcass of a calf on a butcher's stall, and pieces cut off and sold like lights for the concierge's cat! BERLIOZ, *Memoirs*

A complete edition of the score was only published in 1969, the centenary of Berlioz's death.

UNWRITTEN OPERAS

Puccini's unwritten operas include a *Marie Antoinette*, a *Notre-Dame*, and a *Tartarin*. This last project he discussed with the dying Daudet, who was thrilled at the prospect of having his unheroic hero set to music. These three unwritten operas are not nearly a complete catalogue of the subjects which Puccini considered seriously. Indeed, we might say with only a little exaggeration that it would be difficult to find a dramatic subject Puccini did not consider. Puccini was happy only when he was working, miserable as soon as he had written *fine* to an operatic manuscript, and bored with any opera which he had completed. He immediately began the search for a new one. He bombarded all his friends with pleas for suggestions. He searched through books; he ran to see the popular plays. He conferred with D'Annunzio, and relinquished what started out as a promising collaboration only after D'Annunzio had failed twice to deliver a satisfactory libretto. The search took him to so unlikely a subject as *Lorna Doone*, to a play about the actor David Garrick, to a novel called *Two Little Wooden Shoes*, by Ouida, author of *Under Two Flags*, and to *The Florentine Tragedy*, by Oscar Wilde. . . .

One of the strangest of all unwritten operas is a huge project by Wagner. He worked on an opera to be called *The Victors* the year before he began *Tristan*. This was to be an opera on Buddhism, and Wagner studied the religion and the philosophy in preparation for the opera. The sketch for the drama has survived. It is a turgid and vague plot, but its central motive is Wagner's favourite theme, the redemption of the world through Woman. Some characteristics of the heroine, Ananda, were probably made part of Kundry, and one musical motive in the Wotan–Erda scene in the third act of *Siegfried* was originally intended for *The Victors*.

The unwritten opera which might have been most interesting to Americans is a work of Dvořák. When Dvořák was living in New York and teaching at the Conservatory, he became interested in American literature. In a Czech translation he made the acquaintance of a poem which spoke of Indian hunters and the American forest in a strange, beguiling metre. Dvořák was so captured by the *Song of Hiawatha* that he wanted to make Longfellow's legend the basis of an opera, just as he meant to write a symphony in B minor about Niagara Falls. He never did either.

GEORGE MAREK, *A Front Seat at the Opera*

One might add Debussy's Orpheus, Tristan, Siddharta, As You Like It *and* The Fall of the House of Usher *to this list.*

From the evidence of his synopsis, I take the heretical view that Verdi was wise not to pursue the idea of an opera based on King Lear *any further!*

Act I, Scene i

Great Stateroom in Lear's palace. Lear on his throne. Division of the Kingdom. Demonstration by the Earl of Kent. Rage of the King, who banishes the Earl. Cordelia's farewell.

Scene ii

Edmund's soliloquy. Gloucester enters (without seeing Edmund) and deplores the banishment of Kent. Edmund, encountering Gloucester, tries to hide a letter. Gloucester forces him to reveal it. He believes that Edgar is plotting. Edgar enters; and his father, blind with fury, draws a sword against him. Edgar flees, after trying to assuage his father's anger with soothing words.

Scene iii

Hall (or vicinity) of Goneril's castle. Kent is seen dressed as a beggar. Lear arrives and takes him into his service. Meanwhile, the Fool with his bizarre songs mocks Lear for having trusted his daughters. Goneril enters, complaining of the insolence of her father's knights, whom she refuses to allow to stay in the castle. The king erupts with anger when he realizes his daughter's ingratitude. He fears he will go mad . . . but, remembering Regan, he calms himself and hopes to be treated better by her. The arrival is announced of Regan, who has been invited by her sister. Lear approaches her and tells how Goneril has wronged him. Regan cannot believe this and says he must have offended her. The sisters unite to persuade Lear to disperse his followers. Then Lear, realizing his daughters' heartlessness, cries: 'You think I'll weep; no, I'll not weep.' He swears vengeance, exclaiming that he will do terrible things, 'what they are yet', he knows not, 'but they shall be the terrors of the earth.' (The noise of a tempest begins to be heard.) The curtain falls.

Act II, Scene i

Country. The tempest continues. Edgar, a fugitive, banished and accused of an attempt on his father's life, laments the injustice of his fate. Hearing a noise, he takes refuge in a hut. – Lear, Fool and Kent. – 'Blow, winds, and crack your cheeks. . . . Rumble thy bellyful! Spit, fire! Spout, rain! Nor rain, wind, thunder, fire are my daughters. I tax you not, you elements, with unkindness; I never gave you kingdom, call'd you children!' The Fool (still joking): 'O, nuncle, court holy-water in a dry house is better than this rain-water out o'door.' He enters the hut and is frightened when he sees Edgar, who feigns madness and utters cries of woe. Lear exclaims: 'What, have his daughters brought him to this pass? Couldst thou save nothing? Didst thou give them all?' (magnificent quartet). Someone bearing a torch approaches. It is Gloucester who, in defiance of the decree of the daughters, has come in search of the King.

Scene ii

Hall in Goneril's castle. Huge chorus (in various verse metres): 'Do you not know? Gloucester transgressed the command! . . . Well then? A terrible punishment awaits him!! What? . . . to have his eyes put out!! Horror, horror!! Wretched age, in which such crimes are committed.' The events relating to Lear, Cordelia, Kent, Gloucester etc. are recounted, and finally all fear a horrifying war which France will wage against England to avenge Lear.

Scene iii

Edmund: 'To both these sisters have I sworn my love; each jealous of the other, as the stung are of the adder. Which of them shall I take? Both? one? or neither?' etc. etc. Goneril enters and, after brief dialogue, offers him command of the army, and gives him a token of her love.

Scene iv

A poor room in a cottage.

Lear, Kent, Edgar, the Fool, and peasants. The Fool asks Lear, 'Whether a madman be a gentleman or a yeoman.' Lear replies: 'A King, a King!' – Song – Lear, in a state of delirium, continually obsessed with the idea of the ingratitude of his daughters, wishes to set up a court of justice. He calls Edgar 'most learned justicer', the Fool 'sapient sir' etc. etc. Extremely bizarre and moving scene. Finally, Lear tires and gradually falls asleep. All weep for the unhappy King. End of second act.

Act III, Scene i

The French camp near Dover.

Cordelia has heard from Kent of her father's misfortune. Great sorrow on Cordelia's part. She sends messenger after messenger to see if he has been found. She is ready to give all her possessions to whoever can restore his reason; she invokes the pity of nature etc. etc. The doctor announces that the King has been found and that he hopes to cure him of his madness. Cordelia, intoxicated with joy, thanks heaven and longs for the moment of vengeance.

Scene ii

Tent in the French camp.

Lear asleep on a bed. The doctor and Cordelia enter very quietly. '[He] sleeps still. . . .' After a brief dialogue very sweet sounds of music are heard behind the scenes, Lear awakes. Magnificent duet, as in the Shakespeare scene. The curtain falls.

Act IV, Scene i

Open country near Dover. The sound of a trumpet from afar.

Edgar appears, leading Gloucester: moving little duet in which Gloucester recognizes that he has been unjust to his son. Finally, Edgar says: 'Here, father, take the shadow of this tree for your good host; pray that the right may thrive.' (Exit.) Sound of trumpet nearer, noises, alarm; finally the signal to assemble is given. Edgar returns: 'Away, old man; give me thy hand; away! King Lear hath lost, he and his daughter ta'en.' (March) Edmund, Albany, Regan, Goneril, officers, soldiers etc. enter in triumph. Edmund gives an officer a letter: 'If thou dost as this instructs thee, thou dost make they way to noble fortunes.' An armed warrior with lowered vizor (Edgar) enters unexpectedly and accuses Edmund of high treason: in proof, he offers a letter to Albany. A duel takes place. Edmund is mortally wounded: before he dies he confesses all his crimes, and tells them to hurry to save Lear and Cordelia. . . . 'For my writ is on the life of Lear and on Cordelia – nay, send in time.'

Final scene
Prison

Moving scene between Lear and Cordelia, Cordelia begins to feel the effects of the poison: her agony and death. Albany, Kent and Edgar rush in to save her, but too late. Lear, unconscious of their arrival, takes Cordelia's corpse in his arms, and exclaims: 'She's dead as earth. Howl! Howl!' etc. Ensemble in which Lear must have the leading part. End.   VERDI to the librettist Cammarano, 1850

UTMIUTSOL vs.
UTREMIFASOLASIUTUTUT

The rival merits of Lulli (Utmiutsol) and Rameau (Utrémifasolasiututut) are contrasted in this passage from Denis Diderot's novel Les Bijoux Indiscrets *(1748). Compare p. 19.*

Utmiutsol and Utrémifasolasiututut, famous musicians, one of whom was beginning to age while the other was just born, occupied by turns the lyric stage. Each of these original composers had his supporters; the ignorant and the greybeards were all for Utmiutsol, the young and the executants for Utrémifasolasiututut; and the connoisseurs, both young and old, held both in great esteem.

Utrémifasolasiututut, said these latter, is excellent when he is good but he nods from time to time, and who does not? Utmiutsol is more sustained, more even; he is full of beauties; yet he has none of which examples, and even more striking ones, are not found in his rival, in whom qualities are found which are his own and occur nowhere else. Old Utmiutsol is simple, natural, even, too even sometimes, and this is a defect. Young Utrémifasolasiututut is singular, brilliant, complex, learned, too learned sometimes; but this is perhaps a defect in his listeners; Utmiutsol has only one overture, beautiful in truth but repeated at the beginning of all his operas; the other has written as many overtures as operas and all pass for masterpieces. Nature has led Utmiutsol in the paths of tunefulness; study and experience have laid bare to Utrémifasolasiututut the springs of harmony. Who has declaimed and recited as the elder has? Who will give us light *arias*, voluptuous *airs* and character *symphonies* like the younger's? Utmiutsol is unrivalled in his grasp of dialogue. Before Utrémifasolasiututut

391

no one had discerned the delicate shades that mark off the tender from the voluptuous, the voluptuous from the passionate, the passionate from the lascivious; a few supporters of this latter claim even that, if Utmiutsol's dialogue is superior to his, this is less the fault of any inequality of talent than of the difference between the poets they have used. 'Read, they cry, the scene from *Dardanus*, and you will be convined that if Utrémifasolasiututut is given good texts the ravishing scenes of Utmiutsol will appear.' However this be, in my time the whole city ran to the tragedies of the one and crushed to the ballets of the other.

VERDI

Verdi's early reputation for vulgarity and noise was as bad as Rossini's. Nobody today would pretend that Jérusalem *is one of Verdi's masterpieces, but equally nobody would dare call it 'the summit of awfulness'.*

Yesterday they put on Verdi's *Lombardi*, under the title *Jérusalem*, for the first time at the Grand Opera. The libretto has been redone. They've introduced a scene of the knight's devotion – for Duprez [tenor]. Verdi, for his part, has written several new *morceaux* [bits] that are absolutely revolting. I won't tell you about the music, you know it – it's the summit of awfulness. . . .

It absolutely seems that the time of powerful and healthy geniuses has passed; coarse, banal strength is on the side of such facile and productive mediocrities as Verdi. And, quite to the contrary, those to whom the divine fire is given waste away in idleness, weakness, or dreams; the gods are envious: they don't give anyone everything at once. And yet – why then were our fathers luckier than we? Why was it granted to them to be present at the first performances of such things as *The Barber of Seville*, to at least see *Norma*, while we poor things are condemned to *Jérusalems*. TURGENEV to Pauline Viardot-Garcia, 1847

The conductor Hans von Bülow, an ardent Wagnerian despite the desertion of his first wife Cosima, was one of many musical intellectuals who came to a finer appreciation of Verdi's genius towards the end of the century. In this

393

letter of April 1892, he writes to Verdi apologizing for his previous blindness.

Illustre Maestro,
Please deign to listen to the confession of a contrite sinner! It is now eighteen years since the undersigned was guilty of a great . . . great journalistic *bestiality* . . . towards the last of the five Kings of modern Italian music. He has repented in bitter shame – how many times! When the sin in question was committed (in your generosity you may have quite forgotten it) he was not really in control of his own mind – forgive me if I remind you of what may be called an attenuating circumstance. His mind was clouded by an ultra-Wagnerian fanaticism. Seven years later, the light gradually dawned on him. His fanaticism was purified into enthusiasm. Fanaticism is an oil lamp, enthusiasm an electric light. In the intellectual and moral world, light means justice. Nothing is more destructive than injustice, nothing more intolerable than intolerance, as the most noble Leopardi once said. . . .

I have begun to study your latest works, *Aida*, *Otello*, and the *Requiem*, a rather feeble performance of which was recently enough to move me to tears: I have been studying them not only in the letter which kills, but in the spirit which gives life! Well, *illustre Maestro*, now I admire you, love you! . . .

Verdi's reply:

Illustre Maestro Bülow,
There is no taint of sin in you! – and no need to talk of repentance and absolution!

If your former views were different from what they are today, you were perfectly right to express them, and I would never have ventured to complain of that. Besides, who knows . . . perhaps you were right then.

Be that as it may, such an unexpected letter from a musician of your quality and importance in the world of art has given me great pleasure! Not out of personal vanity, but because it shows me that really fine artists form their opinions unprejudiced by schools, by nationality or by period.

If artists in the North and those in the South have different tendencies, then let them be *different*! They should all preserve the *characteristics proper to their respective nations*, as Wagner so well expressed it.

Happy you, to be still the sons of Bach! And we? We too, the sons of Palestrina, once had a great school – of our own! Now it has become bastardized and is in danger of collapsing!

If only we could turn back again?! . . .

Verdi is often praised for his instinctively good writing for the voice – good in the sense of never expecting it to do too much – but in 1893 G. B. Shaw stated the following cogent reservations on the matter.

Verdi's worst sins as a composer have been sins against the human voice. His habit of taking the upper fifth of the compass of an exceptionally high voice, and treating that fifth as the normal range, has a great deal to do with the fact that the Italian singer is now the worst singer in the world, just as Wagner's return to Handel's way of using the voice all over its compass and obtaining physical relief for the singer and artistic relief for the audience by the contrast of the upper and lower registers has made the Wagnerian singer now the best singer in the world. Wagner applied his system with special severity to baritones.

If you look at the score of *Don Giovanni*, you will find three different male voices written for on the bass clef, and so treated as to leave no doubt that Mozart, as he wrote the music, had a particular sort of voice for each part constantly in his head, and that one (Masetto's) was a rough peasant's bass, another (Leporello's) a ready, fluent, copious *basso cantante*; and the third a light fine baritone, the voice of a gentleman. I have heard public meetings addressed successively by an agricultural labourer's delegate, a representative of the skilled artisans, and a university man; and they have taught me what all the treatises in the world could not about the Mozartian differentiation between Masetto, Leporello, and Don Giovanni.

But now please remark that there is no difference of range

between the three parts. Any man who can sing the notes of one of them can sing the notes of the others. Let Masetto and the Don exchange characters, and though the Don will be utterly ineffective in the concerted music on Masetto's lower Gs and B flats, whilst Masetto will rob the serenade of all its delicacy, yet neither singer will encounter any more impossibility, or even inconvenience, in singing the notes than Mr Toole would have in reading the part of Hamlet. The same thing is true of the parts of Bartolo, Figaro, and Almaviva in *Le Nozze*; of San Bris and Nevers in *Les Huguenots*; of Wotan and Alberich in The Niblung's Ring; and of Amfortas and Klingsor in *Parsifal*. The dramatic distinction between these parts is so strong that only an artist of remarkable versatility could play one as well as the other; but there is practically no distinction of vocal range any more than there is a distinction of physical stature or strength.

But if we turn to *Il Trovatore*, we find two vocal parts written in the bass clef, of which the lower, Ferrando, is not a *basso profundo* like Osmin or Marcel, but a *basso cantante* like San Bris or Leporello; yet the baritone part (Di Luna) is beyond the reach of any normal *basso cantante*, and treats a baritone voice as consisting of about one effective octave, from G on the fourth space of the bass stave to the G above. In *Il balen* there are from two hundred and ten to two hundred and twenty notes, including the *cadenza*, &c. Barring five notes in the *cadenza*, which is never sung as written, only three are below F on the fourth line, whilst nearly one hundred and forty lie above the stave between B flat and the high G. The singing is practically continuous from end to end; and the strain on a normal baritone voice is frightful, even when the song is transposed half a tone as it usually is to bring it within the bare limits of possibility. Di Luna is in this respect a typical Verdi baritone; and the result has been that only singers with abnormally high voices have been able to sing it without effort.

As to the normal baritones who have made a speciality of bawling fiercely up to G sharp, they have so lost the power of producing an endurable tone in their lower octave, or of pitching its notes with even approximate accuracy, that they have all but destroyed the popularity of Mozart's operas by their occasional appearances as Don Giovanni, Figaro, &c. I have often wished that the law would permit me to destroy these unhappy wretches, whose lives must be a burden to them. It is easy to go into raptures over the superiority of the Italian master in vocal writing because his phrases are melodious, easily learned, symmetrical, and often grandiose; but when you have to sing the melodious well-turned phrases, and find that they lie a tone higher than you can comfortably manage them, and a third higher than you can keep on managing them for five minutes at a stretch (for music that *lies* rather high is much more trying than music that *ventures* very high occasionally), you begin to appreciate the sort of knowledge of and consideration for the voice shewn by Purcell, Handel, and Wagner, and to very decidedly resent Verdi's mere partiality for the top end of it.

... what I love above all in Verdi's music is the sun in it, its clean beauty, its soaring or leaping phrases, its glorious cantilena. I love it with an immediate, personal love, in the way one loves a human being. And I also love, by a kind of transference that takes no account either of virtues or demerits, Verdi the man, as I love no other composer, not even the greatest, Beethoven.

One of the reasons for this is his sheer humanity. Few have had as keen an awareness of evil as Verdi: but there is a sadness about the music associated with the most evil of his characters – you hear it above all in *Otello* and *Macbeth* – to be found in no other composer, though Britten gets close to it in some of the Claggart music in *Billy Budd*. D'Annunzio wrote the final epitaph for Verdi in his memorial ode: 'Pianse è amo per tutti', 'He wept and loved for all'.

What a joy it is, in spite of everything I have said about the danger of overdoing the Verdi cult, to reflect that there are works by Verdi still to explore, to grow familiar with in the unfolding kind of way that is one of the chief pleasures of musical experience! I had always dismissed *I due Foscari* as more or less worthless, I do not know on what authority, until an evening, some twenty years ago, when I happened to tune in to it on the wireless. At first I went on tinkering away at some sentences I had been writing before dinner, when suddenly – there it came, the great melody, sweet and easy and rounded and strong ('out of the strong came forth sweetness'); and then another and another and another, pouring out, flowing on, with an inevitable prodigality like nature's in spring. So what could one do but just sit there and listen, and beam happily, and bless the old man?

VICTOR GOLLANCZ, *Journey Towards Music*

The time is about 6.50 a.m., and at a Lancashire colliery the night shift has just come up, and the men are in the showers having a wash. Some of them are singing at the tops of their voices all the latest popular tunes. Someone is heard to shout, 'O.K. – the Oath Duet', and out of the noise are heard two voices singing 'Si, pel ciel, marmorio giuro', not perfect, but in tune. Someone shouts, 'Put a sock in it!' but the duettists end their piece of Verdi opera. A pause, then a dark and heavy tenor is heard singing 'Niun mi tema', and at the end, a realistic gasp on the words 'Ancora un bacio'. Both Shakespeare and Verdi have been gone for many years, but here in 1954 at 6.50 a.m. amongst the miners, their words and music are sung with all the love and passion that is in art. It makes one proud to be an opera-lover and a miner. If *Otello* was to be performed in a colliery canteen, he would still be loved as always.   Letter from 'An interested miner', *Opera*, 1954

VIBRATO

Let him learn to hold out the Notes without a Shrillness like a Trumpet, or trembling; and if at the Beginning he made him hold out every Note the length of two Bars, the Improvement would be the greater; otherwise from the natural Inclination that the Beginners have to keep the Voice in Motion, and the Trouble in holding it out, he will get a habit, and not be able to fix it, and will become subject to a Flutt'ring in the Manner of all those that sing in a very bad Taste.   PIERO TOSI, *Observations on the Florid Song*

Some musical historians claim that the vocal music of the Renaissance was sung with a so-called 'straight' tone, but that the vibrato was cultivated and used to ornament or embellish music. Today, when this music is re-created for us, singers who possess relatively vibrato-free voices or the ability to make them so, usually perform it, though there is no actual proof that the early voices sounded in this manner. Writing of singing in the eighteenth century, no less an authority than Mozart has this to say about vibrato in a letter to his father: 'Meissner, as you know, has a bad habit in that he often intentionally vibrates his voice ... and that I cannot tolerate in him. It is indeed truly detestable, it is singing entirely contrary to nature.' Then he adds, 'The human voice already vibrates of itself, but in such a degree that it is beautiful, that is the nature of the voice.'

Mozart lived in a relatively relaxed time when it came to sexual mores. A century later with Victorian morality the dominant influence in parts of the Western world, there is much inveighing against the vibrato. It was sweeping 'through Europe like the influenza' complained the young music critic, George Bernard Shaw, who was not without his prudish side. 'I have the voice of a choirboy,' Nellie Melba once proudly proclaimed, comparing her silvery tones to those piping singers who lack pulsations to their tones. Phonograph records of Melba and other singers of her time attest to the fact that many used much less vibrato than we are accustomed to today. 'The vibrato is popular among the Latin races, while the Anglo-Saxons will not tolerate it.' Dr Holbrook Curtis, a noted American laryngologist, who treated the throats of many singers at the Metropolitan, wrote this in 1909, adding, 'No great singer has ever succeeded in securing recognition in the United States ... who has attempted to secure his effects with a vibrato quality.' Given the time he was writing and his familiarity with the artists at the Metropolitan, it was an odd statement to make. if ever there was a singer who secured 'his effects' with a glorious vibrato quality it was Enrico Caruso, then in the prime of his adulation both in New York and London. Even as late as 1923 the singing teacher and authority on voice, Herman Klein, denounced vibrato as a 'sin'.

Oddly enough it was in the American mid-West where 'sin' does not go unremarked, that a psychologist at the University of Iowa attempted to make 'an objective analysis of artistic singing' during the late 1920s and into the 1930s. Among Dr Harold Seashore's discoveries was the fact that 'individual differences in the capacity for hearing vibrato are very large. In a normal population one individual may be 50 or 100 times as keen as another in this hearing ... Each individual has his own illusion,' he adds, 'and his individual sense of the vibrato determines what shall be good or bad for him.' This statement renders arguments between the fans of various singers over the tone quality of their favorites absolutely ludicrous, since it appears that *no two people hear the same voice the same way.* Measuring an aesthetic response is a dubious undertaking at best, but Seashore declared that a voice to sound beautiful should possess a smooth, regular vibrato of between five and a half to eight pulsations a second – the ideal being about six and a half. Such a conclusion, presumptuous as it may seem to measure beauty of tone, is given credence by the analysis of the vibratos of a number of famous singers of the time made by another investigator. Here are a few of the results:

Singer	Rate of Vibrato per second
Galli-Curci	7.4
Caruso	7.1
Martinelli	6.8
Gigli	6.3

ROBERT RUSHMORE, *The Singing Voice*

VIENNA

In 1716 Lady Mary Wortley Montagu, one of the eighteenth century's great letter-writers, left for Constantinople with her husband, who had been appointed ambassador there. On her return from Turkey, she brought home the theory and practice of smallpox inoculation. The couple went by way of Vienna, where Lady Mary wrote to Alexander Pope:

Don't fancy . . . that I am infected by the air of these popish countries; though I have so far wandered from the Church of England, to have been last Sunday at the opera, which was performed in the garden of the Favorita; and I was so much pleased with it, I have not yet repented my seeing it. Nothing of that kind ever was more magnificent: and I can easily believe what I am told, that the decorations and habits cost the emperor thirty thousand pounds sterling. The stage was built over a very large canal, and, at the beginning of the second act, divided into two parts, discovering the water, on which there immediately came, from different parts, two fleets of little gilded vessels, that gave the representation of a naval fight. . . . The story of the opera is the Enchantments of Alcina, which gives opportunity for a great variety of machines, and changes of the scene, which are performed with a surprising swiftness. The theatre is so large, that it is hard to carry the eye to the end of it. . . . No house could hold such large decorations; but the ladies all sitting in the open air, exposes them to great inconveniences, for there is but one canopy for the imperial family; and the first night it was represented, a shower of rain happening, the opera was broken off, and the company crowded away in such confusion, I was almost squeezed to death.

The Vienna State Opera is much younger than the Scala in count of years, but its place in the life of the city and country is no less central: it is perhaps even more so. When the Opera burned (on March 12, 1945, the seventh anniversary of the Anschluss) as a result of incendiary bombs scattered by a returning mission of the American Eighth Air Force, the starved and shattered city regarded it as the most appalling catastrophe of the whole war. I have been given graphic accounts of how the news traveled through the whole mourning metropolis, and how men and women who had far more personal tragedies upon their minds forgot everything to rush to the center. This was not only because the Opera was a big edifice in the middle of the town: the Bristol Hotel, across the street, is also pretty big and equally central, but its destruction would have meant nothing in particular in the midst of such general disaster.

The reopening of the Opera as rebuilt (November 5, 1955) was the occasion for an outburst of rejoicing just as remarkable. Crowds stood in the streets leading to the Opera all through the day and most of the night, weeping and cheering. At night the illuminations and the general festivities reached a multitude of Viennese and Austrians who could not get into the Opera house and who perhaps (many of them) never will set foot inside it. The American Secretary of State and some of our ambassadors to European countries were there, along with all the potentates of the Austrian State so recently freed from military occupation. The vast crowd listened to *Fidelio* as it came from the loud-speakers in the center of Vienna, and during the hours of the performance I have been told that hundreds of thousands stood in silence broken only by tears. Such a thing is impossible to imagine anywhere else. . . .

The official opening of the Opera took place in the morning of November 5th – a ceremony of great solemnity for invited guests, with the President of the Republic and all the officials present. Mme [Lotte] Lehmann seems to have been even more moved at the ceremony in the morning than at the first performance (*Fidelio*) that night.

'It was an unforgettable moment when the iron curtain rose,' she says of the morning. 'Even now in memory, it chokes me. This wonderful old house which has served only beauty, which has given joy and uplift to thousands of music-loving people, had been mute for so long. Now it lives again. Now the old times will come back again; and I am sure of that. I don't belong to those people who always sigh for the past. Nobody is irreplaceable. Wherever some beauty dies, some new beauty is being born. Much glory lies ahead of this beloved house. If I would not believe this, I would think, "There never will be a time as we have lived through in the past", it would make me very unhappy. Today the house is yet echoing with voices of the past. But soon those voices will fade away in the glory of new voices, as beautiful as ours were. Oh, I am sure of that!

'There were a lot of speeches, and when Ministerialrat Marboe, the General Manager of the two theatres, Opera and Burgtheater, greeted the guests of honor, I felt proudly the surge of love and loyal admiration which came up to my box in big waves of applause. In the end the wonderful Philharmonic Orchestra played the Prelude of the *Meistersinger*. It almost killed me. I was dissolved in tears. I sang at a kind of "trial performance", Eva, as a guest, coming from Hamburg. Standing on the stage behind the closed curtain I wanted to listen to the Prelude. But when the first bars sounded in all their splendor I had the sensational feeling that I had never heard it before. On the wings of this orchestra the music sounded almost unearthly beautiful to me. That was in the year 1914. And the same awesome shock gripped me again now forty-one years later when I listened to this orchestra again.

'In our box of honorary members sat also the first ballerina of former years: Gusti Pichler, now in her sixties, looking simply ridiculously young. I remember so well her birdlike grace, her elflike figure, her radiance. She sat there, tears shimmering in her eyes; and suddenly she leaned forward, touching my hand and whispering, "Your Eva." It moved me very much. After the Prelude, Director Boehm gave an encore which was received with much delight – the "Blue Danube". Oh, how this orchestra played the waltz! And through the music, through the veil of my tears, I saw in my memory the graceful form of Gusti, soaring in her lovely dance. I leaned forward, and, touching her hand, whispered: "I remember you."

'This morning was rather exhausting with all its emotion. I had to go home to the hotel and take a rest in order not to look too terrible in my beautiful gown. I was asked to open the ball of the Philharmonic Orchestra after the *Fidelio* performance that night, but I was sorry to have to refuse. I am accustomed to a quiet life, and three times a day being moved to tears is a little bit too much for me.'

VINCENT SHEEAN, *First and Last Love*

WAGNER

George Eliot wrote this remarkable analysis after a visit to Weimar in 1854, where she heard Wagner's music conducted by Liszt.

Wagner would make the opera a perfect musical drama, in which feelings and situations spring out of *character*, as in the highest order of tragedy, and in which no dramatic probability or poetic beauty is sacrificed to musical effect. The drama must not be a mere pretext for the music; but music, drama, and spectacle must be blended, like the coloured rays in the sunbeam, so as to produce one undivided impression. The controversy between him and his critics is the old controversy between Gluck and Piccinni, between the declamatory and melodic schools of music, with the same difference in comprehensiveness as between the disputes of La Motte and the Daciers about the value of the classics, and the disputes of the classical and romantic schools of literature in our own day. In its first period the opera aimed simply at the expression of feeling through melody; the second period, which has its culmination in the joint productions of Meyerbeer and Scribe, added the search for effective situations and a heightening of dramatic movement, which has led more and more to the predominance of the declamatory style and the subordination of melody. But in Meyerbeer's operas the grand object is to produce a climax of spectacle, situation, and orchestra effects; there is no attempt at the evolution of these from the true workings of human character and human passions; on the contrary, the characters seem to be a second thought, and with a few exceptions, such as Alice and Marcel, are vague and uninteresting. Every opera-goer has remarked that *Robert* is a mere nose of wax; or has laughed at the pathos with which the fiend Bertram invites his son to go to the bottomless pit with him, instead of settling into respectability above ground; or has felt that *Jean, the Prophet*, is a feeble sketch, completely lost in the blaze of spectacle. Yet what a progress is there in the libretto of these operas compared with the libretto of *Der Freischütz*, which, nevertheless, was thought so good in its day that Goethe said Weber ought to divide the merit of success with Kind. Even Weber's enchanting music cannot overcome the sense of absurdity when, in a drinking party of two, one of whom is sunk in melancholy, a man gets up and bursts into a rolling song which seems the very topmost wave in the high tide of bacchanalian lyrism; or when Caspar climbs a tree apparently for no other reason than because the *dénouement* requires him to be shot.

Now, says Wagner, this ascent from the warbling puppets of the early opera to the dramatic effects of Meyerbeer, only serves to bring more clearly into view the unattained summit of the true musical drama. An opera must be no mosaic of melodies stuck together with no other method than is supplied by accidental contrast, no mere succession of ill-prepared crises, but an organic whole, which grows up like a palm, its earliest portion containing the germ and prevision of all the rest. He will write no *part* to suit a *primo tenore*, and interpolate no *cantata* to show off the powers of a *prima donna assoluta*; those who sing his operas must be content with the degree of prominence which falls to them in strict consonance with true dramatic development and ordonance. Such, so far as I understand it, is Wagner's theory of the opera — surely a theory worth entertaining, and one which he has admirably exemplified so far as the libretto of his operas is concerned.

But it is difficult to see why this theory should entail the exclusion of melody to the degree at which he has arrived in *Lohengrin*, unless we accept one of two suppositions: either that Wagner is deficient in melodic inspiration, or that his inspiration has been overridden by his system, which opposition has pushed to exaggeration. Certainly his *Fliegende Holländer* — a transition work, in which, as Liszt says, he only seeks to escape from the idols to which he has hitherto sacrificed, and has not yet reached the point of making war against them – is a charming opera; and *Tann-häuser* too is still the music of men and women, as well of Wagnerites; but *Lohengrin* to us ordinary mortals seemed something like the whistling of the wind through the keyholes of a cathedral, which has a dreamy charm for a little while, but by and by you long for the sound even of a street organ to rush in and break the monotony. It may be safely said, that whatever the music of the future may be, it will not be a music which is in contradiction with a permanent element in human nature – the need for a frequent alternation of sensations or emotions; and this need is *not* satisfied in *Lohengrin*.

As to melody – who knows? It is just possible that melody, as we conceive it, is only a transitory phase of music, and that the musicians of the future may read the airs of Mozart and Beethoven and Rossini as scholars read the *Stabreim* and assonance of early poetry. We are but in 'the morning of the times', and must learn to think of ourselves as tadpoles unprescient of the future frog. Still the tadpole is limited to tadpole pleasures; and so, in our state of development, we are swayed by melody. When, a little while after hearing *Lohengrin*, we happened to come on a party of musicians who were playing exquisitely a quartette of Beethoven's, it was like returning to the pregnant speech of men after a sojourn among glums and gowries.   'Liszt, Wagner and Weimar'

Wagner has just been in Berlin [1871], and his arrival here has been the occasion of a grand musical excitement. He was received with the greatest enthusiasm, and there was no end of ovations in his honour. First, there was a great supper given to him, which was got up by Tausig and a few other distinguished musicians. Then on Sunday, two weeks ago, was given a concert in the Sing-Akademie, where the seats were free. As the hall only holds about fifteen hundred people, you may imagine it was pretty difficult to get tickets. I didn't even attempt it, but luckily Weitz-mann, my harmony teacher, who is an old friend of Wagner's, sent me one.

The orchestra was immense. It was carefully selected from all the orchestras in Berlin, and Stern, who directed it, had given himself infinite trouble in training it. Wagner is the most difficult person in the world to please, and is a wonderful conductor himself. He was highly discontented with the Gewandhaus Orchestra in Leipsic, which thinks itself the best in existence, so the Berlinese felt rather shaky. The hall was filled to overflowing, and finally, in marched Wagner and his wife, preceded and fol-lowed by various distinguished musicians. As he appeared the audience rose, the orchestra struck up three clanging chords, and everybody shouted *Hoch!* It gave one a strange thrill.

The concert was at twelve, and was preceded by a 'greeting' which was recited by Frau Jachmann Wagner, a niece of Wagner's, and an actress. She was a pretty woman, 'fair, fat, and forty,' and an excellent speaker. As she concluded she burst into tears, and stepping down from the stage she presented Wagner with a laurel crown, and kissed him. Then the orchestra played Wagner's Faust Overture most superbly, and afterwards his Fest March from the Tannhäuser. The applause was unbounded. Wagner ascended the stage and made a little speech, in which he expressed his pleasure to the musicians and to Stern, and then turned and addressed the audience. He spoke very rapidly and in that childlike way that all great musicians seem to have, and as a proof of his satisfaction with the orchestra he requested them to play the Faust Overture under *his* direction. We were all on tiptoe to know how he would direct, and indeed it was wonderful to see him. He controlled the orchestra as if it were a single instrument and he were playing on it. He didn't beat the time simply, as most conductors do, but he had all sorts of little ways to indicate what he wished. It was very difficult for them to follow him, and they had to 'keep their little eye open,' as B. [friend of author] used to say. He held them down during the first part, so as to give the uncertainty and speculativeness of Faust's character. Then as Mephistopheles came in, he gradually let them loose with a terrible crescendo, and made you feel as if hell suddenly gaped at your feet. Then where Gretchen appeared, all was delicious melody and sweetness. And so it went on, like a succession of pictures. The effect was tremendous.

I had one of the best seats in the house, and could see Wagner and his wife the whole time. He has an enormous forehead, and is the most nervous-looking man you can imagine, but has that grim setting of the mouth that betokens an iron will. When he conducts he is almost beside himself with excitement. That is one reason why he is so great as a conductor, for the orchestra catches his frenzy, and each man plays under a sudden inspiration. He really seems to be improvising on his orchestra.

Wagner's object in coming here was to try and get his Nibelungen opera performed. It is an opera which requires four evenings to get through with. Did you ever hear of such a thing? He lays out everything on such a colossal scale. It reminded me of that story they tell of him when he was a boy. He was a great Shakespeare enthusiast, and wanted to write plays too. So he wrote one in which he killed off forty of the principal characters in the last act! He gave a grand concert in the opera house here, which he directed himself. It was entirely his own compositions, with the exception of Beethoven's Fifth Symphony, which he declared nobody understood but himself. That rather took down Berlin, but all had to acknowledge after the concert that they had never heard it so magnificently played. He has his own peculiar conception of it. There was a great crowd, and every seat had been taken long before. All the artists were present except Kullak, who was ill. I saw Tausig sitting in the front rank with the Baroness von S. There must have been two hundred players in the orchestra, and they acquitted themselves splendidly. The applause grew more and more enthusiastic, until it finally found vent in a shower of wreaths and bouquets. Wagner bowed and bowed, and it seemed as if the people would never settle down again. At the end of the concert followed another shower of flowers, and his Kaiser march was encored. Such an effect! After the tempest of sound of the introduction the drums came in with a sharp rat-tat-tat-tat-tat! Then the brass began with the air and came to a crescendo, at last *blaring* out in such a way as shivered you to the very marrow of your bones. It was like an earthquake yawning before you.

The noise was so tremendous that it was like the roaring of the surf. I never conceived of anything in music to approach it, and Wagner made me think of a giant Triton disporting himself amid the billows and tossing these great waves of sound from one hand to the other. You don't see his face of course – nothing but his back, and yet you know every one of his emotions. Every sinew in his body speaks. He makes the instruments prolong the tones as no one else does, and the effect is indescribably beautiful, yet he complains that he never *can* get an orchestra to *hold* the tone as they ought. His whole appearance is of arrogance and despotism personified.

By the end of the concert the bouquets were so heaped on the stage in front of the director's desk that Wagner had no place left big enough to stand on without crushing them. Altogether, it was a brilliant affair, and a great triumph for his friends. He has a great many bitter enemies here, however. Joachim is one of them, though it seems unaccountable that a man of his musical gifts should be. Ehlert is also a strong anti-Wagnerite, and the Jews hate him intensely. Perhaps his character has something to do with it, for he has set all laws of honour, gratitude, and morality at defiance all his life long. It is a dreadful example for younger artists, and I think Wagner is depraving them. In this country everything is forgiven to audacity and genius, and I must say that if Germany can teach *us* Music, we teach *her* Morals!

AMY FAY, *Music Study in Germany*

[Hugo] Wolf saw Wagner. He tells us about it in his letters to his parents. I will quote his own words, and though they make one smile, one loves the impulsive devotion of his youth; and they make one feel, too, that a man who inspires such an affection, and who can do so much good by a little sympathy, is to blame when he does not befriend others – above all if he has suffered, like

Wagner, from loneliness and the want of a helping hand. You must remember that this letter was written by a boy of fifteen [viz., in 1875].

I have been to – guess whom? ... to the master, Richard Wagner! Now I will tell you all about it, just as it happened. I will copy the words down exactly as I wrote them in my notebook.

On Thursday, 9 December, at half-past ten, I saw Richard Wagner for the second time at the Hotel Imperial, where I stayed for half an hour on the staircase, awaiting his arrival (I knew that on that day he would conduct the last rehearsal of his *Lohengrin*). At last the master came down from the second floor, and I bowed to him very respectfully while he was yet some distance from me. He thanked me in a very friendly way. As he neared the door I sprang forward and opened it for him, upon which he looked fixedly at me for a few seconds, and then went on his way to the rehearsal at the Opera. I ran as fast as I could, and arrived at the Opera sooner than Richard Wagner did in his cab. I bowed to him again, and I wanted to open the door of his cab for him; but as I could not get it open, the coachman jumped down from his seat and did it for me. Wagner said something to the coachman – I think it was about me. I wanted to follow him into the theatre, but they would not let me pass.

I often used to wait for him at the Hotel Imperial; and on this occasion I made the acquaintance of the manager of the hotel, who promised that he would interest himself on my behalf. Who was more delighted than I when he told me that on the following Saturday afternoon, 11 December, I was to come and find him, so that he could introduce me to Mme. Cosima's maid and Richard Wagner's valet! I arrived at the appointed hour. The visit to the lady's maid was very short. I was advised to come the following day, Sunday, 12 December, at two o'clock. I arrived at the right hour, but found the maid and the valet and the manager still at table. ... Then I went with the maid to the master's rooms, where I

wanted for about a quarter of an hour until he came. At last
Wagner appeared in company with Cosima and Goldmark.
I bowed to Cosima very respectfully, but she evidently did
not think it worth while to honour me with a single glance.
Wagner was going into his room without paying any attention to me, when the maid said to him in a beseeching voice:
'Ah, Herr Wagner, it is a young musician who wishes to
speak to you; he has been waiting for you a long time.'   He
then came out of his room, looked at me, and said: 'I have
seen you before, I think. You are...'

Probably he wanted to say, 'You are a fool.'

He went in front of me and opened the door of the
reception-room, which was furnished in a truly royal style.
In the middle of the room was a couch covered in velvet and
silk. Wagner himself was wrapped in a long velvet mantle
bordered with fur.

When I was inside the room he asked me what I wanted.

Here Hugo Wolf, to excite the curiosity of his parents, broke off
his story and put 'To be continued in my next.' In his next letter he
continues:

I said to him: 'Highly honoured master, for a long time I
have wanted to hear an opinion on my compositions, and it
would be...'

Here the master interrupted me and said: 'My dear child, I
cannot give you an opinion of your compositions; I have far
too little time: I can't even get my own letters written. I
understand nothing at all about music'...

Quoted in ROMAIN ROLLAND, *Musicians of Today*

Tribschen, on Lake Lucerne, was where Wagner completed
Meistersinger; *Houston Stewart Chamberlain was an English disciple of Wagner's who subscribed to anti-semitic
views.*

Visited Tribschen. Toured the rooms. Curious impression.

Dreadful oil paintings, utterly Hitler. One absolutely revolting gigolo of a Siegfried. Nietzsche's *The Case of Wagner* placed next to a copy of *The Birth of Tragedy* under glass, a stupid touch. Interesting photographic group portraits of Wagner's family and friends. A bust of Chamberlain. Magnificence of the view through the windows. Furnishings in better taste than that of the tenants. One upholstered chair he added himself, Bayreuth style. Siegfried in a variety of guises, looking for all the world like a Jew in a more youthful picture. The poem to Cosima that accompanied the *Siegfried Idyll* – one can only say 'hmmm.' Elements of a frighteningly Hitleresque quality plainly discernible, even though only latent and anticipatory, ranging from the overblown kitsch to the Germanic fondness for boys. – Walked in the garden by the lake where Nietzsche and he used to stroll. Hot chocolate in the café of the Kunst-Haus. Walked across the old bridge. The exquisite beauty of the mountains. Drove back and went home by seven.

THOMAS MANN, *Diary*, 1937

One of the more extreme reactions to Wagner was that of the Italian futurist, artist and polemicist, Filippo Marinetti; this blast dates from 1913.

Tristan and Isolde who withhold their climax to excite King Mark. Medicine-dropper of love. Miniature of sexual anguish. Spun sugar of lust. Lechery out in the open. Delirium tremens. Cockeyed hands and feet. Pantomime coitus for the camera. Masturbated waltz. Pouah! Down with the diplomatics of the skin! Up with the brutality of a violent possession and the fine fury of an exciting, strengthening, muscular dance.

Tango, roll and pitch of sailboats who have cast their anchors in the depths of cretinism. Tango, roll and pitch of sailboats drenched with tenderness and lunar stupidity. Tango, tango, a pitching to make one vomit. Tango, slow and patient funeral of dead sex! These words mean nothing to us! We shout *Down with the tango!* in the name of Health, Force, Will, and Virility.

If the tango is bad, *Parsifal* is worse, because it innoculates the dancers swaying in languorous boredom with an incurable musical neurasthenia.

How shall we avoid *Parsifal* and its cloudbursts, puddles, and bogs of mystical tears? *Parsifal* is the systematic devaluation of life! Cooperative factory of sadness and desperation. Unmelodious protrusion of weak stomachs. Bad digestion and heavy breath of forty-year-old virgins. Lamentations of fat old constipated priests. Wholesale and retail sale of remorses and elegant cowardices for snobs. Insufficiency of blood, weakness of the loins, hysteria, anemia, and green sickness. Genuflection, brutalizing and crushing of Man. Silly scraping of wounded, defeated notes. Snoring of drunken organs stretched in the vomit of bitter leitmotivs. Tears and false pearls of Mary Magdalen in décolletage at Maxim's. Polyphonic suppuration of Amfortas's wound. Lachrymose sleepiness of the Knights of the Grail! Ridiculous satanism of Kundry. ... Passéism! Passéism – enough!

WAGNERIENNES

One summer at Bayreuth in the 1890s, when both prima donnas were singing the major Wagner roles, Lillian Nordica had a friend ask the imperious Lilli Lehmann whether she might pay a social call, as one prima donna to another. 'Tell her I am not taking any pupils this season,' Lehmann snapped back, contemptuous and not a little jealous of her American rival's success. Two years later at the Met they were singing in the same performance of Don Giovanni. *Lehmann's dresser was rushing around backstage: Madame had left her black stockings at her hotel – did Madame Nordica possibly have a spare pair? Nordica, magnanimous to the last, obliged. The next day she received the following note: even Lehmann could melt on occasion.*

My dearest Mrs Nordica!

With heartfelt thanks I send back the stockings you lent me last night; I washed them myself so you can be sure they are clean.

I already told your husband that I was so glad to hear your voice is so much better better [*sic*] now as two years ago, I hope you will be pleased.

With much love and thank [*sic*], yours sincerely and affectionately

Lilli Lehmann Kalisch

quoted in IRA GLACKENS, *Yankee Diva*

'I am the most commonplace person in the world. I am not a bit mysterious or unusual or complex,' wrote Kirsten Flagstad. Apart from the fact that she ... had the greatest voice any of us had ever heard – greatest in volume, range, security, beauty of tone, everything a voice can have, and all of one piece, never a break in it, all rolling out with no evidence of effort or strain even in the most difficult passages. The only defect to be found in her remarkable performances was that they did not express what Wagner wrote. The immense audiences which gathered to hear her from 1935 to 1941 did not care a fig what Wagner had written: they wanted to hear this golden flood of tone over the massive orchestra. It is beyond question that they never got from Flagstad any reason for the 'physiological objections' of Nietzsche. The physiological effect of Flagstad was a thrill – a powerful one to be sure – caused by her wondrous singing. She never frightened, alarmed or repelled; she was not in the very slightest degree demonic; she enraptured her audiences, and what did it matter about Wagner?

The curiosity aroused by accounts of Flagstad's triumphs in New York made her London debut [1936] a great occasion, which her own superb gifts turned to more serious account. We were living in Ireland at that time and since my wife was incarcerated in a Dublin nursing home for another week or so, I made a flying trip over to London to hear Flagstad's Isolde.

It was a rare evening in the opera house. Fritz Reiner was conducting (he also conducted her last New York Isolde sixteen years later). Flagstad was beautiful to behold, especially in the first act, and the radiance of her incomparable voice was quite dazzling to one who had never heard it or anything like it before. And yet even on that night, startled as I was at the sheer wonder of all this, I missed a great many meanings that should have been in the part. When I thought it over afterwards (even between the acts) and could hear that voice echoing in my ears, I realized that the meanings were not there because the singer had not put them there.

Isolde's first act is an intricate web of such meanings, suggestions, implications. The rest of the part is simple lyricism by comparison. I do not intend to load down the page with examples; one will do. Isolde in her grief and rage is telling Brangäne what she *imagines* Tristan might say to King Mark on offering to him the captive Irish princess. It is a quotation – it is so marked in the text – and comes from the turmoil of Isolde's mixed emotions, certainly with all the bitterness she can put into it. The words are; *'Es wär' ein Schatz, mein Herr und Ohm...'*

That night after the first act was over this was one of the many passages that echoed in my ears and I perceived that Mme. Flagstad had sung it beautifully indeed, but like a folksong – like *'Heidenröslein.'* The savage mockery, the false sweetness, the snarl: of this nothing was left. It could have been 'The Last Rose of Summer'.... all things considered, it is perhaps not so strange that she failed to give her Isolde and Brünnhilde everything that Wagner wanted; indeed, she may not have been conscious of what he wanted aside from the board lines. It seems downright impossible that any woman could seize the meaning of Kundry in three weeks, although the words and notes (it is short enough) would give no difficulty. It all happened too quickly; there was no time to take it in; Mme. Flagstad's natural calm did not permit instinctive comprehension of these tortured heroines, and the great public – the largest Wagner ever had in the West – did not care anyhow. I see her now in her dressing room at the Metropolitan as I saw her once between the first and second acts of *Tristan:* calm and majestic, smiling kindly, braiding her hair with a vocal score of the opera open on the table before her, an Isolde who had never suffered humiliation of spirit or the wish to die. She had been knitting and put the work down beside the *Tristan* score while she talked to us. After we left I imagine she resumed her knitting until she was called to the stage for, of all things, Act II of *Tristan.* No more tranquil approach to unbridled passion has come under my observation.   VINCENT SHEEAN, *First and Last Love*

WEILL

Robert Craft is characteristically acute in this marvellous paragraph of criticism of Brecht and Weill's major collaboration Mahagonny.

[1963] Hamburg. *Mahagonny* at the Staatsoper, our first evening in a two-week 'Theater Cure.' The staging, by a Brecht pupil, is admirably severe, especially in the groupings of the chorus. After applauding the director, however, one hurries to credit the composer. Though I.S. will say no more than that 'there are good things everywhere in the score, but it is not everywhere good,' the wonder of *Mahagonny* is that so prodigal a musical substance was given to so flimsy a play. (Berg must have been impressed by *Mahagonny*, incidentally, and it seems to me there is a touch of Jenny in Lulu and more than a touch of the athlete in Berg's own funambulist. Perhaps, too, the sax and banjo in the jazz band and the zither in the glutton scene helped to influence the choice of instruments for the 'Garderobe' scene in *Lulu*.) But however good Weill's music may be, what a dispiriting work is *Mahagonny*. After a gay beginning, it plunges unswervingly downward for three far too long hours, until at the end one leaves the theater quite literally in the dumps. And the long decline has a correspondingly deleterious effect on one's judgment, so that most of what is remembered as 'good' seems to have occurred comparatively near the beginning: the boxer's death, for example, and the glutton's, with an '*Er ist tod*,' a 'hats off,' and a that's that; or in the brothel scene, the '*Erst wasch die hände*' and '*Jungens mach rascher*.' But Hamburg is no Berlin-in-the-twenties. Risqué lines and situations meet with uncertain titters, and Herr and Frau Schmidt in the fifth row can be seen exchanging whispers and knowing nudges. The reception as a whole is exactly the opposite of the author's intent, too, for the audience sits back to enjoy it like an operetta or 'musical,' albeit a strangely depressing example of either one.

The Vier Jahreszeiten restaurant, after the performance, could be a continuation of the last scene of the opera. There, the final abasement of society is indicated by pickets whose placards carry slogans of *FÜR GELD!* Here, bellhops in floor-length aprons march about with the same kind of signs summoning people to telephones: *BITTE HERR STOLZ!*

WOZZECK

As I left the State Opera last night I had a sensation not of coming out of a public institution, but out of an insane asylum. On the stage, in the orchestra, in the hall, plain madmen. Among them, in defiant squads, the shock troops of atonalists, the dervishes of Arnold Schoenberg. *Wozzeck* by Alban Berg was the battle slogan. A work of a Chinaman from Vienna. For with European music and musical evolution this mass onslaught of instruments has nothing in common. In Berg's music there is not a trace of melody. There are only scraps, shreds, spasms, and burps. Harmonically, the work is beyond discussion, for everything sounds wrong. The perpetrator of this work builds securely upon the stupidity and charity of his fellow-men, and for the rest relies on God Almighty and the Universal Edition. I regard Alban Berg as a musical swindler and a musician dangerous to the community. One should go even further. Unprecedented events demand new methods. We must seriously pose the question as to what extent musical profession can be criminal. We deal here, in the realm of music, with a capital offense.

PAUL ZSCHORLICH, Deutsche Zeitung, 1925

Injustice – injustice. Wozzeck has been wronged, Berg has been grievously wronged. He is a dramatist of great firmness of purpose, profound truth. Let him speak out! Now he is all torn up. He is suffering. As if cut down. Not a note. And his every note was soaked in blood! ... You ask about the state of opera. Berlin wants to know the same thing. It will advance. ... Not the crashing of instruments. Phenomena made plain. That's its justification. And it will grow with humanity. ... I get across through truth. Truth to the limit. And I believe life has many, many layers; some of them in need of a beautiful sound, too – Schrecker and Schönberg tend to forget that. Truth does not exclude beauty, on the contrary, we need more and more truth and beauty. Above all life. Everlasting youth. Life is ever young. Life is spring. I'm not afraid of life, I love it with a passion!

JANÁČEK, on Wozzeck's Prague première

An example of a musical antithesis to me in my own time is Wozzeck. What disturbs me about this great masterpiece and one that I love, is the level of its appeal to 'ignorant' audiences, with whom one may attribute its success to: (1) the story; (2) Bible, child sentiment; (3) sex; (4) brevity; (5) dynamics, pppp to ffff^n; (6) muted brass, $\wedge$, $\prime$, col legno, etc.; (7) the idea that the vocal line $\nearrow \searrow \curlyvee$ =emotion; (8) the orchestral flagellation in the interludes; (9) the audience's feeling that it is being modern.

IGOR STRAVINSKY, in Dialogues and a Diary (with Robert Craft)

419

die ZAUBERFLÖTE

... the whole opera is one continued and deep river of music, breaking into every possible turn of course and variety of surface, and exhibiting every aspect of the heavens that lie above it. Mozart's genius is here in its most romantic and passionate character, undoubtedly. ... It is to Mozart's other works what the *Tempest* is to the most popular of Shakespeare's comedies.

LEIGH HUNT

Die Zauberflöte will always remain Mozart's greatest work, for in it he for the first time showed himself to be a German musician. 'Don Juan' still has the complete Italian cut; besides our sacred art ought never permit itself to be degraded to the level of a foil for so scandalous a subject.

BEETHOVEN

'Metalogue' to *The Magic Flute,*
composed in commemoration of the Mozart Bicentenary, 1956,
to be spoken by the singer playing the role of Sarastro.

Relax, Maestro, put your baton down:
Only the fogiest of the old will frown
If you the trials of the *Prince* prorogue
To let *Sarastro* speak this Metalogue,
A form acceptable to us, although
Unclassed by *Aristotle* or *Boileau.*
No modern audience finds it incorrect,
For interruption is what we expect

Since that new god, the Paid Announcer, rose,
Who with his quasi-Ossianic prose
Cuts in upon the lovers, halts the band,
To name a sponsor or to praise a brand.
Not that I have a product to describe
That you could wear or cook with or imbibe;
You cannot hoard or waste a work of art:
I come to praise but not to sell *Mozart*,
Who came into this world of war and woe
At Salzburg just two centuries ago,
When kings were many and machines were few
And open Atheism something new.
(It makes a servantless New Yorker sore
To think sheer Genius had to stand before
A mere Archbishop with uncovered head:
But *Mozart* never had to make his bed.)

The history of Music as of Man
Will not to cancrizans, and no ear can
Recall what, when the Archduke *Francis* reigned,
Was heard by ears whose treasure-hoard contained
A *Flute* already but as yet no *Ring*;
Each age has its own mode of listening.
We know the *Mozart* of our fathers' time
Was gay, rococo, sweet, but not sublime,
A Viennese Italian; that is changed
Since music critics learned to feel 'estranged';
Now it's the Germans he is classed amongst,
A *Geist* whose music was composed from *Angst*,
At International Festivals enjoys
An equal status with the Twelve-Tone Boys;
He awes the lovely and the very rich,
And even those *Divertimenti* which
He wrote to play while bottles were uncorked,
Milord chewed noisily, Milady talked,
Are heard in solemn silence, score on knees,
Like quartets by the deafest of the *B's*.

What next? One can no more imagine how,
In concert halls two hundred years from now,
When the mozartian sound-waves move the air,
The cognoscenti will be moved, than dare
Predict how high orchestral pitch will go,
How many tones will constitute a row,
The tempo at which regimented feet
Will march about the Moon, the form of Suite
For Piano in a Post-Atomic Age,
Prepared by some contemporary *Cage*.

An opera composer may be vexed
By later umbrage taken at his text:
Even *Macaulay's* schoolboy knows to-day
What *Robert Graves* or *Margaret Mead* would say
About the status of the sexes in this play,
Writ in that era of barbaric dark
'Twixt Modern Mom and Bronze-Age Matriarch.
Where now the Roman Fathers and their creed?
'Ah, where,' sighs *Mr Mitty*, 'where indeed?',
And glances sideways at his vital spouse
Whose rigid jaw-line and contracted brows
Express her scorn and utter detestation
For Roman views of Female Education.

In Nineteen-Fifty-Six we find the *Queen*
A highly-paid and most efficient Dean
(Who, as we all know, really runs the College),
Sarastro, tolerated for his knowledge,
Teaching the History of Ancient Myth
At *Bryn Mawr*, *Vassar*, *Bennington* or *Smith*;
Pamina may a *Time* researcher be
To let *Tamino* take his Ph.D.,
Acquiring manly wisdom as he wishes
While changing diapers and doing dishes;
Sweet *Papagena*, when she's time to spare,
Listens to *Mozart* operas on the air,

Though *Papageno*, we are sad to feel,
Prefers the juke-box to the glockenspiel,
And how is – what was easy in the past –
A democratic villain to be cast?
Monostatos must make his bad impression
Without a race, religion or profession.

A work that lasts two hundred years is tough,
And operas, God knows, must stand enough:
What greatness made, small vanities abuse.
What must they not endure? The Diva whose
Fioriture and climactic note
The silly old composer never wrote,
Conductor *X*, that over-rated bore
Who alters tempi and who cuts the score,
Director *Y* who with ingenious wit
Places his wretched singers in the pit
While dancers mime their roles, *Z* the Designer
Who sets the whole thing on an ocean liner,
The girls in shorts, the men in yachting caps;
Yet Genius triumphs over all mishaps,
Survives a greater obstacle than these,
Translation into foreign Operese
(English sopranos are condemned to *languish*
Because our tenors have to hide their *anguish*);
It soothes the *Frank*, it stimulates the *Greek*:
Genius surpasses all things, even Chic.
We who know nothing – which is just as well –
About the future, can, at least, foretell,
Whether they live in air-borne nylon cubes,
Practise group-marriage or are fed through tubes,
That crowds two centuries from now will press
(Absurd their hair, ridiculous their dress)
And pay in currencies, however weird,
To hear *Sarastro* booming through his beard,
Sharp connoisseurs approve if it is clean
The F in alt of the *Nocturnal Queen*,

Some uncouth creature from the *Bronx* amaze
Park Avenue by knowing all the *K*'s.

How seemly, then, to celebrate the birth
Of one who did no harm to our poor earth,
Created masterpieces by the dozen,
Indulged in toilet humour with his cousin,
And had a pauper's funeral in the rain,
The like of whom we shall not see again:
How comely, also, to forgive; we should,
As *Mozart*, were he living, sure would,
Remember kindly *Salieri's* shade,
Accused of murder and his works unplayed,
Nor, while we praise the dead, should we forget
We have *Stravinsky* – bless him! – with us yet.
Basta! Maestro, make your minions play!
In all hearts, as in our finale, may
Reason & Love be crowned, assume their rightful sway.

W. H. AUDEN

SOURCES AND ACKNOWLEDGEMENTS

ABC
Quoted by George Marek, in *A Front Seat at the Opera* (London,
  1951). Reprinted by permission of Harrap Ltd and Outlet Book
  Company Inc.
Robert Rushmore, *The Singing Voice* (London, 1971). Reprinted by
  permission of Hamish Hamilton Ltd.

ANTIPATHY
Princesse Palatine, Madame Duchesse d'Orléans, *Correspondance*, ed.
  Ernest Jaeglé (Paris, 1880)
Jane Austen, *Letters*, ed. R. W. Chapman (Oxford, 1952).
Quoted by Jaques Barzun (ed.), in *Pleasures of Music* (London, 1952).
H. L. Mencken on Music (New York, 1961). Reprinted by permission
  of Alfred Knopf Inc.

APPARITIONS
Richard Wagner, *My Life*, tr. A. Gray (Cambridge, 1983). Reprinted
  by permission of Cambridge University Press.
David Drew, in *Peter Pears: A Tribute*, ed. Marion Thorpe (London,
  1985). Reprinted by permission of the author.
The quotation from Montagu Slater's libretto for *Peter Grimes*
  appears by kind permission of Boosey and Hawkes Music
  Publishers.

APPLAUSE
Piero Tosi, *Observations on the Florid Song*, 1723, ed. P. H. Lang
  (repr. New York, 1968).
Michael Langdon, *Notes from a Low Singer* (London, 1984).
  Reprinted by permission of Julia Macrae Ltd.

AUDEN
Robert Craft, *Stravinsky: Chronicle of a Friendship* (London, 1972).
  Reprinted by permission of Victor Gollancz Ltd.
Robert Craft, *Themes and Episodes* (New York, 1966). Reprinted by
  permission of Alfred A. Knopf Inc.

AUDIENCES
Lord Mount Edgcumbe, *Musical Reminiscences of an old Amateur*,
  1823 (repr. New York, 1973).
The Memoirs of Berlioz, tr. and ed. David Cairns (London, 1969).
  Reprinted by permission of Victor Gollancz Ltd.

George Marek, *A Front Seat at the Opera* (London, 1951). Reprinted
by permission of Harrap Ltd and Outlet Book Company Inc.
James Joyce, *Letters*, ed. Richard Ellmann (London, 1966). Reprinted
by permission of Faber and Faber Ltd.

AUDITION
Rosa Ponselle, with James A. Drake, *A Singer's Life* (New York,
1983). Reprinted by permission of Doubleday Inc and the Howard
Buck Literary Agency.

IL BARBIERE DI SIVIGLIA
Stendhal, *Rome, Naples, Florence*, tr. Richard N. Coe (London, 1959).
Reprinted by permission of John Calder Ltd.

BAYREUTH
George Moore, *Hail and Farewell*, 1911 (repr. London, 1947).
Virginia Woolf, *Letters*, vol. i, ed. Nigel Nicolson (London, 1975).
Reprinted by permission of the estate of Virginia Woolf and the
Hogarth Press.

BEGINNINGS
Quoted by O. Strunk, *Source Readings in Music History* (London,
1952). Reprinted by permission of Faber and Faber Ltd.
Claudio Monteverdi, *Letters*, ed. and tr. Denis Stevens (London, 1985).
Reprinted by permission of Faber and Faber Ltd.

BELLINI
Quoted by Herbert Weinstock, in *Bellini* (London, 1972).

BERG
Arnold Schoenberg, *Style and Idea*, 1950 (repr. London, 1975).
Reprinted by permission of Faber and Faber Ltd.
Alban Berg, *Letters to his Wife*, tr. B. Grun (London, 1971). Reprinted
by permission of Faber and Faber Ltd.

BISCUITS
Quoted by Hans Gal, in *The Musician's World* (London, 1965).
Reprinted by permission of Thames and Hudson Ltd.

LA BOHEME
Giacomo Puccini, *Letters*, ed. G. Adami, tr. E. Makin, 1931 (repr.
London, 1974). Reprinted by permission of Harrap Ltd.
Quoted in *Opera*, June 1967.

BOOING
Opera News, 23 February 1980. Reprinted by permission of the
Metropolitan Opera Guild.

BRITTEN
Robin Holloway, in *The Britten Companion*, ed. Christopher Palmer
(London, 1984). Reprinted by permission of Faber and Faber Ltd.

CALLAS
Quoted by Elisabeth Schwarzkopf (ed.), in *On and Off the Record* (London, 1982). Reprinted by permission of Faber and Faber Ltd.

CAMP
Benjamin Lumley, *Reminiscences of the Opera*, 1964 (repr. New York, 1976).
Quoted in *Music since 1900*, ed. Nicholas Slonimsky (London, 1972).

CARMEN
Quoted by Hans Gal, in *The Musician's World* (London, 1965). Reprinted by permission of Thames and Hudson.

CARUSO
Dorothy Caruso, *Enrico Caruso* (New York, 1945). Reprinted by permission of Simon and Schuster Inc.

CASTRATI
Quoted by Angus Heriot, in *The Castrati in Opera* (London, 1956). Reprinted by permission of Martin Secker and Warburg Ltd.

CHALIAPIN
Sir Isaiah Berlin, in *Opera*, February 1975. Reprinted by permission of Curtis Brown Ltd.

CLAQUE
The Musical Times, 1 April 1888.

COLLABORATION
Marilyn Horne with Jane Scovell, *My Life* (New York, 1983). Reprinted by permission of Atheneum Publishers.

COLOUR AND SOUND
Benjamin Lumley, *Reminiscences of the Opera*, 1864 (repr. New York, 1976).

COSTUME
Opera News, 15 February 1954. Reprinted by permission of the Metropolitan Opera Guild.
Shaw's Music, vol. iii, ed. Dan H. Laurence (London, 1981). Reprinted by permission of the Society of Authors.

CRITICS
David Franklin, *Opera*, January 1954.

DEBUSSY
Opera, May 1962.

DEBUTS
Frances Alda, *Men, Women and Tenors*, 1937 (repr. New York, 1971).

DESERT ISLAND OPERA
Quoted in *Saturday Review*, November 1948. Reprinted by permission of *Saturday Review*.

DESTINN
Artur Rubinstein, *My Young Years* (London, 1973). Reprinted by permission of Jonathan Cape Ltd.

DISASTER
Quaintance Eaton, *Opera Caravan* (New York, 1978). Reprinted by permission of the author.
Vincent Sheean, *First and Last Love* (London, 1956). Reprinted by permission of Curtis Brown Ltd.
Bernard Levin, *Conducted Tour* (London, 1981). Reprinted by permission of Jonathan Cape Ltd.

DOCTORS
Michael O'Donnell, in the *British Medical Journal*, June 1984. Reprinted by permission of the *British Medical Journal*.

DONIZETTI
Quoted by William Ashbrook, in *Donizetti and his Operas* (Cambridge, 1982). Reprinted by permission of Cambridge University Press.

DRESSING-ROOM
Marcia Davenport, *Of Lena Geyer* (London, 1949). Reprinted by permission of A. D. Peters and Co. Ltd.

ELEKTRA
Quoted in *Lexicon of Musical Invective*, ed. Nicolas Slonimsky (New York, 1965).
Bela Bartók, *Essays*, ed. B. Suchoff (London, 1976). Reprinted by permission of Faber and Faber Ltd.

ENCORE
Shaw's Music, vol. i, ed. Dan H. Laurence (London, 1981). Reprinted by permission of the Society of Authors.

ESSENTIALS
Piero Tosi, *Observations on the Florid Song*, 1723, ed. P. H. Lang (repr. New York, 1968).
W. A. Mozart, *Letters*, tr. and ed. Emily Anderson (London, 1966). Reprinted by permission of Macmillan Ltd.
Quoted by Hans Gal, in *The Musician's World* (London, 1965). Reprinted by permission of Thames and Hudson Ltd.
Lilian Foerster Loveday, *Opera News*, 25 January 1964. Reprinted by permission of the author.
Hans Werner Henze, *Music and Politics* (London, 1982). Reprinted by permission of Faber and Faber Ltd.

Paul Griffiths, *New Sounds, New Personalities* (London, 1985).
Reprinted by permission of Faber Music Ltd.
Brigid Brophy, *Mozart the Dramatist* (London, 1964). Reprinted by
permission of Anthony Sheil Associates Ltd.

LA FANCIULLA DEL WEST
Quoted in *Music since 1900*, ed. Nicolas Slonimsky (London, 1972).
Igor Stravinsky and Robert Craft, *Dialogues and a Diary* (London,
1968). Reprinted by permission of Faber and Faber Ltd.

FANS
Marina Warner, *Queen Victoria's Sketchbook* (London, 1979).
Reprinted by permission of A. D. Peters and Co. Ltd.
Quoted by Luigi Arditi, in *My Reminiscences* (London, 1896).
Clara Louise Kellogg, *Memoirs of an American Prima Donna*, 1913
(repr. New York, 1978).
Quoted by Mary Watkins Cushing, in *The Rainbow Bridge*, 1954
(repr. New York, 1977).
Peter Medawar, *Memoir of a Thinking Radish* (Oxford, 1986).
Reprinted by permission of Oxford University Press.
Patrick J. Smith, *A Year at the Met* (New York, 1983). Reprinted by
permission of Alfred A. Knopf Inc.

FAREWELLS
Henry Chorley, *Thirty Years' Musical Recollections*, 1862 (repr. New
York, 1973).
Janet Baker, *Full Circle* (London 1982). Reprinted by permission of
Julia Macrae Ltd.

FAUST
John Ashbery, *The Tennis Court Oath* (Middletown, 1962). Reprinted
by permission of Wesleyan University Press.

FEES
Nellie Melba, *Melodies and Memories*, 1925 (repr. London, 1980).
Rupert Christiansen, *Prima Donna* (London, 1984). Reprinted by
permission of the author.

FEUDS
Quoted by Hans Gal, in *The Musician's World* (London, 1965).
Reprinted by permission of Thames and Hudson Ltd.
Jonathan Keates, *Handel* (London, 1985). Reprinted by permission of
Victor Gollancz Ltd.
Beniamino Gigli, *Memoirs* (London, 1957).

FIDELIO
Quoted by George Marek, in *Beethoven* (London, 1970).
Victor Gollancz, *Journey towards Music* (London, 1964). Reprinted by
permission of Victor Gollancz Ltd.

FRANCE vs. ITALY

Quoted by O. Strunk, in *Source Readings in Music History* (London, 1952). Reprinted by permission of Faber and Faber Ltd.

The Memoirs of Berlioz, tr. and ed. David Cairns (London, 1969). Reprinted by permission of Victor Gollancz Ltd.

Robert Rushmore, *The Singing Voice* (London, 1971). Reprinted by permission of Hamish Hamilton Ltd.

Debussy on Music, tr. and ed. R. L. Smith (London, 1977). Reprinted by permission of Martin Secker and Warburg Ltd.

D. H. Lawrence, *Letters*, vol. i, ed. James T. Boulton (Cambridge, 1979).

GESAMTKUNSTWERK

E. M. Forster, *Howards End*, 1910, ed. Stallybrass (London, 1973). Reprinted by permission of Edward Arnold Ltd.

Paul Hindemith, *A Composer's World* (Boston, 1952). Reprinted by permission of the Harvard University Press. Copyright © 1952, 1970 by the President and Fellows of Harvard College.

GLUCK

Quoted by O. Strunk, in *Source Readings in Music History* (London, 1952). Reprinted by permission of Faber and Faber Ltd.

GLYNDEBOURNE

Rudolf Bing, *5000 Nights at the Opera* (London, 1972). Reprinted by permission of Doubleday and Co. Inc.

Damon Evans with David Ellison, in *Glyndebourne Festival Programme Book*, 1987. Reprinted by permission of the Editor.

Ivor Newton, *At the Piano* (London, 1966). Reprinted by permission of Hamish Hamilton Ltd.

GOUNOD

George Moore, *Memoirs of my Dead Life* (London, 1906).

GREAT SINGING

Quoted by Victor Gollancz, in *Journey towards Music* (London, 1964). Reprinted by permission of Victor Gollancz Ltd.

Lilli Lehmann, *How to Sing*, 1902 (repr. New York, 1952).

HOUSE PARTY

Hermann Klein, *The Reign of Patti*, 1920 (repr. New York, 1977).

Blanche Marchesi, *A Singer's Pilgrimage*, 1923 (repr. New York, 1977).

ICONOCLAST

Pierre Boulez, translated anon. in *Opera*, June 1967. Reprinted by permission of *Opera*, *Der Spiegel* and Pierre Boulez.

IMPRESARIO

John Rosselli, *The Opera Industry in Italy* (Cambridge, 1984). Reprinted by permission of Cambridge University Press.

ITALIAN NIGHTS
Stendhal, *Rome, Naples, Florence*, tr. Richard N. Coe (London, 1959).
  Reprinted by permission of John Calder Ltd.
Hans Werner Henze, *Music and Politics* (London, 1982). Reprinted by
  permission of Faber and Faber Ltd.

JANACEK
Quoted by Charles Susskind, in *Janáček and Brod* (New Haven, 1985).
  Reprinted by permission of Yale University Press.
Quoted in *Leos Janáček: Letters and Reminiscences*, ed. B. Stedron
  (Prague, 1955).

JUSTICE
Opera News, 7 December 1973. Reprinted by permission of the
  Metropolitan Opera Guild.

KNOT GARDEN
Paul Driver, in *Michael Tippett: A Celebration*, ed. Geraint Lewis
  (Tunbridge Wells, 1985). Reprinted by permission of the author.
Quoted in *Music since 1900*, ed. Nicolas Slonimsky (London, 1972).

LADY MACBETH OF MTSENSK
Dmitri Shostakovich, *Testimony*, ed. Solomon Volkov (London, 1979).
  Reprinted by permission of Hamish Hamilton Ltd and Harper and
  Row Inc.
Igor Stravinsky, *Selected Correspondence*, vol. i, ed. Robert Craft
  (London, 1982). Reprinted by permission of Faber and Faber Ltd.

LOTTE LEHMANN AND THE LIONESS
Lotte Lehmann, in *Opera 66*, ed. Charles Osborne (London, 1966).
  Reprinted by permission of Alan Ross.

LIBRETTOS
Claudio Monteverdi, *Letters*, ed. and tr. Denis Stevens (London, 1985).
  Reprinted by permission of Faber and Faber Ltd.
Richard Strauss and Hugo von Hofmannsthal, *Correspondence*, tr.
  H. Hammelmann and E. Oesers (Cambridge, 1980). Reprinted by
  permission of Collins Publishers.

LIND
Quoted in *About the House*, Summer 1977. Reprinted by permission
  of the Friends of Covent Garden.
Tony Harrison, *Selected Poems* (Harmondsworth, 1985). Reprinted by
  permission of the author.

LOVE
April FitzLyon, *The Price of Genius* (London, 1964). Reprinted by
  permission of John Calder Ltd.
Peter Heyworth, *Otto Klemperer*, vol. i (Cambridge, 1983). Reprinted
  by permission of Cambridge University Press.

Geraldine Farrar, *Such Sweet Compulsion*, 1938 (repr. New York, 1970).

MAD SCENES
Simon Maguire, programme note for the WNO production of *Lucia di Lammermoor*, 1986. Reprinted by permission of the author.

MALIBRAN
Quoted in Howard Bushnell, *Maria Malibran* (University Park Pa., 1979).
Quoted by Suzanne Desternes and Henriette Chandet, *La Malibran et Pauline Viardot* (Paris, 1969): tr. John Sutro, in *About the House*, Christmas 1979.

MASSENET
Shaw's Music, vol. i, ed. Dan H. Laurence (London, 1981). Reprinted by permission of the Society of Authors.

MAUREL
Shaw's Music, vol. ii, ed. Dan H. Laurence (London, 1981). Reprinted by permission of the Society of Authors.

DIE MEISTERSINGER
Quoted in *About the House*, Summer 1972.
Arnold Bennett, *Things that have Interested Me* (London, 1923).

MELBA
Mary Garden and Louis Biancolli, *Mary Garden's Story* (London, 1951). Reprinted by permission of Simon and Schuster Inc.
Osbert Sitwell, *Left Hand, Right Hand: Great Morning* (London, 1948). Reprinted by permission of David Higham Associates Ltd.

MENOTTI
Igor Stravinsky, *Themes and Conclusions* (London, 1972). Reprinted by permission of Faber and Faber Ltd.

THE MET
Henry James, *The American Scene*, 1907 (repr. London, 1968).
Frances Alda, *Men, Women and Tenors*, 1937 (repr. New York, 1971).
Rudolf Bing, *5000 Nights at the Opera* (London, 1972). Reprinted by permission of Doubleday and Co. Inc.

MEYERBEER
Quoted in *Lexicon of Musical Invective*, ed. Nicolas Slonimsky (New York, 1965).
Cosima Wagner, *Diary*, vol. ii, tr. and ed. Geoffrey Skelton (London, 1980). Reprinted by permission of Collins Publishers.
F. G. Arnstein, in *Opera 66*, ed. Charles Osborne (London, 1966). Reprinted by permission of Alan Ross.

MORALITY
Evening Standard, 14 November 1963. Reprinted by permission.
Daily Mirror, 22 June 1965. Reprinted by permission of Syndication
  International.

MOZART
Michael Kelly, *Reminiscences*, 1826, ed. Roger Fiske (repr. Oxford,
  1975).
Quoted by Howard Mills (ed.), in *Thomas Love Peacock: Memoirs,
  Essays and Reviews* (London, 1970).
Brigid Brophy, *Mozart the Dramatist* (London, 1964). Reprinted by
  permission of Anthony Shiel Associates.

MURDER
M. Eugenia Geib, in *Opera News*, 18 January 1964. Reprinted by
  permission of the Metropolitan Opera Guild.

MUSSORGSKY
Nicholas Rimsky-Korsakov, *My Musical Life*, tr. C. Joffe (New York,
  1942). Reprinted by permission of Alfred A. Knopf Inc.

OBITUARIES
Peter Hemmings, in *Scottish Opera Yearbook 1986–7*. Reprinted by
  permission of the author.

OPERA SERIA
Reprinted by permission of the author.

PACCHIEROTTI
Fanny Burney, *Letters and Journals*, ed. Joyce Hemlow *et al.* (Oxford,
  1972–84).
Vernon Lee, *Studies of Eighteenth-Century Italy* (London, 1880).

PARIS
Peter Conrad, *Romantic Opera and Literary Form* (Berkeley Cal.,
  1977). Reprinted by permission of the Regents of the University of
  California.

PARODY
Jane W. Stedman, in *Opera News*, 6 January 1973. Reprinted by
  permission of the Metropolitan Opera Guild.
George Marek, *A Front Seat at the Opera* (London, 1951). Reprinted
  by permission of Harrap Ltd and Outlet Book Company Inc.

PARSIFAL
Thomas Mann, *Diary 1918–39*. Reprinted by permission of Harry N.
  Abrams, Inc., NY. English translation © 1982 Harry N. Abrams Inc.
  All rights reserved.

PASTA
Stendhal, *Life of Rossini*, tr. and ed. Richard N. Coe (London, 1956).
  Reprinted by permission of John Calder Ltd.

PELLEAS ET MELISANDE
Virgil Thomson, *The Musical Scene* (New York, 1945). Reprinted by
  permission of the author.
Ezra Pound, *Letters 1907–41*, ed. D. D. Paige (London, 1951).
  Reprinted by permission of Faber and Faber Ltd.

PETER GRIMES
Edmund Wilson, *Europe without Baedeker* (London, 1967). Copyright
  © 1947, 1966 by Edmund Wilson. Reprinted by permission of
  Farrar, Straus and Giroux Inc.

PLOTS
Gladys Davidson, *Standard Stories from the Operas* (London, 1940).
  Reprinted by permission of the Bodley Head.
Leo Slezak, *Songs of Motley*, 1938 (repr. New York, 1977).
Quoted in *About the House*, Spring 1967. Reprinted by permission of
  the Friends of Covent Garden.
George Marek, *A Front Seat at the Opera* (London, 1951). Reprinted
  by permission of Harrap Ltd and Outlet Book Company Inc.

PLUMBING
Quoted in *Lexicon of Musical Invective*, ed. Nicolas Slonimsky (New
  York, 1965).
Ronald Duncan, *Working with Britten* (Bideford, 1981). Reprinted by
  permission of the Ronald Duncan Estate.

PREMIERES
Cosima Wagner, *Diary*, vol. i, tr. and ed. Geoffrey Skelton (London,
  1978). Reprinted by permission of Collins Publishers.
Vera Stravinsky, in Igor Stravinsky and Robert Craft, *Themes and
  Episodes* (New York, 1966). Reprinted by permission of Alfred A.
  Knopf Inc.

PRIMA DONNAS
Quoted by Mollie Sands, in *Theatre Notebook*, Spring 1966.
George Hogarth, *Memoirs of the Opera*, 1851 (repr. New York, 1972).
J. H. Mapleson, *Memoirs*, 1888, ed. Harold Rosenthal (London, 1966).

PRODUCERS
Quoted by Elizabeth Forbes, in *About the House*, Spring 1977.

PUCCINI
Ernest Newman, *Testament of Music* (London, 1962).
Giacomo Puccini, *Letters*, ed. G. Adami, tr. E. Makin, 1931 (repr.
  London, 1974). Reprinted by permission of Harrap Ltd.

RAVEL

Colette, *Earthly Paradise*, tr. H. Beauclark etc. (London, 1966).
  Reprinted by permission of Desmond Shawe-Taylor and Martin
  Secker and Warburg Ltd.

RECORDING

Mary Watkins Cushing, *The Rainbow Bridge,* 1954 (repr. New York,
  1977).

REGIME

Piero Tosi, *Observations on the Florid Song*, 1723, ed. P. H. Lang
  (repr. New York, 1968).
Hermann Klein, *The Reign of Patti*, 1920 (repr. New York, 1977).
Robert Rushmore, *The Singing Voice* (London, 1971). Reprinted by
  permission of Hamish Hamilton Ltd.
Mary Watkins Cushing, *The Rainbow Bridge*, 1954 (repr. New York,
  1977).
Lilli Lehmann, *How to Sing*, 1902 (repr. New York, 1952).

REHEARSAL

John Ebers, *Seven Years of the King's Theatre*, 1828 (repr. New York,
  1969).
Quoted in Robert Tuggle, *The Golden Age of Opera* (New York,
  1983).

DE RESZKE

Desmond Shawe-Taylor, in *The Opera Bedside Book* (London, 1965).
  Reprinted by permission of Victor Gollancz Ltd.

RETIREMENT

Adelaide Sartoris, *Past Hours* (London, 1880).
Colette, *Earthly Paradise*, tr. H. Beauclark etc. (London, 1966).
  Reprinted by permission of Desmond Shawe-Taylor and Martin
  Secker and Warburg Ltd.
Gerald Moore, *Furthermoore* (London, 1983). Reprinted by
  permission of Hamish Hamilton Ltd.
Quoted by Patrick O'Connor, in *Harper's and Queen*, December 1983.
  Reprinted by permission of the National Magazine Company.

DER RING DES NIBELUNGEN

Quoted by Hans Gel, in *The Musician's World* (London, 1965).
  Reprinted by permission of Thames and Hudson Ltd.
Robert Zeschin, in *Opera News*, 3 April 1971. Reprinted by
  permission of the Metropolitan Opera Guild.

DER ROSENKAVALIER

Richard Strauss, *Recollections and Reflections*, tr. L. J. Lawrence
  (London, 1973). Reprinted by permission of Boosey and Hawkes
  Ltd.

Arnold Bennett, *Journals*, ed. N. Flower (London, 1932–3).
Iris Murdoch, *The Black Prince* (London, 1973). Reprinted by
permission of Chatto and Windus Ltd.

ROSSINI
Lord Mount Edgcumbe, *Musical Reminiscences of an old Amateur*,
1823 (repr. New York, 1973).
Quoted by Herbert Weinstock, in *Rossini* (London, 1968).
Stendhal, *Life of Rossini*, tr. Richard N. Coe (London, 1956).
Reprinted by permission of John Calder Ltd.
Quoted in Jacques Barzun, *Pleasures of Music* (London, 1952).

SALOME AT HOME
The Star, 7 December 1910.

SCHOENBERG
Constant Lambert, *Music Ho!*, 1934 (repr. London, 1985). Reprinted
by permission of Faber and Faber Ltd.

SCHWARZKOPF
Quoted by Elisabeth Schwarzkopf (ed.), in *On and Off the Record*
(London, 1982). Reprinted by permission of Faber and Faber Ltd.

SELLING OUT
Roland Gellatt, *The Fabulous Phonograph* (London, 1956).
Mary Watkins Cushing, *The Rainbow Bridge*, 1954 (repr. New York,
1977).

STRAUSS
Neville Cardus, *Talking of Music* (London, 1957). Reprinted by
permission of Collins Publishers.

SUPERSTITION
George Marek, *A Front Seat at the Opera* (London, 1951). Reprinted
by permission of Harrap Ltd and Outlet Book Company Inc.

TCHAIKOVSKY
Quoted by Hans Gal, in *The Musician's World* (London, 1965).
Reprinted by permission of Thames and Hudson Ltd.

TEACHERS
Giuseppe Verdi, *Letters*, tr. and ed. Charles Osborne (London, 1971).
Reprinted by permission of Aitken and Stone Ltd.
Blanche Marchesi, *A Singer's Pilgrimage*, 1923 (repr. New York, 1977).

TENORS
Quoted by Henry Pleasants, in *The Great Singers* (London, 1981).
James Joyce, *Letters*, ed. Richard Ellmann (London, 1966). Reprinted
by permission of Faber and Faber Ltd.
Quoted by Robert Rushmore, in *The Singing Voice* (London, 1971).

TRANSLATION
Joseph Addison, *Spectator*, 21 March 1711, ed. D. F. Bond (Oxford, 1965).

LES TROYENS
The Memoirs of Berlioz, tr. and ed. David Cairns (London, 1969). Reprinted by permission of Victor Gollancz Ltd.

UNWRITTEN OPERAS
George Marek, *A Front Seat at the Opera* (London, 1951). Reprinted by permission of Harrap Ltd and Outlet Book Company Inc.
Giuseppe Verdi, *Letters*, tr. and ed. Charles Osborne (London, 1971). Reprinted by permission of Aitken and Stone Ltd.

UTMIUTSOL
Quoted by C. M. Girdlestone, in *Rameau* (London, 1957).

VERDI
Ivan Turgenev, *Letters*, tr. and ed. C. Knowles (London, 1983).
Quoted by Hans Gal, in *The Musician's World* (London, 1965). Reprinted by permission of Thames and Hudson Ltd.
Shaw's Music, vol. ii, ed. Dan H. Laurence (London, 1981). Reprinted by permission of the Society of Authors.
Victor Gollancz, *Journey towards Music* (London, 1964). Reprinted by permission of Victor Gollancz Ltd.
Opera, March 1954.

VIBRATO
Piero Tosi, *Observations on the Florid Song*, 1723, ed. P. H. Lang (repr. New York, 1968).
Robert Rushmore, *The Singing Voice* (London, 1971). Reprinted by permission of Hamish Hamilton Ltd.

VIENNA
Lady Mary Wortley Montagu, *Letters*, ed. R. Halsbund (Oxford, 1966–7).
Vincent Sheean, *First and Last Love* (London, 1956). Reprinted by permission of Curtis Brown Ltd.

WAGNER
George Eliot, in *Essays*, ed. T. Pinney (London, 1963).
Amy Fay, *Music Study in Germany* (London, 1886).
Quoted by Romain Rolland, in *Musicians of Today*, tr. M. Blaiklock *et al* (London, 1915).
Thomas Mann, *Diary* 1918–39. Reprinted by permission of Harry N. Abrams, Inc., NY. English translation © 1982 Harry N. Abrams Inc.
Quoted in *Marinetti: Selected Writings*, ed. R. W. Flint (London, 1972). Reprinted by permission of Laurence Pollinger Ltd.

WAGNERIENNES

Quoted by Ira Glackens, in *Yankee Diva* (New York, 1963).

Vincent Sheean, *First and Last Love* (London, 1956). Reprinted by permission of Curtis Brown Ltd.

WEILL

Robert Craft, in Igor Stravinsky and Robert Craft, *Themes and Episodes* (New York, 1966). Reprinted by permission of Alfred A. Knopf Inc.

WOZZECK

Quoted by Charles Susskind, in *Janáček and Brod* (New Haven, 1985). Reprinted by permission of Yale University Press.

Igor Stravinsky, in Igor Stravinsky and Robert Craft, *Dialogues and a Diary* (London, 1968) Reprinted by permission of Faber and Faber Ltd.

DIE ZAUBERFLÖTE

Quoted by Theodore Fenner, in *Leigh Hunt and Operatic Criticism* (Kansas City, 1972).

Quoted in *Beethoven: Impressions of Contemporaries*, ed. O. G. Sonneck (London, 1927).

Reprinted by permission of Faber and Faber Ltd and the Auden Estate.

While every effort has been made to secure permission, we may have failed in a few cases to trace the copyright holder. We apologize for any apparent negligence.

INDEX OF NAMES

Numbers in italics indicate authorship of an extract; dates of birth and death are given for the major operatic composers; dates for the operas are those of the first public performance of the work, in its most frequently heard form. For further information, the reader is referred to *The Concise Oxford Dictionary of Opera*, ed. Harold Rosenthal and John Warrack (Oxford University Press), which I have taken as my authority.